The Complete Idiot's Reference Card

Billiard Table and Cue Sizes

	Pool Tables	Snooker	Carom
Standard table	$4^1/_2$ '× 9'	6'× 12'	5' × 10'
Home table	$4^1/_2$× 9', 4'4" × 8'8", 4' × 8'	6' × 12', 5' × 10', $4^1/_2$' × 9', 3'×6'	5' × 10', $4^1/_2$' × 9', 4' × 8'
Coin-operated table:	$3^1/_2$' × 7', 4' × 8'	n/a	n/a
Standard cue length and weight	$57^1/_2$" or 58" $18^1/_2$ to $20^1/_4$ ounces	$57^1/_2$" or 58" 15 to 18 ounces	54" to $55^1/_2$" 18 to 22 ounces

Break Shot Pointers

➤ Hit the front ball in the rack full in the face, even if you have to sacrifice speed.
➤ Learn the best breaking position for each game.
➤ After you're in position, scoot your feet forward a couple of inches.
➤ Follow through an extra 6 to 18 inches.

Ewa's 90-Degree Rules

➤ At the moment the cue tip strikes the cue ball, the forearm of your rear arm should be at a 90-degree angle to the cue.
➤ Using a center ball hit on the cue ball (with the cue tip) and medium speed, the cue ball bounces off the object ball at a 90-degree angle to the direction in which the object ball goes after the collision.

Basic Rules of the Game

➤ A game does not begin until the white cue ball touches an object ball.
➤ If you touch the cue ball with the cue tip, it is a shot, even if you're just moving the ball around after your opponent fouled.
➤ On every shot, you must pocket a ball or, after the cue ball contacts the object ball, at least one ball (it can be the cue ball) must touch a cushion.
➤ Hitting any ball off the table is a foul.
➤ In games that require you to hit the lowest-numbered ball first, failing to do so is a foul.
➤ Touching the cue ball with your hand or another body part is a foul unless you're just beginning the game and haven't yet broken the balls, *or* if your opponent just fouled and you have been awarded ball in hand.
➤ Players must have at least one foot touching the floor at the moment when the cue tip makes contact with the cue ball.
➤ Hitting under the cue ball and scooping it into the air is a foul.

Tips for a Good Rack

➤ All balls should be touching their neighbors.
➤ The front ball should be centered on the footspot.
➤ The rack should be properly aligned with the center line of the table.

Tips for a Healthy Cue

➤ Keep your cue tip in good shape with a scuffer, shaper, and trimmer (or a multiple-purpose tool that does all three things).
➤ Shape the tip to the radius of either a dime or a nickel.
➤ Rough the tip just enough that it holds chalk easily.
➤ Apply a thin, even layer of chalk to the cue tip.
➤ Chalk up before every shot.

alpha
books

Closed (Loop) versus V (Open) Bridges

Closed-Loop Bridge

➤ Very stable

➤ Offers more control, especially on power shots

➤ Prevents the cue from lifting up during the stroke

➤ Creates better follow-through on medium and hard hits

➤ Looks more professional

V (Open) Bridge

➤ Makes aiming easier because you can sight down your cue

➤ Easy to make

➤ More likely to pass smoothly through your bridge hand

➤ Can be made by a hand of any size

➤ Can easily be made into an elevated bridge, if necessary

Top-10 Checklist for Your Stroke

1. Did you make all your decisions about the shot before you started stroking?
2. Is your stroke straight?
3. Is your cue as level as possible?
4. Does your cue stay level during the stroke?
5. Is your stroke smooth?
6. Is your cue tip going to hit the cue ball in the proper place?
7. Do your preparatory strokes feel good?
8. When you hit the cue ball, do you follow through 6 to 8 inches?
9. Do you freeze and does your head stay down after you hit the cue ball?
10. Are you consistent in your stroke technique?

Steps of the Approach

1. As you approach the table, focus on the layout of the balls.
2. Place your other hand on the cue.
3. Approach along the line from the cue ball to the object ball.
4. Place your front hand on the table, 6 to 8 inches from the cue ball.
5. Place your front foot at an angle of 45 degrees or less from the cue.
6. Be sure that you're balanced, comfortable, and stable as you bend over the table.
7. Check your alignment (see figure below).
8. Bend as low as you can comfortably go.

What to Get in Line

1. Your eyes
2. The shoulder, elbow, and wrist of your rear arm
3. The back of your rear hand
4. The toes of your rear foot
5. Your cue
6. The cue ball
7. The object ball

Check Your Aim

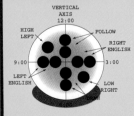

If the cue tip hits the cue ball in the white outer area, you'll likely miscue. Stay on the vertical axis, and the cue ball will behave normally. Stray off to either side (sidespin/English), and the cue ball won't go exactly where you aimed it.

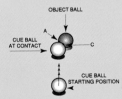

If you aim the center of the cue ball at Point A, they actually contact at Point C. That's why people miss shots when they know that they aimed right.

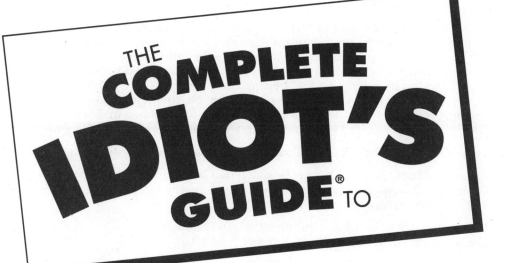

THE COMPLETE IDIOT'S GUIDE® TO

Pool & Billiards

by Ewa Mataya Laurance
& Thomas C. Shaw

alpha books

A Division of Macmillan General Reference
A Simon & Schuster Macmillan Company
1633 Broadway, New York, NY 10019-6785

Alpha Development Team

Publisher
Kathy Nebenhaus

Editorial Director
Gary M. Krebs

Managing Editor
Bob Shuman

Marketing Brand Manager
Felice Primeau

Senior Editor
Nancy Mikhail

Editor
Jessica Faust

Development Editors
Phil Kitchel, Amy Zavatto

Assistant Editor
Maureen Horn

Production Team

Development Editor
Nancy Warner

Production Editor
Kristi Hart

Copy Editor
Kathy Simpson

Cover Designer
Mike Freeland

Cover Photography
Phil Aull

Photo Editor
Richard H. Fox

Illustrator
Jody P. Schaeffer

Instructional Figures
Phil Aull (photography),
Paul Harris (drawings)

Designer
Nathan Clement

Indexers
Sandra Henselmeier, Greg Pearson

Layout/Proofreading
Angela Calvert, Mary Hunt, Cheryl Moore

Contents at a Glance

Contents

Foreword

Today, it seems that everybody is playing pool. Thousands of new billiard clubs have opened up all around the country, and they're grand places, with plush decor, full-service dining, and a modern atmosphere. I've been watching the sports surveys over the past 15 years, and the number of people who report that they play pool has skyrocketed.

And why not? Pool (or *billiards*, as it's now called) is a wonderful game, and you can enjoy it from the moment you first pick up a cue stick. It can be a family recreation, a fun thing to do on a date, a way to relax after a tough day at the office, or a serious sport. The choice is yours—and 44,231,000 people in America made billiards their choice in the past year.

Billiards can be played by anyone, any time, almost anywhere. Millions of people now have pool tables in their homes and enjoy the game with their family members, friends, and neighbors. Parents who worry about the dangers that their teenagers face discover that a billiard table keeps them home—and it's a good way to meet your kids' friends, because you can be sure that they'll be coming over to play, too.

Teenagers aren't the only ones who are attracted to the game, of course. If you hold a party and have a table in your home, I can guarantee you that the table is where people will congregate. You can also play at one of thousands of new billiard rooms, where the atmosphere is enjoyable and friendly. Today there's a room for any mood, taste, or income level. Smoke-free rooms are becoming common, and today, you also see something that you didn't see very often when I started playing: lots of ladies. I think when the rooms got so nice, the ladies discovered billiards, and they've improved the sport tremendously. Now the women professionals are on television more than the men are, and they really know how to play.

That brings up one of the most attractive things about billiards: You don't have to be unusually strong or unusually tall to excel at the game. You don't even have to play very well to enjoy the game, although you'll enjoy it even more if you know what you're doing.

I started playing in 1915, when I was 7 years old, and there was nothing like the book that you're now holding in your hands. In fact, when you'd ask better players how to do something, they'd tell you, "It took me a long time to find out, and now it'll take you a long time." That's not true for you, because you have *The Complete Idiot's Guide to Pool and Billiards*, by World Champion Ewa Laurance and billiard writer Tom Shaw. This book takes you from the very beginning of billiards— making smart choices when you're buying a pool table for your home, buying your first cue, and knowing how billiard rooms work so that you'll be at home when you first walk through the door— to the various games that you can play on a pool table, from 8-Ball to Straight Pool and beyond. You'll find everything that you need to know, including all the basics of playing pool, explained in a clear, simple way, so that you won't get bogged down with technical details. If you ever want to take up the sport seriously, you'll have a firm foundation, but if you just want to know what billiards is all about and how to play the games, this book makes it easy for you.

Pool is great fun, and so is *The Complete Idiot's Guide to Pool and Billiards*. You can read the book straight through or use it as a reference. The whole idea is to make everything as easy as possible and to make you as knowledgeable as possible, as soon as possible. It succeeds wonderfully.

I invite you to discover a sport that will provide you a lifetime of fun, challenges, and entertainment. Welcome to Pool World!

Jimmy Caras
World Champion 1936, 1938, 1939, 1949, and 1967
Member, The Billiard Congress of America Hall of Fame
Brunswick Billiards Player Representative 1933–present

Introduction

In the following pages, you'll be introduced to a sport that is also a recreation, a social game that can be played by you, and a single set of fundamentals that can be used around the world in more than a dozen variations of the basic game. Billiards is easily adaptable to almost any situation, in almost any location.

I'm making the assumption that you know close to nothing about the sport. You've probably heard of 8-Ball, heard someone mention "pool," and know there's such a thing as a pool table. You really don't even have to know that to enjoy and learn from this book. If you do know more—even quite a bit more—you'll still be able to enjoy and learn. There's a lot of information in the following pages, but it has been broken down into logical, simple bites.

You'll find out that there's a great deal more to billiards than just hitting a ball into a hole. You'll be able to pick one of the variations of billiards that matches your mood at the moment. You'll also learn that you can take the sport to whatever level matches your available time and inclination. There's plenty to learn if you want to get serious about the sport, but you don't have to spend a lot of time practicing if you just want to have fun. Billiards doesn't demand more than you want to commit, but it does leave the learning process open-ended so that you can go as far as you want to go. In this book, you'll learn exactly what I mean.

How to Use This Book

With most things, it's better to start at the beginning, and this book is no exception. But if you already have some billiard knowledge you may want to start with a chapter dealing with something that is new to you, rather than go over other subjects with which you're already familiar. Even then, however, it would be a good idea to read through the early chapters when you get time. You may find that the things you heard from other people aren't exactly correct.

Part 1, "Jumping into Pool!" will tell you a little about the game's history and about the correct perception of pool by the media and public. It will also give you some tips about choosing a place to play, and clue you in on the proper etiquette that is peculiar to billiards. If you're thinking of getting a table for your home—or a cue of your own to take to the local billiard room—then Part 2, "The Home Court Advantage" has all the information you need.

Parts 3, 4, and 5 deal with actually playing the game. Because the most important problem that beginning players have to overcome is wobbling, we start out with the techniques for developing a solid stance and stable grip on the cue. Then we move through more logical steps: learning how to swing your cue, how to hit the cue ball, how to aim the cue ball at the ball you want to hit, and where to hit that ball so that it goes into a pocket.

You may have heard the term "English," or the phrase "using English on the cue ball." But whether you have to not, by the time you get through with this middle section you'll not only understand the phrase but be able to do it.

In Part 5, "Ewa's Super Shots," we move on to things like bank shots and combination shots, and I even show you some trick shots that you can learn to do yourself. Then I put it all together in Part 6 when I explain the actual games, giving you the characteristics, rules, and strategy of 8-Ball, 9-Ball, and the other popular billiard games.

Scattered throughout the main text are sidebars containing extra information, definitions of billiard terms, warnings about mistakes, and a few anecdotes. This is what each sidebar title means:

Heard It in the Poolroom

True stories from the billiard world, including personal anecdotes from Ewa.

Pocket Dictionary

These are definitions of billiard terms. Every sport has its own jargon, and these will put you in the know.

Ewa's Billiard Bits

These are facts, figures, records, and other interesting and useful information about the subject of each chapter.

Scratch!

Watch out for these things. These sidebars tell you about problems that could arise. We want to be sure you're forewarned.

Cue Tips

These are extra bits of information that can give you an edge and help you enjoy the game more.

Acknowledgements

A lifetime of advice, support, and friendship adds up to a list of acknowledgements as long as this book. The publisher wouldn't go for that, so we'd like to thank all our friends, supporters and co-lovers of the sport. Specifically, our thanks to Mitchell and Nikki; to Harold Simonsen and Shari Stauch, Publisher and Executive Editor of *Pool & Billiard Magazine;* to Paul Harris, Art Director at the magazine for his fine diagrams; the legendary Jimmy Caras for his Foreword; Jason Akst and the Billiard Congress of America for the BCA Hall of Fame section; and Karen Kaltofen, graphic artist, for her Web site list.

Part 1
Jumping into Pool!

Just because I fell in love with the game of billiards doesn't mean that you will. But it's my guess that it will happen to you, too, after you try it. Like surgery, however, it's more fun if you know a little about it.

In this book, I give you the benefits of learning how to play the game that 44 million Americans played last year. Maybe not all of them played it well (they didn't have this book!), but they all had fun, and that's one great thing about billiards: You can have fun as either a beginner or as a seasoned pro on the tour.

Billiards is more international than you may have imagined, and it's also an older game than most people realize. In this part, I tell you about the broad world of billiards and how it got so popular. I also tell you about the various types of billiard rooms and how to identify them. In addition, I tell you a little about the tuxedoed and gowned tournament players and the colorful hustlers of past eras.

Part 1 winds up in your head. I give you the scoop on pool etiquette, so that you won't make a faux pas on your first trip to a billiard room. As a prelude to actually getting into the equipment and how to play, I talk about the mental aspects of the sport.

Chapter 1

My First Love Was a Game

In This Chapter

➤ How I discovered pool

➤ This is a sport you can play from age 5 to 95

➤ You don't sweat when playing pool

➤ You don't have to be an expert to have fun

➤ A pool league is a social activity

➤ Males and females can play on an equal basis

I have always loved sports. Growing up, I played soccer, basketball, and hockey, and I loved to watch soccer and hockey games on TV with my dad. I also had a passion for track-and-field events, skiing, and some other nonball sports—although sports that use balls always intrigued me the most. I grew up in Sweden and I may very possibly have watched every major championship that Bjorn Borg ever won. All in all, I guess you could say I was something of a tomboy.

When I was introduced to billiards, however, all other sports paled by comparison. From the very beginning, I loved the mystique surrounding the game, as well as the colorful balls, the dramatically lighted table, and the silent intensity with which players tried to solve the layout of the rack. After I played the game twice, I pretty much knew that this was the sport I wanted to be mine—the sport where I would see whether I could become the best in the world. Pool obviously wasn't as physically demanding as, say, Australian Rules football, but what it lacked as a physical challenge, it more than made up for when it came to the mental aspect. At the time, I had no true idea of how much there was to this game, but I believe that's why it is such a great sport for me—and will be for you. It constantly puts you to the test.

I have been a pool junkie for close to 20 years now, and every day I play the game, I learn something new. It remains fascinating no matter how long you play—and you can successfully play over an entire lifetime. Players in their 50s and even 60s have won world championships. The endless challenge is one of the main reasons why I fell in love with the game and the main reason why I will always love it, whether I compete or not. Pool is truly a game for life.

Ewa's Billiard Bits

Irving "Deacon" Crane, who was born in Lavonia (Rochester), New York, in 1913 and is a member of the BCA (Billiard Congress of America) Hall of Fame, won world championships in five decades, from the 1930s through the 1970s. The last time he won the title, he was 59 years old.

Scratch!

Beware of the well-meaning advice of strangers in a billiard room. Their pointers may sound logical when you don't yet have a solid foundation in the game, but they may turn out to be less than accurate.

I Started Playing Because of a Boy

I have a brother named Mats, who is three years older than I am. He was a very good athlete, and when he took up the game of pool, my girlfriend Nina and I did, too. The fact that we had no idea what pool was—in fact, we had never even heard of the sport—didn't cause us a moment's hesitation. We were only interested in the players, not the game. (Nina, you see, had a crush on my brother, and I had a crush on his friend Peter.)

I remember the first time we walked into Gavle Biljarden. The place seemed like one big party, the kind where everyone knows everyone else—except you. Nina and I worked our way to a spot in the corner where we could watch Mats and Peter play, and after a few hours, we got up enough courage to rent one of the tables in the back and try the game ourselves. We laughed a lot, as we tried to imitate the people around us who seemed to know what they were doing. But even on that first day, as awkward as we were, the cue somehow felt right in my hand. We had so much fun that we decided to go back the next day.

That was the day when I decided that I had found the sport for me. We played (and I use the word loosely) for hours. After a while, a couple of the better local players stopped by and offered us some advice. Once we learned the fundamentals, there was no stopping us; we became *regulars*. After only a few weeks, the guys who originally took us to the poolroom were a mere memory.

Although we both loved to play pool, Nina was simply having a lot of fun, but I was getting obsessed with it. It didn't take long before I was spending five or six hours a day practicing. The minute I got out of school, I was at the poolroom. I did my homework when it was my opponent's turn at the table, and I always grabbed the last bus home. Later that year, Nina and I entered our first tournament, which was held in

Sundsvall. It turned out to be the first women's tournament ever held in Sweden, and it was run by Jorgen Sandman, who later became instrumental in getting Olympic Committee recognition of pool. I came in fourth, among 35 entrants. It was about that time that I started beating my brother at the game, and shortly thereafter, he quit playing.

Over the next three years, as the other sports faded in importance, I spent every spare moment playing pool. And I mean every spare moment—up to 10 hours a day. I'd get up early, go to the house of the man who owned the poolroom (Leif Johansson), borrow the key, take a bus to town, let myself into the poolroom, and practice all day and into the evening. That's pretty much how I spent my summer vacations for three straight years. As a result, I started winning some events, with the highlight being the Swedish 9-Ball Championship in 1980. In 1981, after again winning the 9-Ball title—and also winning the 14.1 (Straight Pool) event—I was invited to participate in the European Championships.

Pocket Dictionary

Nine-ball is a game played with the cue ball and nine balls numbered 1 through 9. Whoever makes the 9 ball wins.

I had no idea how winning the European Championship would eventually change my life. My brother, Nina, and my parents—IngBritt and Lennart Svensson, who were so supportive of my pool playing—were thrilled for me. They were even more pleased when they heard the news that I'd been invited to participate in the World Championships in New York City. They were less excited three months later, when I called from a hotel room in New York to tell them that I wasn't coming back home. My dream was about to come true: I was going to be a professional pool player. (I wonder if Peter still plays....)

Pocket Dictionary

The game *14.1* (also called *Straight Pool*) is played with the cue ball and 15 numbered balls. Each ball counts as 1 point, and you play to a predetermined figure (such as 125 points).

Pool Is Cool

When I say that pool is cool, I mean that it's fun and exciting. But I also mean that billiards is a very *in* recreation/sport now—and has been since the mid-1980s, when it was suddenly revived (I talk more about that in Chapter 2). At the time, the abruptness of the billiard boom made a lot of people think that in a year or two, something new would pop up and take it's place as the latest fad.

But billiards surprised people by growing year after year, and it continues to do so today.

No Sweat!

As I got older and my social life flourished, finding time to shower, do my hair, and put on makeup after rolling around on a muddy soccer field became increasingly difficult. Being of a competitive nature and loving sports, I found pool to be the perfect activity. It has all the elements of a great sport without the sweat! You can play with the family or on a date and maintain your cool throughout the entire day or evening. And you can actually talk to each other (when you're not shooting, of course; then you want to let your opponent concentrate).

If you and your date are at different skill levels, you can easily handicap a game to even things up. Pool is similar to golf in many ways (although you never get rained out in pool). People who develop good billiard skills seem to have an easier time learning golf. The reason is more than a matter of mastering hand-eye coordination; it has something to do with the stationary ball, the moving stick, and the feel for the way that spin affects the ball's path.

Not having to sweat makes pool a good social activity as well as a sport—something that can't be said about every sport. There's no additional expense in renting a locker room, and you don't have to waste time taking a shower and changing clothes before you meet your playing partner after a game. Many people stop by a billiard room for lunch or on their way home from work and hit balls for 15 or 20 minutes while they're still dressed in business suits. No sweat. Unlike golf or tennis players, pool players can play a single game in a few minutes or stay as long as they like. In either case, they leave looking just as fresh as they did when they walked in.

Cue Tips

Although you don't work up a sweat playing pool, your hands can become damp, and the cue won't slide smoothly through your fingers. If you have your own cue case, carry a small hand towel. If you don't have a case, talc will be available.

The no-sweat aspect of pool is also a boon to people who have had to turn from tennis to golf to billiards for health reasons. Pool puts little or no strain on your body, letting people continue a lifelong interest in competitive sports even after their doctors have told them to take it easy and avoid physical stress.

Who Plays Pool?

Relaxing (relieving stress) and having fun are two of the most common reasons that recreational players give for taking up billiards. When the billiard boom started in the mid-1980s, yuppies (young urban professionals) were the most-written-about group to invade billiard rooms. The sport became so identified with them that the billiard industry began a campaign to feverishly put out the word that pool was for everyone. The feeling in the industry was that yuppiedom might just be a fad, and when the fad disappeared so would the popularity of billiards. What happened was that the word "yuppie" fell out of favor, but the people and pool still go together well.

Almost anyone can play pool. Age, gender, height, weight, and even physical disabilities are not a problem. You can adopt this sport at the age of 5 and reasonably expect to still be able to play it at the age of 95. You may not play as well, but you can still offer a respectable game and have a lot of fun. With pool, you don't have to be the tallest, the fastest, or the biggest. I have friends in wheelchairs who can beat 98 percent of the pool players in the country.

In every sports survey, billiards continues to rise in popularity among all age groups and both genders. The largest groups are males 18 to 34 and 35 to 54, but the number of female players has increased the most dramatically since the 1980s, to 35 percent of all players now. Depending on the survey, billiards is the number two recreational sport in the country (behind bowling or walking) or the number three sport/recreation (behind bowling and basketball). You're about to join 42,231,000 other Americans who play pool. Out of hundreds of sports and recreational activities, billiards was one of only five that showed significant growth in the past year.

Ewa's Billiard Bits

The fact that billiards is harder than it looks is a problem that TV has only partly overcome. When players miss, they often do so because they're attempting something much more complex than the viewer thinks. Explaining the situation would take a long time and require more billiard knowledge than the typical viewer has.

Looking at the Social Side

Although I think more about the professional side of the sport, I'm keenly aware that the social side is critical to the success of billiards. Few other sports can be so easily turned into casual social recreation, and few are as much fun at the level of a complete beginner. The first time you pick up a cue stick, you'll have fun, and I guarantee that you'll be laughing within 10 minutes. The colorful balls will go in unexpected directions, and you'll be surprised that the game is harder than it looks.

It's Fun at All Levels

The element of surprise delights most new players. Even during professional tournaments, a ball that goes in the pocket by mistake or a winning 9 ball that is sunk on the break brings a sudden burst of amusement and applause. Although the unforeseen is often fatal to a pro player's chance of winning a match, there's no doubt that it really breaks the tension during a tough game.

Luck can happen in any sport, but in billiards, you're playing in a controlled indoor environment, on a precise playing surface that is subject to the rules of physics and plane geometry. You're not hitting a ball into the air, where the wind can catch it and do something to it that you didn't plan, and you're not returning a ball hit to you that was being controlled by your opponent. It's all you. Nothing's moving when you step to the table, so everything that happens is a result of what you do. Knowing that all those physical rules are working and that you can use them to succeed is one of the challenges that gets people hooked on pool. I think it's one of the most intensely personal games/sports I've ever come across.

Because you're essentially butting up against your own skill level every time you shoot, you're always trying to move up a notch and do things that you couldn't do before. That's true whether you're playing the second shot of your life or the 20,000th. That may help explain how someone who is brand-new to the game and someone who has been playing for 50 years can find equal enjoyment playing pool. In the end, the game is really a competition against yourself. There may be an opponent, but that person isn't hitting the ball to you and has no influence on how well you execute your next shot. Consequently, pool is one of the most individual of sports, even when you're playing with someone or playing on a team. But as self-reliant as you are when you play pool, you can easily share the fun, which I think is one of the reasons why it's so popular with families.

As I said at the beginning of the chapter, pool is also a great stress reliever. After a high-pressure day, nothing is as good for unwinding both your brain and your body as a quiet 45 minutes of hitting balls on your home table. Anyone who works knows that life is more stressful than ever before, and many people find that billiards provides the perfect antidote. (Maybe they like the reassurance that the fundamental laws of motion and matter are still working just like they're supposed to—that the world really hasn't gone crazy after all.)

Pocket Dictionary

An *in-house league* is a pool league that holds all its matches in one location.

Pocket Dictionary

A *traveling league* is a pool league in which teams move around, playing teams from other locations.

Leagues of Opportunity

League play is both team play and social play, for the most part. I've seen some teams get pretty serious about their games, and they all put out a full effort to capture the season trophies, but the real appeal of leagues is the camaraderie. Billiards, like bowling, is perfect for leagues because the team members aren't running all over the place. One person is playing, and his or her teammates are usually grouped together, cheering the player on. There's time for banter, getting to know one another, and making new friends from the other team.

There are two types of leagues: *in-house* (sometimes called stationary) and *traveling*. A billiard room or tavern might form its own league, get teams organized, and hold a 13-week (typical) session of matches. That's an in-house league. Occasional customers become regulars, and you get to know everybody, so even when it's not league night, you can find someone you know to play a few racks (games) with you.

A traveling league includes one or two teams from each location that play each other on a visitor-versus-home basis. That way, you get to move from location to location with a group of people you know (your team) and meet people (your opponent's team) whom you might never have run into any other way.

I'm using the word *location* because traveling leagues can be either all-tavern teams or all-billiard-room teams. The reason for the separation is that taverns have small, coin-operated tables ($3^1/_2$ feet by 7 feet), whereas billiard rooms have large tables ($4^1/_2$ feet by 9 feet). If the two types of locations were mixed, one team would have a serious advantage over the other from location to location.

There are several national billiard leagues. The easiest way to find one, however, is to ask the house pro or manager at a billiard room, sports bar, or neighborhood tavern. It doesn't matter if you're a beginner at the game. All leagues have handicapping systems (the different systems are the main difference between the leagues) that attempt to put beginning players on par with experienced players. These systems are what make the leagues practical.

Your teammates (and teams usually are composed of both males and females, by the way) will help you improve your game, and when you reach a new level, your handicap will change. The drawback of any handicapping system is that it can take away some of the motivation to improve. In addition, league play is mainly for social mingling anyway, and the goal is just to have fun, not necessarily to become a better player.

Pocket Dictionary

Handicapping means adjusting the goal that players of different skill levels must reach, so as to even the competition.

I don't want to downplay the fact that some league players take their game very, very seriously; practice often; and place more value on winning the season than on socializing. Some of these players go so far as to buy a home version of the coin-operated small tables (the home version simply has no coin mechanism but is otherwise exactly the same as the commercial version) and spend hours and hours practicing on it. A few places—mainly blue-collar towns in the Midwest—have very few billiard rooms, and almost all the pool activity centers around the small bar tables. These places turn their league championships into events of monumental importance.

The few upscale leagues that exist are in-house leagues at the elaborate billiard clubs. In any kind of league, though, it's not the cash prizes (which are small) but the socializing and trophies (also small sometimes) that really count. In fact, they count so much that thousands of people take a week of their vacations to play in the year-end championships in Las Vegas, where the three biggest national leagues hold their events. Walking into the ballroom during one of these events is one of the most overwhelming sights in billiards. Hundreds of the small 7-foot coin-operated tables are lined, row after row, each with two five- or six-person teams doing battle. Family members and friends crowd the sidelines rooting on their loved ones, and everyone has a ball.

Gathering Around the Family Table

If you have a home billiard table, you'll find that it's a magnet during any kind of gathering, from the kids' birthday parties to a summer cookout. People just can't seem to resist picking up a cue and trying to hit a ball into a pocket. The under-18 group can't be pulled away after they discover that you have a table at home. But adults are equally susceptible to the lure of the shiny balls and deep green cloth. When my parents come from Sweden to visit, my daughter Nikki and her grandfather patiently wait for me to finish my practice session each day so that they can have their big challenge match on our home table.

Cue Tips

Getting an outdoor pool table (three companies make them) can really perk up your summer parties. They have to use different materials in the construction of the tables so they don't play exactly like a "real" pool table, but they still provide a lot of fun.

The game brings families together. Even billiard retailers tell me that one of the big reasons that customers give for buying a table is to give the kids a reason to stay home. (It works!)

One of the most appealing things about billiards—in addition to all those I've mentioned so far—is the fact that it's an active game you play standing up and moving around, but still play indoors. What a great change of pace pool is from surfing the Web, watching TV, or playing cards or a board game. It gets the problem-solving part of your brain working while giving you a little physical activity and friendly competition. It works for me.

Billiards Is Sexy

I'm using the word *sexy* in the current sense of being exciting, emotionally stimulating, and very popular. It's nice to be involved in something that is regarded that way, and I was very fortunate to be born at the right time with the right talents. But you don't have to become a professional player to get involved with something sexy. All you have to do is play, and that's what this book is about.

In most sports, success depends on strength, size, and/or speed. That fact makes the top ranks all male and divides men and women. In the old days, the situation wasn't much of a problem, but today, women are active participants in business, numerous professions, and the entertainment industry. That makes billiards the perfect sport for today's lifestyles because it is does not depend on strength, size, and speed.

Pool reflects the progress of society pretty directly. Before the 1960s in America, it was considered unusual for a woman to get seriously involved with pool (although that wasn't the case in Europe), and a typical room of players was probably 85 percent to 90 percent male. When a pro tournament for women was held (and only half a dozen were held a year, in a good year), it was always as an addition to the men's tournament.

The situation changed gradually during the '70s but it wasn't until the '80s that things really changed in a big way. Women players who owned or managed businesses joined the tour board of directors and worked with the other players to restructure the association and design a marketing plan.

Today, the WPBA (Women's Professional Billiard Association) is the most successful tour in billiards. We have 15 professional tournaments a year (the maximum that we can fit into our schedule), which draw the top women players from all over the world. Tournament purses are being increased every season, and an easy majority of the sponsor-endorsement contracts are signed by female professionals.

Television sponsors even sign contracts with the women's tour and then try to arrange to have the male pros represented in some way. Eighty percent of the non-billiard-industry press coverage of pool is about the women professionals, and close to 100 percent of the guest shots on network and cable talk or entertainment programs feature WPBA pros. I can't think of another sport in which this is the case.

Beyond just making you more knowledgeable about the world of billiards, knowing about the success of the women's tour illustrates the fact that pool is one of the most gender-neutral sports around. Men and women can play on an equal footing, making it great for dates, families, social gatherings, and the world we live in today.

Billiards and Business

Golf is the traditional business game. A few country clubs have a billiard room with expensive tables and English hunting prints on the walls, but I'm surprised that it's not an obligatory feature. A billiard room and a golf country club would go together well, and it would be a nice source of income on rainy days. I suppose the reason is that no one at a country club has the expertise to manage the room. But as a non-running, non-sweating sport, billiards is an ideal way to play a game and conduct business at the same time.

Billiards is a natural for business discussions because you can talk while you play. You're not positioned 20 yards from the next player or running helter-skelter in a dozen directions. You're in a quiet atmosphere, and you're close together.

Billiards at a private club, a private room at a public billiard room, a golf club, or anywhere else is a relatively subdued activity. Taking advantage of one of the many natural pauses in the game, you can break to make a business point, and then get back to your shot and score a billiard point. Knowing how to play can help you with all types of clients and co-workers, as well as help you pocket more balls and have more fun.

Because of the heavy schedule of pro tournaments, charity events, and new billiard-clubs openings that I attend each year, I try to limit my corporate exhibitions to two a month. Still, I can get a very good feel for what Fortune 500 companies think about pool, and I'm struck over and over again by how versatile the sport is and how much everyone loves playing the game. No matter what kind of business an organization does, and no matter whether it's a trade show, a corporate fun day, a seminar series, a corporate party for top customers, or a hospitality evening at an annual meeting, the pool table quickly becomes the focus of everyone's attention, drawing the biggest crowd. I've had a couple hundred people trying to see the exhibition while the trade-show aisles around us were almost empty.

Pocket Dictionary

An *exhibition* is an appearance by a professional player that always includes trick shots and usually includes a "play the pro" session and some instruction.

Sometimes, my appearance has a tie-in with the theme of a company's presentation, and sometimes, it's simply something that will attract (and entertain) a crowd. Sony's theme for its booth at the electronics show in Chicago in the early '90s, for example, was "DO Get Behind the Eight-Ball"—a way of introducing the company's 8mm video format.

I once made an appearance for a tool company called ToolMaster, which called its event "We Knock the Socks off the Competition."

A group called Celebrity Focus asked me to appear at a medical convention for PAT Pharmaceuticals, Inc., to help introduce a new product: a series of six shots (the type with a needle), one per month, that would end endometriosis. The theme of the presentation was "Six Shots to Sink Endo." I invented a bunch of trick shots in which six balls went in on each shot. Many of the doctors told me that they grew up playing pool and had tables at home.

From profession to profession, the reaction is the same. I've heard the same story and gotten the same reaction from engineers; toolmakers; video retailers; McDonald's executives; investment consultants from Goldman, Sachs; the chemists and salespeople at GE Electromaterials; and the bankers at J. P. Morgan; among hundreds of others. It seems that everybody loves to play pool.

Heard It in the Poolroom

A certain mid-level professional decided to start doing exhibitions. His second booking was at a corporate function. His ego got the better of him, so he represented himself as being one of the top players in the world. At the end of his trick-shot routine, he invited the assembled executives to pick someone to play him, promising that he would go easy on their choice. The man who stepped forward was Alf Taylor, the CEO of a rug-importing company, and he proceeded to beat the pro into the ground. It turned out that Taylor had spent the first 25 years of his life as a hustler on the road before turning to the corporate world.

Corporations sometimes use in-house planners for their events, but more frequently they call on outside firms that specialize in party/event planning and marketing. These firms in turn contact either my agent or Brunswick Billiards, and it's always a treat to hear the latest industry that is discovering the appeal of pool.

This appeal even extends to other sports. The National Basketball Association polled its players to help them plan exhibitions and teaching clinics for their outings, and billiards topped the list of the players favorite pastimes. Golfers feel the same way (billiards has often been called indoor golf or golf on a table), and I've been invited to many celebrity pro-am golf charity events. At an Arthur Ashe Foundation event, I was teamed with Dr. J (Julius Erving) and found out that he's a pool nut and has a table at home. Olympic skater Scott Hamilton does, too, and we've become good friends. In magazines such as *Architectural Digest*, you see tables in the homes of virtually all the Hollywood stars. Comedian David Brenner even owns his own billiard club in New York City, and Paul Sorvino, Jerry Orbach, and Bruce Willis are frequent customers.

Sports figures, chemists, salespeople, movie stars, retail-store owners, engineers, marketing specialists…everyone loves playing. Billiards has an amazingly broad appeal, and no matter what business you're in, you'll find that knowing how to play will help you.

A doctor told me he put himself through medical school by playing pool. An investment broker wanted a few tips so that she could get good enough to beat her boyfriend when they went on their next date. An electrical engineer wanted me to sign an autograph for everyone on his pool league team back home. Every corporate exhibition brings a flood of questions from people who want to know how to play better pool. It's hard to tell whether they're asking so that they can make a better appearance in a business-social situation or whether they just got hooked on the sport and want to have more fun by playing better. My guess is that they want both things. Now they—and you—have a book that gives you the help that you need.

Least You Need to Know

➤ Billiards can be played at any age.

➤ Billiards has been very in since the mid–1980s.

➤ Because you don't run or sweat, billiards is a great date and business game.

➤ Billiards is fun at all levels.

➤ Most leagues are more social than serious.

➤ Strength and size are not important, so females can play on the same level as males.

Chapter 2

Welcome to Pool World

In This Chapter

➤ How the game began

➤ The elegant tournament champions

➤ The less-than-elegant gamblers

➤ Hollywood's effect on the sport

➤ Is it *pool* or is it *billiards?*

➤ What billiards is today

The commercial said, "You've come a long way, baby!", and it could have been talking about billiards. It has been a strange and fascinating journey, with strict social divisions giving way to mass appeal, and then that appeal had enough ups and downs to resemble a roller coaster. But in the end, the game prevailed. Today, billiards is at an all-time high in popularity and acceptance, which makes being a professional a real joy.

For some reason, billiards never had the popularity swings in my home country, Sweden, that billiards has experienced in its home country, the United States. The game was accepted in Sweden from the start as being both a sport and a recreational activity. It was popular with all ages and classes. You did have to have a house with a big-enough extra room for a table, which meant having some money, but billiards still didn't take on the image of being most popular with the upper class and lower class, which prevailed in the United States until recent times. The reason may be the Swedish socioeconomic structure, which places great emphasis on a large middle class and discourages the formation of an upper or lower class. Whatever the reason, when I came to America as a teenager, I found pool to be much different from what I expected it to be.

It Started as a Lawn Game

Golf, croquet, billiards, and possibly even tennis and badminton have vague roots in long-lost stick-and-ball games. These games came and went over the centuries. Some billiard historians trace the sport back to ancient Egypt, but there may be some wishful thinking involved in that conclusion.

We do know that the sport started during the Middle Ages as a lawn game that was played only by European royalty and the very, very rich. Then, one day, it rained. Royalty does not look favorably on being denied a pleasure, so somebody came up with a way to move the game indoors, to a table. This move took place in Europe, Scandinavia, and Britain around the early 1400s, so we can say that the sport is at least 600 years old.

The first versions were a little like table croquet, with a hole in the middle of the playing surface, a hoop, and a post. Very likely, it became obvious after a few days that sides would be a nice addition to the tables. Running down those drafty castle corridors after the balls must have gotten old in a hurry.

Ewa's Billiard Bits

In 1606, William Shakespeare wrote a play called *The Tragedy of Antony and Cleopatra*. One character says, "Let us to billiards," so the sport must have been well known by the audience. It may also explain why so many people try to establish the game as having come from ancient Egypt.

In trying to nail down the elusive beginning of billiards, some folks say that the game may be of French origin, because the word *billiard* means "stick with a small hook at the end." This is a good description of the original billiard cues, called *maces*, which looked more like wooden golf putters than modern billiard cues. But that really only means the word *billiards*, which originated in France, was first used in England during the 1500s.

As sparse as the information is about early European play of billiard-type games, billiard history draws a nearly complete blank on the roots of the game in Asia, sub-Asia, Africa, and South America. Colonialists brought their games with them, but they usually discovered that some kind of indigenous table-ball-stick game was already being played. The better-made European equipment dominated, however. Today, you will find billiard games played around the world.

The Hustlers versus The Tuxedos

For the first two hundred years of the game's existence, only royalty and the rich played, but as nonfarm classes developed, so did public billiard rooms. Develop a game of skill, and you eventually get gambling. (This situation is true of golf, soccer, football, billiards, and many other sports.) Get gambling, and you get people trying to get an edge by less-than-honest means.

The term used today is *"hustler,"* and although hustlers hang around the golf courses and the sites of other one-on-one sports, the word has been associated mostly with pool, probably because of the 1961 movie of the same name. Until the 20th century, hustlers were called *sharps* (a word that hangs on today in the word *cardsharp).*

Heard It in the Poolroom

The second-greatest pool-match concentration-breaker of all time was a trick used by the great Indiana gambler, oil tycoon, and pool player Hubert "Daddy Warbucks" Cokes. Cokes favored dark three-piece suits. He would position himself across the table from his opponent, and just as the man was about to hit a crucial shot, Cokes would whip a huge white handkerchief out of his coat pocket. His opponent was lucky to not drop his cue, let alone make the shot.

In America, the first "world championship" (really, the North American pool championship) was held in 1878, but the game was hugely popular from the 1830s onward. During the American Civil War in the 1860s, the results of billiard tournaments often made bigger headlines than news from the battlefront. Players were celebrities, receiving the treatment that Michael Jordan gets today and playing in tuxedos before capacity crowds of 5,000 people. (I can't imagine how anyone in the back rows could see what was going on.)

The 1900s

Although many well-heeled people visited public billiard rooms—and some very fancy rooms existed—the division of the world-class players into tuxedoed tournament types and poolroom gamblers was well established by the turn of the century. After 1910, top players such as Jerome Keogh, Willie Hoppe, Frank Taberski, and the astounding Ralph Greenleaf were household names. Greenleaf won his first world championship in 1919, at the tender age of 20, and held the title 13 times between then and 1937. Only the appearances of Jimmy Caras ("The Greek Wizard") and Willie Mosconi was able to put an end to his reign.

Mosconi brought home the gold 15 times, which would seem to top Greenleaf's 13 world titles. But say that around Straight Pool fans and you're sure to start an argument. Mosconi, you see, played a few of his tournaments on 9-foot tables rather than the 10-foot-long tables that were standard for tournaments before World War II. Further, the cloth and balls changed over time. During the late 50s, Mosconi held the title unchallenged because the popularity of Straight Pool had fallen off and no one scheduled a world tournament. Finally, a world title holder could be challenged (under pre-WWII rules) by the runner-up in the last world tournament, and an additional world title match could be held two months after the first one. That meant that some years Greenleaf was world champion two or three times (these victories are not counted in his 13 years of world titles), but not always consecutively.

As Greenleaf was fading, Mosconi was coming up. Who, then, was the best Straight Pool player of all time? All the variables make it a complicated issue, made more so by the fact that the men were from different generations and didn't play each other. The question has been debated for 50 years, and pool fans will talk about it for the next 50.

While Ralph Greenleaf battered all tuxedo contenders during the Roaring '20s and most of the Depression (1930s), the hustler subculture developed fully, aided by the automobile. Top nontournament players could travel from town to town, play poorly (called "laying down the lemon," in the hustler's world), get the stakes up high, make some side bets, and then clean out the entire pool-playing population of a town. They often used false names and always stayed clear of professional tournaments where news photographers gathered.

Ewa's Billiard Bits

Ralph Greenleaf and Willie Mosconi, the two greatest names in pool in the 20th century, made only one national exhibition tour together. Greenleaf was at the end of his career, and Mosconi at the beginning of his. On the first part of the tour, Greenleaf dominated, but Mosconi won more matches in the second half.

The hustlers played in small towns and big cities. Even a rural community of 8,000 people would have five or six poolrooms in those days. Cities had entire four- and five-story buildings devoted to billiards, with more than 100 tables, plus bowling lanes in the basement.

The two sides rarely played each other. Although many of the tournament stars were not above some occasional gambling, they disdained the hustlers. To challenge them and win proved little, but to play one and lose meant great harm to the stars' reputations. On the other hand, the undercover gamblers weren't eager to play the top tournament players, either. If they won, they would become famous and could no longer deceive opponents into thinking that they played at a modest level. If they lost, it would cost them money, and above all, they were playing to make money. Consequently, the two groups engaged in a war of words, each saying that the other group couldn't play under the conditions *it* had to face and forever arguing about who the best players really were.

Heard It in the Poolroom

The greatest pool-match concentration-breaker, bar none, was used by only one player: a famed gambler of the 1920s and '30s named Bob Cannefax. He was a world-class talent, even though he had a wooden leg. During a match, he would clean his fingernails with a penknife. When his opponent was about to hit a game-winning shot, the gambler would suddenly and violently stab himself in his wooden leg. His unnerved opponents could rarely continue the game. The trick was so shocking that it often worked on the same opponent more than once.

Going to War, Then Pausing for Peace

When World War II started, the tournaments stopped. Famous players turned to entertaining the troops with exhibitions, and professional trick-shot artists such as Charles Peterson, Clarence Anderson, and Jack White took to the USO circuit. The nontournament players started *"jamborees,"* which were congregations of gamblers in one location, usually near a huge military base (such as the one in Norfolk, Virginia).

After the war, the G.I.s came home, bought modest tract houses (too modest for billiard tables), and began raising families. Across the country, 40 percent of the billiard rooms closed their doors, and the owners waited for the postwar Baby Boomers to reach playing age. Hustlers went back on the road, holding jamborees in action towns such as San Francisco or at horse-racing meets in Hot Springs, Arkansas; Louisville, Kentucky; and DuQuoin, Illinois, a tiny town just a couple of miles from the home of Minnesota Fats.

On the tournament side, although Willie Mosconi remained world champion—a title that he first won in 1941—there was little activity. In 1954, and from 1957 to 1962, there were no world-championship tournaments at all. The best players in the world could no longer earn a living at their game. They had to wait until 1961, when the film *The Hustler* opened in neighborhood theaters across America.

Scratch!

Never play pool for money with a stranger named Fats, Slim, or Red.

Everything (Pool, too) Changed in the '60s

Not many people in billiards liked the movie *The Hustler* at first. It seemed to show pool at its worst, and most people involved in the sport regarded it as being a death knell. Surprisingly, the movie turned out to be just the thing that was needed to revive the sport.

Although all of billiards benefited from the movie, it also achieved something else: It brought the traveling gamblers in out of the cold, and the public got to learn a little about their lives. Contrary to myth, many of the "hustlers" hadn't hustled at all—that is, they didn't deceive their opponents. They would go into a poolroom and ask whether anyone wanted to play pool for money. That tactic, called *"declaring,"* wasn't uncommon. Some people, such as New York Fats (in 1961, when *The Hustler* was released, he began calling himself "Minnesota Fats"), did a little of both.

Born Rudolph W. Wanderone, Jr., in the Hell's Kitchen district of New York City, Minnesota Fats sounded just like W. C. Fields and was just as funny. Although he was a world-class nontournament player during the 1930s and '40s, his strong suit was being able to talk people into playing when they had no intention of betting a dime. Fats was past his playing prime when the movie came out, but he started a second career giving exhibitions in which he sometimes never made a shot. He'd start talking, the audience would start laughing, and it was all show biz after that.

I don't like the seedy side of the game and am very happy that it is almost all in the sport's past, but listening to Fats talk was an absolute ball. He was simply hilarious, and I never saw a crowd that wasn't doubled over when he went into his routine. He was a great showman and brought a lot of good publicity to the sport. When he and some of the other colorful characters from his world and his era got together, they told stories that would keep me entertained for hours.

Ewa's Billiard Bits

Paul Newman learned to play pool for his role in *The Hustler* and made some tough shots, but in the shots in which you see only the hands, you're watching World Champion Willie Mosconi shoot. It was Mosconi who suggested Jackie Gleason, an excellent player, for the role of Minnesota Fats.

The Hustler made pool popular again, and it was timed just right, because the Baby Boomers were in their teens and looking for recreation. Even the gamblers thought that prosperity was at hand. Two big regular annual tournaments began: one at Johnston City, Illinois (called The Hustler's Tournament, because it brought all the traveling gamblers together), and the other at the Sands Hotel and Casino in Las Vegas. Both tournaments were promoted by the Jansco Brothers. CBS Sports and ABC's "Wide World of Sports" discovered the tournaments, and suddenly, the hustlers were playing in suits and ties on national television. A few balked at getting their faces on the tube, but most welcomed the move to legitimacy. The promoters quickly changed the event's name to The World All-Around Pool Championship, and even a few of the tuxedo players, such as Irving "Deacon" Crane and Harold Worst joined in. Willie Mosconi, Jimmy Caras, and others stayed away, however.

The late '60s was a unique time in America, and social changes affected the game, which started to decline during the '70s. It would be more than a decade before it revved up to full steam again.

Pool and Billiards Today

The Hustler killed hustling, because it made people aware that the stranger they were playing for a few dollars might be a top player disguising his ability. In the words of one player, "It got to be so bad, as soon as you offered to play for a couple dollars, they'd call the manager, who would ask you to leave." From that time on, people who gambled on pool played with other people who gambled on pool, and rarely did an innocent bystander get taken.

That's not to say that some people don't still try, but only the very naive lose more than a few dollars in a friendly game of pool with a stranger. I give you some advice about that situation near the end of the next chapter, in the section called "How to Spot a Hustle."

To Paul Newman, With Love

In 1986, the game changed into what it is today. As was true of the boom during the '60s, the reason was Hollywood. Paul Newman reprised his role as "Fast Eddie" Felson from *The Hustler* and teamed up with young heartthrob Tom Cruise to make *The Color of Money*. Like its predecessor, *The Color of Money* presented an outdated, almost '50s version of the sport, at least until the tournament scenes in the last part. That's when *Pool & Billiard Magazine*, the official consultant for the film, stepped in and explained how tournaments really worked.

The day after the film's release, the boom began, and it hasn't stopped since. The game went upscale in a hurry, with million-dollar billiard clubs opening around the country. My exhibition schedule tripled overnight, not only for appearances at stylish new billiard clubs, but also for shows at corporate gatherings and sports conferences. Twenty-five years after *The Hustler*, Ol' Blue Eyes had done it again, and this time he walked away with an Oscar for Best Actor.

Scratch!

Don't try to imitate Tom Cruise's cue-twirling dance from *The Color of Money* in your local billiard room. You'll most likely be asked to either stop or leave.

In Japan, where money isn't green, the movie was released as *The Hustler II*, and it sparked almost as big a boom as it did in the States. Japanese businessmen frantically ripped out bowling lanes, video-game rooms, and even restaurants to make room for new "pool bars." The sky-high real estate prices in Tokyo during the late '80s didn't slow the entrepreneurs down; they just charged players $35 an hour!

To a lesser degree, the same thing happened in Europe, Hong Kong, the Philippines, and dozens of other places. Overseas bookings started coming into my agent's office faster than they could be scheduled.

Groups of eight or more female pro players were offered all-expenses-paid trips to Japan just to be in an eight-player invitational tournament (with healthy prize money). In countries that had weak billiard associations, the associations became strong, and in areas that had no associations, groups were started. American manufacturers of billiard equipment began exporting as fast as they could build the tables and cues, and they added on to existing plants or built new ones. One manufacturer shipped 20 9-foot tables, at 1,800 pounds apiece, to Japan via overnight air cargo! (I would loved to have seen that Federal Express invoice.) Suddenly, everything from chalk to tables was in short supply. More than a couple of millionaires were created in a few short months.

The Color of Money was the right movie for the right time. Had it been released five years earlier, when the country was in a different mood and different economic conditions prevailed, it might have had little effect on billiards, but in 1986, it hit a sport that was primed for explosive growth. In fact, the first two million-dollar billiard rooms had opened (in Boston and Atlanta) before the movie was released. That hadn't happened for 30 years. Something was in the air. It may have been the changing age and income demographics of the country. The so-called yuppies were the first group to rediscover the sport in a big way, and they themselves were a new phenomenon. But whatever the ancillary forces were, one guy really made it all possible when he said "Let's go" to Martin Scorsese's movie proposal. So thank you, Paul Newman, from everyone who loves billiards.

It's a Game and a Sport

OK, there was a boom, but was it a booming game, or was it a booming sport? John McEnroe once said that the difference between a game and a sport was that to be a sport, you at some point had to run. Conveniently, that definition fit his game, tennis. I've talked with other sports figures at various sports conferences and seminars, and I've heard everything from the similar "you have to sweat" to the facetious "you get paid for a sport." Some people say that if a physical element is involved (hand–eye coordination, for example), plus a professional body of players playing by prescribed rules, you have a sport—golf, but not chess.

So there is no single definition of the word "*sport*," but there are many opinions. The vast majority of people who play billiards (probably including you), play for fun, recreation, business, or social reasons. There is a large body of serious players, however, and many people such as me who play billiards professionally. Sure, billiards is fun, but professional competition is serious and very, very intense. So I know that billiards has two distinct sides: the game and the sport. In "Shooting for the Olympic Goal" later in this chapter, I tell you how the "Is it a sport?" question was finally settled.

Is It "Pool" or Is It "Billiards"?

Is it *"pool,"* or is it *"billiards"*?

Yes.

Billiards is the name that's used for the collection of cue sports. The three divisions are Pool, Snooker (a game played with 22 balls on a table with rounded pocket openings), and Carom (a game played with either three or four balls on a table with no pockets). So when you play pool, you are playing billiards, but when you're playing billiards, you may or may not be playing pool.

Because the word *pool* is perceived as carrying some slightly negative images, the word *billiards* is being used far more often. ESPN's frequent airing of tournaments is always listed, properly, as "Billiards" in television guides, and that's the term used in association names, tour names, club names, and conversation. *Pool* is used in speech, as in "shooting pool," when the term *billiards* might be awkward. I use the terms interchangeably throughout this book to get you accustomed to real-life use.

Pocket Dictionary

Billiards is the term for any cue sport, including pool, Snooker, and Carom games. The term is also used interchangeably with the word *pool*.

Not to confuse you, but in case you aren't from the United States or if you travel overseas, the following discussion applies to billiards in a global sense. When the British refer to "billiards," they are not using the term the same way that Americans do. The British have a game, which came before Snooker, that they always called simply *billiards*. When people elsewhere in the world refer to that game, they call it "English billiards." Snooker, which was developed as a game to play on an English billiard table, soon eclipsed the basic game. In England, pool is called "American Pool" to differentiate it from the English variety of pool. (In English-speaking Canada, by the way, pool was called "Boston" until the late '80s (it's now called pool), but Snooker clubs are called *pool halls*.)

Pocket Dictionary

Snooker is a game of British origin, played with 21 colored balls and a cue ball on a large pool-type table with rounded pocket openings.

Further, in other parts of the world (too varied to list here but mostly associated with either France or Spain), the term *billiards* sometimes means only Carom games, as it did in the United States until the 1990's. Finally, a specific type of shot in the cue games is called a billiard or carom, so in a pool

Pocket Dictionary

Carom is a game of French origin, played with either three or four balls on a pool-type table with no pockets.

game, you can *billiard* off a ball. (I provide details later in Chapter 20. For now, I just want you to know that this term exists.) *Billiards*, then, can be used interchangeably with the word *pool* in the United States, but not elsewhere in the world.

Take It with You: Pool Is International

Each of the three disciplines of cue sports was popular in separate but influential countries: pool in America, Snooker in England, and Carom in France and Spain. The countries where one of these four nations had influence naturally adopted that country's version of billiards. As a result, Hong Kong, Australia, India, and central and western Canada, for example, adopted Snooker. In Japan, the Philippines, Germany, Puerto Rico, and Panama, the game of choice is pool. Carom has a widespread but weak following in many countries.

Since *The Color of Money* was released, however, pool has become the fastest-growing branch of billiards. The game is more easily played by beginners than either Snooker or Carom but can still be played on a professional level. The tables used are also smaller (Snooker tables are 6 by 12 feet, and Carom tables are 5 by 10 feet, whereas commercial pool tables are 4.5 by 9 feet), so commercial rooms can fit more tables into the same amount of space, thereby increasing their revenue. Another reason for pool's growth is that there are more pool tournaments in America. Finally, the organizations and associations in America can take advantage of the large media and economic base of this country. What that all means is that pool has truly become an international sport, whereas Snooker and Carom are found only in certain countries associated with their colonial pasts, and even there, pool is the growing game.

Shooting for the Olympic Goal

When billiards became so popular around the world, a few people started looking into the possibility of making it an Olympic sport. They found out that the process was long, complex, and expensive. The Billiard Congress of America and Brunswick Billiards picked up the lion's share of the bill and began the process; the world Snooker association (WPBSA) is now adding its financial backing, too, and the Carom association is participating. The first step was to form a world governing body for each of the three divisions (pool, Snooker, and Carom) and then an umbrella governing body for all three. Each division had to meet stringent Olympic requirements, which only seemed to increase as the previous requirements were satisfied.

Finally, in 1996, the International Olympic Committee awarded the WCBS (World Confederation of Billiard Sports) provisional membership in the General Association of International Sports Federations (GAISF). In 1998, the IOC made that status "permanent" and welcomed billiards "into the Olympic family." Being declared a sport by the Olympic committee pretty much settles the "Is it a sport?" question.

Other steps have still to be taken, but billiards is on track for inclusion in the Olympic Games. The IOC is a slow-moving organization and takes the long view, so at this point, the talk is that billiards will debut in the 2008 or 2012 Olympics. Won't it be neat to be able to play an Olympic sport in your family game room or basement?

Discovering the New Image of Pool

Olympic recognition hasn't been widely publicized, but it's an indication of the new image of pool. Two other things have made more impact: upscale billiard rooms and increased television coverage (primarily on ESPN and ESPN2). I tell you about the variety of new billiard rooms in the next chapter, but this is the place to talk about the effect of these facilities on the image of the game. The television coverage speaks for itself.

Unless you're older than 50, you probably haven't been in a billiard room that fits the old stereotype: smoke-filled, dark, and populated by hustlers. With rare exceptions, these places haven't existed for the past 20 years. What you see now are billiard clubs that are large and attractive, located in upper- or middle-class shopping malls in nicer neighborhoods. That is the image of the sport today. (By the way, they may be called billiard *clubs,* but there's no membership involved.)

That image is reflected in the use of billiards in advertising and films. Corporations started using pool scenes in their print and TV ads in a big way in the late 1980s. Nike, Levi Strauss & Co., Price-Waterhouse, Izod, McDonald's, Miller Lite, and hundreds of other companies have found that pool presents a colorful, fun, and positive image to the public. These corporations reinforce this image every time they use billiards in an ad. Hollywood has done the same thing by using a pool table in a TV sitcom or a home billiard room in a mansion in a movie. One billiard writer has tracked the use of film pool scenes from 1920 to now and found a sharp turn away from scenes that involve fights with billiard cues to the use of pool tables as a symbol of the affluent and cultured. In print ads, the tracking reveals that pool has gone from rare appearances to a common symbol for fun and excitement.

ESPN's television coverage of billiard tournaments, whether originating from The Boardwalk at Walt Disney World in Orlando or a billiard club in San Diego, is all nicely packaged and presented. I have the opportunity to be a color commentator for ESPN, so I'm intimately familiar with the work that ESPN does. Because I play in the tournaments (which makes for an interesting juggling act sometimes!), I'm also familiar with the added tensions and concentration-breakers that players face when they have a TV match. The 40-plus hours of coverage is increasing each year as more and more fans discover the game/sport of billiards.

Why I Turned Pro

The modern professional game matches the modern image of billiards, and I probably wouldn't have pursued the idea of playing on the pro tour unless I'd seen improvement on the horizon. When I first considered the idea, the opportunities were sparse. But a combination of a love for the game and the hints of a rosier future were enough to make me take a chance.

Not many people are fortunate enough to be able to love what they do for a living. I consider myself one of the lucky ones. Sure, practicing four to six hours a day gets old from time to time, and there is nothing glamorous about living out of a suitcase, but when it comes down to it, I get to play pool. Whether it's competition, corporate exhibitions, or just me and the table at home or at the local billiard club, playing the game is what I love to do.

When I first started playing, I didn't really have any aspirations to become a professional. I just knew I loved to play. However, little by little, with the encouragement of more seasoned players, I realized I did have a talent for this game. Once I won some competitions, a dream started to take form: I wanted to become a professional player. There were a few obstacles, however. In all of Europe at that time, there was no professional pool circuit. Tournament prizes usually consisted of a trophy and perhaps a toaster (my Mother could soon make toast for the entire neighborhood at one time).

When the opportunity to move to the United States presented itself, it was like a dream come true. I could actually live over here and play on the pro tour! My parents thought that Sweden was a better place for a 17-year-old, but they finally agreed to the move. It turned out that the pro tour in the United States wasn't all I had hoped it would be, although it wasn't long before it broke open. I, along with a small number of other players, was able to enter this sport while the pro tour was still in its infancy, catching it at just the right moment. We've all been part of the incredible growth and positive changes the game has gone through in the last decade and a half. Having served several terms on the WPBA (Women's Professional Billiard Association) Board of Directors, I've had the opportunity to see the improvement first hand.

Things really changed for me in 1988 when I signed an endorsement contract with Brunswick Billiards, the leader in billiard table manufacturing. That was when I was able to truly look on pool as my vocation as well as my avocation. I started doing exhibitions for the company, and with all the upscale billiard clubs opening around the country it seemed as if I was constantly on the road. The size of the billiard boom overwhelmed a lot of people, but the exciting and sustained upward cycle has provided a lot of opportunities and made it possible for the professional tour to succeed.

I still do a lot of shows both here in the United States and internationally, although most are now corporate functions. As big business embraces billiards, I get an opportunity to promote the sport and Brunswick Billiards and have some fun, all at the same time. Along with playing on the pro tour and doing exhibitions, I do color commentating for ESPN, serve on the board of the WPBA and USCBS (United States Confederation of Billiard Sports—the American member of the World organization working on the Olympics), teach, write a monthly instruction column for *Pool & Billiard Magazine,* do charity events, and write books! So, my "pool world" is busy and getting busier, but I love it all because it allows me to play the game for a living, and I love to play the game.

The Least You Need to Know

➤ The first billiard games date back at least 600 years.

➤ The words *billiards* and *pool* can be used interchangeably in America.

➤ Billiards is both a fun recreational game and a serious sport.

➤ Both *The Hustler* (1961) and *The Color of Money* (1986) had a huge positive impact on the popularity of pool.

➤ Hustling decreased drastically in 1961 but it can still happen to you if you play for money with a stranger.

➤ Snooker, a game most popular in Great Britain, is played on a table with rounded pocket openings and a set of balls unique to the game.

➤ Carom, a game most popular in countries connected with France or Spain, is played on a table with no pockets, using three balls.

➤ Billiards is now the term for all cue sports (pool, Snooker, and Carom), so you are playing billiards when playing pool, but not always playing pool when you're playing billiards.

Chapter 3

It's a Home and an Away Game

In This Chapter

➤ The advantages of playing pool at home

➤ The different types of commercial billiard rooms

➤ Other places where you'll commonly find a billiard table

➤ Cautions about betting on billiards

➤ What to expect from a pro shop

I wasn't fortunate enough to have a pool table of my own to practice on when I was growing up. My mother and father were, shall we say, billiard-illiterate. They, as well as my brother Mats and I, had never played pocket billiards or even heard of Minnesota Fats. In fact, we didn't even know that the sport existed. (Some of my relatives in Sweden still call what I do "shooting bowling.") I do have a Gold Crown table at home now, of course, and practice regularly for tournaments. But you don't have to have professional aspirations to enjoy a table in your family room. My daughter, Nikki, and her friends have a ball playing; and when we have friends over, it's a great way for everyone to enjoy themselves (and no, I do not hustle my dinner guests!). I tell you more about the benefits in this chapter, and in Chapter 8, I tell you how to set up a home billiard room.

Learning how to play in my local billiard room brought its own set of advantages. After I started showing up almost every day, some of the top players in the area began offering some helpful advice and instruction that would have taken a long time to figure out in the isolation of home play.

Another great benefit was the opportunity to play on a different table each time I went. Even tables made by the same manufacturer play differently from one another, for reasons as simple as their location in the club. Humidity, for example, greatly affects the way that a table plays, so one near the door is slightly different from one in a corner. A table under an air conditioning/heating duct gives you ball rolls that are not exactly the same as those of the table next to it. Even the number of people in the club affects table play because of the change in humidity.

In addition, a table with new cloth plays differently from one with cloth that has been used a while, and a table in a popular spot has cushions that have been compressed more times. This variety is one advantage of playing in a public room, and I get into more differences in a minute. In this chapter, I want to let you know what home play is all about and how to pick out a commercial billiard room that's right for you.

The Home Game

Not everyone gets a home billiard table with the idea of becoming a very good pool player, although once you hit a few balls, human nature does make you want to be able to make more (put them in the pockets) and miss less. Your original motivation may have been to buy something that looked like fun and that would provide entertainment for family members and friends, but your competitive instincts will soon take over, and you'll start to invite people over based on their playing ability.

In Chapter 5, I tell you what to look for when you pick out a table and what time of year you can get the best prices, but at this point you should know why you should even consider buying a table in the first place.

You can compare having a billiard table to having a computer. Having a computer at the office saves a lot of time, and if you use one there, I'll bet that you also have one at home. You may work on office projects in the evening, or you may just use it for personal things such as e-mail or surfing the Net. Even when you do different things with the computer at home, you're still sharpening your computer skills and adding to your computer knowledge, which makes things easier and better when you fire up your office machine.

Cue Tips

More than a dozen pool-simulation games are available for computers, in both IBM-compatible and Macintosh formats. All of them are fun, and some can actually help your game.

The same thing applies to any sports activity, especially if it's an individual sport such as tennis, golf, or archery. Imagine having an 18-hole golf course in your garage or a tennis court in your basement. (Now imagine your mortgage payments.) Billiards, on the other hand, is a sport that is practical for both home and away play. You can fit a table into your basement, garage, or family room. Granted, a billiard table is a big piece of furniture, and a modest home wouldn't really be able to accommodate a billiard room. That's why so many homes in the northern United States have tables in the basement and why, in the South, garages are converted into rec rooms or family rooms with a pool table as the centerpiece.

The average home has been getting bigger over the past 20 years, a fact that dovetails nicely into the boom in billiards. Larger homes mean more room for a pool table and more families participating in the sport, so when you go to a neighbor's house for a party, you're likely to find a pool table set up in the rec room, basement, Florida room, or billiard room. Knowing how to play will add to your enjoyment and to your host's.

Billiards is not only a sport that fits a home, but also an affordable sport. The initial investment in a table is like your investment in your dining-room set; it's furniture that will last many, many years. Like any other piece of furniture, the better quality you buy, the longer it will last, and it's not uncommon for a really good table to become an heirloom, handed down to the next generation.

After you buy a table and the proper accessories, the only costs that you'll incur are for the occasional replacement of the table cloth and (years down the road) new cushions for the rails. Billiard tables have remained pretty much the same over the past hundred years or so, and I don't expect them to change much in the next hundred years. There will be new designs and styles for all the exterior portions, of course, but the playing area will remain constant, so you'll be able to use a table for as long as it lasts. A very good table may even increase in value after 40 years, when it becomes an antique.

Picking a billiard table for your home involves looking at those styles and designs. I get into that topic, and some other options that are offered, in Chapter 5, but for now, all you need to know is that appearance isn't a problem. There are tables to match every furniture style that you can imagine, with hundreds of different wood stains, different woods, and so on. You can match anything in your house or make your billiard room unique by getting a table, chairs, a light, and cue stands that are completely different from the furniture in your living areas. The choice is yours, and the selection is large.

When you have a home table, you're a hot candidate for a serious case of billiard fever. This common disease is similar to Internet-itis and hobby obsession. Stick a toe in, and before you know it, you're neck-deep and loving every minute of it. You'll be inviting neighbors over just to beat them at 8-Ball. Then they'll turn around and invite themselves over to practice. Before you know it you'll be venturing out to the local billiard establishment to strut your stuff...which brings me to the next topic: choosing a billiard club.

Scratch!

Most people buy 8-foot-long tables for their homes but run into 9-foot-long tables at billiard rooms and end up missing a lot of balls without knowing why. Now you do.

The Away Game

Whether or not you have a home table, you'll eventually want to play in a commercial billiard *room* (also called a billiard *club,* although membership is not required). You may just want to get out of the house, go someplace where things are happening, or try your hand on other equipment. If you bought an 8-foot table (the most common

Pocket Dictionary

The words *club* and *room* are interchangeable when you're talking about commercial places where the game is played.

Cue Tips

If you choose a table against a wall or one in a corner, you'll have fewer people walking by while you're playing.

size for home use), you're sure to want to try the 9-foot models that are used in tournaments and in commercial rooms. (Most rooms now also have 8-foot models along with the 9-footers.) You'll discover that simply adding 12 inches to the length and 6 inches to the width of a table (making it $4^1/_2$ by 9 feet) makes a lot of difference.

The table brand may be different and therefore may play differently, and you may be playing with house cues rather than your own familiar cue. Added to those differences are the distractions of playing in a public place. There's a lot of movement close by as people play on adjoining tables. The wait staff and other customers will be walking by just when you have a critical shot. A pair of couples will burst out in sudden laughter or shout as something happens on their table. You also have to contend with the music from a CD jukebox or internal sound system. It's a wonder that anyone makes a ball. But the reality is that in a billiard room, you learn to focus and make your surroundings fade away—either that, or you join in the fun and start rooting for your partner and laughing when balls roll in unexpected directions.

All those distractions exist to varying degrees, depending on the type of billiard room you choose. Before World War II, there was lots of variety, but from 1940 to 1960, few new rooms were built, and many of the old, ornate billiard palaces closed. The '60s were busy, and new rooms opened, but by '68 and '69, that boom was over, and billiards slipped into a negative period that didn't end until 1985–86. What this means to you is that of the thousands and thousands of billiard rooms around the country, probably 85 percent have been built since the mid-'80s. Almost any commercial room that you see will be new (or fairly new) and targeted to a specific market.

Entrepreneurs took advantage of modern marketing techniques and developed a series of categories designed to meet the needs of specific segments of the population. In the following sections, I break billiard rooms into six types. You can pick the one that appeals to you.

Upscale Rooms

Most upscale rooms are on the affluent side of town (and in the hip part of downtown, if that exists). The location is the easiest way to spot an upscale room from the outside. On the inside, you'll probably find a full restaurant (with a wine list) and a posh bar, along with anywhere from 20 to 45 furniture-style billiard tables. The design theme may be anything from rustic English to technopop, but it will look expensive and

trendy in one way or another. The majority of the
crowd will be professionals, entrepreneurs, or other
up-and-comers in their 20s and 30s—the same mix
that you'd find in any fashionable watering hole.
That's not to say that there won't be some good
players, but for the most part, it's a dating atmosphere or just an enjoyable way to spend an
evening. During the day, you might find people
entertaining business clients or people of sufficient
means that they don't have to work.

Pocket Dictionary

Furniture-style billiard tables are
ornate tables that look like (and
are) fine furniture, as opposed to
the utilitarian look of some commercial tables.

An upscale room may or may not have a pro shop.
The rooms that do have pro shops rarely carry
instructional materials. Instead, they sell a few of the better lines of cues and cases,
along with billiard clothing and small accessories (see Chapters 6 and 7).

By the way, you don't need any special clothing to play pool. A few things work better
than others, as I tell you at the end of the next chapter, but no special shoes or gloves
are required. The type of billiard clothing sold in pro shops is normal clothing (polo
shirts, jackets, T-shirts, and so on) with billiard artwork or slogans.

Most of the upscale rooms have private rooms for rent by companies or individuals,
offering catering and a function organizer who can help you with details. These rooms
are rented for product introductions, press conferences, birthday parties, bar-mitzvah
or bas-mitzvah parties, small family gatherings, and even for entertaining a single
client. One billiard room rents the space to a law office every Friday from 4 to 7 p.m.
What a great way to unwind at the end of a tough week!

The private room(s) in a billiard room may have one table or two, and some clubs have
two or three private rooms with sliding walls that can be opened, making one large
private room. Other billiard rooms have a section divided from the rest of the room by
waist-high walls, with or without planters on top. That way, when the section is not
being used for a private function, it can be open to the public.

A billiard room in this category most likely has a waiting list for tables on Friday and
Saturday nights that can stretch to a couple of hours or more. That may even be the
case on Thursdays and Sundays as well. If you want to play at an upscale club on the
weekends, I suggest that you call first and find out whether you can reserve a table. A
few clubs have waiting lists seven nights a week, although early in the week, the wait
may be only 10 or 20 minutes.

Upscale clubs rarely have video machines or pinball machines, no matter how in those
games are at the moment. You also rarely see anyone under 18 or 21 years of age. Each
state has different laws about whether minors can play in a billiard club that serves
alcohol, but even if minors are allowed, most of the upscale clubs have their own rules
banning underage customers. A few notable exceptions (mostly in California) pop to
mind, but generally, you won't find teens in upscale clubs in the evenings.

The cost to play in this type of room varies a great deal, as it does in all the categories. To say that it's higher than other types of billiard rooms is no surprise, but that also doesn't tell you too much. The cost is never sky-high, however. About the most you might expect to pay is about $14 an hour for two people or $16 an hour for the table time, regardless of the number of people playing. In some upscale clubs, the cost may be half that, and during the day, prices are usually substantially lower—say, $5 an hour for one person and $7 for two or, if the club charges by the table, $6 to $8 an hour. Sometimes, steeper discounts are available during the lunch hour and during happy hour.

Scratch!

If you decide to take a break from playing to have something to eat and drink, be sure to check your set of balls back in at the desk. Tables are rented on time, not on whether you're actually playing, so you could be charged for table time while you were sitting in the restaurant or at the bar.

Neighborhood Rooms

Neighborhood rooms are the biggest category, with the broadest definition. This category is a catch-all group, including all rooms that don't fit in the other classifications. These billiard rooms are in the suburbs, have 15 to 50 tables, and cater to the middle and upper middle class. You'll find them in strip malls and in special-purpose freestanding buildings. They're new (or newish), stylish without being overly hip, lean toward being bright and exciting without going to the point at which people over 50 feel out of place, and attract a broad segment of the surrounding population.

Neighborhood rooms almost always have a pro shop, which frequently is very well stocked. Billiard supply stores in the same town regard the pro shops as direct competition, because a big pro shop sells everything short of actual tables and lighting. They sometimes even tread on the traditional supply-store strongholds of re-covering tables with new cloth and doing cue repairs.

Every now and then, you can find a room of this type that does sell tables. I can think of a couple of billiard rooms that are next door to a full-scale billiard supply store; these companies are owned and operated by the same people, and bolster each other's business. A couple of large rooms are the local dealers for whatever brands of table you find on their billiard-room floors. That's the kind of test drive that can't be beat.

The house pro (this type of room is likely to have one) may do cue repairs; man the pro shop; and help players with tips, occasional lessons, and general billiard information. They also act as directors for any local, state, or regional tournaments that take place at the room. Depending on the business, the house pro may also organize and direct an in-house league or captain the room's team in a traveling league. All these activities are typical of a neighborhood room, and if there's no house pro, the room manager handles these tasks. (Actually, the range of activities is one thing that sets this type of room apart from the others in this chapter.) There's a lot to get involved in at a neighborhood billiard room, but you can ignore all of it if you'd rather just play a quiet game by yourself or with a friend.

Most of these rooms are fairly large, running from 13,000 to 30,000 square feet—a size that allows them to include other features. Aside from the pro shop, a neighborhood room has amenities such as food and drink service of some kind. Finger foods are always available; there's usually a grill; and sometimes, there's a full restaurant and bar. Local liquor licensing laws, the competition in the immediate area, and the goals of the owners are the deciding factors. In some states, alcoholic beverages are limited to beer and wine or to an attached microbrewery.

If no alcohol is served, or if alcohol is downplayed for whatever reason, the room usually has a video and pinball game room off to one side. Nearby are the small coin-operated, 7-foot tables that are the mainstay of taverns. These tables are used for league play and by teens and preteens. Coin-op tables are most common in the Midwest, where there is heavy league action.

Again, it's difficult to say what it will cost to play at a neighborhood room, because rooms vary so much in their approaches to the billiard business. The presence of alcohol can mean a lower price for pool; the tables are used as an inducement to get people into the room, and half (or more) of the profits come from the sale of drinks. Evening play should cost about $3 to $4 for one person or $5 to $6 for two; if prices are by the table, you might pay $8 an hour per table for as many people as are in your party. The cost could be slightly more on Friday and Saturday nights and less during the day.

Ewa's Billiard Bits

A chain of poolrooms called Pink-E's, which started in the western United States, has only coin-operated tables in its rooms, but the rooms have 50 to 100 tables per location, and all the tables are covered in pink cloth!

Sports Bars

The sports-bar phenomenon has created a mix of rooms that rivals the variety in the neighborhood-room category. Although sports bars may not seem to be billiard clubs, they often devote a large percentage of their floor space to pool tables. I'm using the term *sports bar* loosely here, because I've visited some places that I might call billiard rooms with a sports bar, rather than the other way around. These establishments advertise billiards and big-screen TVs with equal enthusiasm, and they have the biggest crowds on game days. Still, pool is what draws people inside most of the time, and it's the major constant attraction.

A billiard room/sports bar probably won't have a pro shop, but it will have a gift shop or at least a gift display. The establishment may sell some clothing, mugs, and caps, and may have a dozen cues on display, but will have little of the expertise that a first-time buyer needs. Other amenities include fast food, finger foods, and a large bar area. At the bar, and scattered around the room, big-screen TV sets are tuned in to regional, local, and national sporting events. Sports bars like coin-operated machines, so shuffle-board, electronic darts, video games, and pinball machines are common.

35

Heard It in the Poolroom

Sports bars are wonderful places for WPBA (Women's Professional Billiard Association) professionals. More than a few of us have been known to challenge the more macho guys to a game, be met with laughter, and then clear the table. We call this process "taking egos."

The prices for pool are pretty much in line with what the neighborhood rooms charge. One thing to watch for are beer promotions. Sports bars like to get involved in promotions, and beer companies thrive on them as well. Watch the ads, and you could find half-price pool days or even free pool during selected hours during the promotion. If you're looking for a boisterous crowd, that's the time to go. If you like to play pool in relative peace and quiet, the specials are a "Do Not Enter" sign.

Club Rooms

Country clubs, Boys' Clubs, Girls' Clubs, YMCAs, YWCAs, YMHAs, Elk's lodges, Moose lodges, skiing lodges, downtown athletic clubs, men's clubs, summer resorts, youth camps, student unions, sorority houses, fraternity houses, military O clubs, NCO clubs, enlisted-men's clubs…there's almost no end to the places where you'll commonly find a billiard table. On my way to a recent billiard-industry convention, I sat next to a man who was flying to Las Vegas to play in the American Indian 8-Ball League Championships. It turns out that there are pool tables at all the reservation community houses around the country, and pool is one of the most popular activities among all the tribes—so popular that the various tribes got together and formed a national Indian pool league.

From American Indian community houses to ski lodges to university student unions, there's such a diverse group of locations that I can't tell you what to expect at each of them. The equipment (and its upkeep) varies. Sometimes, you can play free just because you're a member; sometimes, two or three tables are available; and sometimes, you have to reserve a lone table days in advance. When you see a billiard table at a club where you're a guest, wouldn't it be nice to be able to have the skill to pick up a cue and have people gather around to watch—or stand in line to play you?

Tavern Pool

During the late 1960s and throughout the '70s, the coin-operated tavern table was the most popular model in America. The game best suited for the coin table is 8-Ball, which became the dominant game among recreational players. Tavern play—and the game that many people know as *stripes and solids* or *highs and lows*—kept pool in business for many years and still exists today.

Coin-op tables can be found in taverns, places where teens play, and anywhere else someone can stick a table. League play started around tavern tables and is still stronger in taverns than in billiard rooms. Although tavern coin-operated tables kept the sport alive, they also fixed it as being associated with drinking and all the problems that arise in that kind of situation.

Heard It in the Poolroom

This anecdote has been attributed to several professional players, including Harold Worst (who was a world champion during the 1960s) and the legendary Willie Mosconi (who was world champion 15 times). Both men were purists who played on professional 9- or 10-foot tables. One or the other was shown his first coin-operated 7-foot table and was asked what he thought. "Well, there are six pockets and green cloth and 16 balls," he said as he surveyed the table. "But it isn't pool."

Tavern pool is still very popular, but because of the small table (coin-operated tables are $3^1/_2$ by 7 feet rather than $4^1/_2$ by 9 feet), the unusual cue ball (it's either weighted or larger than the other balls, as I explain in Chapter 5), and the fact that it's difficult or impossible to play certain advanced games on the table (such as Straight Pool and One-Pocket), it's not considered to be *real* pool. Think of tavern pool as being a miniature version of pool.

The cost of a game on a coin-op table varies from location to location. In the 1960s, the cost was 25 cents. But like everything else, the cost of coin-op pool went up over time. Today, the coin mechanism must be fed with anywhere from three to eight quarters to release the balls for a game of pool.

A Blast from the Past: The Action Room

When the sport of billiards almost died during the 1940s and 50s, and then again during the '70s, a huge number of rooms closed. During the first part of the 20th century, New York City had more than 5,000 billiard rooms; by the 1970s, it had two. (Not two thousand—just two rooms.) What kept those rooms, and others like them all across the country, alive was the fact that they were action rooms. If you enjoy playing pool for money, the action room is your destination. (It's also your destination if you want to watch people play for money, or if you just want to take a trip in a time machine back to the less-savory days of two generations ago.)

You can find an action room in most cities with a population of half a million or more. These rooms hang on, defying all the trends of the past two decades. In truth, there probably aren't more than 25 or 30 of these establishments in the entire country, and that number is slowly shrinking every year. To locate one close to you, check out billiard rooms in the telephone book, and call around. Sooner or later, you'll find someone who has heard of such a place and can give you general (if not specific) directions. If your city has an action room, it will be in a less-than-prosperous neighborhood and probably not doing jam-up business.

A room of this type has no pro shop, no house pro, no amenities except strong coffee and secondhand smoke, and no pinball or video games. The equipment will be old but probably very well taken care of, because serious money can ride on how well it plays. There'll be no jukebox, either. Especially no jukebox.

The cost to play depends on whether you're foolish enough to bet on a game. If you're not, table-time rates are probably low. If, as an outsider, you do decide to test your skill and back it with money, you'll end up as an anecdote. Colorful characters—and action rooms are definitely populated by colorful characters—tell colorful stories, so it will be an embellished anecdote, and not too complimentary to you, but at least you'll have reached some level of fame.

Everyone wants to know about the possibility of danger in a place like this, but I can't really tell you much. Although you can gamble on just about anything, anywhere, the true action rooms hardly exist anymore, and they're not places that I suggest you search out.

How to Spot a Hustle

You can get hustled in anything you do, but since the Paul Newman movie in 1961, the word *hustler* has been closely associated with pool. OK, it's an unfair association, but that's the way it is. The irony is that the popularity of the movie practically put an end to most pool hustling, because it wised up the naive mid-century American public. Today, betting on a game of pool for any really significant amount of money is relegated to people who do that for a living (and to their financial backers). They don't hustle; they gamble.

That's not to say that people don't try to get an edge by saying how badly they've been playing and so on, but that all takes place before the actual game. The old gambit from the movie—playing poorly at first; then raising the bet and playing well—is a nonstarter in these situations. Hardly anyone is going to purposely lose when playing for four or five figures; it just doesn't make sense. Hustling also doesn't involve the public, so it's unlikely that you'll have a chance to see it.

On the other hand, plenty of people bet on sports, and pool is a sport. These people, too, try to get an edge. One way to do that is to get involved with someone who has less knowledge than they do. (The same thing occurs in every other sport, as well as a fair number of businesses.) To avoid getting into a trap like that, never play for money. If a stranger offers, decline.

But suppose that you do want to make the game more intense by betting on your skill and that such betting is legal in your state (which is not the case in most states). What kind of thing would a very good player do to get your money? These days, your opponent might do something like give you a loose rack of balls to break open at the beginning of the game. A loose rack absorbs the power of the cue ball that hits it, and balls are less likely to go into a pocket on the break. How many players know to check the rack of balls to make sure each is touching its neighbor before breaking?

Cue Tips

If you do hear of a money match, try to watch it. You'll see some of the best playing around and will pick up a lot of tips just by watching.

Another trick is tapping the one-ball (the ball at the front of the rack of balls) into the cloth with another ball to make sure that it stays in place, but really lowering the center of the ball by putting it in a dimple in the cloth. When the center of the one-ball is below the center of the cue ball, the power of the cue ball on the break is partially directed down into the table, again lowering the chance that a ball will be made on the break. This mismatched centering also causes the cue ball to jump up when it hits the rack of balls, increasing the chance that it will fly off the table. That's a foul against you and gives your opponent an advantage.

Those are a couple examples of how easy it is to do something that's apparently innocent but that can give one player an edge over the other. I hope it also shows you that it's foolhardy to gamble on pool until you know everything possible about the game.

For serious, legitimate competition, check out local tournaments, which are a real test of your skill level. If tournaments are held too infrequently, or if your room doesn't stage anything for players at your level, try playing other customers. In a billiard room, you don't need an introduction. Someone may prefer to practice alone to hone a particular skill, and that's fine; just ask someone else. Talk to the house pro or counter person, and ask who is about equal to you or perhaps just a little bit better. Matching up with other room regulars—or anyone else as long, as it doesn't involve money—is the way that most people get the maximum enjoyment out of the game and improve their skills at the same time. As you become a regular you'll learn how well other people play and whether they favor a particular game, such as 9-Ball or 8-Ball.

Pro Shop Till You Drop

I've mentioned pro shops a couple of times, and it's worthwhile to take a second to tell you what billiard pro shops are all about. You'll see quite a variety, and when you're looking for a particular item, such as a new cue, case, or cue-tip tool (see chapter 6), it would be natural to think of going to a nearby billiard room to see what it has to offer.

I've seen pro shops with as many as 600 cues, at prices ranging from $65 to $6,500. Some shops have 50 cue cases, a full range of accessories, the latest pool and billiard magazines, books and tapes of billiard instruction, clothing, chalk, balls, and a full cue-repair facility. I've also seen so-called pro shops that have half a dozen cues and little else. Retailing is something that not all billiard rooms embrace with enthusiasm. Many rooms would rather leave that end to the local billiard supply store, which is designed to handle a large quantity of merchandise (including tables), so you have to check each pro shop out individually.

Pocket Dictionary

A *billiard supply store* is a retail store that carries a large quantity of billiard supplies, ranging from tables and lights to chalk, and that also sells barstools, jukeboxes, and other merchandise for your home billiard room and rec room.

Billiards is not a sport that requires a lot of gear (to the chagrin of billiard retailers). It is a sport in which the technology is pretty stable. If someone invented a new material for billiard balls, it would have to play exactly like the material in balls that already exist, and because current balls last for 20 years (except cue balls, which get hit on every shot) and are reasonably priced, there's little incentive to change things. After you get the basic items, you'll have things that last a long time and won't need to be replaced. That's true even if you have your own table at home.

What you find in a billiard shop, then, are items that you may want but don't have to have. You can get clothing with billiard designs or a tool for shaping your cue tip that works a little better than the one you already have. You can find a fancier cue, one with a design that strikes you as being more appropriate to your personality, or even one with a taper that works better for your playing style, but after you buy it, you won't have to replace it for many, many years.

The only billiard item that needs regular attention is your cue tip. The tip wears out and must be replaced fairly often: once a year for a casual player and every four months for a regular player. Large pro shops have a cue-repair facility, and small ones have arrangements with a local cue-repair person. The ferrule (the white portion, about an inch and a quarter long, just behind the cue tip) may crack every couple of years and will have to be replaced.

You can also find instructional materials in a pro shop. But beyond the few items mentioned in the preceding paragraphs, the stock consists of items that you may want but that won't make you play any better.

The Billiard Mail Mall

The '90s brought something new to billiard players—mail-order billiard supplies. Local billiard supply stores and national equipment wholesalers both began looking at the mail-order market. Entering it was as easy as advertising in the leading billiard publications, and they discovered that mail-order was a low-overhead way of doing business. At first, players in small towns became their customers because these players could then get items that no one carried locally. Business expanded, and today there are dozens of companies selling through ads in billiard publications.

Smaller companies realized that they could follow the same path as the big dealers and wholesalers. Many of them weren't large enough to attract dealers for their products, but they didn't need to be large to buy an ad and take orders over the phone. They, too, started a mail-order operation. Custom cue makers have been the biggest manufacturing entities to benefit, but today you can buy anything from chalk to a table through mail-order. Prices are competitive, even with shipping costs, and the only drawback is one that plagues every mail-order customer: You don't get to hold the item before you buy it. But that's a small problem because you can see (even use) almost anything you want to buy at your local billiard club first. If you can't find the actual model (a particular cue design, for example), you can usually find another model by the same manufacturer and get a very good idea of what yours will feel like.

The Least You Need to Know

➤ A home table is affordable, fun, and a social center, and it can also be used for serious practice.

➤ Home tables are usually 8 feet long, but commercial and professional tables are 9 feet long.

➤ Upscale rooms usually feature private rooms for business or social functions.

➤ Neighborhood rooms offer the most activities (leagues, tournaments, house pros, and so on).

➤ Taverns feature small, coin-operated tables that play differently from regular pool tables.

➤ You can buy equipment such as cues and chalk at a pro shop, by mail order, or at a billiard supply store.

➤ Never play a stranger for money.

Chapter 4

Polite Pool

In This Chapter

➤ Avoiding pool gaffes

➤ Good sportsmanship in pool

➤ Building playing confidence

➤ Tuning out distractions

➤ The mystery of deadstroke

➤ Dressing for billiards

Over the past 20 years, the nonphysical part of sports has come under a lot of scrutiny. That's what I'm going to tell you about in this chapter, but I'm also including (along with info on the mental game) some of the special rules of behavior, so that you won't be guilty of committing a billiard blunder. By the time you're done reading this chapter, you'll know all about how to act both at the table and around the table. I'm even going to throw in a few tips on how to dress for the sport. You don't need pads or spiked shoes, but some things will make your experience more pleasant.

The topic of the mental game is especially close to my heart. After playing pool for as long as I have, with the success that I've had, the game is now 99 percent mental for me. From a good day to a bad one, a good tournament to a poor one, the difference is rarely in my stroke, but in my head. If you're just taking up billiards, this may not seem to be important, but it is. From the moment that you pick up your first cue and attempt to hit the cue ball into an object ball, you've engaged your brain in the game. Even if you're going to be playing strictly for fun, you'll find yourself concentrating on tough shots and trying to do better each time you step to the table. Having the right mental attitude makes it easier to be successful.

The New Haven: Etiquette

Perhaps because there have been so many millions of new players since the mid-1980s, there has been a lot of emphasis on proper billiard behavior lately. Newbies run into regulars, and the regulars are sometimes quick to point out what should and should not be done. There are a lot of rules for professional tournament play, but for nontournament play, the rules are fairly simple. Most of the things that you need to know are just common sense and courtesy, but you should know about a couple of billiard-specific circumstances. It's better to be forewarned than to end up behind the social eight ball.

Heard It in the Poolroom

During the early rounds of a national tournament in Ohio, while play was under way on a dozen tables, one of the big lighting fixtures broke loose and crashed down in the middle of a table. The noise was explosive, as the fluorescent tubes disintegrated and dust and bits of glass flew in all directions. The player at the table naturally jumped back, but the pros at adjoining tables were so focused on their matches that they barely glanced up.

Don't Move!

A common-sense rule is not to cause a distraction that might make a player miss a shot. Sudden loud noises or movement are the most common problems, but one rule is especially important: Don't stand in, or pass across, the shooter's line of sight. The *line of sight* is the line that runs from the player's eyes and down the cue through the cue ball to the wall. If you're two or three tables away, you're out of range, but if you're playing at the next table, keep nearby players in your peripheral vision so that you'll know when they have a shot that requires them to face your table.

If you're already in a player's line of sight when he or she gets down to shoot, simply freeze until the shot is complete. If you freeze, and the player looks up at you, just step away four or five feet. Some players object to having even a motionless person in their line of sight, because part of their mind will be wondering whether that person knows enough to stay still through the shot or will suddenly move at the critical moment.

This rule also applies to the people who are playing at your table, of course. If you're in the shooter's line of sight, stay motionless until the shot is complete.

Use a little caution when moving around the table, too. A person who is concentrating on a shot may suddenly spread his legs and get down into shooting position, or jerk his cue back without looking behind himself. You could end up with a bruise on your hip or get your feet tangled with the player's.

Should you and a person at the next table find that you have to occupy the same place to be in position to play your next shot, it is better to let the other person go first. It's polite, sure, but there's more to it than that. The theory—and it has some validity—is that the person who goes first may not be able to focus totally, because she's aware that someone else is almost standing over her shoulder, waiting for her to finish. The person who shoots last, however, has no such distraction. The advantage, then, is to the person who politely stands aside and lets the other player shoot. (Mom was right when she said that politeness pays.)

Pocket Dictionary

Line of sight is the line from the shooter's eyes and down the cue through the cue ball to the nearest wall.

Don't Stall

Taking unusually long to decide how to shoot a shot is irritating to some people. Among serious players, it's sometimes used as a stalling tactic to throw off an opponent's rhythm or to get his or her goat. Among less-serious players, it just lessens the fun.

Pros use a 45-second shot clock for televised tournament matches, and that's not an unreasonable length of time for beginners who are shooting an average shot. If the situation on the table is complex, feel free to take longer. If you're a naturally slow player, or if you're just learning the game and are at a loss about what to do when you're faced with a shot, just hope that the person you're playing with will understand.

When you become a regular at a billiard room, you'll find out the playing style of other regulars and can spot the playing speed of new players, so you can match up with someone who is not only at a comparable skill level, but also plays at a comparable speed. A game that matches a slow player with a fast player can be agony for both of them.

Chalk It Up

When you chalk your cue tip, place the chalk on the table rail, so that the open side is neither up nor down. If you place it down, the chalk leaves a blue mark on the rail, which transfers to the clothing of the next person who bends over that section of the rail. If you leave it up, the chalk marks other players' clothing directly.

Scratch!

Chalking your tip after you play your last shot and again before your next shot can deposit a too-thick layer of chalk on the tip. A caked tip actually slides off the cue ball rather than grips it, which is exactly what you *don't* want.

Another tip: Don't get into the habit of chalking your tip *after* you shoot. That's when the incoming player needs the chalk. It's surprisingly easy to get into this habit as a way of making sure that your tip is always chalked, but it really doesn't work, because you'll chalk it again before you shoot anyway.

Don't walk away from the table with the chalk in your hand, either. Chalk your tip, put the chalk on the rail, and then shoot, repeating the process until you miss—at which point, you take your seat. The exception to this rule is when you're playing in Great Britain, Canada, Australia, or Hong Kong. In those places, chalk cubes are sold, not provided free to patrons, as they are in America. As a result, people in those countries keep their chalk with them when they return to their seats.

Keep It to Yourself

Giving advice on playing techniques or strategies can be touchy. In team sports, advice is easily accepted, in most cases, but in individual sports, it's better to wait until you're asked—or at least to test the waters with minor, tentatively offered advice. If you're playing with your date, spouse, or someone else whom you know very well, your knowledge of that person's personality will tell you whether to make a suggestion or offer information.

On the other hand, if there is a pro player or even a serious player who plays at your club, it's not really correct to *ask* for advice—and it's never correct when that person is playing. The best approach is to ask the counter person or manager whether the expert is the kind of person who enjoys giving advice and tips or would rather be left alone.

Certain clubs, especially in Los Angeles and New York City, have a large number of celebrities as regular customers. Management tends to be protective of these folks, because they're there to enjoy themselves like everyone else, and they don't want to have to keep interrupting their games to sign autographs and make small talk. Be polite; don't bother them.

Cue Tips

Many people resent verbal advice, especially when they're playing. A smoother way to offer advice is to make a present of a copy of this book. That's called a shameless plug, but seriously, it's a good idea.

The guidelines about giving advice also apply to comments on equipment. Although it's fine to compliment the appearance of a cue (even the cue of a stranger) and then to ask how it plays, it is not acceptable to inform the owner that the brand is balanced wrong, has a lot of built-in deflection, or is not suitable for the game that he or she is playing. The same common-sense approach applies to your host's tables and cues, when you're playing at someone else's home.

Odds and Ends

It's bad form to try to play either a jump shot or a massè shot (I explain these shots in Chapter 21) on someone's home table. Many billiard clubs prohibit them, too, although they look the other way if the shots are played by experienced players who can execute them properly. The reason for the restrictions is that both types of shots are very difficult, and if the slightest thing goes wrong, they can damage the equipment. Ripping the cloth means replacing the entire cloth set (playing surface and cushion cloth), to the tune of $200 or $300. A poorly executed jump or massè shot can also chip the slate, which could cost $1,000 or $2,000 to replace.

Talcum powder is meant to be used very sparingly in billiard rooms. It's purpose is to make the cue slide smoothly through your fingers, and you want to avoid using too much, getting it on the table, or spilling it on the floor.

Finally, there's the issue of eating and drinking around a pool table, which can mess up the equipment for you and the other players. Twenty years ago, most commercial tables had rounded rails, so it was impossible to set a drink on the rail, but that's no longer the case. Rounded and flat rails are used in both commercial and home billiard tables, with flat rails being far and away the more common. Although these rails can hold a drink, you should never place one there.

The same applies to foods and snacks of any kind, especially greasy finger foods. Although the latter are often available in billiard rooms (along with greasy, salted chips), they're death to a pool table. Even a tiny amount of oil on a pool ball, piece of chalk, cue tip, or the cloth can ruin the game and possibly the equipment. If you choose to eat finger foods or snacks while you're playing, be sure to wipe your hands very thoroughly before picking up your cue to play. Your fellow players will appreciate the gesture, and it make the game better for everyone.

Billiard Sportsmanship

Sportsmanship, in most cases, is really just honesty. The most common situation in billiards is calling a foul on yourself that your opponent didn't see. One general rule that applies to all billiard games (9-Ball, 8-Ball, Rotation, and so on) is that after the cue ball contacts an *object ball* (the one that you hit with the cue ball), a ball must go into a pocket, or a ball (it can be the cue ball) must touch a cushion. When a ball is pocketed, that fact is obvious. It's not always obvious in the second situation, when a ball is not pocketed—such as when you hit the cue ball into the cushion, the cue ball bounces back and hits the object ball, the object ball goes into a group of three or four balls, and they all move a couple of feet. If someone isn't paying attention, it would seem that one of the balls must have touched a cushion, and there's the impression that the cue ball did. But the rule is that *after* the cue ball contacts the object ball, a ball must be pocketed or touch a cushion. Your opponent may not have been paying full attention and, with all the ball movement, may have just assumed that a ball touched a cushion when it didn't. It is good sportsmanship to call (tell) that foul on yourself.

I tell you more about what constitutes a foul in billiards when I go over the rules of the games later in the book (Chapter 9, Part 6, and Appendix D), but it's enough for you know now that it is proper and good sportsmanship to call a foul on yourself when your opponent didn't see it. That call may lead to your losing the game, which opens an area that is common to all games: being a gracious winner and a calm, complimentary loser.

Because billiards is such a personally intense game, it is easy to get emotionally involved. If you mess up, you have no one to blame but yourself. Playing at your peak all the time is impossible, and during the inevitable valleys, frustration will rear its ugly head. That's when your level of self-control is tested and when the true sportsperson exhibits civility. Just as often (more often, I hope!), you'll win and be tempted to gloat, especially if your opponent did a lot of bragging beforehand. I don't need to tell you that gloating is not good behavior, either.

The one area in question is whether to tell your opponent that he or she is about to make a mistake. In a rotation game (such as 9-Ball or Rotation), for example, you are required to hit the lowest-numbered ball on the table first. If the 1 and 6 balls were sunk on the break the players must shoot at the 2 ball, and one of them must make it before aiming at the 3 ball. In a game, one of the balls may be at the far end of the table and go unnoticed by a player. If the player aims at the 3 ball while the 2 ball is still on the table, should you say something?

Pocket Dictionary

Any billiard game that requires players to put the balls in the pockets in numerical order is considered to be a *rotation game*.

There's no rule of proper behavior for this situation. Popular convention is that if the game is just for fun, you mention it, but if it is a serious game (during a tournament, a money match, grudge match, or so on), you do not say anything. You let your opponent commit a foul, after which you do mention it and take the advantage.

If you decide to play in a league, in a local room tournament, or a city, state, regional or national tournament, it's inappropriate to complain about the equipment. Because your performance is based 100 percent on your execution, there's a tendency to blame something else if you execute poorly, and the equipment is the logical choice. To a regular player, however, this excuse is transparent (everyone is playing on the same equipment, even the person who beat you) and a sign of a unsportsmanlike beginner.

Heard It in the Poolroom

During a major tournament in a game that is now famous as the Phantom Five Rack, Jimmy Mataya broke so hard that the balls flew in all directions, and the 5 ball slammed into a pocket and popped back out. Because a ball wasn't pocketed, the opposing player, Larry Hubbart, should have stepped to the table, but both players thought that a ball had been made. Mataya went on to clear the table and win the game—even though it wasn't his right to continue shooting. It was only when the players viewed the videotape later that they saw that the phantom 5 had disappeared into a pocket, swirled around, and jumped back out.

My Mental Game

Recently, being incredibly frustrated with my game, I realized that spending five to six hours a day practicing was not enough. As soon as I was under any kind of pressure, my game simply did not hold up. I seemed to be stuck on a roller coaster. No matter how well I played one day, the next day, I would struggle to make two balls in a row. I tried everything known to man, including changing my stroke, my stance, and even my timing. Everything seemed to work for a short time—a few minutes to a few days—but nothing had a lasting effect. Finally, I realized that the problem was in my head. Great revelation, but how do you fix your concentration when it's broken down? What store do you go to buy a package of focus, and where is confidence on sale?

This had happened to me once before, when I first came to the United States as a teenager. Thinking back on that, and the solution that I found, helped me get through the recent situation. Telling you about my experience may save you the trouble and frustration of analyzing your own periods of poor play.

Cue Tips

Three things that helped me get over my recent slump were the support of my husband, Mitchell; resuming my workout schedule; and quitting smoking—proof that the physical effects the mental part of the game.

Cueing with Confidence

Teenagers are very optimistic. Full of enthusiasm and confidence, they often feel they are invulnerable and can do anything. A short time after starting to play pool, they may find themselves making great shots. A seasoned player, watching a young hotshot, will often say, "He doesn't know how to miss," meaning that the young player hasn't experienced enough missed shots to weaken the confidence he has in his abilities. True, hand-eye coordination may be at a peak during those years, but it's really the confidence that is the main factor in a teenager being able to make great shots after they've only been playing a short time. The same young hotshot will probably try a very difficult shot—one that should be avoided—simply because she doesn't know how difficult it is—and she'll probably pocket the ball!

Confidence is a critical factor in your success in billiards (and just about everything else), and I'm going to go over some legitimate ways to build your confidence in your playing abilities. There are less attractive ways, too. For example, you'll sometimes hear players telling themselves—and everyone in earshot—that they're the best player that ever lived. It sounds like arrogant bragging, but it's really just simple (and crude) self-confidence building—positive thinking on steroids. They have learned how important it is to believe you can do something before you actually do it. They just haven't learned how to express that confidence in a non-offensive manner.

I don't think that I was like that when I moved to the States. The truth is that my situation was almost the opposite. I'd had great success in Europe, but when I came here, I lost that confidence. I felt as though I was under a great deal of pressure to prove myself to a new (and, I suspected, critical) audience. At the same time, I was coping with the culture clash that anyone who moves to a new country faces. *Everything*, from taxes to transportation to foods, was new to me and needed to be understood—all in a language that was only somewhat familiar to me. My comfort zone had been jostled. My game went downhill, and it was then I first realized how important confidence is to playing pool.

Ewa's Billiard Bits

Today's top players look calm, cool, and collected on TV, but they weren't necessarily always that way. When I was 14 years old, I entered my first tournament, and in a tied game I made the winning 9-Ball—and scratched! I was so mad I turned around and kicked the wall. I had to walk on crutches for two weeks, and endure the questions of everyone at school about what had happened to my foot!

The first thing that you have to be confident about is the fundamentals of the sport. (I tell you about those fundamentals later in Parts 3 and 4), when I describe the proper stance, grip, stroke, and so on.) Just having the knowledge adds to your confidence. You won't be thrown off stride when something happens with the balls, because you'll know why it's happening. When something doesn't happen the way that you expected it to, you'll be able to say what went wrong and know what to do the next time. If you get the fundamentals down to the point at which they are automatic, you'll know that you have a rock-solid basis for your game. You won't have to worry about them or be distracted by them. At that point, you can put your attention on your mental game.

The second thing that you have to do is establish a confidence level. Going around saying that you're the best works for some people, but frankly, being around somebody like that is a pain, so I don't recommend that you go that route. But telling yourself that you're a good player and can make the shot in front of you isn't a bad way to get your mind working in the right direction. Keeping these thoughts to yourself might be called polite positive thinking.

Naturally, a lot of practice is also a big help in establishing a high confidence level. I've seen pros set up easy shots and shoot them over and over just before a match, simply to build their confidence and establish a positive attitude toward their abilities. If conditions allow, you'll also see them go to a practice table, set up a shot that they missed in a match, and shoot it over and over until they feel that they own it—that is, until they feel that they won't ever miss it again. That's confidence-building. They've eliminated a negative thought in their billiard brains ("I missed that shot") and replaced it with a positive one ("I can make that shot now").

As someone who's just starting to play the game, all shots may appear to be tough to you at the moment. But you can still apply the same principles. After you've read this book, you'll know how to establish a firm set of fundamentals. Practice them with the cue ball and object ball as close together as you want, with the object ball as close to the pocket as you want, and build your confidence while you build your fundamentals. Make the easy shots over and over until you *own* them; then move to the next level by making the shots a little tougher. In no time at all, you'll be scoffing at the simplicity of your first setups. Because you have the confidence, you can make them with no problem.

Pocket Dictionary

In billiards, *owning a shot* means that you're confident that you'll never miss it, whereas *owning a player* means that you can beat him at will, even though he thinks he can still win.

Dealing with Distractions

Distractions come in both external and internal forms. Because billiards is a nonreactive sport, there's plenty of time for your mind to wander. Personal situations, both positive and negative (although the negatives seem to dominate!), can bubble up in your brain and get your mind off the game. Suddenly, you find that it's your turn to shoot, and you realize that you have no idea what your opponent just did. You walk to the table, and what you see is a total surprise.

It can even happen while you're shooting. If you don't have control of your concentration, and you have a pressing personal concern, you can go blank even while you're stroking in preparation to hitting the ball.

The secret, I've found, is to stay in the game every second. Professional athletes talk about focus so often that the term has become trite, but the fact that they talk about it so much means that focus is critical to their success. When I say that you should stay in the game every second, I'm talking about both when you're at the table and when you're seated and your opponent is playing. Watch what the other player does and what happens to the balls. Think about what's happening. Thinking gets you focused. Think about what you would have done if you had been at the table. Think about why the cue ball behaved as it did. (I tell you all about cue-ball behavior later in the book.)

When you're at the table, continue the thinking stream. Establish a playing rhythm by using the same number of preparatory strokes on every shot before striking the cue ball. Familiarity breeds comfort and confidence, which is your goal. That's how you stay in the game, how you beat distractions—and how you become a better player.

That kind of focus has a great way of beating external distractions, too. During a televised match, I face the prospect of camerapeople walking all around the table, followed by people dragging the heavy camera cables. Sometimes, the director feels that the best TV shot is to plant a handheld camera directly over the pocket and aim back at me down my line of sight! It's the worst pool faux pas but apparently makes for good home viewing. Anyway, it's a super distraction that professionals learn to deal with by tightening our focus and by having experienced it more than once.

You won't run into that particular distraction when you're playing at home or in a commercial room, but you'll probably find something almost as bad. The thing is, once you get into the game, even the external distractions fade. Another tip is to be aware of the possibilities and then tune them out in advance. By that, I mean notice whether there is a group of boisterous people two tables over, and realize that they may make sudden loud noises. Then muffle them mentally. When the noises occur, they won't be a surprise and won't be much of a distraction.

Scratch!

One of the biggest temptations while your opponent is shooting, especially if he's a slow player, is to start watching the game on the adjoining table. That can destroy your focus and your chance of winning your match.

Ewa's Billiard Bits

I was playing Jean Balukas in a tournament in Charlotte, North Carolina, in 1985 when I went into such a hyper-focused mental state that I was aware only of the table and balls. After winning a game, I put up my score and got ready to break the next rack of balls. When Jean came up to me and stuck out her hand I didn't have the vaguest idea what she was doing—or why. My focus was so centered that I hadn't realized I'd won the match!

Something else may happen along the same lines as the internal distraction, but this one isn't a stray thought or disassociated problem. This one is billiard-oriented, and it goes like this: The better you get at playing the game, the smarter and more realistic you become when you're faced with a tough shot. A little voice in your head can't wait to point out how tough the shot is and all the negative things that could happen if you miss it.

This distraction is a major one, and this is the time to talk back. I mean it. When the negative voice finishes saying its piece, talk back. Actively think that you know the shot is a bit difficult, but that you've made it before and you'll make it now. Something as simple as finishing your preparatory strokes on this positive note can have an incredible impact on the outcome of your shot. I use this technique all the time in pro matches, and it really works. As simple as it sounds, give it a try, and I think you'll see what I mean.

Deadstroke

In all sports and many other endeavors, a mental condition occurs in which the person involved is so confident and so focused that she slips into a trancelike state. This semi-trace can be so deep that the person honestly cannot recall the exact things she did during that time and is not aware of how much time has passed. You don't have to be playing at a professional level to have this happen to you, although it does happen more often at that level. The event is simply focus that is so intense that you almost hypnotize yourself, and the reason why it happens more often at the pro level of any sport is that professionals have learned to focus better. But it can happen on your job or while you're engaged in your favorite hobby, too.

I'm not talking about your mind drifting and sort of shutting down while you're inactive, and more time passes than you realize. This situation is the opposite. You end up doing something at a very high level compared with your regular abilities. In pool, this phenomenon is called *being in deadstroke*.

Let me emphasize that deadstroke can happen at any level of play, from complete beginner to world champion. If it happens while you're alone and practicing, you may only be aware of the fact that more time passed than you realized. If you have a witness, however, he can tell you whether you played over your head—that is, better than you've ever played in your life.

Pocket Dictionary

Deadstroke is a semi-trance condition in which you play better than you ever did in your life but aren't fully aware of doing it. Playing pool at your peak level or beyond is called *playing over your head.*

If deadstroke is so great, why doesn't everybody do it all the time? First, and ironically, it's not much fun. You don't enjoy it (although you may come out of it with a sort of adrenaline rush), because you aren't really aware of yourself while you're in deadstroke. Comparing it to being under hypnosis is a little strong, but it's sort of like that. Second, it's very, very difficult to put yourself in deadstroke at will. If you try to focus very narrowly and very intensely, you're alert to focusing. You almost have to turn your brain off in some manner and just let it happen. The danger in that, of course, is that you'll make more mistakes with your brain in pause if things aren't just perfect for induced deadstroke.

One thing that I've noticed about the condition is that it seems to be defensive in nature. When you've focused too long and too hard, the brain apparently modifies some of its perception and processing features with a sort of buffer. Time, light, motion, and thinking don't seem to register, and all your actions are a bit robotic. If your fundamentals are strong, and the knowledge of the game is present (in other words, if you've read this entire book!), the fundamentals take over, and you simply do everything right. Now, if only someone could figure out a way to get into deadstroke at will and enjoy it while it's happening....

Dressed to Skill

Pool has no uniforms or clothing-related equipment, which makes it great for impulse play, dating, and all the rest. But I can give you a few tips about what kind of clothing might cause some problems.

Games can be played with either of two types of rules: cue-ball fouls only or all-ball fouls. The rules are determined beforehand by the tournament director (if it's an organized tournament) or by the individual players (if you're playing with friends). *All-ball-fouls* means that if you touch any ball with your hand, cue, or clothing, you've committed a foul (except, of course, for touching the cue ball with the cue tip when you hit it). *Cue-ball-fouls* means that touching the cue ball with any of those things is a foul, but if you touch any other ball, it's within the rules. If your touch makes the ball move, you and your opponent agree on where it was and put it back before you shoot.

All-ball fouls can cause problems. Loose clothing—especially baggy sleeves or shirts and blouses that billow out at the waist—can easily touch a ball when you're leaning over the table for a shot, and that can be a foul. You don't have to move the ball; if you just touch it, you lose your turn. Cue-ball-only fouls rarely cause a problem. On the other hand, clothing that's too tight can bind and restrict your movements, both for your upper body and lower body. I suppose you could say that as long as you avoid anything too baggy or too tight, you can play pool in just about any type of clothing.

Scratch!

Female players should be aware that bending over the table makes scoop-necked and low-cut blouses more revealing. The same is true of short skirts.

Sometimes, within a couple of games, you'll find yourself reaching for a shot and lifting one foot off the floor to make hitting the ball more comfortable. If the floor is wood, it can be slippery. Even carpeted floors can be slippery. That's why I suggest avoiding leather-soled shoes when you're playing billiards. Because you're on your feet quite a bit, footwear should also be comfortable and offer good support.

The Least You Need to Know

➤ Don't stand in or move across a player's line of sight.

➤ Good sportsmanship means a more enjoyable time at the table.

➤ Playing poorly may be as much mental as it is physical.

➤ Build confidence by knowing the fundamentals and practicing them.

➤ Focusing on the game, even when it's not your turn to shoot, helps your game.

➤ When you're planning to play billiards, avoid wearing clothing that's very tight or very loose.

Part 2
The Home Court Advantage

Having your own pool table at home is about the neatest thing in the world. Adults love it as a centerpiece for parties or visits by family members or friends. It can keep the kids at home—yours and the neighbors'. You can even fold laundry on it. Now, that's a versatile sport.

In this part, you find out how to buy your first billiard table. A billiard table is not as expensive as most people think, and its appearance can match your furniture (unless you have futons). With a table, of course, you also need cue sticks, balls, and a few other trinkets, all of which I tell you how to pick out.

Next, I help you design your home billiard room—upscale, recreational, big, small...whatever suits your budget and needs. You can buy special billiard furniture (such as spectator chairs) and either fancy lights or plain lights to put over the table. It's up to you whether to get creative or go utilitarian, and I give you information about all your options.

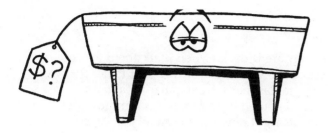

Buying Your First Table

Of all the pool tables sold in America, 98 percent are for use in homes. That's a pretty powerful number, considering the thousands and thousands of billiard clubs around the country, but it really makes sense when you realize how much fun a home table can be. At home, I have a 9-foot Brunswick Gold Crown—the table that you see in most television tournaments, at world championships, and in many upscale billiard rooms.

When I signed with Brunswick, they told me to pick out any table I wanted, and I was tempted to pick out one of their beautiful home furniture–style tables with leather pockets, and that's what I'll probably get when I retire and turn in the Gold Crown. At that point I'll be more interested in matching the furniture style in the rest of my home than in tuning up my competitive play. Still, there are many people who buy the commercial model for their homes because they take the sport very seriously and are highly competitive by nature.

In this chapter, I tell you how to pick out a table that's just right for you and your family. The number of choices may surprise you, but I'll make you a smart shopper in a few pages.

Tracking Table Trends

All billiard tables are twice as long as they are wide, so when I talk about a 9-foot table, you'll know that it's 4^1/$_2$ feet wide. That ratio was true of the 12-foot tables that were popular up to the Civil War; the 11-foot tables that were popular for about five years during that war; the 10-foot tables that were used in tournaments until just after World War II; and every other table made, right down to the small coin-operated tavern tables. Even toy tables are twice as long as they are wide.

The 9-foot table is the professional and commercial size, but nothing says that you can't have a table that size in your home—nothing except the size of the room that you're going to make your billiard room, of course. That's the reason why tables have been shrinking. People had so much fun playing in public billiard rooms that they wanted to play at home, and manufacturers began making smaller tables to accommodate the size of a home game room. The 8-foot model became the home standard.

Tables not only got smaller when they moved into homes, but they also got prettier. The old stereotype was that Dad wanted a pool table and Mom agreed only if they could find one that matched their furniture. Table makers were quick to catch on, so today, you can buy a table in any style from Art Deco to Duncan Phyfe and beyond.

Ewa's Billiard Bits

The first billiard table in the president's home, the White House, was ordered by John Quincy Adams in 1826. It cost $50, and he billed the government.

Matching Mom's furniture means more than the style of the table; it also means the wood and color. The trend is toward opening up options and getting away from the traditional dark, dark wood and dark green cloth. Today, you can find a table made of bleached maple, white oak with a whitewash stain, jet-black laminate, or any of a thousand colors and hues. One manufacturer makes billiard-table cloth in 60 colors. Let me tell you, you really haven't taxed your ability to focus until you've played on a shiny chrome table with pink cloth.

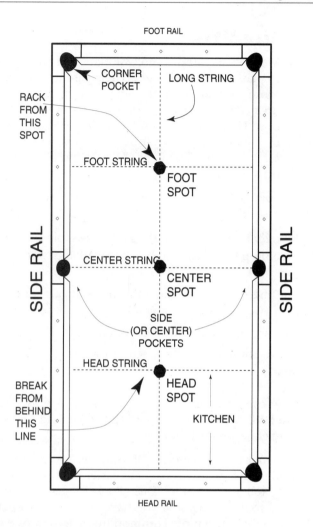

FOOT RAIL

CORNER
POCKET

LONG STRING

RACK
FROM
THIS
SPOT

FOOT STRING

FOOT
SPOT

SIDE RAIL

CENTER STRING

CENTER
SPOT

SIDE RAIL

SIDE
(OR CENTER)
POCKETS

HEAD STRING

BREAK
FROM
BEHIND
THIS
LINE

HEAD
SPOT

KITCHEN

HEAD RAIL

An overhead view of a standard pool table, no matter what size. Many of the "strings" will not be marked on the cloth, and of the three spots, usually only the foot spot is marked.

Sizing Up Your Situation

I always like to encourage people to get the biggest table—up to 9 feet—that they can fit into their home billiard rooms. My Gold Crown is the 9-foot model, because that's the size and brand I play on at professional tournaments, but it would be the size that I'd get even if that weren't the case. My reasoning is that when I go out socially to a billiard club, most of the tables there will be 9-foot models, and I want to be comfortable playing on that size. It's also the only way to see how really well you can play compared with the pros you see on TV.

Size Wise

Most of the famous professionals over the years learned to play at very early ages. Their parents owned billiard rooms or had tables at home, and the future stars picked up a cue and began banging balls around at the age of 5 or 6. They learned on full-size (9-foot) tables, standing on a box to shoot. As long as you take the necessary safety precautions, your children can also learn to play on a big table.

Following are four exceptions to getting the biggest table that fits:

➤ If you play almost exclusively in leagues, buy the same-size table that you use there—usually, a 7-foot coin-op style. These tables are available for the home without the coin mechanism.

➤ If your game of choice is American Snooker or golf (the pool game, not the game played on fairways), buy a 10-foot Snooker table.

➤ If your game of choice is Carom, buy a 10-foot Carom table.

➤ If you want to play outdoors, buy one of the special all-weather tables. Three manufacturers make them.

Houses have been getting bigger over the past 20 years or so, and it's now easier to fit a full-size 9-foot table in a room. Still, the vast majority of the tables sold for home use are 8-foot models, and there are good reasons for that.

It's easier to make balls on an 8-foot table than on a 9-foot table, and making a lot of balls is where the fun is in pool. (You can also make balls easier on a table that has bigger pockets—an option that I tell you about in "Deep Pockets" just ahead) It's also true that not all styles come in 9-foot models, so if you have your eye on a particular style, you may be able to buy it only in the more common home length of 8 feet.

It's also surprising how often you can fit a smaller table in a room but end up really cramped with the larger one. A foot in length (and half a foot in width) doesn't sound like much, but it's often the deciding factor.

The standard pool-table sizes are:

➤ $4^1/_2 \times 9$ feet

➤ $4^1/_4 \times 8^1/_2$ feet (called a Big Eight)

➤ 4×8 feet

➤ $3^1/_2 \times 7$ feet (coin-operated tavern table)

To figure out whether you can fit a table into your would-be billiard room or family room, remember that you need at least 5 feet on all sides of the table to be able to play. That means an area 19 feet × 14^1/$_2$ feet for a 9-foot table.

When you figure in seating—and perhaps a TV and VCR stand, where you can watch instructional tapes while you're at the table, or maybe a wet bar—you're talking about a big room.

Convertible Tables

If you are pressed for space, there are other options. A dozen or so table manufacturers make variations of what are known as multi-use game tables or convertible tables.

A *multi-use game table* is basically a pool table with one or more tops. When the top is in place, the table becomes a table-tennis table or even an air-hockey table. A *convertible table* is one with a top that turns it into a dining table. This conversion doesn't usually work smoothly, because it makes the dining surface higher than normal, and it's often difficult to get chairs underneath without bumping your knees. I suggest using a convertible table as a buffet table. If this versatility appeals to you, be sure to evaluate those two problem areas carefully.

Commercial-Style Tables versus Home-Style Tables

If you do choose the 9-foot size, the billiard supply store's salesperson may ask whether you want a commercial style or a home style. What he or she is really asking is whether you want a table with heavy construction that will last a lifetime or a lighter-duty table with a furniture appearance. The answer depends on what kind of use the table will get, how long you intend to keep it, and how much you want to pay. I give you some guidelines on prices in the sections to follow.

With the upscale billiard boom that began in the mid-1980's, the distinction between commercial and home tables began to blur. Fancy furniture designs got beefed up by the manufacturers and started appearing in the posh new billiard rooms. Because millions of new players were discovering the game—and because customers are happy when they can make balls—these rooms also began adding 8-foot tables, something that had previously been popular only in the South. So there is now a new animal on the scene: the 8-foot commercial table. It's a heavy-duty table that looks like fine furniture. The neat result is that it gives you more options.

Table Options and My Recommendations

I'll do some quick and easy math for you to give you an idea of just how one-of-a-kind you can make your home billiard table. Then I'll show you what each option means. By the way, I'll use fairly conservative numbers.

Ewa's Billiard Bits

A custom table on pivots was made for an ocean liner during the early 1900's. As the ship rocked, the table was supposed to remain level. It didn't.

Pocket Dictionary

Drop pockets are billiard-table pockets that are shaped like cups. *Ball-return pockets* are a type of billiard-table system that includes pockets with holes in the bottom and a series of channels that send the balls to a central collection point at the foot of the table.

Suppose that a certain billiard table is available in 20 finishes, with 6 styles of legs ($6 \times 20 = 120$). That table comes with rails in two widths ($2 \times 120 = 240$), four pocket styles ($4 \times 240 = 960$), eight woods ($8 \times 960 = 7,680$), four lengths—7 feet, 8 feet, Big 8, and 9 feet ($4 \times 7,680 = 30,720$)—and either circular or diamond-shape rail sights ($2 \times 30,720 = 61,440$). A line of tables from one manufacturer may contain 10 styles ($10 \times 61,440 = 614,400$), and the company may offer 30 colors of cloth ($30 \times 614,000 = 18,432,000$). A single table manufacturer, then, could make more than 18 million tables and not make two exactly the same.

Some manufacturers will make a table in any wood that you specify and match any color stain you send them. The delay is usually only a couple months, and in the end you'll have a table that looks like it came with the other furniture in your home.

Deep Pockets

Pool tables have two types of pockets: drop pockets and ball-return pockets. They don't affect the play of the game, but they do affect the table's appearance, the cost of the table, and the ease with which you gather up the balls after clearing the table.

Drop pockets are less expensive to build than ball-return pockets are, and they look better to most people. They're made of either an inexpensive rubberized plastic or leather. The leather versions can get pretty fancy, with tooling and fringe and custom work (such as your initials), and you could end up spending as much money as you would on a ball-return system. But in their basic form, drop pockets are inexpensive to make and inexpensive to replace. Another characteristic of drop pockets is that they are much quieter than ball returns. This can be a consideration if you want to play at home after everyone is asleep (and why I chose drop pockets for my home table).

Traditional ball-return pockets are common only in the northeastern United States, and they come as options (if at all) on a limited number of tables in any manufacturer's line. The newer versions, which you'll see more often, have the same appearance as drop pockets.

A ball-return pocket has no bottom, and when you make a ball it drops into an angled trough or channel. The channels come together at a shelf at the foot of the table, where you rack the balls, saving you from walking all the way around the table and emptying each pocket individually, as you have to do with drop pockets. The only drawback with ball-return pockets is that balls sometimes get stuck in the channels; a piece of chalk (or anything else) that is accidentally dropped into a pocket blocks their path. To get a blocked ball, you have to kneel down, bend low, look under the rails, find it, and then push it on its way. The maneuver takes an agile person.

Both styles of pockets come in a variety of sizes, measured at the mouth (opening) of the pocket. The Billiard Congress of America (BCA) publishes an acceptable range of sizes, rather than a specific size, which allows manufacturers to offer different sizes and still advertise tables with pockets that meet BCA specs. The largest opening ($5^1/8$ inches wide at the entrance for a corner pocket) makes pocketing balls relatively easy and is a good choice for beginner tables at billiard clubs. After players develop a few skills, they have a choice of moving to tables that have slightly smaller pockets. The small end of the range ($4^7/8$ inches for a corner pocket) is a little tough. I suggest that you request 5-inch corner pockets for your first home table. (By the way, pro tournaments are usually played on tables that have either the minimum-size opening, which is $4^7/8$ inches or on tables with even smaller pockets, such as $4^1/2$ inches.)

Cue Tips

You may find tables with different-size pockets in a typical billiard club. Look for the better players; they usually congregate on the tables that have the tightest pockets.

Cushion the Blow

The *cushions* of a billiard table are the cloth-covered walls around the playing surface. There are no cushion options when you're picking out a table, but there are a few things that you need to know.

When the table installers (they're called *mechanics*) finish putting your table together, stand across from each of the four sides, and see whether the cushion points are parallel with the bed of the table. Check the cloth where it butts against the wood or laminate rail, and make sure that it is flat and smooth. Hit a ball against the cushion every 3 or 4 inches, and listen for a sound that resembles either a dull thud or a double click; either of these sounds indicates that the cushion is not firmly attached.

Ewa's Billiard Bits

In the beginning, wood boards kept the balls on the table. Manufacturers tried cushions of cloth filled with horsehair, and when those failed, they tried cushions of pure rubber, but the rubber got hard and cracked. In 1839, vulcanized rubber was formulated, and that has been the standard billiard-cushion material ever since.

It's Not Felt

I'm sure that someone, somewhere, used felt for a billiard table, but I haven't a clue as to how it became the popular term for table cloth. To set the record straight, billiard cloth is either pure wool or a blend of wool and nylon polyester. It has never been felt, which is a rough, unwoven, coarse material. You are now permitted—nay, encouraged—to roll your eyes and smile knowingly around anyone who uses the word *felt* to describe billiard-table cloth.

The most expensive table cloth is 100 percent worsted wool—the same material used in fine suits or skirts. It is so fine, in fact, that even a lightly hit ball rolls for a very long time—too long for most games. In billiard terms, that type of cloth is called a *fast* cloth. Different weaves, which create a nap, and a thicker cloth slow the roll. Non-worsted wool and a nylon–polyester mix (anywhere from a ratio of 60/40 to 90/10, wool/nylon) in a thicker cloth slows the roll even more.

The slowest cloth of all is on coin-operated machines in arcades and other places where teens and preteens play. This material is a blended cloth with a rubber backing. It takes rough abuse and, if torn, is fairly easy to repair. I don't recommend it, though, even if you're buying your table for your kids. Because it plays so slow, you have to hit the ball harder, and with the rubber backing, even a slight downward stroke will make the cue ball take to the air and fly off the table. To be completely safe, you'd need rubber-backed walls, rubber-backed carpets, and a rubber-backed opponent.

The fastest cloth is for Carom games—games that are played on tables without pockets (see Chapter 27). Almost all professional pool tournaments are played on a medium-fast pure worsted wool cloth, and even though people may think of it as being a professional cloth, I suggest that you specify it when you buy a home table. It wears a long time, gives good value for the money, and provides smooth and consistent play. Long wear is important, because re-covering a table costs $150 to $350 (depending on the part of the country, the size of your table, and the quality of the cloth). If short-term cost is the most important factor, go with the nylon/wool blend, but in any case, I would avoid the two extremes of very fast cloth and rubber-backed cloth.

Dark green is the traditional color for billiard-table cloth, although it's probably traditional only because billiards started as a lawn game. In recent TV tournaments, ESPN experimented with a two-table format—men on a table with green cloth and women on a table with dark blue cloth—so when the camera switched, even to close-up shots, you knew that you had gone to the other match. Some recent experiments showed that a tan cloth showed the balls better on TV.

Pocket Dictionary

Tiny balls of wool that form on new cloth when it's first used are called *pills*.

In short, there's no restriction—official or unofficial—on the color of cloth that you use for your billiard table. My own experience is that the brighter colors produce some eye fatigue and that some colors match a ball color too exactly, making it hard to shoot that ball. Aside from that, any color cloth that strikes your fancy is fine.

When you have the new cloth installed and start playing on it, you may notice that tiny balls of material start appearing all over the table. These balls are called *pills,* and they're no reflection on the quality of the material. A sweater trimmer, or even an electric beard trimmer, shears them off, and then you can vacuum them up. You have to be careful not to cut the cloth, of course, but if you have a good trimmer, the operation is simple. If you're the least bit skittish about this and can put up with slow shots rolling off line because they hit a pill, you can just be patient. The loose pills disappear each time you brush the table down, and like visiting relatives, they'll eventually all be gone.

Bed Rock

The cloth covers the bed (the flat playing surface) of the table, which is made of slate. At first, it may seem to be a little crude to be playing this finesse game on rock, but if you've ever seen the process involved in creating table slate, you'd quickly change your mind. The last step is a milling process with a diamond cutter that leaves the surface level over its length to $7/1000$ inch. If a billiard ball rolls off a straight line, it's far more likely to be the result of a buildup of chalk dust beneath the cloth or the presence of pills than an unlevel spot in the slate.

Do you need a slate table bed? Yep. You can buy tables with anything from a honeycombed cardboard bed and plastic panel top to a machined high-tech artificial stone bed, but modern science still hasn't come up with anything that lasts as long or plays the same as slate.

In 8- and 9-foot billiard tables, there are actually three pieces of slate. These pieces are aligned, doweled, and machined at the quarry, and your table mechanics will fit them together flush when they put your table together. One piece of slate is used in 7-foot tables.

Almost all modern tables use slate with a thickness of $3/4$ inch to $1\frac{1}{4}$ inches. Which thickness of slate should you look for? Thicker slate is, naturally, heavier and therefore makes a more stable table, assuming that the support design is the same, but aside from that, I suggest going with anything in the preceding range. The thinner slate makes the table less expensive but certainly doesn't present a problem. I've never heard of a slate cracking during normal use just because it was too thin, even with a table that had a $1/2$-inch slate bed.

Scratch!

Dropping anything heavy or sharp on the bed of a billiard table can easily chip the slate. Although slate is rock, it's brittle.

Ewa's Billiard Bits

The first billiard table on record, made for Louis XI in 1470, had a bed of wood. Wood parquetry, which mitigated warpage, was used for 400 years, until the introduction of slate during the 1850's. Some wood-bed tables, including Benjamin Franklin's, still exist today in private collections.

Table Prices

The tables sold at department stores and some sporting-goods stores are usually relatively light-duty. If a table folds up when you're done using it or costs less than $800, it won't give you the full experience of the game. Tables of this type are better than nothing, but then, so is Ping-Pong.

You can buy a quite acceptable 8-foot table for less than $1,200, and it should last for a decade or more. For a hundred dollars a year, it will provide a lot of family fun. The table probably will be simple, perhaps made of plywood with a laminate exterior, and fairly light-duty. A few manufacturers are also making simple furniture-style tables in this price range. For another $100 to $200, you can get the 9-foot model.

A furniture-style table or home–commercial table costs $2,000 to $9,000 and lasts for 40 years or more. This type of table is heavier and more stable than the other kinds; if you lean against the side, it won't shift. The cushions are made of better-quality rubber and give you a true rebound for a longer time than a less-expensive table does. The construction is solid wood or a combination of solid wood and high-end plywood, and it looks like a nice piece of furniture.

For a hand-carved, high-tech antique reproduction, a one-of-a-kind table, or simply an upscale design, you'll have to pay $6,000 to $100,000. About two dozen table makers serve this upscale market, and some of the tables that they produce are really astounding.

The price of a table may or may not include a basic accessories package, consisting of balls, a rack, and some cues. It also may or may not include delivery and installation. These are often areas of negotiation when you're buying a billiard table, so don't assume that these vital items are included in the posted price. Upgrading the accessories package is something that can alter the stated price of a table. If you want a wooden rack instead of a plastic rack, a better set of balls, and more and better cues to go with your table, be prepared to shell out an additional $100 to $350. On the other hand, the upgrade may be free as long as you're paying list price for the table. If you're looking for sale prices, the best times to shop are Father's Day, Christmas, and the dog days of summer.

Move It or Leave It?

Moving a pool table is a very tricky business. If you try to move it yourself, even a couple of inches, you run a high risk of chipping the slates. If the slates can be repaired (and they often can't), the repair will cost $200 or more. Even trying to lift the table can cause serious damage (to you as well as the table; tables weigh half a ton). The only solution is to call the mechanics who installed your table and tell them what you need to have done. With some tables, mechanics can use a special table dolly to raise and move the table from one room to another without disassembling it.

Most billiard supply stores mechanics will transport a table within a radius of a hundred miles or so. If you're selling your home, you'll have to make a decision about whether to take your table with you, and if you're moving out of state, that could be a problem. In any case, moving from one house to another, no matter how close or far, requires that the table be disassembled and reassembled. This process can cost $200 to $500 dollars (depending on whether the cloth can be saved and how difficult that model is to disassemble and reassemble), plus travel expenses.

Home buyers often find that a billiard room is an attractive feature, and most of the people I know ended up leaving their table with the house and then getting a new table at their new location, which is easier all the way around.

Cue Tips

Lifting a billiard table from the ends is far more likely to cause damage than lifting it from the sides. Lifting from the ends pinches the slate, causing the edges to shatter.

The Least You Need to Know

➤ All billiard tables are twice as long as they are wide.

➤ The most common home-table size is 4 × 8 feet, but the commercial-room and pro size is $4^1/_2$ × 9 feet.

➤ Everything from the style of the table legs to the size of the pockets is optional.

➤ A slate-bed table costs anywhere from $900 to $100,000.

➤ If you must move your table, call a professional.

Chapter 6

That's Your Cue!

In This Chapter

➤ The cues you'll find in a billiard club

➤ The features to look for in your personal cue

➤ The special cues for special shots

➤ Choosing a cue case to meet your needs

➤ The importance of the cue tip

➤ How to chalk a cue tip

Finding a cue that feels right for you is as important as finding a person with whom you could comfortably spend the rest of your life. Well, maybe not exactly as important. Maybe not even close. But if you want to excel at this game, it is very important that you select a cue that does what you want it to do and plays as though it were an extension of your arm.

When I started playing as a teenager in Sweden, few billiard books were available in my native language. That's probably just as well, because most of the books are pretty vague in this critical area, and some are downright misleading. Many options are available, and I'll help you sort through them so that you'll make a good choice.

The first cue I owned was a beautiful hand-carved piece of art. It was nice to look at, but it played like a piece of art. On my 15th birthday, my biggest fans—my Mom and Dad and Leif Johansson, the owner of the billiard club where I was a member— presented me with a two-piece custom cue. Although it was a great cue, as I became a better player, I learned that it wasn't right for me. I later found one that *was* right. Now let's find out what's right for you.

The One-Piece Billiard-Club Cue

Almost all billiard rooms have racks of one-piece cues on the wall, called *house cues*, and you can use them without charge. The weight of the cues, in ounces, is stamped on or cut into the cues. That's all the information you get from the cue, but there's more that you should know.

The most important part of a cue is the tip, but the tips on house cues are rarely maintained carefully, because room owners know that serious players have their own cues. So the tip is the first thing to check on a house cue. There's a little bit involved in checking the tip, and it applies to personal cues, too, so I made it a separate section at the end of Chapter 8, the equipment-maintenance chapter (see the section "Keep It Clean").

The second-most-important thing to check is whether the cue is straight. The traditional method is to roll the cue on the table, but this method has fallen out of favor lately. The in way to do it is to hold it up like a rifle and sight down the length while slowly rotating the cue. Rolling it on the table, as long as you roll it slowly, is every bit as revealing; it's just not as cool-looking. No doubt your optometrist would go with the safer table method.

Cue Tips

For the beginning player, an inexpensive, well maintained one-piece cue will play as well as a two-piece cue.

Pocket Dictionary

Shaft papers are small squares, usually made of plastic, that are used to clean cue shafts. They are color-coded, from coarse to fine.

The third thing to notice about a house cue is whether it is smooth. Perspiration and dust combine to make a cue bumpy—especially the small end, called the *shaft*. That is not only a distraction, but also unpleasant. If you can't find a cue in the wall racks that is glass-smooth, take your choice to the desk and ask for shaft papers or sandpaper. Shaft papers, which are specially made for smoothing and cleaning cues, are far less abrasive than sandpaper, and simple to use; just rub the papers up and down the small end of the cue, as though you're sanding a piece of wood.

When you bought your home table, you probably also purchased an accessories package that included two or more one-piece cues. There are different quality levels for one-piece cues, but you're safe in depending on the billiard supply store's salesperson (although maybe not the clerk at the sporting-goods or department store) to tell you which is the better brand. The best cues have a maple shaft and cost no more than $18 each—a real steal. Because you will have these cues at home, you can keep them clean and straight, and keep the tips in good shape. I tell you how to do that in Chapter 8.

More and more billiard rooms, especially the newer ones, have replaced their house cues with two-piece rental cues. If that's the case at your local room, you'll get to play with a better-quality cue. The average rental rates are very reasonable. The most I've ever heard of—and it was at only one location—was $1 an hour. More typically, the cues rent for $1 for as long as you play. These are lower-end two-piece cues, but they have the characteristics that I tell you about in the following section.

Two-Piece Cues Aren't Just for Professionals

A two-piece cue unscrews into two pieces of equal length, called the *shaft* (the smaller end, with the tip) and the *butt* (the thicker end, with a rubber bumper at the end). That design makes carrying the cue easier—the main advantage of a two-piece cue and the reason why they were invented.

When people began owning their own cues, they realized that they could get them altered or custom-made to the specifications they thought were best for them. Today, that's what the two-piece cue is all about. You can not only get the shapes and materials that you believe work for you, but also have the cue made with any style of inlay or design work that pleases you. If you get carried away, you can pay as much for a pool cue as you did for the family car.

At the low end, the prices of two-piece cues range from about $40 to $90. The shaft is generally ramin wood (a cheap maple substitute from Asia), graphite, or a lesser grade of maple. I personally would avoid ramin wood. Both graphite and lower-grade maple play very well and are quite acceptable. Most people start in this range and move up as they get more into the game.

The butts on lower-end cues tend to be fairly plain. A trend over the past five or six years is to use *decals* (also called *transfers*) that appear to be wood, metal inlays, or hand-applied artwork. Because the butts of all cues are covered with a clear protective coating, it's sometimes hard to tell a decal from the real thing. It's something to watch out for when you're buying a cue, although all dealers I've ever talked with will tell you if you ask. Now you know to ask.

Midrange cues sell for $140 to $450 and are the most common among regular players. The shaft wood is a better grade and always maple, which means that it looks better (has fewer blemishes and imperfections) and stays straighter longer under equal conditions.

You will find some decals used in the butt designs of cues at the lower end of this range, but by and large, all the designs that look like inlays of exotic woods really *are* inlays of exotic woods. You can choose among the offerings of a hundred cue

Cue Tips

Comparison-shop for two-piece cues. Check the telephone directory for billiard supply stores; check the pro shop at your billiard room; and see the ads in the billiard publications, such as *Pool & Billiard Magazine*. Summer is the best season to shop.

makers, each providing 10 to 60 designs, and customize your cue by choosing different colored wraps, stains, weights, tip sizes, and joint styles. Some of the choices are cosmetic, but some affect the play of the cue, as I'll explain after I tell you about the high-end cues.

Cues that cost more than $450 (and you can pay up to $150,000 for a cue) don't play any better than midrange cues. You're paying extra for the beauty of the instrument, the rare materials in the design (gold, semiprecious and precious stones, and so on), and (at prices over $5,000) the fact that your cue is unique. The shafts—you get a spare at this price, needless to say—are of highest-grade maple.

The parts of a two-piece cue.

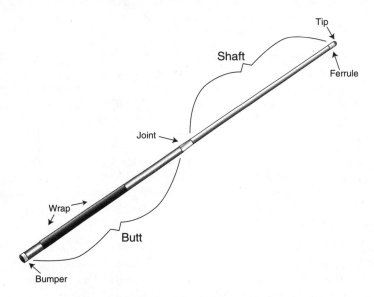

Used cues are hard to come by, so I can't give you any price guides that are really practical. For some reason, people who play pool will buy new cues but rarely have an interest in selling their old cues. It's fairly common to find a longtime player who owns 5 or 10 cues. A cue, if taken care of, will last 30 years or more, so not many go by the wayside because of age.

Picking Out Your Two-Piece Cue

You should consider three areas when you pick out your first two-piece cue: comfort, personal preferences, and playability.

Two Matters of Comfort

The wrap on the butt of a cue is there to make your back hand grip more comfortable. Absorbing moisture is a big part of that. The wrap also adds to the appearance of a cue and can make your grip less likely to slip. You can often pick the color of the wrap.

Following are the materials that are used for a cue butt wrap:

➤ *Rubber*—inexpensive, common only on cheap pool cues and quality Carom cues, nonslip

➤ *Nylon*—the least expensive and longest-wearing, the most popular in lower-end cues, moderately comfortable

➤ *Irish linen*—absorbent, regarded by many people as being the best-looking, comfortable, the most popular

➤ *Leather*—less common, around $50 to $100 more than other choices, absorbent, natural feel, very comfortable

➤ *Cork*—very absorbent, not as long-wearing, not always available

Cue Tips

A few cue makers spray the entire butt with a clear protective coating *after* the wrap has been put on, eliminating all advantages of the wrap material except appearance. The coating, however, is relatively nonslip, so it's not quite as bad as it first sounds. Cue shafts are coated only near the joint; the rest is bare wood.

The diameter of the butt is another comfort variable in two-piece cues. A trend toward slimmer butts (with diameters around $1\frac{1}{8}$ inch) began around 1992. Test the cue before you buy it to discover what thickness feels best to you. Each brand usually uses the same thickness throughout the entire line, so you may have to switch manufacturers to get a different size.

Matters of Personal Preference

The following items are personal preferences. I could tell you what I think looks good, but it's your cue, and the design you pick will express who you are, not who I am. The important thing to know is that *none of these items makes a cue play better or last any longer*. They are, for the most part, matters of taste and appearance.

Following are cue options that do not affect the way that the cue plays:

➤ The materials used in the construction of the butt (various exotic woods, metals, and plastics)

➤ The color of the stain used on the butt woods

➤ The design on or in the cue butt

➤ Whether to get a second shaft

➤ The number of points in the cue butt

I recommend that you purchase a second shaft if you expect to use the cue for more than 10 years or to play twice a week or more. A cue tip can pop off during a tournament or another important game, and you'll want the ability to simply change shafts rather than *go to the wall*—that is, have to use a house cue from a wall rack. Getting a worn tip replaced may take at least a couple of days, and you can use your second shaft in the meantime.

Scratch!

Never lean your cue against the wall, get it wet, or subject it to high temperatures. Those things warp the shaft, and a replacement shaft can cost $80 to $140.

A traditional cue butt has a design of *points*, which look like stiletto blades emanating from the front of the wrap to the joint of the cue. You can buy a cue that has anything from 2 to 10 points (except 7 points, because 7 doesn't divide evenly into 360 degrees). The more points, the higher the cost.

Designs range from intricate wood inlays that involve 500 pieces of wood of various species to create an Art Deco motif, all the way to hand-painted wildlife scenes. The creative imaginations of cue makers is awesome.

Things That Affect the Way That a Cue Plays

Other features vary from model to model and cue maker to cue maker, and many of these features affect the playability of the cue. Exactly what effect they have is the subject of long-standing debates, and I won't mire you down in things that haven't been resolved and don't really matter at this point. Instead, I'm going to put the features in an easy-to-read list and follow that list with some notes.

Following are optional cue features that affect the cue's performance (each described following the list):

➤ The diameter of the tip

➤ The hardness of the tip

➤ The material used in the *joint rings* (the area where the halves of a cue screw together)

➤ The taper of the shaft

➤ The length of the cue

➤ The weight of the cue

➤ The balance point of the cue

Tip diameter. The most common tip diameter used to be 13.5mm, but in the past 10 years, that has changed to 13.125mm (always called 13^1/$_8$ rather than 13.125mm), 13mm, 12.75mm, and 12.5mm. I prefer the 12.5mm, and I would suggest that you get the same or just slightly larger—certainly nothing larger than 13mm, even though you'll find a lot of the larger sizes for sale in pro shops and billiard supply stores.

Tip hardness. This subject is so important that it deserves a section of its own, and by golly, I'm going to give it one. It's near the end of this chapter (see "Cue-Tip Hardness").

Joint material. Your choices are various metals or plastics (also called *fibre joints*). Go with a nonmetal joint. The reasons are technical, but for every level of play, from tyro (beginner) to professional, I believe that the plastic/fibre joint is better. You don't see too many players who use a metal joint except for Straight Pool players in the northeastern United States.

Cue-shaft tapers. A house cue is tapered straight from one end of the cue to the other. A two-piece cue has a *pro taper*, which means from that from the tip to a certain distance up the shaft (which varies from cue maker to cue maker but averages 10 to 18 inches), the diameter stays constant. Then the taper begins and grows evenly to the very back end of the cue.

Cue length. People have been getting taller faster than cues have been growing in length. In the past few years, the standard length has increased to 58 inches from $57^{1}/_{2}$ inches, but you can easily find the shorter version, or you can custom-order any length that you believe suits your height. The time that it takes to get a cue made varies from maker to maker, but expect it to be at least a couple of months. Either $57^{1}/_{2}$ inches or 58 inches will suit everyone from 5 feet 4 inches to 6 feet 1 inch tall.

Cue weight. This feature, too, has been changing over the past decade. The standard now ranges from $18^{1}/_{2}$ to $19^{1}/_{2}$ ounces, which seems to work well for most people, regardless of strength or age. The standard used to be 20 to $20^{3}/_{4}$ ounces. If you're going to get something outside the current standard range, go for lighter rather than heavier.

Balance point. This has a lot to do with how a cue feels when you take your warmup swings and then hit the ball. If you hold your cue horizontally on one finger, you can quickly find its balance point. The most common balance point of a cue is about $18^{1}/_{2}$ inches from the rubber bumper at the end of

Cue Tips

A few players use a larger-diameter tip—and, therefore, a larger-diameter shaft, for their break cue. The diameter may be 13.5mm or even 13.75mm. This size gives them more stiffness and strength for the demanding power of the break shot.

Pocket Dictionary

The *balance point* of a cue is the place on a cue (usually, 18 to 19 inches from the butt end) where one end of the cue weighs the same as the other end.

the butt. If the balance point is more toward the butt end, the cue is called *back-weighted*, and it is said you have to *steer* it when hitting a ball. I personally don't care for a back-weighted cue; I like a balance point close to 18 to 19 inches from the butt end. A *front-weighted cue*, of course, has a balance point a little farther from the butt than the popular 18^1/$_2$ inches.

My Recommendations for Your First Cue

I suggest that you start close to where you should finish. Buy a good two-piece cue—something in the $120-to-$350 range—within the specs in the list below. If you get a less-expensive cue, you may be unhappy with it a couple years down the road. Then, if you want to get something nicer at a later date, you'll have some experience and information behind you before spending the extra money.

Following are my recommended specs for your first two-piece cue:

➤ 18^1/$_2$ to 19^1/$_2$ ounces

➤ 58 inches long (57^1/$_2$ inches, if you're less than 5 feet 7 inches tall)

➤ 12.5mm to 13mm tip

➤ Pro shaft taper of 8 to 18 inches

➤ A soft, medium-soft, or medium tip

➤ A back-hand-grip wrap of Irish linen, leather, or nylon

➤ A nonmetal joint

Following are my Brunswick playing-cue specs:

➤ 18^1/$_2$ ounces

➤ 58 inches long (I'm 5 feet 10 inches tall)

➤ 12.5mm tip

➤ Pro 18-inch shaft taper

➤ Medium tip hardness

➤ Leather grip

➤ Plastic joint

The specs on my Brunswick break cue are exactly the same.

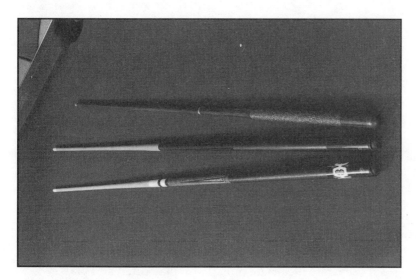

The three cues that I carry to every tournament or corporate exhibition. On the bottom is the Brunswick cue that I use 99 percent of the time. The center cue is my Brunswick break cue. Both cues have leather wraps. On the top is The Frog, a special cue for jump shots.

Special-Purpose Cues

People who play frequently often carry two or three cues with them, or if they have a table at home, they keep a couple of special cues separate from the rest. Neither of these extra cues is an absolute must-have unless you're very competitive or play on the pro level. Still, there are advantages to owning both of these additional cues, and you can make up your own mind after you read about them.

Breaking Cues

A break shot can be either an open break or a safe break, depending on the game. Straight Pool and One-Pocket are two of the few games in which you break the rack of balls (that is, the balls as they are positioned in a group at the beginning of the game) very gently. That's called a *safe break*. In all the other games, such as 8-Ball and 9-Ball, you break to smash the rack of balls wide open and send them flying in all directions, hoping that at least one will land in a pocket. That, for obvious reasons, is called an *open break*.

A safe break (or *safety break*, as it's sometimes called) is like any other shot during the game. Your regular playing cue is fine for this type of break. An open break, however, requires that you hit the rack of balls with the cue ball as hard as you can—much

Cue Tips

The "Sneaky Pete" is a unique cue with a very special purpose. It has all the qualities of a custom two-piece cue, but the joint is hidden, so it looks like a one-piece cue. Why make a pro cue that looks like a house cue? To sneak up on unsuspecting opponents. Beware the player who has a Sneaky Pete!

Pocket Dictionary

An *open break* is when, at the beginning of the game, you hit the cue ball into the rack of balls as hard as possible. A *safety break* is when, at the beginning of the game, you just graze the rack of balls and make the cue ball go to a position where no ball can be pocketed when your opponent comes to the table for his or her turn.

harder than any shot you would shoot during a game. This huge force can destroy a cue tip, flattening it or making it pop off the cue stick. Trying to play the precise shots of pool after subjecting the cue tip to that kind of battering is very difficult. Hence, we have the *break cue*. Although it's not always used even once a game (your opponent breaks the rack of balls for some games), this cue takes the punishment of the open break shot and leaves your regular playing cue free of potential damage.

Do you need a break cue? If you have a table at home, you can designate one of your one-piece cues as your break cue and then play the game with your two-piece cue or a different one-piece cue. In a billiard club, you can use a one-piece house cue from the wall racks as your break cue. You need to buy, carry, and maintain a separate break cue only if you play often and play seriously.

Many players use a break cue that is the same length, tip size, and balance as their playing cue, on the theory that their muscle memory is familiar with these characteristics. The weight should be similar; some players prefer half an ounce lighter, and some like half an ounce heavier.

Jumping Cues

Sometimes, you can't hit the ball that you want to hit, because another ball is in the way. It's possible to jump over that ball, and I tell you how in Chapter 21. There are special cues for this purpose, called *jump cues,* and they are legal to use in some circles and illegal in others. The design of these cues makes it easier to jump the cue ball over the *blocking ball* (a ball between the cue ball and the ball you want to hit).

Heard It in the Poolroom

Sammy "Jumpin'" Jones, pro player and husband of former World Champion Loree Jon Jones, unscrews his cue and jumps balls with only the shaft of the cue. He's so proficient that he can place the cue ball less than half an inch from the object ball and make the cue ball jump over the top without ever touching the object ball.

Jump cues are easy to recognize, because the butt is only one-fourth to two-thirds as long as the butt of a regular cue. If you're going to play in a league or local tournament, check the rules before you begin. If you (or your opponent) want to use one of these special cues, it pays to know whether it's permissible. If not, you'll have to try the jump shot with your regular cue. That's tougher, but still possible.

The Case for Cues

A cue case is designed to protect and transport your cue. Ideally, the case will keep the cue cool even in your trunk on an August day. (Heat is the leading cause of cue-shaft warpage.) Even if you have a table at home, you'll sometimes want to play at one of the local billiard rooms, or maybe to take your cue on vacation and find out what they're playing in Tokyo (Pool), London (Snooker and Pool), or Rio (Carom, Pool, and Snooker). You'll need a case.

Cases can cost as little as $9 for a vinyl-covered soft case with padded interior or as much as $895 for a custom exotic-wood case with exterior designs that match your cue's inlay work. The first type of case is too light-duty for any real traveling (it's for transporting the cue to and from your local billiard room), and you probably wouldn't take the other one out of your house. Between the extremes, however, is a range of very practical and attractive cue cases.

Scratch!

Hard cue cases have solid foam interiors with tapered holes for the shafts and butts of cues. Never force a cue into the holes; you may never get it back out.

The typical leather-covered hard cue case costs about $350, and the heavy-duty vinyl-covered hard case is half that price. Although cases have different names from manufacturer to manufacturer, most of them also have a standard numerical code attached to the model name. This code is in the form of two digits, the first of which designates the number of butts that the case holds; the second digit indicates the number of shafts. A 24, for example, is the most common type of case; it holds 2 butts and 4 shafts. Common designations are 11, 12, 24, and 36. One company may produce the Excalibur 24 and another company, the Pretty Close to Waterproof Titanic 24; each case will hold two cue butts and four cue shafts.

Hard cases almost always have one or more outside zippered pockets for holding the tools that you use to shape and rough your cue tip, a small hand towel, your own chalk, and whatever other items you want to keep handy.

If you had a cue custom-made to a length of 60 inches or more, as have many professional basketball players and pool players who are 6'2" or taller, each half (shaft and butt) is at least 30 inches long. You'll have to get a cue case custom-made, because standard cases won't hold anything larger than a 58- or 59-inch two-piece cue.

Among the monthly professional tour stops, the world championship, overseas invitation events, and a full schedule of corporate exhibition appearances, my case sees a lot of overhead baggage compartments on a lot of airplanes. It's a 24-style hard case, and I've had it for over 10 years and it still looks good. I'm searching for a new one now only because the newer ones offer the same protection but weigh less—something that's a big factor for my lifestyle.

Cue-Tip Hardness

The most important factor in how well a cue plays is how good a tip you have on the end of the cue. I've heard seasoned pros say that they could play with a broom handle, just as long as it had a good tip on it. That statement is a little exaggerated, but it does tell you how important the cue tip is.

Although people have experimented with, and marketed, cue tips of manmade materials, none has duplicated the products of Mother Nature. Whether the source is water buffalo, yak, or bovine, leather is the standard material for all cue tips.

Special tools are available for shaping and roughing your cue tip, as I tell you in Chapter 7. Right now, though, I want to deal with the tip itself and with the most important characteristic that you have to know about: tip hardness.

Ewa's Billiard Bits

Before 1807, it was impossible to put spin on the cue ball, because there was no such thing as a cue tip. Captain Francois Mingaud invented the tip while he was in prison on political charges. When Mingaud was released, he made a career out of exhibiting shots that no one else could make. His 1827 book is so rare that it's priceless. Nowadays, you can buy a tip for a buck.

I suggest that you begin with a soft or medium-soft tip. Developing a pool stroke takes time, and until then, you can spin the cue ball when you need to, using a soft tip. If you practice seriously, you'll reach the point at which you're frequently putting too much spin (English) on the ball. That's when you should consider switching to a tip of medium hardness, which gives you more control of spin without having to alter your stroke.

You'll have to trust me on this point, because all this talk about spinning the ball doesn't mean much to you now. (It will, starting with Chapter 15.) But if you've heard the phrase "putting English on the ball" or just the colloquialism "put a little English on it" (meaning to spin the facts), you'll have a clue as to what I'm talking about.

The hardness of cue tips can be measured, and you can use the following two charts as relative guidelines. The Mueller Sporting Goods chart was created by a national billiard-supplies retailer. The BB Chandivert chart was created by a French cue-tip manufacturer.

The Mueller Sporting Goods, Inc. Cue-Tip Hardness Chart

1 = Softest, 4 = Hardest

1.0 Elk Master
1.0 Blue Knight
2.0 Royal Oak
2.5 Match
2.5 Triumph
3.0 Le Professional
3.5 Champion
3.5 Crown
3.5 Triangle
4.0 Rocky

The BB Chandivert Cue-Tip Hardness Chart

1 = Softest, 10 = Hardest

1 Snooky
2 Rond
4 Match
4 Eureka
6 Champion
6 Super-Royal
7 Crown
7 Comprime
10 Rocky

The Chandivert tips are made in France. In the United States, #6, the Super-Royal, is called the quarter-pounder with cheese.

Chalk It Up!

The tip is the most important part of the cue, and chalking up is the most important thing that you need to do to the tip. Among nonprofessional players, an unchalked tip is the most common reason for miscues. (It's a lapse of concentration for pros, but we're also sometimes guilty of failing to chalk up properly.)

Chalking is fairly simple. You apply the chalk to the tip, in the words of Minnesota Fats, "like a beautiful woman puts on her lipstick." In other words, carefully make sure

Cue Tips

If the edge of your hand turns greenish–blue when you play pool, it's not from the dye in the cloth. It's from excess cue chalk that has fallen off cue tips onto the bed of the table. Never chalk your cue over the table or apply too much chalk.

Pocket Dictionary

A *miscue* occurs when the cue tip glances off the cue ball, either because of a lack of friction caused by not chalking the tip or because the cue ball was struck too close to the edge.

Ewa chalks her tip with a wiping motion or, in the words of Minnesota Fats, "like a beautiful woman puts on her lipstick."

that the chalk covers the entire surface that's supposed to be covered, without going to excess.

Use a wiping motion rather than a grinding or drilling movement. Trying to drill the cue tip into the depression in the cube of chalk creates a very uneven layer of chalk, parts of which will drop off the tip and get into the cloth of the table. An uneven or too-thick layer of chalk doesn't adhere well to the leather tip and, therefore, won't grab the cue ball—and the purpose of chalk is to provide friction between the cue tip and the cue ball. Without that friction, the cue tip slides off the cue ball, causing a miscue. If you're attempting to put spin on the cue ball, you'll fail.

The best way to remember to chalk your tip before each shot is to make it part of your preshot routine. It quickly becomes a habit. Another good habit is picking up the chalk cube and carrying it with you after each shot. When you place the chalk back on the table, place the open side on the side. If the unwrapped side is face-up, you'll get it on your clothes while bending over the table, and if you place it face-down, it will leave chalk on the rail, which will transfer to your clothing.

By the way, the best billiard chalk in the world is American-made and is exported in huge quantities. During my overseas travels I've tried locally produced chalk and haven't found any that met the quality of domestic brands.

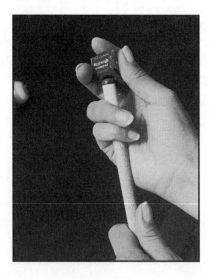

The Least You Need to Know

➤ An $18 one-piece cue is perfectly good for beginners and recreational play.

➤ You have many options when you choose a two-piece cue, but standard selections fit almost everyone's needs.

➤ A good two-piece cue should be stored and transported in a protective case.

➤ A soft to medium-soft tip is best for beginners and intermediate players.

➤ Chalk your cue tip before every shot.

Chapter 7

Having a Ball with Accessories

In This Chapter

➤ How to buy balls for billiards

➤ The other accessories you'll need for your home table

➤ Necessary accessories for your cue

➤ Tools that touch up your tip

➤ Picking a cue case that matches your needs

When you play billiards away from home, you'll find that the location—whether it's a billiard club, the billiard room at the country club, or even the tavern table at your neighborhood bistro—supplies all the basics. Bringing your own balls and rack would be awkward and unnecessary, but in the case of smaller items, you may want to use your own rather than the ones supplied. I carry my favorite brand of chalk, hand talc, a tip tool, and a mechanical bridge head in the accessories pocket of my cue case. You may also find a nail file and some gum, but that's not important. In this chapter, you find out what *is* important and what will be best for you.

Buying a table for your home game room means that you also have to pick an accessories package. You often have a choice among two or three packages that offer different amounts (two, four, or six one-piece cues, for example) and qualities of accessories. Even if only one package comes with your billiard table, you'll always have the option to upgrade individual items. The choices will be easy after you check out the rest of this chapter.

Additional accessories typically have to be purchased separately, such as a pool-table light, which is a substantial item in and of itself. I think that other things don't get included because the salespeople don't want to load you up with too much at one time. Some people never find out about these very useful accessories. I won't let that happen to you.

Buying Balls

You can play all the common pool games with a single set of standard balls, consisting of 15 numbered balls and a cue ball. Snooker and Carom—two billiard disciplines that I mentioned in previous chapters and explain in more detail in Chapter 27— require special sets of balls. They also require special tables, which may be one reason why the games are not common in America.

The standard set of pool balls is numbered 1 through 15. The first seven are solid-colored, the 8 ball is solid black (the only black ball), and the last seven balls (numbers 9 through 15) are white with a colored stripe around the equator. In every set, the same color progression is used. The 1 ball is always solid yellow, and the 9 ball (the lowest-numbered striped ball) is always white with a yellow stripe. The 2 ball is solid blue, and the second striped ball, the 10, is white with a blue stripe.

Ewa's Billiard Bits

The first billiard balls were made of stone, which was quickly replaced by wood, which in turn was replaced by ivory. The first attempt at nonivory balls produced a product that, when hit with enough force in a room with a certain humidity level and temperature, tended to explode. This distracted the players, and they were not popular.

The standard colors for pool balls are:

Yellow	1 ball (solid) and 9 ball (stripe)
Blue	2 ball (solid) and 10 ball (stripe)
Red	3 ball (solid) and 11 ball (stripe)
Brown	4 ball (solid) and 12 ball (stripe)
Orange	5 ball (solid) and 13 ball (stripe)
Green	6 ball (solid) and 14 ball (stripe)
Maroon	7 ball (solid) and 15 ball (stripe)
Black	8 ball (solid)

Spotting Quality

Do you really need a high-quality set of balls? If you're just playing recreationally, with no intention of becoming skilled at the sport, even the cheapest set of balls will be fine. If you want to play competitively at your billiard club and practice at home, I suggest that you buy what a commercial room would buy: a medium-high grade. The acknowledged cream of the crop are the Brunswick Centennial Balls, and their price reflects the workmanship involved in making them.

Balls should be as close to perfectly round as possible, their size and weight should be consistent from one ball in a set to another, and they should be color-consistent. The last characteristic is the easiest to see. Compare the blue in the 2 ball with the blue in the 10 ball, and if the blues differ, you know that the balls are of a low grade. The other three characteristics are tougher to judge.

Ball roundness, balance, and consistency of size and weight within a set can be measured only with special instruments, so there is no way to evaluate those features when you buy balls for your home billiard room. Price, however, is a very reliable guide. I've never found a set of billiard balls whose quality level didn't match their price level.

Lower-quality, less-expensive balls are always made of polyester, which develops flat spots sooner than phenolic resin—the material used in better balls. Polyester also ages faster than phenolic resin; the whites turn yellow, and the balls shrink slightly. Ask the salesperson which material is in the set that comes with your table. He or she will be glad to tell you, and probably will be pleased to have such a well-informed customer!

Scratch!

Balls should be cleaned occasionally; but if you wax them at all, use only billiard-ball wax. If you use other types of wax, then every time you hit the ball, it will mark the cloth with a white dot that is almost impossible to get out.

All Cue Balls Are Not the Same

At the age of 14, when I picked up my first cue stick and hit a cue ball, I thought that that ball was the same as the other balls on the table except for the fact that it was solid white—if I even thought about the matter at all. It's the natural assumption that most people make. When you play with the cue ball that is a part of the set you bought, you're right. In a billiard room or tavern, you may be wrong.

A cue ball is very personal; it's the ball that does the job and the only ball that your cue touches. At various times in history, but especially over the past 50 years, companies began manufacturing cue balls that were different from the other balls in the set. Some weigh a fraction of an ounce more than standard balls, some weigh close to half an ounce more, and one weighs a tad less than standard balls. Experienced players will notice that the weight of a cue ball makes a tremendous difference in their games, although the difference may not be apparent to beginners.

Cue Tips

All billiard balls change color over time, but if you keep them clean and keep them out of direct sunlight, they'll stay new-looking longer.

The other reason why manufacturers began producing cue balls separately from ball sets is that the cue ball is the first ball to wear out. The white ball is the one that gets slammed in every open break shot and the only ball to hit another ball on every shot. This relentless punishment is why the cue ball develops tiny flat spots before any others do. In a commercial room, cue balls should be replaced every few years, but they'll last a decade in home use. The 1 ball, which is usually placed at the front (or *apex*) of a rack of balls, is hit the hardest and most often of any ball other than the cue ball, so it wears out second-fastest. But a phenolic resin 1 ball still lasts close to 15 years in home use. The rest of the set lasts 10 to 15 years (polyester balls) or 20 to 40 years (phenolic balls).

You're more likely to find that a billiard room has replaced all the standard cue balls with slightly heavier versions if the room is a hangout for serious players. The heavier cue ball gives the regulars an edge over new customers, because they've grown used to the different angles in which a heavier cue ball travels. The more important reason, however, is that experienced players can manipulate a slightly heavier cue ball better. Social, upscale, and recreational rooms will more than likely use the cue ball that came with the set.

Coin-operated tavern tables, which are sometimes called *bar boxes* by players (but never by manufacturers), are unheard-of in Sweden, so they were a surprise to me when I came to America. I quickly discovered that these tables use cue balls that are different from the other balls on the table. The reason is very simple: All pocketed balls end up in a locked tray on coin-operated tables, and when all the balls have been pocketed, you have to put in more coins to release them for another game. But what happens if the cue ball accidentally goes into a pocket (called a *scratch*) before the game is over? If customers had to put in more money every time that happened, they'd soon quit. The only solution was to make the cue ball different from the other balls in some respect.

Ewa's Billiard Bits

The "red dot" and "red circle" cue balls are currently the most popular with serious players.

Pocket Dictionary

A *scratch* is when the cue ball (the white ball) goes into a pocket. This is one kind of foul.

Manufacturers have two main solutions for this problem. One is to make the cue ball slightly bigger. Pocketed balls travel down a chute with a hole in it. Other balls fall into the hole, but the bigger cue ball rolls over the hole and out an opening where players can retrieve it. The other solution is to place a magnet or a piece of metal in the exact center of the ball when it was being formed at the factory. A magnet in the table pulls the ball out of the path to the locked coin-operated tray, and it drops into a hole where players can get it and resume play.

The Fashion Ball

Dozens of special pool-ball sets are available. One set consists of clear balls with cards suspended in the center that have the ball numbers printed on them. Another set looks as though it were carved from marble, with the colors swirling in a white background. Other sets have designer circles around the numbers. Although the first set is really a novelty item (the cards make the balls unbalanced), the rest play just like standard pool balls.

You may also see balls with playing-card designs on them, all the way up through the Jack, Queen, King, and Ace. These balls are used for a special game called *Poker Pool*. Other games that require special ball numbering are being invented on a regular basis, but none has caught on permanently. If you feel adventuresome, you may want to buy one of these sets for special games and give the game a try. Rules are always included with the balls.

Money Balls

A standard set of pool balls (1 white cue ball and 15 numbered colored balls) costs $70 to $195. A low-end set will do the job, but balls are really a one-time investment, and a phenolic-resin set ($110 and up) will last longer and be a better value over the long run. A solitary cue ball costs $3.95 to $14.95 (the resin versions start at about $7). If you lose a numbered ball (it does happen; I think that cats eat them), you can buy a replacement for about the price of a cue ball.

Because balls last so long, they aren't fast-moving items for a billiard supply store and are rarely put on sale. The best time to strike a deal is when you're buying your table.

Must–Have Table Accessories

Let there be lights—and let's make sure that they cover the table. You can choose among hundreds of styles, but be careful not to forget that billiard-table lights have a job to do. Some of the fixtures on the market are more attractive than functional.

Heard It in the Poolroom

Johnny Irish (whose real name was John Lineen) was a shy, slim, unambitious pool player during the 1940s and '50s who died young. He also happened to be one of the best players who ever lived. Even though he weighed less than 140 pounds all his life, when he broke the balls open in 8–Ball or 9–Ball, two men would have to hold the table lights off to one side. The tremendous power that Irish achieved would cause the cue ball to smash into the racked balls and then fly straight up in the air as high as 8 feet!

In an ideal world, I prefer a table-lighting fixture that's 8 feet long, even though I have to use a little caution in swinging my cue around at the ends of the table. But I realize that a lighting fixture that big isn't always practical or attractive. Some 6- and 7-foot-long lights do a very good job, but I would think twice about anything smaller.

You have a choice between fluorescent tubes and incandescent lighting (light bulbs). The traditional three-cone lighting fixture uses bulbs, and the long box styles are either incandescent or fluorescent. You can purchase fluorescent tubes that give off a light similar to natural outdoor light, and fluorescents cast a softer, broader light with fewer harsh shadows than incandescent lights do. But incandescent light fixtures are generally more attractive and can be made in more styles, making it easier to match your home billiard room's decor. If function is your main interest, or if you can find a fixture that looks right for you, I recommend buying billiard-table lights that use fluorescent tubes.

A billiard-table light should be suspended 30 to 32 inches above the flat playing surface (bed) of the table. If your home billiard room is well lighted, aside from the table light, the distracting and unattractive shadows cast by the table light disappear.

The prices of table-lighting fixtures are all over the place, from a bare 6-foot fluorescent unit that you can pick up at a hardware store for less than $30 to beautiful hand-crafted, custom stained-glass units costing thousands of dollars. A more common range is $120 for a simple brass bar with three cones to $450 for a more elaborate glass-enclosed box design.

Pick Your Rack

Balls are arranged at the beginning of each game by means of a device called a *rack*. The triangle is the standard shape, which is why some people refer to the rack as *the triangle*. There's also a diamond-shaped rack for arranging the balls for a 9-Ball game, but I wouldn't bother getting one because it's easier to do with the triangular rack, which gives you room to put your fingers inside the rack and push the balls into place. The object is to get the balls in a tight grouping in which all balls touch all adjacent balls. This arrangement is called a *tight rack*.

Pocket Dictionary

You *rack* at the beginning of every game. The numbered balls are placed in a group inside of a triangular or diamond-shaped frame called a *rack*. *Rack* is also slang for a single game, as in "José is ahead by two racks." *Rack* is also used as a verb, as in "I'll rack the balls, and you break."

Although you can buy designer racks made of stainless steel, chrome, or hand-carved exotic woods, as well as racks that have ball bearings in the base, by far the most common materials are plastic and domestic hardwoods such as maple and oak.

A plastic rack is cheap (costs about $6) but doesn't really do a very good job, especially after it has been used for a few months. The sides begin to bow under pressure, and you can't achieve a tight rack. The solid-wood rack is your best bet. This type of rack costs around $12.95 for a lightweight model and will last a lifetime if it's not abused. Make it a habit to place the rack on the hook provided at the end of the table under the rail—or on a carpeted floor under that rail—instead of just tossing it onto a shelf, credenza, or barstool. All the designer racks that I've seen (and I think I've seen them all) have very sturdy sides and will give you a tight rack.

Billiard Bridges

The mechanical bridge, a device that helps you reach faraway shots, is basically a cue and a slip-on or screw-on head that's shaped like a very skinny bridge. You place the tip end of your cue in one of the grooves in the bridge, and the bridge acts as your front hand.

Cue Tips

Most triangular racks are large enough to hold all 15 balls plus your fingertips so that you can push the balls together tightly. But if you rack the balls with either of the other two points in the forward position, the angle of the point of the rack is slightly off, and you'll have trouble getting all the balls to touch one another as they should.

There are metal, plastic, and composite bridge heads. Look for a head that is smooth and, when you set the bridge on the table, stable. When checking out a new design, I try to wiggle the bridge back and forth, and if it's difficult to get the bridge to tip over, it's a good design.

I often carry my favorite bridge head in the accessories pouch of my cue case, just in case the bridges at the place where I'm going aren't up to snuff. I especially want to avoid a bridge head that has a nick or burr, because it can scar my cue shaft. The head of my bridge, like most, slips snugly onto the tip of any house cue, giving me an instant bridge.

Almost every table, home or commercial, has hooks on the long side, under the rail, and that's where you keep the bridge. Some tables have hooks on both sides. If your table doesn't, you can easily get the hooks installed. I like a bridge on both sides of my table. It's not laziness. When I'm playing, I'm very focused, and if I need the mechanical bridge, I want to be able to reach for it without thinking and without finding that I'm on the bridgeless side of a table. It's a concentration-breaker to have to move away from the shot to get the bridge on the other side. But even during recreational play, having bridges on both sides of the table is simply more convenient.

A bridge head costs about a dollar for a plastic model and $8 for the brass version, and a complete bridge (head and 58-inch cuelike handle) costs from $8 to $18.

Spots

Only two spots on a pool table are marked. One is the center of the bottom half of the table (where the balls are racked), and the other is the center of the top half (where you put the cue ball to break the balls open at the beginning of the game). Both spots are very, very thin canvas with a glue backing. The spot at the head of the table is around $^1/_4$ inch in diameter, and the spot at the foot of the table may be $^3/_4$ inch to $1^1/_2$ inches in diameter. There don't need to be any specs for spots, so each manufacturer makes a slightly different size.

Both spots should be applied to your table after it has been assembled and the cloth has been put on. The table mechanics (installers) then draw a line from one side of the table to the other, directly through the spot at the head of the table (the *head spot*) and parallel to the end cushion. This line is called *the headstring* or just *the line*, as in "You have to break from behind the line."

Over time, the edge of a spot can come loose and curl up. Don't try to reglue it; you could easily create a slight bump that will cause balls that roll over it to change direction. Then you'd have to have the table re-covered with new cloth—a $250 job that takes half a day. Billiard supply stores sell new spots for a few pennies. Pull up the old one, and apply the self-sticking new spot in the circle that the old spot left. Ten seconds, and you're done.

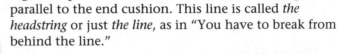

Pocket Dictionary

Spotting a ball is when you place an illegally pocketed ball on the spot at the end of the table where the balls are racked. A *spot shot* is when you place the cue ball behind the headstring and shoot a spotted ball off the spot.

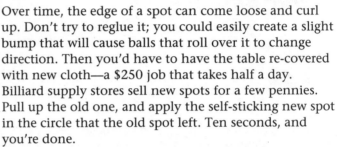

Ewa's Billiard Bits

Before 1960, removing the covers from billiard tables in commercial rooms was a morning ritual that was carried out in a solemn, silent fashion. Only when all the covers had been removed did play begin. Today, most billiard rooms don't even cover their tables at night.

Table Cover

Covering your table when it's not in use is a good idea. Mail-order billiard stores, online supply stores, and the place where you bought the table all sell covers in a variety of colors and qualities. As long as you pick one that fits your table ($4^1/_2 \times 9$ feet, 4×8 feet, and so on), you can get any style you like. A cover keeps the table free from dust, making the cloth last longer and look better. It also protects against whatever someone may put on the table. Nothing should be placed on the table, but it's going to happen sooner or later. The phone will ring while you're carrying a box or a bird cage or something, and you'll quickly put whatever you're carrying on the table and forget it.

Pool-table covers cost $18.95 for a thin plastic sheet to $100 for a fitted, heavy-gauge vinyl in a color that matches your walls.

Must–Have Tableside Accessories

You'll need a couple more things to play billiards at home, things that I'll call tableside accessories. The number of things that you *can* have, of course, is almost endless, from art and memorabilia for your walls to wet bars carved with billiard scenes. I tell you about appropriate furniture and the like in Chapter 8, but first things first. The items described in the following sections are must-haves.

Cues for Company

In the accessories package that came with your table, you got some one-piece cues. Four cues is the typical number, which probably seemed like plenty because the game is best suited to one to four people. But people like to have choices. Everyone who's playing may prefer the same-weight cue, for example, or one or more of your cues may be at the pro shop getting a tip replaced or having some other repair.

So how many one-piece cues satisfy your basic needs? I would say 6 or 7, but 10 is not an unreasonable quantity. Buy different weights, ranging from 17 ounces to 20 ounces. Most one-piece cues come in steps of a full ounce, so 2 of each would give you a total 8 cues, and you could pick up a couple extra 18- and 19-ounce models.

The best one-piece cues run around $18 apiece, and the best time to negotiate price is when you're buying your table.

Cue Keepers

What do you do with a dozen cues? You can't just lean them in a corner; they'll warp. You need a cue rack, and you can choose between two general types: wall racks and floor racks. Most are wood, but you can find metal racks.

The least-expensive option is the two-piece wall rack, which is simply a bar of wood at the top with holes drilled in it and a bar of wood at the bottom shaped like a little shelf. Screw the two pieces into the wall, the appropriate distance apart. Slide the tip of the cue into a hole in the top piece, and rest the base of the cue on the shelf at the bottom. This type of rack is simple and inexpensive (about $30), and it lets your wallpaper or paint show through.

More-expensive wall racks are one piece, with a solid-wood backing. Some racks have mirrors in the backing, which looks pretty neat. There's a lot of variety in racks of this type; you can choose among different woods, stains, and decorative carvings and designs. Again, you can get something to match your table and any decor.

You can find floor cue stands that are round and twirl like a lazy Susan, as well as square stands and stands that are shaped like a fan for placement in a corner. A floor stand may have places to set drinks

Cue Tips

If you own a valuable two-piece cue that you use at home and at the billiard club, put it away in the case when you're done playing, even when you're using your own table. That way, visitors will pick a one-piece cue from your wall rack and won't start using your personal cue by mistake.

and store a set of balls. A typical price would be $140, but as with any furniture, there's a broad range of prices and styles available.

Chalk It Up

The only thing you need to know about choosing cue-tip chalk is to buy American-made brands. The quality is the best, and the prices are very reasonable. A box of a dozen cubes of chalk lasts the average family a year or more, even if you chalk up before every shot. (You *do* chalk up before every shot, don't you? I certainly hope so.)

A dozen cubes of cue chalk cost around $4.

Talc About Smooth

The older, traditional poolrooms used to have a few cones of talc placed around the room, and players would rub the cone to get talc on their fingers. The talc made the cue slide smoothly while they were playing. Manufacturers purified the talc, converted it to powder form, and put it in containers, giving it the name talcum powder. Talcum powder is what players use today.

The problem with talc, as it's still called, is that it's messy. Modern rooms rarely have a talc cone or powder dispenser, because one out of a hundred people is going to go overboard and create a white dust storm that settles on the table.

Scratch!

Excess hand talc gets on the balls and cloth, ruining the needed friction, which creates miscues and missed shots. Also, white handprints on dark-green cloth and clothing are ugly—a sure sign that a thought-less and unknowledgeable player has passed that way recently.

I prefer to keep my hands free of moisture simply by keeping a dry towel next to me while I play and wiping my hands between shots. It works. But at times, the humidity is so high, or the game so full of tension, that I need a small amount of talcum powder. The operative word is *small*. Please. And avoid using baby powder. As you know, baby powder is designed to cake up when it's hit with moisture, and ultimately, it will make things worse than using nothing at all.

Some great products are available, only a couple of which are talc-based and some of which you apply directly to the cue shaft. Experiment and find the one that you like. Or just use a dry towel, as I do.

Tool Time for Tips

Keeping your cue tip shaped and roughed is critical to playing the game, whether you play for fun or take the sport seriously. The better you get, the more important the condition of the tip is, but it counts even for a complete beginner. I'll keep the explanation brief but give you enough information that you can see what I'm talking about.

The sides of a new cue tip are flush with the sides of the cue, but after you use it for a while, the tip will flatten a little and the sides will mushroom out. When you hit the cue ball anywhere but dead-center, you'll be using both the mushroomed part of the tip, which has nothing behind it, and part of the tip that is supported by the cue shaft. The ball goes slightly to the right or left of where you aimed, and you miss the shot.

A hard, smooth tip does not accept chalk well. When you hit the cue ball anywhere but dead-center, it has the same result as hitting it with the mushroomed cue tip: The ball veers off to the side.

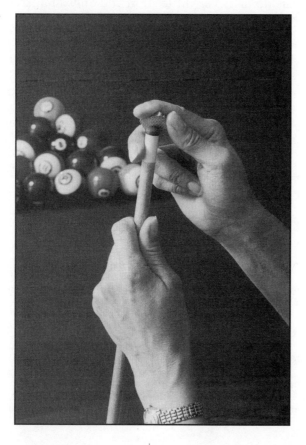

Here I'm using a small device which slightly roughens the cue tip so it will more easily accept chalk. You can chalk a smooth tip, and the chalk may cover the tip, but the appearance is deceptive because chalk won't bond to a smooth tip and will flake off as soon as the tip touches the cue ball.

A flat tip—and all rounded tips flatten with use—must have the same result if you hit the cue ball anywhere but in the center.

Billiard companies produce dozens of products to deal with these problems. Scuffers are made to rough up the tip so that tip chalk will adhere to it. Other devices poke tiny holes into the tip to achieve the same result. Shapers grind down the edges of the tip to make the top rounded again. Trimmers cut off the mushroomed edges. A multitude of combination devices do two or all three of these jobs. I like the dual-purpose scuffer-shapers because those two tasks have to be done most often. A tip has to be trimmed only once, and a tip can last an occasional player six months to a year. I carry a scuffer-shaper in my cue case but leave the trimmer at home.

Pocket Dictionary

A *scuffer* is a device that roughs a cue tip so that it accepts chalk. A *shaper* is a device that converts a flat tip to a crown shape. A *trimmer* is a cue-tip tool that cuts off any part of the tip that is wider than the cue shaft.

When you see a tip tool, you'll immediately understand how to use it; the tools are that simple. The only thing I'll caution you about is grinding away too strongly with either the scuffer or shaper. Shaping or roughing up a cue tip takes very little effort and only a few seconds. If you grind too hard, you'll quickly wear out the tip and have to replace it.

The single-purpose and multiple-purpose tools are all small enough to fit in your pocket or purse—or in your cue case's accessory pouch. Single-purpose tip tools are priced from $4 to $10, and the multiple tools cost $8 to $30. Unless you become addicted to the game (and you may!), tools will last 10 years or more.

The Least You Need to Know

➤ If you want to try playing snooker or caroms, you need special balls and a special table.

➤ Install your pool-table light fixture 30 to 32 inches above the playing surface.

➤ Get 8 to 12 one-piece cues, in weights ranging from 17 to 20 ounces, when you buy your pool table.

➤ If you must use talc, use the smallest amount that will get the job done.

➤ Chalk your cue tip before every shot.

➤ A cue-tip scuffer and a tip shaper are must-have items.

Chapter 8

Your Billiard Sanctuary

> **In This Chapter**
>
> ➤ Picking a room in your home for your pool table
>
> ➤ Special chairs for billiards
>
> ➤ Other games commonly found in a home billiard room
>
> ➤ Keeping your table clean
>
> ➤ Cleaning cues

Basements aren't common in Europe, and my parents didn't want to trade the dining-room table for a pool table, so I grew up in a home without the sport that later became such a large part of my life. As I mentioned earlier in this book, I started playing in the local billiard club and moved to America as a teenager. It was then that I discovered basements being used as family rooms and game rooms and billiard rooms.

When my husband, Mitch, and I began planning to build a house, the most important room (to me) was what builders are now calling the bonus room. My Brunswick Gold Crown table is there, on the second floor above the garage, in a space that's 20 feet by 20 feet and that also doubles as an office. One of the nice things about having a billiard room at home, by the way, is the fact that it can serve other purposes. As I mention in Chapter 5, manufacturers make tables that can be converted for Ping-Pong, air hockey, or some buffet/dining configuration.

In this chapter, I give you a few ideas on how to approach designing your home billiard room. Remember that it can be used, at various times, as a getaway room where you can quietly practice by yourself and unwind from a stressful day, or as a social center for the family or gatherings of friends. A lot depends on the space that you have available.

How Much Room for Your Billiard Room?

You need at least 5 feet on each side of the pool table. This space gives players enough room to get in their stances and go through the swinging of the cue (called *the stroke*) without hitting the wall. Having $5^1/_2$ feet is even better. You know from Chapter 5 that most home tables measure 4 feet by 8 feet, although the commercial and professional size is $4^1/_2$ feet by 9 feet. Add the depth of any furniture that you intend to put in the room to figure the size that the room must be.

This doesn't mean that all you can do in, say, a 20-by-20-foot room is play pool. Desks, for example, are a couple of inches lower than the top of a billiard table, and the desk chair can go into your 5-foot clearance area when you're not playing. Low bookshelves work, too. If you have a little extra space, you can do what a lot of people do: add a bar to the billiard room.

The actual room that you designate is up to you. People use basements, which they remodel into a billiard room, game room, den or combination of all three. Where no basement is available, people wall in their garages and make a family room/billiard room in the space. Florida rooms are also popular locations. A large spare bedroom, the bonus room, or a room that the builder may have designated as a den or library is also commonly used. If your house is large enough, you may have a couple of extra rooms to choose between. Generally, you want the billiard room to be easily accessible to the entire family and guests, but not adjoining a room where someone may be sleeping.

Scratch!

Don't set up your table without finding out whether the ceiling beams are in the right position to anchor the table light. The light has to be perfectly centered and aligned with the table, and it is heavy enough to require more than just a plasterboard or drywall sheet for the support screws.

I've seen homes with poolhouses and outbuildings converted to billiard rooms, and I've seen houses for which the easiest thing to do was build an addition. One couple whom I know, who own a historic house, use their basement. The problem is that the house is more than 100 years old, and the basement is only 6 feet high. But they love the game, and the basement was the only place they could fit a table, so they play until they get claustrophobic.

Another couple I know converted their dining room to a billiard room. Their problem was a built-in counter with a circular section that stuck out. They could play shots from anywhere around the table but that particular point, because the section blocked them from drawing the cue stick back to shoot. They installed the table anyway and just made a house rule that if the cue ball ended up on a certain spot, it could be moved 2 inches.

A man I know retired to Florida and bought a condominium. It was too small for a billiard table, so he rented a small storefront in a nearby building and put a table there. Tourists do a double-take when they walk by, but he's also found some interesting people to play against that way. The long and the short of it is that you can be as creative as you want when it comes to picking a place to set up your own billiard table.

A Multiple-Table or Multiple-Game Room

If the room is large enough, entertain the thought of using two tables. I've seen home billiard rooms that have up to four tables—a rather impressive sight. The second table could be the same size and type as the first or a table for another of the billiard games (such as snooker or carom). The latter two games, which I explain further in Chapter 28, require tables that have different features.

A snooker table has rounded cushions near the pocket, and a carom table has no pockets at all. People who enjoy playing either of these games try to put in one of the appropriate tables along with a standard pool table. If you do a considerable amount of entertaining at home and expose your guests to your billiard room, everyone will want to take a whack at the game—even people who have never picked up a cue in their lives. Two players is a perfect number, and four people can play comfortably, but if you have any more than four, the wait between shots for each person gets to be too long, and interest dwindles.

Two tables will occupy eight people. In a bigger group, players can mingle and act as the audience while they wait to get a chance at banging balls around. It's really neat to have a group of friends cheering when you make a good shot.

Heard It in the Poolroom

During the 1950s, a businessman in Hot Springs, Arkansas, liked to gamble on pool but wouldn't gamble at a poolroom. He always insisted that his opponent gather up lots of money and come to his house for an evening of money games. Players who could beat him usually lost, for a reason that went beyond having a simple home-court advantage. The man had set up his table so that one corner pocket was a tad lower than the rest and one side pocket was a tad higher. He also used an uncommon cue ball that was a couple of grams lighter than a standard cue ball. These subtle differences took even experienced players a while to discover and then adjust to— but by then, they were broke, and it was too late.

A two-table home billiard room can make sense for the right lifestyles, but if that doesn't fit your scheme of things and you have a large area left over, other things typically belong in your sanctuary. One of the most popular additions is a jukebox. You can find antique reproductions, ultramodern designs, and compact versions. You can load in your favorite CDs and punch up whatever kind of music makes your play or your party more enjoyable.

Other games that are typically put in a home billiard room are full arcade-size video games and pinball machines. Arcade video games are having a tough time, because the new games are now coming out on home computer CD-ROMs at the same time as the arcade versions. (Once, games were introduced in the arcades and appeared in home-computer versions a year later, but that's rarely the case now.) The decrease in arcade sales has lowered the prices of the big machines, especially for used models, and for people who first played a video game in an arcade, they're almost nostalgic, even when the games are only 5 or 10 years old.

Pinball machines are a different story. There's no way to get the same feeling playing a home-computer version of pinball, and maybe for that reason, they've had something of a comeback. Prices reflect that fact, but they're still within the budget of someone who has a home game room. The one thing to watch out for—and this applies to arcade-size video games also—is that everyone eventually gets tired of a single game, and the machine sits idle until new friends come over.

This situation isn't true of a billiard table, however, possibly because you can play so many different games on one table. The *Billiard Congress of America Official Rules and Record Book* lists the 8 most popular games, plus 16 others, but more than 50 other games aren't included. Also, the nature of billiards is so different from that of a video or pinball game that you simply don't get tired of it. If anything, the opposite is true: The more you play, the more you want to play.

The final game that you often see in home billiard rooms is darts. A dartboard takes up almost no space when it's not being used, and the game is fairly simple to play. Not easy, especially if you play at a serious level, but not difficult to understand or enjoy. The only reservation I would have applies to families that have small children.

Darts are available in the traditional models, usually with tungsten shafts and sharp points, or the soft-tip models with plastic or plastic-coated points. Even with the soft tips, you still have to take care not to let darts get into the possession of children or pets.

Cue Tips

If you have a TV set, computer monitor, glass-top pinball machine, or glass-front video arcade machine in your billiard room, invest in covers that have hard fronts, just in case a ball flies off the table in that direction.

Billiard Balls Are Harder Than Glass

The orientation of your billiard table is something to consider if your would-be billiard room has glass windows or doors. Balls sometimes fly off the table, and they shatter glass in a flash. The best thing to do is place the *head of the table*— the end where you stand when you get ready to break the balls at the beginning of a game—near the glass. Most flying balls go off the foot of the table, and it happens most often during the opening shot, when the balls are smashed in all directions.

If you have a large billiard room that includes a den, think about the possibility that someone will be sitting there, and place the table so you're breaking away from the den. In an office situation, especially if the office has a computer, you want to direct the break away from the monitor and CPU. These are common-sense things, but many people don't think about them when they have their tables installed.

Carpet is a super idea, not only because it is less tiring to stand on than a hardwood floor, but also because if a ball does drop off the table, it won't harm the floor or the ball. An option that looks really good is to have a different color or section under the table. If you're lucky enough, you may find a pattern with a rectangular design in the middle that is roughly 4 feet by 8 feet, but I wouldn't count on it. Your carpet salesperson can tell you the cost of installing a carpet with a cutout section that will match your table and can give you an idea of what color to put in that section. Having a carpet custom-made for a billiard room is a little expensive, but it looks spectacular.

Pocket Dictionary

The end of the billiard table where you stand to break the balls at the beginning of the game is the *head* of the table, except in snooker where its called the foot of the table.

Scratch!

Be aware that a carpet will compress under the weight of a billiard table, and the table will have to be re-leveled and checked a week or so after it's installed. Check it again in a couple months.

Home Room Seating

When players aren't shooting, they should have a place to sit, which makes the game more enjoyable and gives them enough rest to play longer. When you're deciding how to furnish your home billiard room, you can use regular kitchen-type chairs, dining-table chairs, living-room-style sofas and love seats, or any other seating that suits your taste. But regular furniture is low, and while you're playing pool, you'll be getting in and out of your seat all the time. Something higher is much more practical.

Pocket Dictionary

Spectator chairs are chairs made specifically for billiards. They're as high as barstools but built like chairs.

Barstools are commonly used in home billiard rooms; you can buy them through pool and billiard magazines and at billiard supply stores. Specific chairs are made for billiard rooms, however. You see them in commercial billiard clubs and can also buyo them for home use. These chairs usually are called either *spectator chairs* or *observation chairs*, and they are about as tall as barstools. The difference is that they are chairs, not stools.

Spectator chairs have arms and often a cutout place in the arm to hold your drink. They look like chairs with long legs. The seat is padded and upholstered, but the rest is usually stained wood. There's a crossbar where you put your feet. After those basic features, the styles vary. Some chairs have small built-in shelves on one side. Some are wide enough for two people to use. Others come in an attached set with a shelf between the two chairs to hold drinks, a towel, and whatever else you want to keep at hand. Watch for one that has a place to rest your cue in an upright position (often, just a U-shape notch in the shelf or arm)—a very handy feature. You can leave your cue there while you rack the balls or do other things.

When you pick out seating, try to get at least enough for four people. True, one person will always be playing, but everyone wants his or her own seat. If you give a lot of parties, think about surrounding your table with billiard spectator chairs. They're elevated enough for the viewers to be able to see all the action. The old-style 1930s billiard rooms had spectator benches 8 to 12 feet long. I don't know of any company that makes these benches today, but you can easily line up two or three two-seaters. Because almost all of these benches have a shelf attached, they work well for small parties and after-dinner play. Spectators can nibble on munchies and have their drinks at hand.

Ewa's Billiard Bits

Most professional pool players have a table at home, but they still go to their local billiard clubs to play. If you play only at home, you can get too used to the personality of your personal table and become less able to adapt to a strange table, as you have to do at tournaments.

Optional Furniture and Decorations

Turning your game room into a gaming room is relatively easy, as long as it's legal in your state. Most governments permit you to have a gaming room if it's just for amuse-ment and nobody can actually lose any money. Slot machines (both new and used), a blackjack layout, a card table, and maybe even a roulette wheel can be a ball when you use them for fun. This setup presumes that you give a lot of parties, of course, but if that's your style, a one-armed bandit can add excitement to your game room.

Antique or faux-antique bars have become very popular for home billiard rooms over the past few years. Owners match them up with authentic antique tables (if they're lucky enough to find those tables) or the many modern reproductions of classic tables. You can go all the way and find antique lights for the table, antique-looking spectator chairs, and even a shiny spittoon. Whether or not you go the antique route or get all the accessories, if your room is large enough, a bar is a nice, popular addition.

After buying your table, table light, and furniture you can turn to wall decorations. You have thousands and thousands of things to choose among—and that's just in terms of billiard-themed items. The possibilities include signs from early-20th-century billiard clubs; framed posters of billiard scenes from motion pictures; neon art; graphics; artwork of the members of the Billiard Hall of Fame; action or publicity photos (signed or unsigned) of past and present stars; lithographs; billiard floor and table lamps; cases for displaying collectible cues; tournament posters; and a ton of billiard paperweights, ashtrays, and statuettes.

Billiard-room television sets are popular among people who take the game seriously. If you have a VCR, you can run an instructional tape or one of the thousands of tournament tapes and set up the shots to practice on your own. Seeing whether you can get the same result as a touring pro is a fun way to practice. You can even stop the tape before the shot is actually made and, with the balls set up in the same position as they are on- screen, figure out what you would do. Then hit the Play button and find out whether you and the pro reached the same conclusion. With instructional tapes, you can actually shoot the shots that the instruction shows you, rather than just watch the tape and hope to remember everything when you finally reach a table.

Scratch!

You can even buy underwear, ties, and suspenders with billiard designs. Just don't wear them to your billiard club, if you value your reputation.

Keep It Clean

A couple of things need to be done in your billiard room that are different from standard housekeeping chores. A table can be dusted and the wood can be polished just like any other piece of furniture, but the cloth and the cues need special attention.

Dust from the air and chalk dust from cue tips settles on the cloth. Most of it works its way through the threads and settles on the slate, where it does the most damage. Most people are surprised to find out that billiard cloth wears far more from the underside than it does from the top. What happens is that dust settles—especially chalk dust—and, being abrasive, cuts and wears at the material every time a ball rolls over it. The dust makes the cloth thinner, separates tiny chucks that are whisked away with a brush or picked up by the vacuum cleaner, and spoils the dark-green coloring. I recommend a pool-table cover, which eliminates a lot of the air dust but doesn't do much for the biggest culprit: chalk dust.

Cue Tips

Don't clean your cue tip or ever get it damp, but the white area just behind the tip (called the *ferrule*) can be cleaned with soap and water. A toothbrush and toothpaste work well, too, and a final swipe with bleach makes the ferrule bright white.

Overchalking your cue tip adds chalk dust to the cloth, but just normal play builds up a fine layer between the slate and the cloth. If chalk didn't separate from your cue tip when you hit the cue ball, you'd have to chalk up only once before each session. So the existence of chalk dust is inevitable, and the question is how to get rid of it. A carpet vacuum cleaner (even a canister model) looks like overkill, and it is. That much power just sucks up normal fibers and makes your cloth threadbare in no time. Handheld vacuums are far better suited to the job. Buy one that has no beater bar and no burrs or sharp edges on the part that glides over the cloth. Remember that billiard cloth is the same material used in fine clothing, not carpets. Vacuum after every 20 to 30 hours of play, and you'll be keeping your cloth in good shape.

Before quality hand-held vacuums were popular, billiard clubs (then called poolrooms) used to brush down the tables at the beginning of each day. (You see this done in the 1961 movie *The Hustler*.) Brushing was better than nothing—but not a lot.

Billiard brushes are still sold and are very popular with commercial rooms. They're cut in a special profile to make sure that they can get under the angled cushions surrounding the flat bed of the table. The idea used to be to brush the dust off the cloth and into the pockets, which worked, to some extent. One substantial drawback was that the first ball into the pocket picked up a lot of the dust and put it back on the table. Another problem was that the act of brushing itself caused pressure and helped the tiny chalk particles cut through the threads.

But the real problem with brushes is that they get only part of the dust (and you may have a miniature dust storm on your hands if you wait too long between brushings). When you buy your table, one of these brushes may be included, but I don't think I'd bother using one. Even the cheapest handheld vacuum cleaner does a better job.

Cloth also develops gray areas after a significant amount of use. These gray areas can be caused by excess wear—the line that is formed around the perimeter of the table bed, just below the point of the cushions, for example—or by burning. Cloth is said to have been *burned* when it turns gray in an area around the headstring. The *headstring* is the line across the head of the table from the second diamond on one side to the second diamond on the other side. That's where you put the cue ball to make your opening shot. The cue ball is hit harder for that shot than any other, and it gets hit into and across the fibers. Whether a cloth is actually burned is debatable, but if you break from the same spot over and over, the cloth certainly turns gray for the first few inches past the line. The discoloration occurs faster on a polyester/wool cloth than on a worsted-wool cloth, but it occurs on all types of cloth eventually. Because the areas around the perimeter of the table and along the headstring are the first to wear, they're a good thing to use to evaluate the condition of your cloth.

When your billiard cloth first develops gray areas, try splashing water on the cloth. (You have to wet the entire bed to avoid leaving water marks.) Rub the water around with your hands, especially around the gray areas, and then blot it up. Let the cloth dry thoroughly and then vacuum with a handheld vacuum cleaner. Although this technique is a bit risky (there's a chance of leaving water marks), it can partially convert the gray back to green.

Cleaning cues is an easier process. The advice of certain cue makers is to never use any liquid on a cue shaft. The cue butts are coated with a clear protective layer that resists moisture, but the shafts are bare wood. Moisture is absorbed by bare wood, and moisture can warp the shaft and deteriorate the wood. Actually, I've found it safe to follow the suggestion of the other group of cue makers, who say that it is effective to wipe down the shaft of a cue with a damp cloth and then follow with a dry cloth. If you do this after each session, the shaft remains clean and smooth. A sticky or bumpy shaft is very distracting to use, and if the shaft isn't cleaned, it will eventually turn dark gray and look terrible. Cleaning the cue shaft on a regular basis takes only a minute and lengthens the life of your cue.

You should clean balls the same way that you clean a cue shaft. A damp cloth, followed by a dry cloth, takes off all the chalk and dust. Dirty balls cause odd things to happen when they collide; they cling together for a moment, rather than sliding off or bouncing off each other as they should. Then the balls go in slightly incorrect directions and can make you miss shots. After you read Chapters 15 and 16 on putting spin on the cue ball, you'll appreciate the fact that even one chalk mark on a ball affects the way that the ball acts if that chalk mark happens to roll around and be at the point of contact when the cue ball and the object ball collide.

On the Level

When you have your home table installed, it will be leveled. If the company that you bought the table from is any good, it will make an appointment to return and check to see whether the table needs re-leveling. Tables weigh half a ton or more, and they settle, whether they're on carpeting or not. Even on a stone floor, a table settles just under its own weight. This settling may be even all around, as the frame is symmetrical, and it may not need any adjustment. Chances are, though, that one place will settle a little more than another. The installers may decide to come back in a couple of days or a couple of weeks, depending on the table model and the flooring in your home.

Scratch!

You may be advised to spray the cloth with a silicon spray. The spray does make the balls roll farther and smoother, but it can gum up cloth over time.

Pocket Dictionary

When a very-slow-moving ball deviates from a straight line, the table is said to have *rolloff*, and the ball is said to have *rolled off*.

Over time, the table may need another adjustment. There's no way for me to tell you how long a period to wait before having it checked, because so much difference exists among models and locations, but there is an easy way for you to check it yourself. Stand at the head of the table, and slowly roll a ball down the right side of the table bed. Watch to see whether the ball rolls off the straight line that it should follow. Then roll a second ball down the center of the table, with just enough speed to reach the end cushion. Try the same on the left side. Then switch and follow the same procedure across the table, from side to side.

Be sure that the cloth is clean, because hitting a tiny (and I do mean tiny) clump of piled-up chalk dust can cause a slow-moving ball to deviate from its path. If you don't see any *rolloff*—that is, deviation from the straight line—the table is level or very close to level. If you do see rolloff, vacuum the cloth again and move the ball over an inch or so before trying it a second time. I suggest moving the ball over an inch because the cloth can have a pill (a clump of loose fiber on a newish cloth) or a worn spot (on used cloth) that will mess up the roll of a slow-moving ball.

Try this test a couple of weeks after your table is releveled; then try it again every six months or so. After a quality table has settled, it probably won't go out of level for many years. Cheaper department-store-type tables may go out of level in a few weeks or a few months.

Cue Tips

Don't use a cue ball or a 1 ball for this test. These balls are hit the most often and are the most likely to have minute flat spots. If a ball is rolled very slowly, an almost-imperceptible flat spot is enough to make the ball roll off line. (The possibility of rolloff, by the way, is why you don't see players delicately baby very many shots; we'd rather hit them with a firmer stroke.)

The Least You Need to Know

➤ Locate ceiling studs for the table light before installing your billiard table.

➤ Place the table so that any window or other breakable object is at the head end—not the foot, where the balls are racked.

➤ Regular furniture is too low for a billiard room; billiard spectator chairs work much better.

➤ If your room is large enough, it's appropriate to add other games or to also use it for other purposes, such as an office.

➤ Use a handheld vacuum cleaner with no beater bar to clean your table cloth after every 20 to 30 hours of play.

➤ Clean your cues with a damp cloth, followed immediately by a dry cloth.

Part 3
Let's Get Physical

Now that you've picked out a place to play, and maybe have even purchased a table for your home, you need to know how to go about this billiard thing. How do you stand? Do you just walk up and whack the ball, hoping that something interesting happens? Not quite. Billiards, like all sports, has special stances, grips, and swings (although in billiards, swings are called strokes). That's the kind of stuff that I tell you in this part.

First, you have to know what you're permitted to do and what you're not permitted to do (illegal things, according to the rules). This is foul stuff, I admit, but you don't want to incur a penalty, so I give you the do's and don'ts of billiard play.

Next, I tell you how to stand. I know that you've probably been doing that since you were 18 months old, but you haven't been doing it with the idea of making a billiard ball go into a billiard-table pocket—something that requires standing in a special way. Also, you've probably held a stick or two in your time, but maybe not a finely balanced cue stick. That's why this part includes a chapter on the various grips that will put you in the winner's circle.

I wrap up this part with a chapter on the stroke. In many sports (golf, baseball, '40s big-band dance music), swing is critical, and it is in billiards, too. Developing a stroke is essential to success, and I tell you how to do that at the end of this part.

The General Rules

Knowing the rules before you play is critical for any game or sport, and as in many sports, the rules of billiards change from time to time or place to place. The game of 9-Ball, for example, has become much more popular than the traditional Straight Pool because it is a faster-moving game. (The specifics of these games are explained near the end of the book, in Part 6.) As professionals changed to 9-Ball for tournaments, they felt that rule changes needed to be made to bring the game up to tournament standards. These changes have been gradual, and at times, changes have been tried and then we switched back to the old way. It's all a refining process to meet the needs of the game and the circumstances of the moment.

One game, 8-Ball, is notorious for being played by a thousand different rules. Within a single town, three or four leagues play by different rules, one tavern sets rules slightly different from the next, and individual players decide which rules they like before they chalk up. The reason for the chaos in 8-Ball is that it was never a professional tournament game. Anyone could, and did, make up rules as they went along. When the game was taken overseas, those countries developed their own rules to fit their cultures. Although professional 8-Ball tournaments have been held occasionally, the game is not really fast enough for TV, so I don't see a broad acceptance of one set of rules anywhere in the near future.

Ewa's Billiard Bits

An interesting thing about 8-Ball is that when it was introduced in Great Britain, the rules were modified to (sort of) match British snooker rules. Then the balls were changed from the various colored solids and stripes to half-red and half-yellow (leaving the 8 ball black). The British changed the rules to make it a defensive game, and because it's played on a coin-operated table, they now get the maximum for their money.

The WPBA (Women's Professional Billiard Association), in which I'm a touring pro, has a standard set of rules that we use from tour stop to tour stop, but we make an exception at special events. Pro–celebrity charity events and special-event TV programs come to mind. The various men's tours have somewhat-stable rules, but then, there are several men's tours, so there's no single set of rules.

In Appendix D of this book, you'll find the *Billiard Congress of America General Rules of Pocket Billiards*. The BCA also publishes the rules for specific games (such as 8-Ball and 9-Ball) in its rulebook. The rules are a good fundamental set, and they're used as the default standard if no other rules are being imposed by the powers that be at a particular tournament (local or professional). The BCA rulebook is usually behind the counter at all billiard rooms, and it's the reference that people use when a question arises during play.

In this chapter, I give you an idea of the rules that apply to all games. Even if you're playing a specific game (such as 8-Ball) in a specific place (such as a league), the stuff in this chapter gives you a basic understanding of the rules of the sport. You can then pick up the special differences imposed by the site or the event that you're involved in. This chapter gives you a general understanding of the game. Near the end of the book in Part 6, I tell you about each individual game (Straight Pool, 9-Ball, and so on), the special rules, the object, and winning strategies.

Legal Shots

Let's start with a positive. I'll get to fouls in a minute, but you can't really understand what you did wrong unless you understand what you should have done. Right now, you need to know that you can touch the cue ball only with the cue tip; that you can touch it only once per shot; and that when you touch (hit) it, the cue ball must touch the correct object ball, and then one of the numbered balls must touch a cushion or go in a pocket, or the cue ball must touch a cushion.

That last part is something that is hard to grasp at the beginning. The cue ball hits the object ball. You hope that it goes into a pocket, and if it does, that's a legal hit. If it doesn't, some ball (any of the balls on the table, including the cue ball) must touch a cushion.

Here's a kind of trick example to show you what I mean: You hit the cue ball (the white ball) into the 1 ball, the 1 ball hits the 2 ball, and the 2 ball hits the 7 ball. No balls go into any pocket. The 7 ball rolls up against the cushion, but the cue ball and the object ball (the 1 ball, in this case) never touch a cushion. Is this a legal hit? Yep. After contact occurs between the cue ball and the object ball, *any* ball can touch a cushion and make the shot legal.

In some games, you have to hit the lowest-numbered ball on the table first. You can make the other balls before the lowest-numbered ball by hitting the lowest-numbered ball into a higher ball and having the higher ball go into a pocket, but you must make contact with the lowest-numbered ball first. This is true for 9-Ball, Rotation, and a few lesser-known games in the rotation category. In 8-Ball, you must hit one of your balls first: one of the solid balls (lows, 1 to 7) if you have solids or one of the striped balls (highs, 9 to 15) if you have stripes. Sometimes, you're allowed to hit the 8 ball first (the 8 ball is considered to be *neutral* if this is the case), and sometimes, you're not. (See, I told you about those flexible 8-Ball rules.) As long as you do that and fulfill the rest of the preceding rules, the hit is legal.

At times, the stipulation *call shot* is put on a game. The object is to eliminate luck and to stop players from just slamming into the balls, hoping that something goes in—as though every shot were a break shot. Call shots come in two forms:

> ➤ You must call the ball that you intend to pocket.

> ➤ You must call the ball that you intend to pocket and also the pocket that you are going to put it in.

You can miss, and it's not a foul. You can accidentally hit the ball into another pocket, and it's not a foul. In both cases, you lose your turn, but there's no penalty; you simply failed to do what you tried to do. Missing in a call-shot game is a legal shot (once again, as long as you meet the specs described earlier).

Pocket Dictionary

A *call shot* is a condition sometimes imposed for games, requiring you to either name the ball that you intend to pocket or name the ball and also the pocket that it will go into.

Fouls

Fouls can be classified as being fouls of the general rules, fouls of the specific game's requirements, and fouls of the current rule variations that you're playing under. Fouls are not really common, considering all the little things you can do that fall under that name. In almost every shot, you'll meet the requirements of a legal shot and not commit a foul. Besides, a foul committed by relatively inexperienced players has almost no detrimental effect.

Pocket Dictionary

Ball in hand means that after your opponent commits a foul, the cue ball is placed in your hand, and you can place it anywhere on the table that you desire.

Scratch!

In Straight Pool, your first foul costs you 1 point, and a second consecutive foul costs you 1 more. A third consecutive foul, however, costs you 16 points!

The penalties for fouls are very few and very simple. They're such that when experienced players are shooting, a foul is usually the difference between winning and losing that game. But for someone who's just beginning the game, the biggest harm is that you lose your turn.

The penalty for most fouls is *ball in hand*. That means that the incoming player can take the cue ball and put it anywhere on the table, playing the first shot from that position. For experienced players, that penalty is enough to start a string of pocketed balls, so that they clear the table and win the game. For inexperienced players, the penalty means that your opponent can usually make one ball and then will be back to facing a difficult shot.

Another penalty for a foul is *ball in hand behind the headstring*. The headstring, as I said earlier, is a line across the head of the table from the second diamond down on one side to the second diamond down on the other side. In billiard slang, the headstring is sometimes called *the kitchen* (see diagram in Chapter 5).

Under today's rules, the ball-in-hand-behind-the-headstring rule usually applies only in 8-Ball. In snooker, ball in hand means that you can place the cue ball anywhere inside a half-circle that is drawn at the head of a snooker table (see diagram in Chapter 28). In Straight Pool, a foul causes a deduction of 1 point from your score and a loss of turn. In the game called One-Pocket, you don't get ball in hand; instead, one of the balls that you previously pocketed is returned to play. Loss of turn is common to all fouls, regardless of what other penalty also applies. A foul causes a loss of turn under every circumstance, no matter what additional penalty exists.

It's a Table Game

Knocking a ball off the table is a foul in any billiard game. Penalties vary. Some billiard clubs, firmly establishing that the game is one of order and niceties, post signs saying that house rules are that a ball off the table is an automatic loss of game. Officially, though, if you hit a ball off the table (any ball, including the cue ball), you lose your turn, and the incoming player gets to place the cue ball anywhere on the table for the first shot (ball in hand).

When you're playing with friends, it's a good idea to use that penalty, and when you're playing at home, it's a good idea to mimic the billiard rooms and use the loss-of-game option. You really don't want to encourage players to shoot so carelessly that balls end up flying around your billiard room.

Behind the 8 Ball

The popular phrase "behind the 8 ball" means that you're in a hard-luck situation, unable to do anything positive to achieve your goals. The term comes from pool, of course, and more specifically from the game of 8-Ball. In that game, you have to hit one of your group of balls, either the stripes or solids. Under most rules, you cannot hit the 8 ball first; if you do, you foul. If you're behind the 8 ball, then, you've got a problem. If you decide beforehand that the 8 ball is neutral, however, or if the rules of the league or tournament state as much, you can hit the black ball first, in which case being behind the 8 ball is not a bad thing at all.

The following fits into a general class of fouls that doesn't have a particular name. In games in which you have to hit a particular ball first, your opponent can get an advantage by placing the cue ball in such a position that you can't do what you have to do. When he does this, he is shooting a *safety*. If you fail to hit the ball, you're required to hit, and then your opponent gets ball in hand and can start *running* (clearing) the table. If you commit that foul, it's said to be simply not a legal hit.

I go into the nuances of safety play later in Chapter 22. Until then, all that you need to know is that in some games (8-Ball, 9-Ball, Rotation, and a couple more-obscure games), you are required to hit a specific ball, or one ball in a specific group, before the cue ball touches any other ball, and that failing to do so is a foul. In Straight Pool, the numbers on the balls have no meaning, because every ball is simply worth 1 point. Consequently, you can't commit this type of foul in Straight Pool.

Pocket Dictionary

A *safety* is playing a shot not to make a ball in a pocket, but to place the balls—especially the cue ball—in such a position that the opposing player cannot make a ball or (better) even hit the ball that he needs to hit.

One Foot on the Floor!

I get asked about this rule all the time. Is it really an official rule that you have to have one foot on the floor while you're shooting? It sounds like a funny rule (for all I know, it was created by billiard-room proprietors to keep their equipment from being damaged), but it is enforced in all tournaments, league competition, and even among friends playing a game. There is an official rule in the *Billiard Congress of America Official Rules and Records Book* (see section 3.1.2 in Appendix D) that explains their position. Even when players are not following the BCA rules, however, this rule is assumed to be in effect. It's a common sense rule, and the only parts that are ever debated is whether or not the foot on the floor has to be flat on the floor, and whether or not contact with the floor existed at the precise moment the cue tip made contact with the cue ball.

The Intentional Foul

At times, in particular games, it is to your advantage to take an intentional foul. There's nothing underhanded or wrong about this, although among beginners it might be called *dirty pool*. It's really a legitimate part of playing strategy. Just so you'll understand what I'm talking about, I'll give you two examples.

Two rules are important for understanding the following 9-Ball example:

➤ You must hit the lowest-numbered ball on the table first.

➤ Whoever makes the 9 ball wins, whether or not any of the other balls have been made.

Now imagine a situation in which Player A breaks the balls but nothing goes in. You are Player B, and when you come to the table for your turn, you see that it is almost impossible to hit the 1 ball. You also see that the 9 ball is sitting right in front of the pocket and that the 1 ball is just a few inches away. If you fail to hit the 1 ball (as you undoubtedly will because of the position of the cue ball), your opponent will have ball in hand. He or she will place the cue ball in line with the 1 and 9 balls and hit the 1 into the 9, and the 9 will go in the pocket. Your opponent will have won the game. The intentional foul that you take is to hit the 9 ball into the pocket (it is brought out and put on the spot at the foot of the table, an act called *spotting the ball*) or to simply hit it away from the pocket opening. Your opponent still gets ball in hand but no longer has an easy game-winning shot.

Cue Tips

Imagine that your cue ball is in such a position that you can't hit the ball you are required to hit. Giving your opponent ball in hand would let him win the game, so consider using your cue ball to nudge two balls together so that neither can be made. This strategy is a foul, but it prevents your opponent from winning and is a good defensive move.

You need to understand two rules to understand the following Straight Pool example:

➤ You can hit any ball at any time.

➤ You don't get ball in hand when your opponent fouls (unless he or she *scratches*, which means hitting the cue ball into the pocket). Instead of ball in hand, you simply play the cue ball from where it ends up. If your opponent leaves you in an almost-impossible position, you may want to take an intentional foul.

Now suppose that all the balls are at one end of the table, but none is near a pocket, and your opponent has left the cue ball frozen tightly against the cushion on the other end of the table. You're in trouble. When a ball is frozen against a cushion and you have to shoot away from the cushion (as opposed to hitting it from the side and aiming it along the cushion), you can hit only the top 40 percent of the ball. When you have to do that, you can easily hit the ball poorly and end up leaving it where your opponent can pocket a ball, then another, then another, and so on. Good Straight Pool players can run 50, 60, or even 100 balls or more without missing—enough, in other words, to win a game to 100 points in one turn.

You don't want to give your opponent that opportunity, so nudge the ball out from the cushion a little bit and take an intentional foul. The idea is to make the shot easier but still very difficult, so that your opponent is tempted to shoot it. You lose 1 point but maybe save the game.

Spotting a Rack of Balls

Balls are placed in a triangular or diamond-shape configuration at the beginning of each game. The result is a *rack*—a word that is also used to describe the device that shapes the group of balls and that is synonymous with a single game. All the balls should touch all adjoining balls, and the rack should be correctly aligned. If you have a full rack of 15 balls, for example, the back row of five balls should be parallel with the foot cushion. If you have a 9-Ball rack (nine balls in a diamond shape), the line down the center of the rack should be parallel with the side cushions.

Just as a table has a headstring, it also has a footstring, but unlike the headstring, it is rarely drawn on the cloth. If it were, it would pass across the table from one side to the other, beginning at the second diamond from the end (on the long rail, called the *side rail*) on one side to the second diamond on the other side. The spot is placed in the center. Just as the footstring is rarely drawn, the spot that might go in the center of the headstring is rarely placed there (it is called the *head spot* if it is). In other words, you typically find a line but no spot at the head of the table and a spot with no line at the foot of the table. Sometimes, you find the whole ball of wax, but because the head spot and footstring aren't used for anything, they're usually left off (see diagram in Chapter 5).

So you place the first (front or apex ball) ball in the rack on the foot spot, make sure that it's aligned correctly, and make sure that all the balls are touching. But which ball is the first ball—and does ball order matter? Well, in some games, it does, and in some games, it doesn't. In the rotation games, the 1 ball (solid yellow) is always in front. In games such as Straight Pool and One-Pocket, in which each ball is worth 1 point regardless of the number printed on it, any ball can go in front. In 8-Ball, it's traditional to have the 1 ball in front, but it doesn't have to be there.

8-Ball and 9-Ball also have one ball that is special (the 8 ball or the 9 ball), and that ball always goes in the middle of the rack. The rest of the balls can go anywhere, by the rules.

How you place the balls in the rack does make a difference, however, and a smart player doesn't just dump them into the rack and roll them in place. I tell you about those little tricks in the chapters on the specific games, but as far as the rules of racking are concerned, you now have the requirements for ball placement.

Questions about miss-hit cue balls on the break shot pop up when you're first learning the game. The break shot is so different from the others that you can easily mess up. Following are some common questions:

➤ If you hit the edge of the cue ball, and it starts rolling slowly toward the rack in what you know is going to be a pitiful break shot, can you grab it, place it back where it was, and try again?

➤ If you miss-hit the cue ball, and it misses the rack completely, can you try again?

➤ If you try going through your warmup strokes very fast to get some power, and you accidentally punch the cue ball forward a foot or two, or just move it a little, can you put it back and regroup?

Scratch!

An applied spot is glued to the cloth, making it higher than the rest of the playing surface. A ball that is rolled very slowly over the spot can change directions when it hits that material.

Pocket Dictionary

Lagging is when two players each hit a ball (without using a cue ball) down the table and return it to the head cushion to determine who breaks the balls for the first game.

The answer to all these questions is yes. The game doesn't officially start until an object ball has been struck by the cue ball. In 9-Ball, the game doesn't start until the 1 ball has been struck, so you can even hit the cue ball into the side of the rack, and it doesn't count. In that case, you re-rack the balls and start again.

The spot has another use, aside from telling you where the rack belongs. In some games, an illegally pocketed ball must be brought back up from the pocket (or ball-return tray, if your table has that feature) and placed on the spot. The same spot you used for racking. If the spot is occupied or partially occupied by another ball, the illegally pocketed ball goes against that ball, along a line from the spot to the back cushion. That procedure is called *spotting a ball*.

Who's on First?

In the pro arena, the tour usually sets rules about who breaks the balls in the first game. The exception is for special events, such as created-for-TV tournaments. For amateur events, the promoter or league decides. For nontournament events, the players involved decide. Socially, whether you're at a billiard club playing with a stranger or playing at home, you have no set rule to go by.

The opening break can be determined by making a casual "Go ahead and break" statement or by flipping a coin. The third method is a skill-based method—and the preferable one, if you take the game at all seriously. This method is called *lagging*. Two players place balls (any balls) on the headstring, one on each side of the table; then they shoot the balls the length of the table to the far rail (the foot rail) and back. The player whose ball ends up coming back and stopping closest to the head rail wins the right to break (or not break; in Straight Pool, it's a disadvantage to break).

The ball, by the way, can come all the way back and hit the head rail and bounce off, or it may not be hit hard enough to come completely back to the head rail. Either way counts, and the final resting positions are all that matter.

Also, there's no rule that requires the players to shoot the balls at the same time, but fairness and good sportsmanship dictate that one player should not wait until he sees how well the other player hit the ball before shooting his own ball. Players should shoot at approximately the same time.

Lagging for the break is also a good way to see whether the table is playing fast or slow. That concept is probably a bit much to throw at you at this moment, but humidity and other factors can alter how hard you have to hit a ball to make it go a fixed distance. A table on which you have to hit a ball only lightly to make it go to Point A is said to play fast. A table on which you have to hit the ball harder to get to that same point is said to be playing slow. The lag can give you that information, which is helpful for your first few shots, after which you will have found out how the table's playing anyway.

After you've played one game, who breaks the next rack of balls? With two players, you have only two options: The winner breaks, or the loser breaks. You could choose to alternate breaks. For the second game, it would mean that the loser breaks that rack. Establish the format that you're going to use before you start playing. If you choose winner breaks, you run the risk of giving an advantage to the better player of the two. (Having the opportunity to break is good, because the key ball may go in—the 9 ball in 9-Ball or the 8 ball in 8-Ball—and the second player may never get to break.) If you choose loser breaks, you're leveling the playing field slightly by giving an advantage to the loser. The scores will tend to be closer as a result. Alternate break gives only slight assistance to the lesser player.

Rules, Rules, and More Rules

There are more general rules, of course, and more still for specific games, but they're the kind of things that don't come up often. When they do, you can refer to the *BCA General Rules of Pocket Billiards* in Appendix D. Some of the BCA's explanations are written in a way that assumes billiard knowledge on the part of the reader, however, so I'm going to talk about those rules in a clearer way—one that doesn't assume that you have been playing the game for a while.

I said that you can hit the cue ball only once per shot, and that's true. But suppose that you accidentally hit it twice. If the object ball and cue ball are very close to touching, it's likely that you'll hit the cue ball twice, perhaps without even knowing it. Hearing the rapid double-click takes a trained billiard ear. This double hit is a foul. It can also happen if you have a jerky, unsure stroke. You hit the ball forward in a tentative way and immediately try to recover by moving the cue forward faster and hitting the cue

Ewa's Billiard Bits

It's ironic that the push shot is now illegal, because in the early days of the game, it was the only shot that *was* legal. Billiards was played by pushing a ball on the table, sort of the way that shuffleboard players push the puck. Cues as we know them weren't used. Instead, players used sticks with heads, similar to golf clubs.

Cue Tips

You can find rules for wheelchair billiards in the BCA rules book, along with rules for international snooker and three-cushion billiards (Carom). The BCA's address is in the back of the book under Appendix B. I provide an easy guide to Snooker and Carom, along with all the common pool games, in the final chapters of this book. For now, you're pretty well set with all the basic rules of pool.

ball twice. That's a foul. (Actually, that probably won't happen to you, because you'll read Chapter 12 and know how to develop a clean, smooth stroke in no time.)

Another rule involves your stroke. You must hit the ball, not push it. The difference is sometimes a gray area, but most of the time, it's pretty clear what happened. Pushing is a foul; hitting is not. This type of foul happens frequently to beginning players, because they're unsure about what they're doing. Without any understanding of how to stand, how to grip the cue, how to stroke, and how to develop focus and confidence (all things that you learn in the chapters immediately following this one), beginners are apt to push the cue ball sometimes instead of striking it.

Something that comes up from time to time is a *hanging ball*, meaning a ball that's precariously balanced on the edge of a pocket opening. Hanging balls have been known to pause there for many seconds and then drop in. Does the shot count or not? Rules vary, and the BCA rules set a 5-second limit, but that limit has turned out to be impractical. Who's ready with a watch that has a second hand? A good guideline is to use a point of action that is not controlled by either player.

Suppose that Player A shoots a ball that hangs on the edge of the pocket. If he made a second ball on that same shot, he would continue shooting, so he would continue to be in control of the table when, and if, the hanging ball dropped. But if the hanging ball is the only ball that he hit to a pocket, he loses control of the table when the cue ball stops moving. If the other player is in control of the table and the hanging ball drops, it counts as his, not Player A's. That solution seems to be practical, especially for friendly competition.

Every now and then, something happens that makes you wonder. A ball will seemingly move on its own. It's really weird when you're aiming at the object ball and you're in the middle of your stroke. The ball moves only a fraction of an inch, but when it does so without anybody's bumping the table or otherwise causing it to happen, the least you've got to wonder is whether the ball should be put back in place before you shoot. The answer is no. The rules say that you should shoot the ball as it is (or, if it's not a ball that you're aiming at, just leave it where it is).

The reasons why this otherworldly movement occurs are fairly simple. One reason is that the ball came to rest on an area that had a minute hill of chalk dust beneath the cloth, and the weight of the ball compressed the chalk slowly until it caused the ball to roll a millimeter or two to the side (downhill). A second reason is that uneven cloth wear and the weight of the ball compressed the fabric. A third reason is that the ball was made slightly out of balance—a defect that shows up only when it stops on a certain axis. But no matter what the reason, the rules say to leave the ball where it ends up.

The Least You Need to Know

➤ In all games, you must hit the object ball with the cue ball, and then some ball must touch a cushion.

➤ In some games, you must hit a specific ball, or a ball in a specific group of balls, to score a legal hit.

➤ Ball in hand, which is the penalty for many fouls, is a significant advantage to the player who receives it.

➤ At times, you want to foul intentionally.

➤ Each specific game has rules for racking the balls.

➤ Before play starts, decide whether you will let the winner or the loser break the next rack, or whether you're going to alternate breaks.

Chapter 10

Taking a Firm Stand

In This Chapter

➤ Approaching the table

➤ Finding a comfortable shooting stance

➤ Learning to align your body

➤ The alternatives to stretching for a shot

➤ Special stances for special shots

Most sports require proper body positioning, even if it's on the run, such as a quarterback throwing a football. For the static sports (golf, billiards, archery, and so on), there is a proper stance, worked out over the years. Even motion sports, such as baseball, basketball, and boxing, have moments (batting, free throws, and so on) when not simply form but also stance come into play. The billiard stance is a static stance and is fairly simple, but it's also easy to undervalue, and for that reason, I've made it a separate chapter.

To help students picture the properties of a good stance in pool, I sometimes use the story of a photo that I took—or almost took, that is. My daughter, Nikki, was playing with her puppy, and it was a classic Kodak moment. To get the correct angle, I had to put the camera tripod at the base of the stairs, shortening one leg to put it on the third step up. Something about this arrangement caught my eye, and I realized that it was a great illustration of the basic billiard stance: two legs, spread equal distance, and an arm extended to the tabletop. While I hesitated, the puppy ran off, and the picture was lost forever, but I did get an illustration that I could use when teaching the stance. After people hear it, it seems to stick in their minds.

The Approach, Coach

Before you get into your shooting stance, you should think about how to approach the table. This, by the way, is sometimes called *approaching the shot,* but that phrase also means how you choose to deal with a shot, so I'll stick with *approach the table.* I just want you to know that sometimes, it's called something else, so if you hear that something else, you won't be confused.

Cue Tips

Use your approach to the table and the way that you get into your stance to establish a playing rhythm. It's surprising how much this technique can help your game.

Many players use the few seconds that it takes to walk to the table to begin their turn, or to make their next shot, for getting focused on the positions of the balls. It can be a mental psyching-up time, but for most players, it's more a period of easing into the situation. (I tell you about that in Chapter 4, where I cover the mental game.) Along with the mental part of the game is a physical part that is connected to the stance. If you watch players who have played for some time, you'll see them stare at the table when they approach and almost subconsciously place both hands on the cue, forming a bridge and back grip, and then raise the cue in preparation for putting it down on the table. That's a good approach. It's what drill instructors in the military call a *port-arms position.*

This is the port-arms position, *used by some players from the moment they get out of their seat to walk to the table. It's a good position to be in while you study the way that the balls are positioned, just before you put your hand down on the approach line.*

As you're approaching the table, focus on the cue ball and the object ball (the ball that you want the cue ball to hit), and draw a line through them, extending toward you. Just like an aircraft finding a landing approach signal, you should find that line and approach the shot directly. You want to be looking down that line; it will be an important element of your stance.

This is also a great time to reach for the chalk and chalk up, If you make chalking up part of your preshot routine, you'll do it automatically and never miscue because your tip was too slick.

I cover the grip and bridge in Chapter 11. For right now, when I talk about your bridge (the way that you hold the cue with your front hand) and grip (the way that you hold the cue with your back hand), just grab the cue in any way that's comfortable to you. Neither the grip nor the bridge really affects your stance. Simply hold the cue with one hand about half a foot from the tip and with the other hand 8 or 10 inches from the butt. I'll show you the correct methods after you nail down the stance.

Pocket Dictionary

An *object ball* is the first ball that the cue ball hits. Sometimes, the word is used loosely to refer to any ball other than the cue ball.

When you're close enough (and you should already be gripping the cue with both hands at this point), place your front hand on the table about 6 to 8 inches away from the cue ball. (Sometimes, another ball will be in that position, as I explain in Chapter 11, but this example covers the most common situation.) If you're right-handed, the front hand is your left hand. At the same time, or just before you place your left hand on the table, move your left foot forward and to the left at about a 45-degree angle to your cue.

Describing the stance makes it sound a little more complicated than it really is. Timing is totally unimportant, and you'll move naturally. The point is that you should end up like the camera tripod I described earlier in this chapter. Your front arm should be straight, and less than one-third of your body weight should be supported by that arm and hand. Your back foot will end up near the butt end of the cue or past it, depending on your height, and your front foot will be slightly off to the side. If you're accidentally bumped while you're down for a shot, you shouldn't find yourself knocked to the floor.

The trend over the past 20 years has been for players to turn more toward the cue, so the front foot may be on the line or only 10 or 20 degrees away from it, rather than 45 degrees. That's the stance I prefer, but I think that the variations you see are probably a matter of body configuration and agility. If you avoid standing with both feet at a 90-degree angle to the cue, and you feel balanced and comfortable, go with what works for you. What's important is not strict form, but the result: the balance, comfort and solidness.

You'll find that once you get into the proper stance, you'll have an even distribution of weight

Scratch!

Don't be mislead by standard player photos. They usually show a player as though she's about to make a shot, using a very upright stance. But that pose is used only so the player is facing the camera. During an actual shot, she'll be bent low.

on each foot (about 40 percent on each, with roughly 20 percent on the hand on the table). One goal is to be balanced, relieving the stress and distraction of having to try to remain steady while you shoot. A second goal is to be solid. During your strokes, nothing but your eyes and rear arm move; the rest of the body is still. If you're balanced and your stance is solid, you won't have to be concerned about wiggling. The third goal is to have a stance that permits you to stroke without your rear hand running into your body during the follow-through. Putting everything in place during the approach takes care of all those elements.

How a beginner might stand if she'd never read this book. Almost everything is wrong, and making a successful shot from this position would take as much luck as anything else.

Ah, this is more like it: stress-free, balanced, solid, aligned, and allowing for full arm movement through the entire stroke.

Part of your approach also includes looking at the shot and deciding what you're going to do, but I'm getting a little ahead of myself, because those kinds of decisions must be based on knowledge that you won't have for a few chapters. At this point, just know that you will be making that decision before you bend over the table and that the time to do it is during your approach.

For some players, or for all players on particular shots, it's a great advantage to walk around the table and view the balls from different angles before deciding what shot you're going to make. In fact, it's not a bad idea to do that on the majority of your shots, especially when you're first learning to play. It gives you a nice feel for the angles involved in playing pool and helps you decide exactly where you want the cue ball to hit the object ball.

Technically, this isn't part of the approach, but deciding how you're going to shoot the cue ball is something that you must do before you can have an effective approach. Many players never get good instruction and end up down on the table, going through their warm-up strokes, without having a clear and specific idea of exactly what they're going to do. I always like to stop new students at this point and ask them their plans. It brings home the idea of not making a shot without first making a decision about precisely what that shot will be. Then, when you hit that approach line, you can do so with confidence and purpose.

Cue Tips

A shot clock, usually set for 45 seconds, is being used more and more often in tournaments, both professional and amateur. The timing starts when the cue ball stops, and you must strike the cue ball for your next shot before the time expires. If you plan to play in city or room tournaments, or in leagues, find out in advance whether a shot clock is being used. If so, get into the habit of staying within the time limit.

Following are the items that will be on the line:

1. The ball that the cue ball is going to hit (called the *object ball*)
2. The cue ball
3. The cue tip
4. The entire cue
5. Your back hand
6. Your back arm and shoulder
7. The toes of your rear foot
8. Your right eye, left eye, or nose

To test your alignment, swing the cue a few times. It should go smoothly and naturally along the line leading to the cue ball and the object ball. If you have to use any muscle, no matter how slightly, to keep the cue from going off to one side, no matter how little, you're not on line. If, however, the cue follows the line with no effort, you're perfect.

127

Aligning Your Body

Approaching on the line that runs from the object ball through the cue ball to you assists you in getting all the parts of your body in the proper place before you actually bend over the table. From a few feet away, you're just generally on line, but as you get closer to the table, begin noticing certain items. Your head, right shoulder (if you're right-handed), back hand, and cue should begin to get on the line at this point. By the time you're actually bending over, everything should be where it is supposed to be.

"Supposed to be," however, doesn't mean that it's always that way. Sometimes, you'll get down for a shot and find yourself just a little off balance or feeling a little off in some other way. Never hesitate to get back up, step away, and then reapproach. If you're not on line, and you go ahead and shoot anyway, you're very likely to miss the shot. Professionals do this often in tournaments, although usually for a different reason: They're not completely comfortable with the shot that they chose before they bent down. Rather than shoot the wrong shot or shoot without confidence, they stand up and rethink the possibilities. Also, the shot sometimes looks different from table level than it did when you were standing up and looking at it. If that's the case, stand up and realign.

My sighting preference is to have the cue centered directly under my chin, but some people play better by centering either their right or left eye over the cue.

One of the body parts that you get on line is your head, and I need to be a little more specific about that. The purpose of getting your head on the line is to be able to sight down the cue at the cue ball. Most people have a dominant eye, however, as they have a dominant hand, and many instructors tell you to line that eye over the cue.

For years, instructors told students to find their dominant eye and then place that eye over the cue. Well, it turned out that not everyone has a dominant eye, and that even people who do instinctively place their head over their cue in the proper position, dominant eye or not. You'll do that, too, so don't worry about billiard-room experts who try to persuade you to change the position of your head to get the proper eye over the cue. The only thing that you need to worry about in this area is consistency. After you've played for a few months, take note of where you naturally place your head; then always place the same eye (or your nose) over the cue. I play with my head perfectly centered on the cue line.

The shoulder, elbow, and hand of your rear arm should also be on the line. A common pair of faults in players who have never had any instruction is to either pull the cue in toward their body or hold it too far away from their body in a slight sidearm fashion. A few famous world champions, such as Willie Hoppe (1887–1959), had a sidearm stroke, but that's only because they learned how to play as children, and the only way they could swing the cue was sidearm. So it can be done; it just means that you have to have a whole lot of natural talent to overcome a faulty form. Don't put that burden on yourself. Use a classic approach, lining everything up properly, and you'll be making more balls right from the start.

Cue Tips

You can tell which eye is dominant by holding one finger up in front of you and then closing each eye in turn. The finger moves less with one eye open than with the other eye open, and the eye that shows less finger movement is your dominant eye.

Ewa's Billiard Bits

Although the number of people who have a dominant right eye is about the same as the number who have a dominant left eye, observation has revealed that a far larger number of top-flight players sight with their inside eye (left eye, for right-handed players) than with their outside eye. There are a lot of theories, but no one really knows why this is so.

Your front arm should be straight (but obviously not on the line, because it comes from your opposite shoulder). This isn't a hard-and-fast rule, however. For some shots, you have to scrunch up a little and bend your arm. That's not a problem as long as you maintain your balance and stability, but try to keep your front arm straight when space permits. You may see world-class tournament players bend their elbows a little even when they have plenty of shooting room, but if you watch carefully, you'll also see that the bend is consistent, shot after shot.

129

Getting Down

The distance between your feet depends on your height. At first, you'll probably stand like a boxer, golfer, or baseball player at the plate, and that's not an entirely bad position, especially if you're shorter than 5'8". The difference between those other sports and billiards is that you have to bend over the table, and for most people, a widening of the stance would make that a lot easier.

With a little experimentation, you'll find the right distance for you. Just avoid modifying the height of your hips by bending both knees in a semi-squat, which is tiring and unstable. But if you've ever seen soldiers on a parade field toppling over like trees at a Canadian woodcutter's championship you'll know that you shouldn't lock your knees for long periods, either. A slight bend of the knees, even locking your back knee, is ideal. If you need to get lower, spread your legs more rather than bend your knees more.

Cue Tips

Overweight players find it difficult to breathe easily when they're bent over in the classic stance. If that's a problem for you, try spreading your legs farther apart, and if that's not enough help, try a more upright position. It worked for Minnesota Fats and a lot of other players.

Another part of your form is keeping your back relatively straight. I qualify "straight" because I want you to avoid having a stiff, straight back, which leads to a distracting discomfort. By the same token, you play more comfortably, can play longer, and maintain a proper relationship to other body parts (front hand to back hand, for example) if your back is relatively straight. It's hard for most people to think of the body's adopting a fairly strict form, staying frozen while nothing but the back arm is moving, and calling that comfortable. But the reality is that the classic form I describe in this chapter really is the most relaxing and most effective position to use while playing billiards.

When you're in position, bending over the table, how low should you bend? I like to have my chin touch the cue stick as it slides back and forth. During the first half of the 20th century, most players stood almost upright. Today, they get as low as they can (depending, again, on their body's abilities). Getting low makes sense to me, because I want to see what the cue sees—or as close as possible to what the cue sees, anyway. I even have a small mark on my chin from repeated contact with the cue. So my advice to you is to go as low as you can comfortably go.

Sighting down a cue is often compared with sighting down the barrel of a rifle. The difference is that when you're target-shooting, you stand in a spot and extend the rifle comfortably in front of you, so the position of your body dictates the placement of the rifle. It's the other way around for a billiards stance. You place the cue where it has to be, extend your arm, and lower your head, and if you feel bunched up or hunched, then you move your feet back, adjusting your stance to the position of the cue.

Special Stances for Special Shots

There are exceptions to every rule, and you'll run into situations on the billiard table in which you'll have to break a lot of the rules I just told you about. You'll stand closer to upright rather than getting low to the cue. You'll place your front hand 1 inch from the cue ball, rather than 6 to 8 inches away. There's even one shot for which you'll purposely stand off balance. But all the exceptions are part of the fun of the game, and learning how to tackle them makes those difficult shots much easier.

Standing Up to the Break

In the games in which you have to smash the balls wide open at the beginning (9-Ball and 8-Ball especially), you'll be hitting the cue ball very hard. You want as much power as possible, so that the balls will roll longer and therefore have a better chance of rolling into a pocket. You can achieve this effect by using a heavier cue stick or increasing the speed of the stroke. The first choice is the old choice. Today, as I mention in the chapter on cues (Chapter 6), the choice is speed.

Increased speed means an increased chance that things will get out of control. To counter that risk, players use a slightly tighter back and front hand grip. They also stand differently. Because you'll be throwing your body into the break (I discuss different breaks for different games in Chapter 18), you'll have to stand up straighter—not erect, but straighter than you would for a normal shot. That's the only way you can get your body behind the forward thrust of the cue. Because some bodies are short, some tall, some skinny, and some round (not to mention short-waisted, long-waisted, muscular, and so on), there's no way to say exactly how much you should straighten up. But you now know that you have to find a point somewhere between your low shot-making position and your normal standing position.

You should also be off balance at the start of your stroke (swing). The best advice on this subject was given by world champion Luther "Wimpy" Lassiter (1919–1988), who advised players to get into their normal playing position and then scoot up a little.

Scratch!

The cue ball flies off the table more often on the break shot than at any other time. Don't hit the ball too hard or too fast until you are sure that you have your stroke under control.

Ewa's Billiard Bits

Luther "Wimpy" Lassiter (so nick-named because he, like the old comic-strip character of the same name, always ate hamburgers) was a soft-spoken North Carolina gentle-man of the old school. His courtly manners were deceiving, however. At the table, he displayed a devas-tating stroke and a killer instinct that crushed opponents. He dominated much of the sport during the 1960s.

Just move your feet forward an inch or so. That's all it takes. You'll be just a tad off balance, not enough to make you really unstable. But when you thrust that cue forward at maximum speed, you'll find that you can get your body behind the shot much more effectively. As your arm swings forward, your balance changes and the scooting that you did before the shot helps you get more speed and power into the shot.

The Mechanical-Bridge Stance

Using the mechanical bridge alters your stance, partly because you have to hold what amounts to an additional cue and partly because the cue ball is so far away from you.

When you can't comfortably reach the cue ball, use a mechanical bridge. Notice how I place my hands, and also notice that I keep the forearm of my shooting arm parallel to the table.

A mechanical bridge is used when you can't reach a shot. Check out how I use the mechanical bridge, and you'll see that it would be awkward at best for me to shoot the 5 ball by stretching. But when I have to use the mechanical bridge (just called *the bridge* most of the time), I have to change my grip and stance. I discuss the grip in Chapter 11.

Because the bridge head on the mechanical bridge is higher than the bridge that you'd make with your hand, you have to elevate the butt of the cue to hit the center of the cue ball. When the butt is elevated, you can't swing the cue underhanded, as you normally would. You have to use an odd-looking stroke that starts in the center of your chest and moves toward the cue ball. To make the stroke smooth and accurate, the forearm should be parallel to the table. All these elements require that you stand up straighter, which means that your feet are now closer together. At the same time, you need to keep the bridge still, which you do by pressing down firmly on the end of the bridge handle. The result is a stance that breaks almost all the rules of the classic shooting stance described earlier in this chapter.

Problems with using the mechanical bridge don't usually arise from the stance, which comes naturally, but from the oddness of the stroking action. If you have trouble making balls or even hitting the cue ball when you use this piece of equipment, try slowing your stroke and hitting the cue ball gently. I've seen people practice by playing with the bridge on every shot for 15 minutes a day. After a week, they rarely have another problem.

Cue Tips

When using the mechanical bridge, shorten the forward and backward movement of your cue during your stroke. Shortening the stroke makes the shot easier.

Getting a Leg Up

It is legal to play with one leg on the table as long as one foot is touching the floor. That foot can even be on tiptoe, and it can leave the floor after contact has been made and broken between the cue tip and the cue ball. In other words, during the follow-through, you don't have to be touching the floor at all.

The stance for this type of situation is whatever works for you. I've seen some double-jointed, very thin people work their legs into amazing positions just so they could reach the cue ball and avoid having to use the mechanical bridge. Keep in mind that you always want to be balanced and stable—and try hard to maintain alignment of all the critical body parts that I talk about earlier in the chapter. Without alignment, you'll probably miss the shot and maybe even miss the cue ball! But aside from the real fundamentals (and the rule of touching the floor with one foot at contact), if you feel comfortable putting a leg on the table and don't touch any balls with that leg, the position that you get into is totally up to you (and your body's abilities to bend and twist).

Scratch!

When you put your leg on the table, there's a good chance that you'll fall forward at the end of your shot. During the follow-through, your weight shifts, and if you're already precariously perched, this stance could be messy and dangerous.

The Jumping Stance

The jump shot is a specialty shot that I tell you about in Chapter 22, but I want to briefly talk about it in this chapter, because it requires a stance that breaks the rules in a way that is different from both the break-shot stance and the mechanical-bridge stance. It's a very difficult shot to control or even to make and absolutely not for the beginner, although you see it in professional matches on TV. Like the massè shot (which I tell you about in Chapters 11 and 21), you strike the cue ball from above, but as difficult as the jump shot is, it is still easier than the massè.

When shooting a jump shot, you have to elevate the butt of your cue anywhere from 30 degrees to 80 degrees. Alignment is the same as in the standard stance, but your rear arm is as high as it can go and still execute a stroke. The greatest practitioners of this shot can almost shoot directly down onto the cue ball and make it jump over another ball that is less than half an inch away. That elevation of the butt of the cue creates the need for a different stance.

Unless you're very tall, when you elevate the cue butt as high as is necessary for the jump shot, you'll be standing with one foot flat on the floor and will be on the toes of the other foot. Balance becomes a real problem, and although pool is renowned for not requiring a player to be in great physical condition, on this shot, it helps to be in shape. If you're too large, too weak, or too short, you'll find the jump-shot stance to be very difficult to execute successfully. Sustaining rock-solid steadiness while standing on one foot and leaning forward is the toughest part of this stance.

Standing Up to Combinations

A *combination shot* is one in which the cue ball hits an object ball and the object ball hits a second ball, which goes into the pocket. (See Chapter 20 for information on when to shoot a combination, how to aim, and so on.)

For combination shots in which the balls are close together (less than 18 inches from the cue ball to the second numbered ball), I recommend standing up straighter than normal. Looking down on the balls helps you see the angles clearer and helps you aim better. This is one case in which looking down the shaft may not be the best method. Occasionally, you may find it beneficial to actually get directly above the balls; after you plot the angles in your head, you can get down in your normal low stance to actually shoot the shot. Generally, though, stand a little straighter to shoot combinations when the balls are fairly close together.

The Least You Need to Know

➤ Extending a line from the ball that you want to hit through and beyond the cue ball establishes your approach line.

➤ Stand in a firm, stable, comfortable position, with your legs slightly spread.

➤ Your cue, the toes of your rear foot, your entire rear arm, and your right eye, left eye, or nose should be on that line.

➤ Take some warm-up strokes to test your positioning on the line.

➤ After you're in position, if your stance feels wrong in any way, stand up and step back for a second.

➤ For some special shots, you have to break the rules of the basic stance.

Chapter 11

Get a Grip on It

In This Chapter

➤ Where to grip the cue with your back hand

➤ Ewa's First 90-Degree Rule of Pool

➤ How to make the two basic front-hand bridges

➤ How to make a bridge on the table rail

➤ How to elevate your bridge

➤ The special bridges for special shots

Beginning players die by their own hand. Usually, the front hand—the one on the table—is the culprit. It wobbles, it teeters, it wiggles, and it twitches. The players stroke, miss the shot, and assume that they aimed wrong when they really wobbled and sent the cue off in an unknown direction. It happens to all of us at first, and it's caused by not knowing how to make a solid bridge. I'm going to fix that for you in less than a minute.

Bridge, by the way, has three meanings in billiards:

➤ It means the configuration of your front hand, which is called your *bridge hand*. You can make different bridges, which are among the main things that I want to show you in this chapter.

➤ It means the distance between your front hand and the cue ball, which varies from player by player and among the different types of shots. You might hear a TV commentator say, "She's using a short bridge on this shot," meaning a short distance between the player's front (or bridge) hand and the cue ball.

➤ It means a device called the *mechanical bridge,* which is used to reach shots that can't be comfortably reached by stretching a little. Instead of *mechanical bridge,* most people just call it *the bridge.*

I'll be using the word in all three ways in this chapter, but it will be clear what I mean.

By the way, you can become a champion by using an unorthodox bridge and grip, but you're needlessly making it rough on yourself if you follow that path. Billiards has progressed much like other stick-and-ball games, such as golf and tennis. On all three pro tours, you're more likely to see an unusual style used by older players who learned before modern instruction and swing analysis were developed. Stick with what I'm about to show you, and you'll find it much easier to hit the balls into the pockets. Making balls is half the fun in this game. (The other half is making the cue ball go where you want it to go after it knocks a ball into a pocket. That's called *position play,* and although I touch on it in Part 4, I really zero in on the topic in Chapter 22.)

The Back Hand

When you first picked up a cue and took a few practice strokes, you were probably more concerned about getting your front hand to stop wobbling than you were about where or how you gripped the cue with your back hand. But I want to start with the back hand, because knowing how to establish the proper grip there will make it easier for you to master the front (bridge) hand.

Pocket Dictionary

The word *grip* has two meanings in billiards. First, it's the way that you hold the cue with your back hand. The area where you hold the cue (usually covered by Irish linen, nylon, or leather) is also called the grip or cue grip.

To give you an idea of how important the back hand is to playing good pool, just think of the fact that a player grips the back of her cue with her dominant hand—the right hand, for a right-handed player. The longer you play, the more important that hand and arm become. The back hand is the one that actually aims the cue, determines the speed and power of the stroke, delivers the cue tip accurately, and puts the timing into a pool stroke. The front hand may be the one that gives you problems at first, but when you've been playing a while, you'll come to appreciate that about all it does is provide a guide for a cue that is being controlled by the other hand and arm.

Loose as a Goose

Offhand, I can't think of another stick-and-ball sport in which the players hands are as far apart as they are when you're holding a cue. The players of those other sports either use one hand (tennis), or if they use two hands (golf and baseball), the hands usually are close together. Yet there are similarities, and whether you're tearing up the golf course, taking a stab at fencing, or playing billiards, one piece of advice is consistent:

loose hands. Playing with a white-knuckled grip is performance suicide. I hesitate to even write the words for fear that my brain will consider it a possibility.

How loose? You obviously don't want to drop your cue in the middle of a stroke or, worse, turn it into an unguided missile heading for the heart of your opponent. Think in terms of holding a toddler by the hand. You'd be as gentle as possible, but you wouldn't want to lose control. I tell students to think of two words: *relaxed* and *controlled*. During the latter part of your stroke, your hand will naturally tighten slightly, and that's all you need to keep the cue in your grasp. I tell you more about that in Chapter 12, when I tell you how to develop a good stroke, but for right now, just try to avoid holding the cue too tightly with your back hand.

You'll find that a loose grip doesn't include all your fingers. I don't need to tell you that the fingers wrap around one side of the cue and the thumb around the other. The useful opposing thumb is what makes us humans able to handle such delicate tasks as open-heart surgery and 9-Ball. But how many fingers actually grip the cue?

Some old-timers use only the first finger and the thumb, although all the fingers end up gripping the cue as they go into the follow-through. But I recommend that you start with the classic grip: the cue resting in a cradle composed of the second and third fingers, with light shining through at the very top. How can you tell whether light is shining through? You have to get a very dear friend to adopt a very embarrassing position and tell you—that, or pay a stranger an inordinate amount of money.

Cue Tips

If you want to get a head start, try practicing your grip and the V bridge with a slender broom handle on the kitchen table.

Ewa's First 90-Degree Rule of Billiards

When you're holding the cue properly, it's time to think about *where* you hold it. Your hand may seem to fall naturally at the same place time after time, but it's probably not the right place. Beginners are often told to grip the cue 6 to 8 inches behind the balance point, but that advice works only for a very limited number of people. It's worth the time to know why, and even more valuable to find out what spot is the correct spot for you. The *why* is covered in Chapter 12, where I talk about the stroke, but the *where* can be easily determined with what I call Ewa's First 90-Degree Rule of Billiards.

Getting into Position to check the 90-Degree Rule

1. Bend over at the table, and get into position to hit the cue ball.

2. Place your front hand 6 to 8 inches from the cue ball. Don't worry about how you hold the cue with your front hand. Just lay your hand on the table and lay the cue on top of it, if you want.

3. Move the cue tip forward until it is just touching the white ball; then twist your head around and look at your back arm.

Here's the 90-Degree Rule: Your back forearm should be at a 90-degree angle to your cue. If it's not, slide it forward or backward until it is. When you've found that position, you've found the correct place to grip the cue. Your grip position won't be the same as someone who has longer or shorter arms or a different shoulder width. That's why the classic bit of billiard-room advice (and you're sure to hear it sooner or later) about gripping the cue 6 to 8 inches behind the balance point is correct only for a small percentage of people. (I showed you how to find the balance point of a cue back in Chapter 6.)

Heard It in the Poolroom

During the 1930s, a player named George Sutton gave exhibitions throughout the Northeast and Midwest. Although he was never a top player, Sutton did enter tournaments and reached a respectable level, surpassing the average local player and playing at professional grade. During his trick-shot exhibitions, he made shots that few people could duplicate. But what made him truly unique was the fact that he had lost both arms at the elbow and held the cue with the remaining portions of his arms.

The Human Grip for the Mechanical Bridge

When you say *bridge* in billiards, you sometimes mean a device called the mechanical bridge, which I tell you about in Chapter 7. When using the bridge, you use a special back hand grip, just as you use a special stance (covered in Chapter 10). Your front hand doesn't come into play, except to add whatever stability it can. Most commonly, the front hand holds the mechanical bridge flat on the table, so that the bridge won't move while you go through your warmup strokes. Your grip hand, meanwhile, out of necessity holds the cue near the end, giving you as long a reach as possible. The configuration of your back hand on the cue is the same that you'd use to hold a pen or pencil, though obviously enlarged to match the thickness of the cue butt.

The First 90-Degree Rule of Billiards comes into play, but there's a variation. Your forearm should still be at a 90-degree angle to the cue when the cue's tip is almost touching the cue ball, but it doesn't determine where you grip the cue, as it does when you're playing without the mechanical bridge. Because you're trying to reach as far as possible, you're always gripping the cue at or near the end. The only way to establish the 90 degrees, then, is to move your body. You'll find yourself standing behind the cue, sighting down the length of it. Keep the forearm of your back arm parallel to the floor, and that's all there is to it.

The Bridges of Billiard County

Now I'll deal with the wobbler: the front hand. If you're right-handed, you place your left hand on the table, which provides balance when you bend over and also guides the front of the cue when you make a shot. The guiding is accomplished by making your hand into what is called a bridge. There are two basic bridges, and in this section, I tell you how to make each of them and when to use them.

When you're done reading, you'll own the two fundamental bridges for all cue games known to humankind.

The two common bridges are the *closed bridge* (also called the loop bridge, the circle bridge, and the standard bridge) and the *open bridge* (also called the V bridge). Each has its own advantages.

The closed bridge has these advantages:

➤ Very stable

➤ Offers more control, especially on power shots

➤ Prevents the cue from lifting up during stroking

➤ Creates better follow-through on medium or harder hits

➤ Looks like something that a serious player does (hey, let's not undervalue the superficial)

The open or V bridge has these advantages:

➤ Allows you to see down your cue easier, making aiming easier

➤ Can be made by hands of any size, including children's hands, and by people who have stubby and very thick fingers

➤ Easy to make

Scratch!

It may be stylish now for teenage girls to wear a ring on every finger, but rings make it very difficult to create a smooth bridge.

Cue Tips

If the cue doesn't slide smoothly through your fingers, try a cue glove. You lose some sensitivity, but the cue will definitely slide like a quarter on ice.

The V Bridge

I'll start with the V bridge, because it's as easy as anything you've ever done. This bridge is the one that everyone tries when they first pick up a cue, but it usually wobbles. Read on, and you'll look smooth and polished the first time you pick up a cue. (You can even practice on the kitchen table for 30 seconds, using the handle of a large wooden spoon or something similar, before your first billiard outing.)

To make a V bridge, follow these steps:

1. Bend over the table and stretch out your arm, placing your hand flat on the table, as you see in Illustration A.

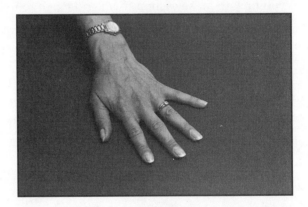

Illustration A: The first step in making a V bridge.

2. Raise the knuckles off the table, as you see in Illustration B, while keeping your fingertips and the heel of your hand firmly pressed down into the cloth.

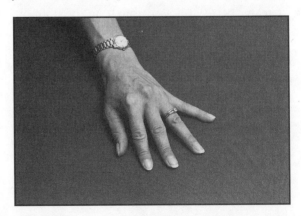

Illustration B: Raise your knuckles off the table.

3. Move your thumb up against the side of your hand, as you see in Illustration C, and drop the cue into the V shape formed by your thumb and hand. Keep pressing your fingertips and the heel of your hand into the cloth, and you'll have a rock-solid bridge.

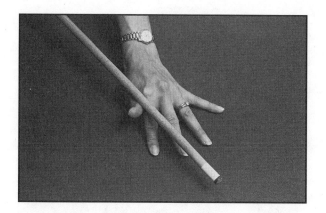

Illustration C: The complete V bridge. The cue shaft rests in the V formed by the end of your thumb and the top of your first finger.

Because you have the right grip on your cue now (refer to Illustration C), are using a well-balanced stance (refer to Chapter 10), and can now make a solid bridge, you have the beginnings of a pretty good billiard stroke. I'll tune that up for you in Chapter 12, but you're ahead of the class at this point.

Because the V bridge is easy to make, don't think that it's just a beginner's bridge. World-class snooker players rarely use anything else, and pool pros use it very often. Because I get down lower than the majority of players, I find that it is the best bridge for me, allowing me to look down the cue without the obstruction of a closed bridge. The cue is also is less likely to bind while sliding through your fingers, which is especially useful in humid or tense tournament conditions.

The V bridge is also especially good for soft, delicate shots in which the cue ball doesn't travel far, as well as for shots in which there are a lot of balls close to the cue ball and you want as few fingers as possible to be in the way. The only problem I ever see beginners encounter is the tendency to simply put their hand on the table without getting a hold on the cloth with their fingertips. Because the cloth is stretched tight over the slate, getting that grip seems to be impossible. Try pressing down with the tips of your fingers and then pulling the cloth toward you just a millimeter or two—not so far that it disturbs the cloth, but enough so that you feel you have a solid footing and your bridge hand isn't going to shift or slide.

Ewa's Billiard Bits

One world-champion pool player had a disease that made his hands shake. He was so used to it that he could time his strokes to hit the cue ball when the shake was at a certain point. He rarely missed making a ball.

Cue Tips

When they can't reach a shot, many players switch hands. If you try this technique, leave your hand in a fist and use the closed bridge.

Make a Fist

Making a fist is the first step in making a closed bridge. To make this bridge, follow these steps:

1. Place your fist on the table, as you see me doing in Illustration D.

Illustration D: The first step in making a closed bridge is making a fist.

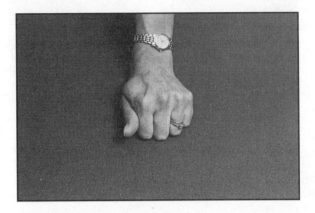

2. Spread three fingers, leaving the finger closest to the thumb in its original position (see Illustration E).

Illustration E: Spread three fingers, but leave your thumb and first finger as they were.

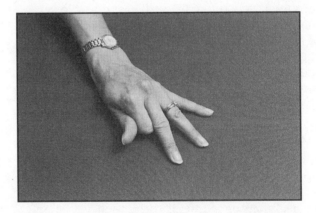

3. Lift that finger and slide the thumb underneath it, as you see in Illustration F. Illustration G is a side view, with the thumb moved out of the way so that you can see how my first finger is lifted just a bit more.

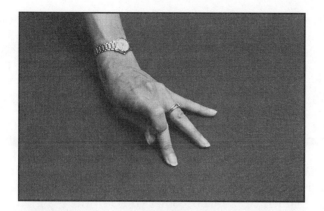

Illustration F: The next step is to make a loop, or circle, of your first finger and your thumb.

Illustration G: The side view of my hand may help you see things better. You can put your thumb on the table before putting the cue in place.

4. Now turn your hand slightly (wrist moving to the left, if it's your left hand), and slide the cue shaft through the loop created by your first finger, keeping the tip of your thumb pressed against the tip of the first finger. That's it (see Illustration H)! It takes months for a lot of people to learn what you just learned in the past minute.

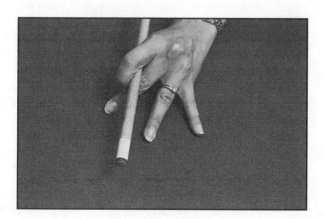

Illustration H: The final product: a closed bridge. You can also see why some people call it a loop or circle bridge.

There are some variables, based on how a person is built. In the last step, for example, some people rest the tip of the first finger on the third finger, or partly on that finger and partly on their thumb. The degree to which you cock your wrist is another variable. The thickness and length of your fingers and your dexterity enter into the final positioning. You can make whatever adjustments you need, as long as you don't stray far from the basic configuration.

Although I like a V bridge for almost every shot, I know that many players prefer the closed bridge, especially when they're going to hit the cue ball fairly hard. The break shot comes to mind, but once again, I find that I can still get better accuracy and power by using the V bridge. When you're just learning the game, you might find your cue popping out of your V bridge. A closed bridge would stop that from happening. The bottom line, however, is that which bridge becomes your favorite is a matter of personal preference, but you should learn to be comfortable with both.

The Rail Bridges

When the cue ball is near one of the cushions, you'll have to make a bridge on the rail to hit it. Although I have seen the rare player use a modified closed bridge when forming a rail bridge, the vast majority of players use a V bridge (also called an open bridge). It's worthwhile to learn how to make these variations so that they work for you. A regular closed or V bridge raises your cue too high, and you'll strike the cue ball from an elevated position, which will make the ball scoot off to the side, rather than follow a straight path to the ball that you want to hit with the cue ball. If you use one of the variations that I'm about to show you, and hit the cue ball softer rather than harder, you'll greatly increase your chances of success.

The first rail bridge is shown in Illustrations I and J. Rather than raise the knuckles of your hand, you leave them flat against the top of the rail, and rather than raise your thumb, you raise the first joint of your first finger. That way, the cue is guided on a straight line by the finger and the knuckle of the thumb. This technique also works if (space permitting) you slide your hand forward so that the ends of your fingers curl over the edge of the cushion. If the cue ball is flush against the cushion, you can revert to the standard V bridge.

Just remember three points: Make the cue as level as you can under the circumstances, hit the ball as softly as you can while still achieving your goal, and shorten your stroke (that is, the backward and forward movements of your cue).

Pocket Dictionary

A *rail bridge* is a bridge formed on the railing and cushion of a billiard table.

Scratch!

On cheaper or older tables, the pocket may be made of a rubberized plastic that will mark your cue. If you have to shoot out of a pocket, as shown in Illustration K, check your cue after doing so, and if it has black lines on the shaft, think about getting the pockets replaced.

Illustration J is a variation that adds a bit more control over the path of the cue. If you're just starting to play, the bridge shown in Illustration I may not offer enough lateral control for you, so you can use this equally valid variation. The cue still glides on the rail, so you haven't created any harmful elevation. Slide your thumb under your hand, keeping it straight and letting it serve as a stop against any cue movement to the left. Drape your first finger over the cue, stopping any movement to the right. Now the shaft should slide smoothly forward and backward in a straight line. This maneuver won't mark either your cue or the table.

Illustration I: This is the variation of the V bridge that you use when the cue ball is close to the cushion. Notice that the cue is guided along the full length of my first finger.

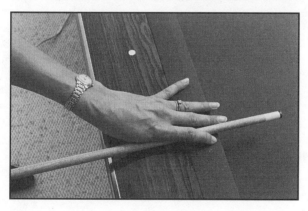

Illustration J: Looping my first finger over the cue and guiding the cue shaft against my thumb (hidden by my palm in this shot) gives me far more control over accidental sideways movement of the cue.

The toughest bridge is the one that you have to make when you're shooting out of a pocket. Now that you know about rail bridges, however, you'll have no problem. As you can see in Illustration K, this bridge is just another modification of the V bridge. The only thing to watch out for is the fact that the material used to make most pockets isn't as slick as the material used in the rails, so your cue probably will not slide as smoothly.

Illustration K: Making a bridge over a side or corner pocket of the table is a little more difficult, but it's still the basic V bridge with a little adjustment.

Spanning the Specialty Bridges

Cue Tips

You should always make sure that your tip is chalked before shooting, but this is even more critical when you're using a rail bridge. It's more difficult to hit the cue ball near the center, which makes a miscue more likely.

In special situations, extreme versions of the two basic bridges come into play. The more extreme the variations, the more difficult it is to maintain stability in your bridge and the more likely you are to miss the shot. For these reasons, if you don't have a good shot, it is to your advantage to leave the cue ball in such a position before your opponent comes to the table. This is a type of safety play, and I tell you more about that in Chapter 22. But until then, all you need to know is that a *safety* is leaving the balls in positions where your opponent cannot make a ball or, better yet, cannot even hit the ball that he or she is required to hit. It also helps if your opponent has to bridge awkwardly to hit the cue ball. The downside, of course, is that your opponent will do the same thing to you, forcing you to use an extreme variation of the basic open bridge.

Lifting the Bridge to Shoot over a Ball

A common situation is finding the cue ball next to another ball, lined up in such a way that you're shooting away from the other ball. To hit the cue ball, you have to bridge over the other ball, and to do so, you have to elevate your bridge, as I'm doing in Illustration L.

It's pretty plain that this bridge can be a little shaky. Depending on the shape of your hands, you may want to pull the shortest finger in and have it touch the table under your palm, or even curl it into your palm and take it totally out of the picture. Some people can get their thumbs up really high in this position, and if you're fortunate enough to have this ability, it makes the bridge a lot easier.

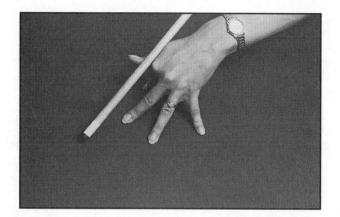

Illustration L: The elevated V bridge, used to shoot over a ball.

But no matter how you elevate your hand and no matter how stable the bridge is, you're still shooting down on the cue ball, which means that it can scoot off to the side if you're not very accurate in your aim. You'll also have to use a very short stroke and hit the cue ball as softly as you can while still sending it on its way with enough force to reach the ball that you want it to hit.

Consider using a mechanical bridge for this type of shot if you feel that your hand will be unsteady. All bridges are designed to turn on their side, giving you enough height to shoot over a ball. Although a mechanical bridge is designed for shooting the cue ball when it's out of comfortable reach, nothing says that you can't use the bridge when you have to shoot over a ball, just as I'm doing in Illustration M. The mechanical bridge takes the place of your elevated bridge and may give you a little more stability.

Cue Tips

Though the bridges in this chapter have been proven over centuries you can still create your own bridge—as long as it works for you.

Illustration M: Using a bridge head to help you shoot over a ball, even though you could reach the shot with it, eliminates the possibility that your bridge hand will shake.

The Suspended Bridge

There is a special shot called a *massé* (pronounced mass-say) in which you actually shoot straight down at the cue ball. It looks like you're trying to drive the ball into the table, but you actually hit it off center. The result is that the ball takes off in one direction, and then suddenly turns and heads in a different direction.

Although it's quite spectacular, and a shot that will get you out of certain very tough situations, a massé shot is also very dangerous. This is a shot that can damage your cue, rip the cloth, or chip the slate bed of the table. Billiard-room owners often post signs prohibiting massé shots for that reason. Still, I wouldn't want you to have read this book and not at least know about a massé. You'll see massé shots used in trick-shot exhibitions and occasionally during a match on TV or at your billiard club.

Remember that you're holding the cue in a vertical position and shooting straight down on the ball. The grip used for this type of shot is the closed bridge, but instead of putting your hand on the table, you place it against your body while holding the cue in a vertical position. The grip of your back hand is optional. The two most common methods are to hold the cue just like you would if it were a normal horizontal stroke or to circle the grip area with a thumb and one finger. Either method is tough, as you can imagine. Even tougher is having to shoot this shot when the cue ball is away from the edge of the table, and you can't press your bridge hand against your body. Then the bridge is suspended in midair and can wiggle all over the place.

Although I'm not advising you to shoot a massé shot at all, I'll be very firm in telling you to never shoot a *suspended massé*. Even in the hands of expert trick-shot players, these shots are very, very difficult and can easily damage your equipment.

The Least You Need to Know

➤ Your back hand should be placed so that your forearm is at a 90–degree angle to the cue when the cue tip is touching the cue ball.

➤ Your back hand should be loose but still control the cue.

➤ Use your dominant hand as your back hand.

➤ Your front hand should be solid and steady.

➤ The two basic bridges are the V (or open) bridge and the closed (or loop) bridge.

Brushing Up Your Stroke

In billiards, it's cailed a *stroke*, but it's very closely associated with what many other sports call a *swing*. Having a smooth, authoritative stroke is what separates the women from the girls (or the men from the boys, as the case may be). Keeping the cue stick as close to parallel to the playing surface as possible, following through with your stroke as far and as straight as you can, and keeping your head down are all very critical fundamentals. But every bit as important is the timing in your stroke, not to mention finding your own stroke rhythm. It's the difference between an awkward-looking tyro and a seasoned player. But never fear—I'm going to help you look like that seasoned player in record time, possibly before you even approach a pool table!

When you watch experienced players, you'll see variations in stroking technique that are caused by either body configuration or some early instruction. I'm not going to suggest that you toe a rigid line in those areas, but I'll explain them so that you'll know what will work best and what styles make it difficult to progress rapidly.

I'm going to get a little strict in a couple of areas, however. If you learn them—and they're simple—you can go on to develop your natural stroke. There's nothing tough about the stroke, but it is one of the most critical areas to master if you want to play good pool.

Ewa illustrates the proper stance, with the cue drawn back during the stroke.

This is the position of your arm when the cue tip is about to strike the cue ball: perpendicular to the floor. During your warmup strokes, you want to go this far forward. Just be careful not to hit the cue ball until you're ready!

The cue ball has been hit. Ewa follows through and freezes at the end of her striking stroke.

The Hit and the Pendulum

In billiards, *hit* refers to several things. It can describe the way that a cue plays ("It has a good hit"), meaning how natural that cue feels in your hands, how much feedback (feeling) you get when you hit a cue ball, and how easy it is to control the cue ball with that particular cue. In a game, it can also refer to whether the cue ball hit the proper object ball. A *good hit* means that it did.

What I'm talking about when I associate the hit with the stroke is whether you struck the cue ball with the cue tip in the exact place where you intended to strike it, and whether the tip hit the ball in such a way as to achieve the desired result.

The most common reason for a bad hit, especially among those who are just beginning to play billiards, is a wobbly front hand. I fixed that problem for you in the last chapter. Another reason is a lack of focus or confidence in what you're doing. If a player is tentative or hesitant, he probably won't get a good hit on the cue ball, and the result will be anybody's guess. Confidence comes with knowledge and practice, and I'm going to fill in both those areas before the book is over. So you can check off the major reasons for a bad hit. The final bad guy that I'm about to shoot down is a poor stroke.

By establishing the correct stance, and by using the correct grips for your front and back hands, you're in the perfect position to execute a good stroke.

Pocket Dictionary

A *hit* can be a few different things. A cue that performs well can be said to hit well. A player who contacts an object ball with the cue ball within the rules is said to have made a good hit. In stroking, *hit* means hitting the cue ball with the cue tip where you aimed, and stroking it well.

While you're bent over the table, in position, think of your back elbow as being a pivot point. Let the forearm of your back arm swing loosely. When you swing the cue back, the elbow shouldn't move very much, if at all. When the arm is straight down, perpendicular to the floor, the cue tip will be in contact with the cue ball (or at least within a few millimeters of it), and the elbow is still in the same position. After you actually strike the ball, your elbow will drop somewhat as you follow through, but you can still think of the motion as being a pendulum swing.

Scratch!

Many beginning players have heard that you have to keep the cue level, so they try to raise and lower their elbows during the entire stroke to achieve this effect. This practice, however, will ruin your stroke. The cue definitely needs to be level from the middle to the end of a stroke, but you raise it slightly at the back of your stroke.

If you own a cue, you can practice getting into the proper stance and creating a pendulum swing. Use the V bridge that I described in the last chapter. Take 20 or 30 seconds 3 or 4 times a night for a few nights, and you'll have a good, natural feel for the proper stroke when you approach your first billiard table. I don't recommend working on your stroke while you're playing against another player, however. I know that many people don't like practicing by themselves, but it's the fastest (and perhaps the only) way to really improve.

Avoid being tight when you're practicing or playing. Yes, the elbow shouldn't move until the cue tip strikes the cue ball, and you should maintain a proper stance, but if everything is done right, it's a stress-free feeling rather than a tense one. Tense muscles make for a jerky, uneven stroke, which is what you want to avoid. You're aiming for smooth, silky, and natural.

The Preparatory Strokes: Your Test

Taking warmup strokes, or *preparatory strokes*, is called *feathering*. The word isn't used a great deal, and like so many other words in the sport, it has two meanings. Just so you'll know if you hear someone use it, it can also mean hitting the cue ball so that it barely touches the side of the object ball, as though a feather had touched it. Used to describe strokes, *feathering* means the swings that a player takes just before the one on which she hits the cue ball with the cue tip.

The warmup strokes are an opportunity for you to test the position of your hands, your cue, and the rest of your body. Do things feel comfortable? Are you forcing yourself into line or leaning a little off balance to get the cue in the right position? Is the cue naturally headed in the right direction?

The warmup is also an opportunity for you to make sure that your line of sight is unobstructed. You should decide where you're going to hit the object ball with the cue ball before you get into position, but this is the time for a quick check of that situation. If you don't feel sure of the shot, you haven't yet committed yourself. You can still stand up, regroup, and get back down into position when you feel confident about your shot decisions.

The final thing to check is whether the cue tip is hitting the cue ball where you want it to. When you start to play, that spot will be the middle of the cue ball, but later, you may at times want to hit it below center, to the right of center, and so on.

An overhead shot of the middle position of the stroke. This illustration shows how Ewa lines everything up properly so that at the moment the cue tip strikes the cue ball, she has given herself the optimum chance for success. Emulate this technique, and you'll be popping balls into the pockets one after another.

The Rhythm Method

Every player has to find his or her own rhythm, which means finding the pace and system that work for them. *Pace* is simply the speed of your stroking, and having a *system* refers to pauses or speed variations in the warmup process.

I recommend that you use a slower *backstroke* (when you're pulling the cue tip away from the cue ball). Having a slower, controlled pullback

Pocket Dictionary

The *backstroke* is pulling the cue tip away from the cue ball during warmup strokes.

promotes an equally smooth delivery. Many players use the same speed when they pull back as when they swing the cue forward. Some players actually make a very short pause at the end of their backstroke before delivering the final stroke. Others pause with the cue tip almost touching the cue ball before their final complete stroke (backstroke and forward stroke). Some players use three or four short jab strokes and then pull back full-length for the striking stroke.

There are different ways of finding your groove, but the classic (and logical) approach is to draw back fully on each warmup stroke. The most important things are to find out what feels comfortable and natural to you and then do it every single time you get down on the table for a shot.

The break shot is instructive, because it's both an unusual shot and an exaggerated shot. You hit the cue ball harder—much harder—for the break shot than for any other shot. Because the shot has a special goal (power), you have to vary your stroke.

One option is to move the cue very fast during your warmup strokes. The theory—and it seems to work for a lot of people—is that this technique sends a message to your muscles that you're about to demand a lot from them. Because your cue changes directions at the back of your stroke (from pulling back to going forward), you are accelerating the swing much more. The key is to develop the proper timing that lets you be at your peak speed, or a hair below, the moment your cue tip touches the cue ball.

The same is true of regular strokes; it's just that the speed is so much slower that it's not as obvious. When you're hitting a soft, delicate shot, you will likely reach your peak speed inches before you hit the ball, but in the vast range of shots, the tip makes contact at the peak speed.

The important points in cue acceleration are:

➤ Make the speed increase smooth and uniform.

➤ Reach the peak speed (even if it's slow) at contact.

Do you want to use the same warmup-stroke speed on all shots? I'm excepting the obvious extreme situations in which you have to slam the ball on the break and just baby it forward a couple of inches on a delicate shot. But for all other shots, should your warmup-stroke speed be consistent?

Only you can answer this question. I can tell you that consistency is critical in billiards. But if you carefully watch players who insist that they use the exact same speed for their warmup strokes and change the stroke speed only on the striking stroke, you'll see that even they use a range of speeds; it's just a more limited range.

I recommend that you fit your warmup strokes to the requirements of the shot, but not vary the speed too much. Keep your warmup strokes in a relatively limited speed range—a little faster for hard hits and a little slower for softer hits.

Rhythm in stroking is part of your overall playing rhythm. I've talked about standardizing your approach to the table and your chalking-up, and how that standardization helps establish a playing rhythm. Warmup strokes fit right into the same picture. Put it all together—it helps tremendously in getting into the game, getting a feel for playing, and feeling confident about making the shots. Stroking rhythm is the most important part of the package, but none of the parts should be neglected.

Part of your rhythm and timing involves establishing a certain number of warmup strokes and sticking with that number. Three is a very workable number. The first one is general and gets you in place. The second one settles you in. The third one is the final test. On the fourth stroke, you *pull the trigger*, as we say in pool. In other words, you shoot the shot.

If you use fewer than three preparatory strokes—and especially if you only use one— you run a serious risk of not having given yourself enough time to really know that everything is right. Four, five, or six strokes are not unreasonable. On occasion, you can even use a couple more, such as when you find, during the second or third stroke, that you're not 100 percent sure that everything is OK. You may feel slightly uneasy about your shot selection, balance, or movement in your peripheral vision. Or maybe you have a very difficult shot in front of you and want to take a little extra preparation. Playing under the combination of tournament tension and television tension, as I do, makes me want to be very sure that everything is perfect before I strike the cue ball, and I may use eight or nine strokes.

It's OK to break your routine slightly and add a stroke—or two, or three. The idea is to make those times the exceptions and to try to stick to a set number on the vast majority of your shots.

Scratch!

Beware of taking too many warmup strokes, even if the shot is very difficult. After a certain point, extra warmup strokes become destroyers of confidence and focus, rather than helpers.

Following Through

The last part of the stroke begins when you hit the cue ball with the cue tip. That's the beginning of your follow-through, and just as you do in any other sport that requires you to swing your arm or an object, you have to follow through. Anything else gives you a wimpy, ineffective hit.

A stroke is not a jab. A good stroke keeps the cue moving for another foot or more after the hit. After contact, your elbow drops so that you can maintain a level stroke; if it didn't, you'd be lifting the back of your cue. If you break your wrist, as you do when you're swinging a baseball bat, the tip will go into the cloth and possibly rip it. (Actually, the ferrule would rip it—not the tip, as most people think.) If you lock your wrist, the cue will jump up in the air, right out of your front hand. So if you see either of these things happen—in your own play or in somebody else's—you know what went wrong.

Drop the elbow at contact, keep the cue level, and follow through as far as is comfortable for you. It's not a bad idea to establish a standard follow-through length, but be aware that you can't use it on some shots. The balls may be too close together, for example, or you may be stroking toward a close cushion, in which case hitting the cue ball into an object ball may make a ball almost instantly come back over the follow-through area and hit your cue if you haven't shortened your follow-through on that shot. But in a never-ending quest for consistency, I suggest that you seriously try to standardize your follow-through length and use it on as many shots as physically possible.

The follow-through concept changes on the break shot and is unusable on a few other shots in billiards. I'll give you some concrete examples.

On the break shot, players extend their follow-through, but how they do it is a reflection of their personality, physical makeup, and personal feelings about what gives them the most power. World Champion Mike Sigel, who won more tournaments during the 1980s than any other player, broke into the cloth. That means that he drove the cue tip down after contact on the break shot, lifting the rear of the cue and actually bending the shaft in an arc, as though he were trying to break it. The fibers in his cue shaft ripped each time he did this, however, and the cue eventually became too limber to use. He replaced the shaft on his break cue every couple of months.

Ewa's Billiard Bits

Ripping the cloth on a billiard table is not nearly as big a problem as cartoons would have you believe. If your leather cue tip and especially your cue's ferrule are properly maintained, it would be very difficult for you to rip billiard cloth. Doing so would not be impossible, but the situation is not as common as folklore suggests.

Other players, caught by still cameras at the end of their break-shot follow-through, look like ballerinas. They've thrown their bodies so far into the shot that they end up on one toe with both arms in the air and the cue 6 feet off the ground, aiming at a faraway point of the ceiling. (That technique doesn't work when you have table lights—only when you have high lights under tournament conditions.)

You may naturally lift your back leg, bend it at the knee, and kick it up behind your body on your break shot; lots of people do. There are no real rules of form when it comes to the body on a break shot. Still, with all these variations, players follow through in one way or another.

When shooting one type of shot you purposely don't follow through—that's the punch shot. Punching (also called bunting or nipping) the cue ball is a very short stroke. It is used when the cue ball and object ball are very close together and the cue ball makes contact with the object ball very quickly. When the contact happens the cue ball stops dead, and if you were to follow through you would hit the cue ball a second time with your cue tip. Hitting the cue ball twice on one shot is a foul. Instead of following through, therefore, you want to just punch the cue ball and quickly withdraw your cue tip.

Stay Down!

Staying down simply means that at the end of your follow-through, you freeze. It's amazing that this matters. The cue ball was contacted long before, so how could anything you do thereafter make any difference? You could whistle "Dixie" at that point, and the cue ball wouldn't change direction. The same could be said for the follow-through but it *does* make a difference.

What's probably happening is that you're changing the end of the sequence if you don't follow through, or if you follow through but jump up at the end of the follow-through. The middle parts of any sequence tend to be smoother and more uniform; if any part deviates, it is either the beginning or the end. By freezing at the end of your stroke sequence, you don't subconsciously prepare to move off line immediately after contacting the cue ball. Not moving at the end of the sequence is a very important part of the stroke. And by the way, when players know that they aimed a little wrong or hit the cue ball a little off the mark, they often jump up after the hit and twist and turn their bodies, in an effort to make the ball go where they wanted it to go. This phenomenon is jokingly called body English (spin), and at times, you'll wish it really worked.

How long should you stay frozen? Peg your freeze to one of the things that occur after you hit the cue ball: the moment the cue ball stops rolling, or the moment the object ball either stops rolling or goes into a pocket. Stay down, freeze at the end of your follow-through, and watch the balls until one of those things happens. Then stand up and prepare for your next shot.

Pocket Dictionary

Body English is when a player mis-aims or mis-hits the cue ball and jumps up off the shot, twisting his or her body in a futile attempt to make the errant cue ball change its path. The term is used jokingly.

I don't care for the method that some players use, which is to count off a given number of seconds to themselves while they're frozen. The distance of shots and the movement of balls vary too much for you to attach the length of your freeze to a fixed length of time. I recommend using the movement of the object ball or cue ball, as I just described.

Along with extending your sequence—and, therefore, making your stroke smoother and straighter—the freeze is a good opportunity to see just how straight your stroke was. Look quickly, and you can sight down the shaft to check the object ball (unless you hit the cue ball hard, in which case the object ball will already be gone). A good check is to put an object ball on the table spot, place a cue ball 18 inches away, in line with the object ball and pocket (a straight-in shot, in other words), and then shoot. Your cue tip should end up directly over or on the spot. If it does, your stroke was straight, and your follow-through was perfect.

Cue Tips

If you find that your game has suddenly gone to Tallahassee, a good way to get it back on track is to check the elements of your stroke. Chances are that you got a little lax in one area and simply need to get yourself back in order.

Stroking: The List

The stroke is what makes a player succeed, and it's also what makes you look like a player. When you have a good, solid, comfortable stance, and when you develop the proper rear-hand grip and front-hand bridge, the stroke almost falls into place. (At least, it becomes much easier to stroke correctly than incorrectly.) Your pre-shot routine (approaching the table down your sight line, chalking up, and so on) can now include a few checks on your stroke.

The best time to check your stroke is during individual practice. But if things are going awry during a game, go ahead and get down for the shot; then run through a dozen warmup strokes while you go over the following checklist. One time should be enough.

Following is Ewa's Stroke Checklist:

❏ Are all the sight-line body parts in line (back elbow, back hand, cue, eyes, front hand, and cue ball)?

❏ Is your back elbow stable during the pullback and to the point at which the arm is perpendicular to the floor?

❏ Are your warmup strokes fluid and unwavering?

❏ Have you made all the decisions about the shot (how hard to hit it, where to aim the cue ball, and where on the cue ball you want the cue tip to make impact)?

❏ If you include a pause either at the front of your stroke or at the back of it, are you doing it consistently?

❏ Do you believe in the shot that you're about to shoot?

❏ Have you followed through so that your tip is at least a foot (and preferably a foot and a half) past where the cue ball was?

Take the tearout reference card (found at the beginning of this book) with you when you go to play. A quick reading will remind you to check the items I've listed here. Follow them all and you'll pocket many more balls when it's your turn at the table.

The Least You Need to Know

➤ Develop consistency in your stroke routine.

➤ Keep your cue level and your stroke smooth.

➤ Keep your body solid and comfortable, but relaxed.

➤ Increase cue speed smoothly, and contact the cue ball at its peak.

➤ Warmup strokes develop timing, confidence, and a straight hit, and give you time to check your form.

➤ Follow through.

➤ Freeze at the end of your follow-through until the cue ball stops moving or the object ball has gone into the pocket.

Part 4
Rack 'Em Up!

You picked a billiard room, you bought a table for the house, and you know how to stand and swing the cue. Now let's hit some balls! Part 4 is where I tell you how to do that. You can do a lot more with a shiny white cue ball than just hit it into another ball; you can make it dance. In this part, I show you how to turn the cue ball into Fred Astaire or Ginger Rogers.

A fascinating aspect of this game is the fact that with the tiny tip of the cue, you can hit a ball, and after the ball is no longer contacting anything in your hand, you can still make it spin, twist, turn, and bounce. This part of the book talks about control of that ball. I show you the secrets of that magic thing called English that you've probably heard about. English is a type of spin, and you're going to able to use it to control the cue ball just a few pages from now. It will put you on a level above the majority of the recreational players in this country. You'll amaze yourself with the things that you'll be able to do.

Sound cool? Let's rack 'em up!

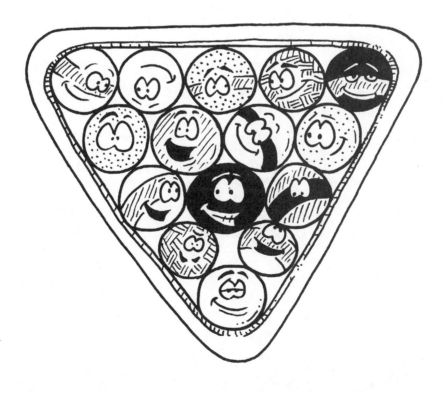

Chapter 13

An Aim That's True

In This Chapter

➤ The secret of aiming in billiards

➤ How to find the contact point

➤ How to find the aiming point

➤ How to aim at a cushion

➤ Intuitive aiming

➤ What to be looking at when you shoot

When giving lessons, I've always found explaining how to aim to be one of the most difficult things to put into words. The fact that you strike one round object that then makes contact with another round object complicates things quite a bit. Figuring out what point to hit on the object ball is fairly simple; the tricky part is understanding which part of the cue ball will strike that spot. Remembering that you're dealing with two spheres, you realize that if you aim at the object ball and hit it—on anything other than a full-in-the-face, straight-in shot—the equator of the cue ball will actually hit the equator of the object ball in a place other than where you aimed it.

I admit that this concept is tough to grasp. It's overwhelmingly important, however, so I'm going to break it down for you. I'm also going to use a concept called the *ghost ball* to help you figure out every correct angle on every shot that is not straight in. By the way, the phrase to describe those shots is cut shots, and when you shoot one, you *cut the ball in*. When you just skim the edge of the ball, it's a *thin cut*. You'll also hear players say that they *sliced the ball*. So I'll get the Slice-O-Matic ready, and we'll go make some balls.

The Contact Point versus the Aiming Point

Because this concept is so important, I've decided to break the procedure into a list of steps, so you can clearly see how to establish the aiming point and contact point of any cut shot (almost every shot, remember, is a cut shot).

1. Put a cue ball and a numbered ball on the table, a couple of inches apart.

2. With your hand, slide the cue ball straight into the object ball, and notice how small an area of the balls actually meets.

3. Go back to the starting position, and slide the cue ball into the object ball in such a way that the object ball heads off at a 45-degree angle. Notice the point on the object ball where the two balls met, which will be different from where they met on the straight hit.

4. Now repeat the process a third time, but this time, draw an imaginary line through the cue ball that is aiming directly at the second point you noted (when you hit it so that the ball went at a 45-degree angle).

5. Aim the imaginary line at the contact point on the object ball, and slide the cue ball to it. You'll see that the cue ball actually touches the object ball in a different place. That's because the balls are both round.

That description makes it for some of my students, but not all. You have to think about it, and I want to emphasize that it's really worth the time. This is the secret of aiming in billiards. If you don't grasp this physical fact of colliding spheres, mastering the game will take a lot longer. You'll have to depend strictly on experience and intuition, and even they will let you down at times.

A critical factor in making balls is learning that on any cut shot, the contact point is different from the point you aimed at—the thinner the cut, the more this is the case. A straight-in shot is the only time that this doesn't matter, and straight-in shots are pretty rare. You have some kind of angle on virtually every single shot you play.

Pocket Dictionary

A *cut shot* is any shot that is not straight on. A *thin cut shot* is when you hit only the edge of the object ball with the cue ball.

If the cue ball were shaped like a needle, you could aim at a point, and the needle tip would hit that point. But balls foul up that scenario. They bulge in the middle, so the equators meet first, sort of getting in the way of the balls meeting at the aiming point.

If it's hard to grasp the written explanation—and I'll be the first to admit that it is—and if you don't happen to have two spheres at hand to put the preceding words into tangible form, the following illustrations should get you over the hump. I suggest that you pause here, read the figure caption, and then pick up at the following paragraph.

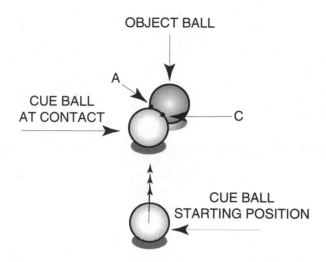

OBJECT BALL

A

CUE BALL
AT CONTACT

C

CUE BALL
STARTING POSITION

The cue ball is aimed at the point on the object ball labeled A. But when it actually hits it, the fact that both objects are balls makes them contact before that point. The actual contact point is labeled C.

The goal is to cut the object ball so that it goes off to the right. Pretend that's where the pocket is, and you're trying to hit the object ball into the pocket. You can see that to make the object ball (let's just call it the *OB* for short) go in that direction, you have to hit it on its left side. You pick out Point A (in the illustration) as the correct point and aim the middle of the cue ball at Point A.

It's all simple and obvious so far, right? But when the cue ball actually heads toward Point A and comes into contact with the OB (object ball), the balls meet at a different point. I've labeled that Point C (for contact). Hitting the OB at Point C makes it go in a slightly different direction (a different angle) than it would if it had been hit at the intended point (A). The result is a missed shot.

This concept can drive you nuts when you start playing ("I hit it right but it didn't go where it was supposed to!"). Seems that way, but what throws everyone off is the fact that the aiming point and the contact point are different on every shot except a straight-in shot. This is what makes a fine cut shot (a hit on which you just skim the OB ball) one of the most difficult simple shots in the game. The thinner you hit the OB, the more difference there is between the aiming point and the contact point. On the other hand, if you're shooting an almost-straight-in shot, there's not much difference at all.

Another thing to consider about angles is that the more distance is involved after the hit, the farther off target the OB goes. In other words, if the OB in the illustration were sitting right in front of the pocket, it wouldn't matter whether the cue ball hit the OB at the aiming point or the contact point. That's why it would be called an easy shot. If the shot is made and the OB has to travel a long distance to the pocket, however, any little error in direction will be magnified over distance. By the time the OB reaches the area of the pocket at the other end of the table, the ball could be 2 or 3 feet off course. That's why a shot with the cue ball and the OB near each other, and the intended pocket far away, is more difficult than the other kind of long shot—the one where the

167

Scratch!

Hitting the cue ball anywhere but in the center makes all shots much more difficult. An off-center hit makes the ball go in a direction slightly different from where you aimed it.

OB is at the other end of the table from the cue ball, but the OB is close to a pocket. This is good to know when you're deciding whether to shoot one of these shots.

Look at the illustration again, and make sure that you fully understand, and are comfortable with, the knowledge that on any kind of angle shot (cut shot), the aiming point and the contact point are different. The next time you're in a position to have two billiard balls handy (this is one of the great things about having your own table at home), try the example that I give at the beginning of this section, using your hand to slide the cue ball into the OB (object ball). Then hit the cue ball with your cue.

Aiming with the Ghost Ball

When you see what's actually happening and understand the reason for it, you probably say, "Great! But then how do I find out where the contact point actually is? And where should I actually aim to make the object ball go where I want it to—short of picking up the cue ball and putting it against the object ball? That's probably illegal." You'd be right—it is illegal to do that during a game. So let's get metaphysical....

This is the shot. You want to send the object ball down the intended path. Because it's a cut shot, you now know that the contact point will be different from the aiming point. The next illustration shows you how to use the ghost ball to make this shot.

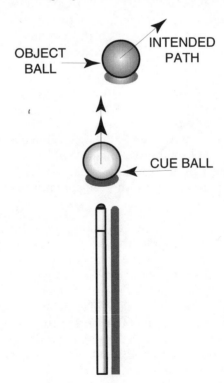

The *ghost ball* is an imaginary cue ball. It's a substitute for picking up your cue ball and placing it against the object ball, and it works great. (Some people call it a *phantom ball*, just so you'll know.) I'm going to work your imagination some more here, because I not only want you to picture an imaginary cue ball, but also want you to draw some imaginary lines:

1. Draw the first imaginary line from the center of the pocket where you want the OB to go through the center of the OB. The place where the line comes out of the backside (the side away from the pocket) of the OB is the contact point.

2. Place (mentally) your ghost ball against the contact point, as you see in the next illustration. Pause here and check it out.

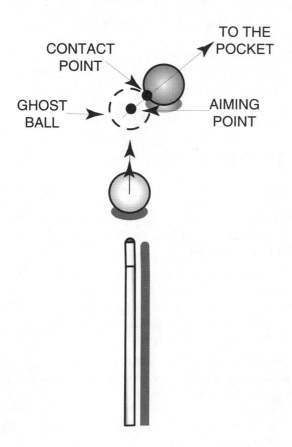

By creating a ghost ball and placing it on the line from the pocket to the object ball, you'll reveal where you should contact your cue ball.

You see the line to the pocket and where the ghost ball should be: touching the contact point. It's easy as pie so far, and there's only one more step, which is just as easy.

3. Picture the center of the ghost ball, and you've found your aiming point.

169

Ewa's Billiard Bits

For one of the shots that I use in my exhibitions, I place two balls together, aimed at a pocket, just like the ghost-ball setup, but with a real ball instead of a ghost ball. When the contact point is real, you can hit the second ball (the one farthest from the pocket) almost anywhere, and the one that it's touching is guaranteed to go in the pocket.

The aiming point is in the air, because the ghost ball is imaginary, and some people have a problem with that concept. If you can picture it, go for it, but if you're like most folks, that's a bit difficult.

So think of it this way: You're going to replace the ghost ball with your real cue ball. In other words, you'll hit the cue ball to the place occupied by the ghost ball, and that will give you the correct hit on the OB so that it goes down the intended path to the pocket. You just replace something imaginary with something real. The result is that you make the ball.

Actually, after you master the ghost-ball concept, you'll just fly past figuring out the contact point and go right to the aiming point. You'll know where to aim, which is what does the job. But I believe that it's always good to understand why things are happening and why you should use certain techniques. If you get into a jam, you'll have the knowledge to get out.

Working the Ghost Ball Concept

The first three illustrations are some of the most important in this book, but for all their importance, after you master the concept and start using it to pocket balls, you'll find yourself automatically figuring out where the aiming point is. With a limited amount of experience, you won't even have to think about it anymore. But without it, getting on the right track is almost impossible.

Millions of people who play the game know nothing about the difference between the contact point and the aiming point, and they've never heard of the ghost-ball concept. Straight shots and short shots become relatively easy for them, but cut shots and longer shots are mostly a matter of luck. In fact, when they don't hit the OB exactly where they aimed, they're more likely to make the ball in the pocket.

Not knowing will stop your progress cold, and you'll struggle slowly to ever improve. I imagine that it would take average players four or five times longer to reach a better level of play simply because they don't know that the aiming and contact points are different. Cut shots and long shots won't be as difficult for you, however, because you now know the secret of aiming in billiards. You know where to hit the OB, and it's just a matter of executing your stroke properly.

Here's another tip in the same area. This technique is especially useful when the OB is a long distance from the cue ball and must be cut fairly thin (meaning that you hit the edge of the ball):

1. Use your cue to establish the intended path of the object ball and the contact point.

170

2. Go to the end of the table where the OB is lying.

3. Place your cue tip on the table (on the side of the OB opposite the pocket) near the object ball, and move the cue until it's on the intended path. This step gives you a visual reference for the intended path, making an imprint on your mind, and shows you the contact point.

4. Visualize the ghost ball, and get the aiming point.

Using your cue this way (and it's done by world-class players on difficult shots, so don't feel self-conscious about it) is a great method of getting comfortable with the shot and knowing where to aim.

You can use the ghost ball on almost any shot. You don't need it on a straight-in shot, but it can be handy even on some advanced shots. I go into more detail on how to tame those toughies in Chapter 20, but an illustration of one of those possibilities now will show you how valuable the ghost-ball concept can be on complex shots.

In a lot of games, you're allowed to pocket a ball that you didn't hit first, as long as you made a legal hit on the ball that you *did* hit first. In 9-Ball, making the 9 wins the game, but you're required to hit the lowest-numbered ball on the table first. An opportunity arises when you notice that if you hit the cue ball into the 1, the cue ball bounces off toward the 1 ball and hits the 9 ball into a pocket, winning you the game. This shot is called a *carom* or *billiard*. (If the 1 went into the 9 ball instead of the cue ball, it would be called a combination.)

Now you need to figure out at what point you want to hit the 1 ball so that the cue ball bounces off it in the correct direction to hit the 9. Follow these steps:

1. Imagine the ghost ball placed against the 1 ball, but instead of using the intended path of the 1 ball, use the intended path of the cue ball after the two balls collide.

   If you draw a line between the center of the 1 ball and the center of the cue ball, the cue ball will go at a 90-degree angle to that line. (See Ewa's Second 90-Degree Rule in Chapter 15 for a more detailed explanation.)

2. Move your ghost ball around until the path that it will take is just the right one to sink the 9 ball.

You have used the ghost ball to establish the contact and aiming points on the 1 ball. Instead of basing it on the intended path of the 1 ball, however, you've based the positioning on the intended path of the cue ball after it hits the 1. Another job well done by a ball that doesn't exist!

Aiming at the Cushion

At times, you won't be aiming at a ball. Suppose that the game requires you to hit the 2 ball next, but the direct path is blocked, and the only way that you can get to it with your cue ball is to bounce your cue ball off a cushion first. You then have to aim at the cushion instead of a ball. The cushion is straight, so in this case, the contact point and aiming point are pretty much the same. (There's more to this concept, such as how hard you hit the ball, which affects the aiming point, but I'm saving that information for Chapter 20.)

I qualified the statement about the contact and aiming points ("pretty much the same") because the cue ball is still round, and if you hit the cushion at a sharp angle (closer to parallel with it, rather than straight into it), the contact point and aiming point do diverge. I recommend that you use the ghost ball again to help you visualize where on the cushion to aim. Sometimes, it helps to imagine the ghost ball moving from where the real ball is to where you estimate that you should hit the cushion. Freeze it in your mind, and draw an imaginary line from the center of the real cue ball through the center of the ghost cue ball. Continue the line until it touches the cushion. That's your aiming point.

Pocket Dictionary

Kick shots are when you hit the cue ball into a cushion so that it bounces off and hits the ball that you want to hit. You use this shot when the direct path is blocked.

These kinds of shots come up often in 9-Ball and Rotation, and occasionally in 8-Ball. Knowing how to use the ghost ball to aim can be a big help. It takes some practice, and you should read the section on *kick shots* (which is what these shots are called) before putting it all together. A simple little added element such as bouncing off a cushion is not at all as simple as it looks.

I'll tease you with an example: Hitting the ball into the cushion at a 45-degree angle doesn't mean that the ball will ricochet off at 45 degrees. You can exert a lot of control over the rebound angle when you make decisions about how to hit the cue ball.

Aiming to Cheat

Cheating the pocket is a perfectly legitimate thing to do; it's just an unfortunate phrase. What it means is that you hit the object ball toward one side of the pocket rather than into the center. As you see in the next illustration, a pool table's corner pocket is wide enough to accept two balls.

Pocket Dictionary

Cheating the pocket means hitting the object ball into one side of the pocket or the other, rather than dead-center.

There are a variety of pocket sizes. My home table is the one in the picture, and it has relatively tight (small) pockets. You'll see some pockets in social billiard clubs that are much wider (the owners know that patrons have more fun if they make more balls), and most home tables have wider pockets that can accept two balls and sill have lots of space left over. Cheating the pocket is easier on a table that has bigger pockets, of course, but it's done all the time (intentionally) on tough professional-level pockets like the ones in the picture.

On my home practice table, two balls (standard 2-inch-diameter Brunswick Centennial balls) fit snugly in the corner pocket. At billiard rooms or on standard home tables, you'll usually see pockets up to an inch wider. I use narrower pockets to tune my shotmaking to the toughest possible conditions—those frequently found in pro tournaments.

If you hit an object ball (OB) toward one side of the pocket, you strike it at a different angle than you would have if you'd aimed toward the other side of the pocket. The different angles of the hit mean that the cue ball, which bounced off the object ball when the two balls collided, will go in slightly different directions after the hit, just as the OB did. Both shots pocket the object ball.

To get closer to your next shot, you might prefer one path for the cue ball over the other and therefore will choose to cheat the pocket. At the beginning stages of learning the game, this concept won't be much of a concern; you'll just be trying to get the ball into the pocket any place it will fit. But as you gain control of your accuracy, you'll start to consider how to improve things, and cheating the pocket is one popular way.

As your aiming abilities improve, you can use dual ghost balls: one to help you aim the cue ball, and the other to determine where you want the object ball (OB) to go. Think of this concept as replacing the first ghost ball with the cue ball and then replacing the second ghost ball (located at the opening of the pocket) with the OB.

Ewa's Billiard Bits

The longer you play, the less frequently you will actually figure out where to aim. Experience will build up a catalog of shots in your head, and you'll hit the easiest ones without picking out a contact point or going through any of the rest of the process. The more experienced you become, the more this becomes the case. Sometimes, intuitive shooting can get out of hand, and you shouldn't intuitively aim at every shot. That's one reason why players miss difficult shots.

173

What's the Last Thing You Saw, Ma'am?

When you've picked out an aiming point and settled down on the shot, going through your warmup strokes, you should be flipping your eyes back and forth between the OB and the cue ball. Don't move your head. This technique gives you the relationship between the balls and connects them mentally. At this point, some players picture the shot successfully going in; others picture a tube from the object ball (OB) to the pocket and imagine that the tube is the only place where the ball can go. Most visualizers (and visualizing is a good thing to do) picture their shot before they get down on it. They examine the table, choose their shot, find their aiming point, and picture the ball being hit into the pocket. Only then do they get down to shoot. They may or may not visualize the shot again at this point, but I think that doing so is a good idea; it gets your brain on the right page.

Now you're looking back and forth, getting closer and closer to the time when you're going to make your final stroke and hit the ball. Do you look at the cue ball or the object ball at this point? Always look at the object ball. Your muscle memory and brain have already set up your stroke, you're sure that everything is in line, and you've decided how you're going to hit the cue ball. What you want to be concentrating on is the aiming point on (or very near) the cue ball. So that's the last thing you look at before you pull the trigger.

After you develop a good stroke, you can actually close your eyes just before you shoot and have just as successful a shot. Everything is locked in. But you close your eyes more to check your stroke than to check your aim, and in actual play, you should look at the aiming point on the object ball last.

The Least You Need to Know

➤ The aiming point and the contact point are different on every shot that's not straight into the pocket.

➤ If you don't know how to find the aiming point, you can miss the shot.

➤ You can find the contact and aiming points by using an imaginary ball, called the ghost ball.

➤ You can hit the object ball into one side of the pocket or the other; you don't have to hit it dead in the middle.

➤ The last thing that you should be looking at before you shoot is the object ball.

Chapter 14

Watch Your Speed

In This Chapter

➤ Why ball speed is important

➤ How to master the speed of your stroke

➤ Why a soft hit on the cue ball is usually better

➤ When a soft hit is dangerous

➤ The transfer of cue-ball speed to object-ball speed

Now that you know how to aim and, therefore, how to make a ball, you're probably eager to get on with the fancy stuff—the magic of billiards in which you hit a ball, and the cue ball startles everyone by coming back to you rather than following on. Or you may want to learn how to hit a combination shot, with one object ball going into a second object ball and the second one flying into the pocket. Well, I'm going to introduce you instead to the MOBD: the Mystic Order of Billiard Development.

Sure, if you want to hit the road and join the pro tour, the spectacular shots are all necessary. But they're nowhere near as important as learning to manipulate the cue ball simply by using speed control. Why do you want to manipulate the cue ball at all? Because if you can make a ball and get the cue ball to go to a place where you can

Pocket Dictionary

Position play is hitting the cue ball in such a way that after it pockets a ball, it goes to a position in which another ball can be pocketed, thereby extending your turn at the table.

easily make another ball, you can keep going until you've won the game. That's called *position play* or *playing shape*, and it's the next big leap in your game.

One of key elements in position play is controlling the speed of the cue ball. In Chapter 15, I start the fancy stuff. Right now, I need to give you a good understanding of one more basic point: speed control.

Speed is one of the easiest things in the world to describe, so I won't take a lot of time with it. What I'm going to do is tell you why it's important, how to use it, and how to develop control of the speed on your cue ball. So let's get on with it!

What Do *Hard* and *Easy* Mean?

Before I start talking about billiard-ball speed, I'm going to tell you what some of the terms that I'll be using mean in actual play. These aren't official definitions or anything like that, but they are meanings that are accepted by a lot of people, and they give you a good idea of what hitting the ball hard means, as opposed to hitting it soft.

Go to the table, and set up the cue ball as I have done in the following illustration. Hit the ball to the other end of the table (toward the camera and the nameplate on the table rail). When the ball stops close to that cushion, that's roughly what I mean by a *soft hit*.

This is the starting position that you'll use to determine the meaning of a hard, medium, and soft hit in billiards. You can also use this as a speed drill, as I explain in the text.

Shoot the shot again, this time with more power, making the cue ball hit the cushion close to the camera and come back to you. That's what I'll be calling a *medium hit*. It's the amount of power that you'll be using on more of your shots than any other. There could be games in which you don't use a medium hit at all, but in the scheme of things, I imagine that you'll hit 60 percent at this speed.

Shooting up the table hard enough so that the ball goes three table lengths and ends up near the camera end is what I'll be calling a *hard hit*. About 5 percent to 10 percent of your shots will be this hard, although in different games, the percentages will vary. These are very ballpark figures, and I'm trying to give you an idea of what I'm talking about when I say hard, medium, or soft hit.

Now the terms have some concrete meaning for you. And by the way, the three shots that I used to explain the three terms are a good way for you to practice your speed. Trying to end up tightly against one of the cushions forces you to learn exactly how hard to hit a ball to achieve a certain distance. When you're on the table playing, you'll have better control of the force that you use.

Cue Tips

Use the medium speed practice shot for determining the speed of your hit to measure the accuracy of your stroke. Freeze after you hit the ball. If it goes to the far cushion and comes straight back, and the center of the ball hits your cue tip, you'll know that your stroke was straight and your aim was true.

From the Tortoise to the Hare

Most people hit the ballstoo hard…because it's fun, frankly—sort of a "Let's see what happens!" thing, sure to produce some surprises. What it won't produce, however, is a string of winning games. As your cue-ball speed goes up, your accuracy goes down. So one of the simplest things that you can do to improve your play right from the start is to hit the balls with less speed (power).

As you develop your stroke, you'll find that the ball seems to go farther at the same speed than it did when you were hitting it roughly. It's an optical illusion. A good stroke is so smooth that it doesn't look like the player is hitting the balls at the speed he or she is actually using.

In billiard games, one of the main goals is to get control of the balls on the table. This control starts with the cue ball, which moves on every shot to the balls that it hits. You sometimes even want to exert control over balls that you won't have to hit for a while.

In 9-Ball, in which you hit the balls in numerical order, you may face a layout where the 8 ball and 9 ball are *tied up*—that is, touching in a way that neither of them can be shot into a pocket. Even when you're shooting the 1 or 2 ball, you may want to send the cue ball into the 8 and 9 so that it breaks them loose and separates them. Then, when you get through with the other balls, you can shoot them without a problem. In that way, you can be said to be controlling the position of the 8 and 9 ball.

Because control of the balls is so important, hitting the balls as softly as possible and still achieving the desired result (usually, that's to pocket a ball) is the best approach. Hitting the balls hard usually puts them out of control.

Pocket Speed

If you've watched billiards on ESPN or one of the other networks, you may have heard the commentators say something like "He (or she) shot that with *pocket speed.*" *Pocket speed* is hitting the object ball just hard enough for the ball to reach the pocket and drop in. Pocket speed is used for a few reasons:

➤ You have more control on a softer hit.

➤ A ball can be hit hard enough to bounce back out of the pocket—especially if the pockets were not installed correctly or are of poor design.

➤ If the object ball was on the cushion, and the player hit it down the cushion into a corner pocket, he ran the risk of mis-hitting the ball slightly and driving it into the cushion just a tad. Because the cushion is made of rubber, the ball would bounce off the cushion slightly, which would be enough to ruin the approach angle. The ball would hit the inside of the cushion opening and dance back and forth across the jaws of the pocket in a pinball-like motion without ever dropping into the pocket.

All of the preceding are good reasons to use pocket speed when you make a ball.

I mentioned position play earlier, and that is one good reason *not* to use pocket speed. Sometimes, you have to get the cue ball to travel a good distance after it pockets the object ball, and to do that, you have to hit it firmly, so you can't use pocket speed. The choice is made for you. But if you can get the cue ball to go where you want it to go for your next shot by pocketing the current shot either hard or soft, choose soft.

In Straight Pool, 8-Ball, and One-Pocket, you'll discover that shooting soft goes with the nature of the game. In 9-Ball, there's a lot of variety, but soft shots still dominate. When you see the cue ball travel a long distance—say, hitting two or three cushions as it travels almost all

Pocket Dictionary

Pocket speed is hitting the object ball just hard enough for the ball to make it into the pocket.

Ewa's Billiard Bits

An enterprising promoter in England first staged a *speed pool* competition, and the idea is slowly catching on elsewhere. The idea is to rack all 15 balls; set a stopwatch; and then see how fast you can break the rack and pocket all the balls, using only legal hits. The records don't mean much at the moment, because they've been done on different-size tables with different-size balls and even different rules. So although speed pool is still a novelty event, it's a lot of fun to watch—and try!

the way around the table—you'll probably also notice that the ball that was pocketed was hit very thinly. A thin hit transfers very little energy to the object ball so the cue ball didn't need to be hit hard to cover a lot of distance. It's also likely that sidespin was used, but that topic is a little advanced. You'll have to wait until Chapter 16 to find out how sidespin affects the way that a cue ball travels.

Speed Transfer

Line up your cue, the cue ball, and an object ball. Put the balls about a foot apart. Hit the cue ball dead-center with the cue tip and drive it into an object ball. This shot is called a *straight-in shot*. What you saw happen was a complete transfer of energy. The cue ball had X amount of energy, but when it struck the object ball, it stopped dead, and the OB scooted away with X amount of energy. (If you place the balls farther apart, this won't work unless you add another element, called backspin or draw, which I tell you about in Chapter 15.) Within reason, you can hit the cue ball at medium, hard, or soft speed, and it will still stop dead on a straight-in shot.

Set up the balls the same distance apart, but this time, just skim the object ball with the cue ball. The OB moves over a couple of inches when it's contacted, and the cue ball goes on its way almost unaffected. Very little energy was transferred, of course.

Now hit a half-ball shot (in which you aim the center of the cue ball at the edge of the object ball), and roughly half the energy is transferred.

As you get more advanced in your technique—and that's going to happen in just a couple of pages, so look out!—you'll be able to add to this shot a few other factors that will change the dynamics considerably. But this example shows transfer of energy in its simplest form.

By thinking about this energy transfer before you shoot a shot, and by applying the speeds that you learned earlier in this chapter, you'll be able to mentally compute how far both the object ball and the cue ball will travel after they make contact. What's neat about that ability is the fact that you'll be able to alter your speed to make the balls go only as far as you want them to go. That control includes making the cue ball travel to a point where you have a good shot on the next ball that you want to play.

Slow—Curves Ahead

In a perfect world, a ball would always roll straight. But we don't live in a perfect world, and we have to figure out how to overcome imperfections. On a billiard table, new cloth can *pill*, as I told you in an earlier chapter (Chapter 8). *Pilling* is the formation of tiny balls of cloth material, and it happens with some types of cloth more than others.

At the other end of the wear scale, an old cloth will have areas that are worn more than other areas. One area that's likely to show extra wear is around the rack, where the balls are guaranteed to be in every game. Cloth this worn will be uneven. In the middle era of a cloth's life, there will be minute build-ups of chalk dust unevenly spread under the cloth, on top of the slate. Vacuuming the cloth regularly eliminates most of the buildup, but not all of it.

Finally, balls will veer from a straight line if the table settles unevenly. A pocket (or even an entire side) can be just a tad higher or lower than the rest of the table.

Ewa's Billiard Bits

Mark Twain, who was a great billiard fan all his life, played mostly on his home table. (When he hired his butler, the only qualification was that the man be a good billiard player. In a short story, Twain wrote that in the Old West, he ran into a table that was a horror, but he liked it because the true test of a skilled player was to be able to conquer all conditions.

All these conditions can cause a ball to roll off its path if it's moving too slowly—the single downside of a soft hit. Under perfect conditions, you can hit the ball as soft as you like and not fear that it will deviate from a straight line. But real conditions mean that untrue rolls will happen on some tables at some times. Experienced players watch for roll-offs, both when they're shooting and when their opponents are shooting, so they can adjust their strokes to overcome any imperfections in the playing area.

The way to overcome the problem is simple: hit the ball a little harder in that area. A ball hit at medium speed won't roll off unless the table looks like a topographical map of the Rockies. But no matter how hard you hit the ball, it will gradually become a slow roller, subject to imperfections. Keeping your home table clean and covered in nice cloth, and playing at commercial billiard rooms that take good care of their equipment, are both well worth the effort.

The Least You Need to Know

➤ Master the speed of your stroke, and you can move the cue ball in position to make the next ball.

➤ Choose the soft hit over the hard hit if either will do the job.

➤ Controlling the balls gives you a better opportunity to win.

➤ A soft hit gives you more control of the balls.

➤ A soft hit can roll off-line on some areas of some tables.

➤ The speed of the cue ball transfers 100 percent to the object ball when you hit it in a straight line.

Chapter 15

Hit 'Em High, Hit 'Em Low

In This Chapter

➤ Why hitting the cue ball in the center is your best shot

➤ Ewa's Second 90-Degree Rule of Billiards

➤ Predicting the path of the cue ball

➤ How to follow the object ball with the cue ball

➤ How to make the cue ball come back to you after it hits the object ball

➤ Using draw and follow to position the cue ball for the next shot

Now we're going to get into some of the fancy stuff— still in the area of fundamentals, though. I'm going to tell you how to establish some control of the cue ball after it leaves your cue tip. That control will force the ball to do certain things that are different from what would happen if you'd just hit it. These things do look a little fancy, but they're not showoff things. They're very practical, and knowing how to do them will elevate your abilities to a new level that's even more fun than before. Dare I call them "Fancy Fundamentals"?

By making the cue ball spin when you hit it, you'll cause it to move differently than it would if it were just rolling naturally. By hitting it at different speeds and with different amounts of spin, you determine *where* that different behavior takes place. Some of that behavior is even transferred to the first object ball that the cue ball strikes, and then that ball behaves differently than it would have if you'd just rolled the cue ball into it. Intriguing? I hope so, because it's another part of the real fun of pool.

After you get past the enjoyment of being able to stand in a professional-looking stance, after you experience the feeling of confidence when you make a smooth and level stroke, and after you've had the thrill of knowing how to aim and pocket balls, you'll move to a whole new level of pleasure. You'll take control of the table and be able to do things that the vast majority of recreational players don't know how to do.

People with good hand–eye coordination take to billiards naturally, and they'll quickly be able to pocket balls. If they play a lot of sports—especially ball-and-stick sports such as golf, tennis, baseball, lacrosse, and table tennis—they'll be able to transfer much of that knowledge and experience to the pool table. They'll miss the tough shots, or the ones in which the difference between the aiming point and the contact point is substantial, but if they put in enough time playing billiards, their memories of missing will help them correct some of those shots. But if they haven't been exposed to the material in this book, it will be tougher for them than for you after a certain point.

If you're one of the people who has experience in those other sports, you've probably progressed faster than the average player so far. But now you're going to play with the big boys and girls. This is the beginning of real pool—and real enjoyment.

Getting Centered

The reference point for all the spin shots in this chapter and Chapter 16 is the center ball hit (no spin). Hitting the cue ball exactly in the center is tougher than it looks, but if you have your front-grip hand at the proper level, and if all the rest of the elements are what I taught you in previous chapters, you'll be able to do it with a little practice. A smooth and level stroke, a solid stance, a solid bridge hand, and a confident delivery are the keys to this shot (and every other shot).

There are two easy ways to see whether you actually are hitting the cue ball in the center. Find the symbol on the cue ball (a tiny red circle, a tiny blue dot, or so on), and turn it so that it is in the center of the ball—that is, when the ball is on the table and you're down on the shot, the symbol is an equal distance from the right and left side, and from the top and bottom of the ball. Now chalk up and hit it softly. Retrieve the ball and look for a chalk mark circling the symbol. If the mark is off-center, wipe the cue ball and try again.

The second way is to use a striped ball as a surrogate cue ball. Place the ball on the table with the stripe horizontal to the table surface. Use a medium stroke. It should slide for a few inches before it catches on the cloth and begins rolling. If you hit the ball off-center (high, low, left, right, or any combination of those), the stripe will not stay horizontal, but will wobble in the first few inches while the ball is sliding. If the stripe rolls neatly from bottom to top, you hit it perfectly. If it turns into a swirling mess, you were off the target.

Use a striped ball as a substitute for the cue ball to determine whether you are hitting the ball in the center, as described in the text.

The center ball hit is a reference point for all other hits. Try to use it exclusively during your first few months of play, so that you get used to how the cue ball acts when no spin is applied. You just saw that the ball slides for a fraction of a second before it catches and starts to roll. The point at which it catches is determined by the newness of the cloth (new cloth lets it slide farther), the cleanliness of the cloth (a clean cloth offers less friction), and how hard you hit the ball (the harder the hit, the longer the slide). This is important, because a ball sliding into an object ball (or cushion) behaves in a way that is different from the behavior of a ball that is rolling. I'll get into that later in this chapter, in the section "Drawing a Ball," when I show you the stop shot.

The second reason why you should favor the center ball hit as often as possible is that a cue ball hit in the center, by the cue tip, behaves pretty much as you would expect a ball to behave. If you hit it off-center, odd things start happening. Odd things can be good if you can predict and control them, but you should use them only when necessary. So stay with the center ball hit whenever you can.

A center ball hit assures you that the cue ball will bounce off the object ball at a predictable 90-degree angle. This piece of knowledge is so vital that I'm going to call it *Ewa's Second 90-Degree Rule of Billiards*. (The first 90-Degree Rule, covered in Chapter 11, is to have your back forearm at a 90-degree angle to the cue when the cue tip is almost touching the ball.) The second rule tells you where

Scratch!

Every now and then, an object ball skids for a couple of inches before it catches and rolls. This skid can throw off the shot and make you miss a close one. No one knows for sure why an object ball skids, but guesses range from static electricity to imperfections in materials.

the cue ball is going to go if you don't do anything to alter its path. Although altering the cue ball's path is what this chapter and Chapter 16 are all about, you first have to know what its unaltered path will be. That's the 90-Degree Rule. I gave you a little teaser on it in Chapter 13 and promised a fuller, but still-easy-to-understand explanation here.

Put a cue ball and an object ball together, as they'd be at the moment of collision in a shot. Draw an imaginary line from the center of one to the center of the other. Then, where the balls meet, draw another imaginary line at a 90-degree angle to the first, bisecting it. If you remember your high-school plane geometry, you'll recall that that line is called a *tangent line*. The cue ball goes along that line, either to the right or left, when the balls collide. The contact point is always where the 90 degrees starts, regardless of the angle from which you approach the object ball. Just clip the side, and the 90 degrees still are measured from the contact point.

I told you how this phenomenon can be useful in a game situation in an example in Chapter 13. You can make the cue ball hit the 1 ball, and then have the cue ball go sink the 9 ball and win the game. That's called a *carom* or *billiard* shot (see Chapter 20 for more of an explanation on using a carom shot). You figure it out by knowing the Second 90-Degree Rule of Billiards. As long as the cue ball isn't spinning in some unnatural fashion, the rule is rock-solid.

Now you're going to build on that rule by breaking it. Your reference point is the center ball hit. When you hit the cue ball above or below center, you can make the cue ball deviate from the 90-degree line. Sometimes, you need to do that to get the cue ball to the next object ball.

Picture a crosshair, like you'd see in a telescopic sight on a rifle. The circle is the cue ball. There are two lines: one splitting the ball vertically and the other splitting it horizontally. Where the lines cross is dead-center. The up and down line is the *vertical axis*, and the line from left to right is the *horizontal axis*.

I'll be talking about where on the cue ball you make contact with the cue tip by using those terms. In this chapter, I'm going to tackle the easiest hits: the ones on the vertical axis. Striking the cue ball anywhere along the vertical axis produces specific ball behavior, but it does not drive the cue ball off the straight path to the object ball. Hitting the cue ball to the right or left of center,

Cue Tips

Develop your own reference shot. It should be a center ball hit, medium speed, using the same cue all the time, if possible. Repeat it until your muscles have memorized the feeling. With that foundation, you always have a point to which to return if things start going awry.

Pocket Dictionary

A *tangent line*, in billiards, is a straight line coming out from a point (the contact point) on the edge of a circle. The line is at a 90-degree angle to the circle's radius and is the path that the cue ball follows after it hits the contact point of the object ball.

however, does drive the cue ball off the straight path, and it can very easily cause you to miss the shot even though you aimed correctly.

In Chapter 16, I'll talk about hitting the cue ball on the horizontal axis (to the left or right of center). The reason why I'm splitting the discussion into two chapters is that the two types of hits are very different.

I'll introduce you to cue-ball spin by starting with non-center ball hits on the vertical axis: the "safe" zone.

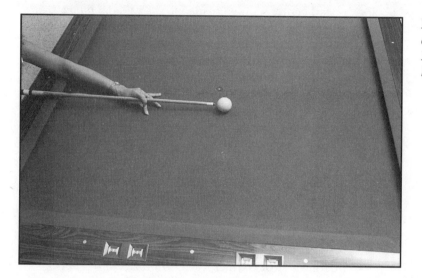

Ewa gets ready to hit the cue ball dead-center. Notice the bridge and the levelness of the cue.

By the way, when very knowledgeable players talk about a *center ball hit*, they can just as easily mean a hit anywhere on the vertical line as they do a hit that's actually dead-center on the cue ball. You'll hear an instructor, or an expert commentator on television, say this from time to time, and it can throw you off a little. One time, the cue ball hits the object ball and then follows it after the hit; the next time, the cue ball hits the object ball and then returns toward the shooter. The commentator could call both types of hits center ball hits. In this case, the meaning is a hit anywhere on the *vertical* center line (axis).

There's a horizontal center line, too, as I showed you when I used the example of the crosshairs on a rifle scope earlier in this section, but striking the cue ball on that line is somehow not considered to be a center ball hit. The better instructors and house pros speak a little more carefully, saying something like "That was a high center ball hit" or "a low center ball hit." But I thought I'd warn you about how this term is used, so that somebody won't accidentally confuse you later.

Are You Following Me?

The reason why you may want to strike the cue ball above or below dead center is that doing so makes the cue ball go off its natural path after it strikes an object ball (or cushion). If the natural path doesn't take you to a place on the table where you can pocket another ball, you need to alter that path. Hitting the cue ball above or below center does the job. All you have to do is know how that works, so that you can figure out how to adjust the variables that affect the path of the ball.

When you hit the cue ball above dead center, you've made what's called a *follow shot* (sometimes called *hitting it high*, *using high English*, or even *using a high ball*). You've run into this situation before. One action may have a lot of words to describe it, or many things are all described by the same word (*rack*, for example). In a way, this is kind of one of the in things about billiards. The sport has a language all it's own, as many sports do, and after you get into the game, you can bandy those words around and talk pool with the best of them. At the beginning, the terms complicate things and exclude the uninitiated (by design?), and my goal is to try to simplify those terms. Still, I don't want to leave you in a position where you won't know what people are talking about when they talk billiards.

Pocket Dictionary

Hitting the cue ball above center so that it spins forward faster than it's rolling forward is called a *follow*.

Ewa's Billiard Bits

When a top player shoots a power follow shot, watch closely. The cue ball will hit the object ball, stop dead for a fraction of a second, hop once as the ball rebounds, and then catch the cloth and rocket off. This jumble of direction changes take place in the blink of an eye.

This book is both simple and complete, so I'll tell you all the alternative definitions, such as the various ways to describe hitting a cue ball above dead center, and then settle on the most common one (or two) to explain what's going on.

The follow shot is much easier than the *draw shot* (hitting the cue ball on the vertical axis *below* center), and maybe for that reason, it's undervalued by too many players. The shot seems to be too simple to bother practicing. But it can do magical and useful things, so don't pass it by. Besides, because it's the easiest off-center hit in billiards, the follow shot is a great place to start learning how to spin the cue ball.

Picture the cue ball as a globe. Follow spin occurs any time you strike the cue ball above the equator—somewhere around Des Moines, say. I'm going to stick with the vertical axis in this chapter, because a hit anywhere else above the ball's equator gets a little complicated for now.

What happens when you do this, and why would you want to do it? First, the cue ball spins faster than it would have if you'd just rolled it along the cloth. This spin doesn't have much effect until the ball contacts something—usually, the object ball. You found out in Chapter 14 that all the energy is transferred to an object ball if the cue ball hits it full in the face (straight on). The cue ball stops dead, and the object ball travels forward at the previous speed of the cue ball.

But with follow, something else happens. The cue ball is still spinning forward and grabs the cloth, taking off after the object ball. Extreme follow is a pretty weird sight. The cue ball hits the weight of the object ball, the object goes forward, the cue ball pauses to grab the cloth, and then the object ball scoots off after it like a cartoon cop car going after the bad guys. That's why the shot is called *follow*.

How far does the cue ball travel after striking the object ball? In Chapter 14, I showed you that the different percentages of power and speed transferred to the object ball depend on how much of the object ball was hit by the cue ball. If the cue ball just skims the OB (object ball), hardly any energy was transferred. In a straight-on collision, however, all the energy is transferred. When you add follow spin to the cue ball, you're adding more energy, so this extra energy comes into effect even on a full hit.

More important are the amount of spin that you put on the cue ball and how hard you hit the cue ball. A lot of spin, not surprisingly, makes the cue ball go farther after the collision. A harder hit on the cue ball means more energy in the spin, which also makes the ball go farther.

Following are the three factors that determine how far a cue ball with follow spin goes after contacting the OB:

➤ How hard you hit the cue ball (how much energy you supplied)

➤ How high you hit the cue ball (how much spin you applied)

➤ How much energy was transferred to the OB (how full you hit the OB)

Hit the cue ball higher and harder, and it goes farther. You could probably sit down and calculate the amount of energy transferred in a shot with a 45-degree intended path for the object ball, hit with so many grams of force, with the cue tip striking the cue ball so many millimeters above center, and so on. Actually, that's been done. Advanced math and physics majors have written papers on the subject, and scientists have written books. But I think that all you need to know—and all I need to know—is why and how. You know that you can use the follow shot to make more balls and have more fun, and that's what the sport's all about.

You'll use the follow shot to get the cue ball to go to a place on the table where you have another shot (this is called *position play*, remember). You do so by hitting the cue ball above center on the vertical axis. The distance that the cue ball goes is changed by how high above center you hit the cue ball, by how hard you hit the cue ball, and by how much of the object ball is hit by the cue ball.

Cue Tips

Remember to chalk your tip before each shot. Chalking is more important than ever before when you're hitting the ball off-center.

An easy way of picturing where the cue ball will go is to think back to the Second 90-Degree Rule. With a center ball hit, the cue ball bounces off the object ball along the 90-degree line. With follow spin, the cue ball goes over the line in a compromise between 90 degrees and straight. With draw (reverse spin), as you see in the following section, the cue ball comes back some, to the closer side of the 90-degree line. The amount of follow (how high up you hit the cue ball) determines how much away from the 90-degree line the cue ball goes.

One final note about the follow shot, which concerns your bridge. Check out the following illustration, and refer to the chapter on making the front-hand bridge (Chapter 11), and you'll see where raising and lowering your bridge comes into play.

Elevate your front-hand bridge for a follow shot by bringing your fingertips toward the palm or heel of your hand. That action raises the front of the cue. Keep the cue level, and chalk up before each shot.

You raise the bridge simply by pulling your fingertips toward your palm. On the follow shot, you raise your bridge until the cue tip is as high as you want it to be. The higher you go, the more follow spin you put on the cue ball. You can go too high, of course, in which case the cue tip will just skip off the top of the ball, causing a mis-hit and a loss of turn at the table. How high you can go depends on your skill level, and in the beginning, I suggest that you stop halfway up from the center of the cue ball. Later, when you get more experience, you can edge it up a little from there.

For a better visual guide, use a striped ball as a surrogate cue ball, placing the stripe horizontally. You can split the top edge of the stripe with your cue tip (half the tip above, half below), and that's about as high as you want to go. Your bridge determines how high the striking point will be. Always keep the cue as level as possible; that gives you a better chance of a good, clean hit.

Drawing a Ball

I remember when I was first learning to play and saw my first draw shot. It dazzled me, but I found out quickly that it would also cause me a lot of grief. No other shot, in any sport, has been more difficult for me to master (except perhaps the severe downhill chip shot in golf). I wish there were some other way to learn this shot, but you're simply going to have to pay your dues with hours at the table before you can effectively add the shot to your quiver.

The effort is worth your while, though The draw shot is not only very useful, but also looks incredibly flashy. You shoot the cue ball forward, it hits the object ball, and then it comes back to you—like your kitten that got left behind at your vacation home and showed up at your door three months later. Only faster.

The draw shot is common in billiards, and it's really very simple. You just hit the ball below dead center. When given an option, the majority of good players hit the ball low rather than use right or left spin (called English; see Chapter 16). The shot gives you a strong feeling of control, and that's not small potatoes in a game that (after you get some experience under your belt) is more mental than it is physical.

The "Why" of hitting the cue ball low is the same as the reason for hitting it high: to make it go to a place where you can make another ball. Sometimes, follow spin won't get you there, so draw is the next option that you should consider. Using a lot of follow shots looks graceful, because the ball rolls smoothly around the table and into position. But using a draw shot looks powerful, because you're forcing the ball to move opposite it's natural direction (you hit it forward, but it comes back) and making it go where you want it to go. Looks aside, there are situations in which the follow shot bumps into balls and doesn't get the cue ball where you want it. A draw shot might to the trick.

The mechanics of a draw shot are basically the same as those of a follow shot. You lower your bridge instead of raise it, and that's the only real difference. Why, then, is this shot so difficult to master? If you hit a follow shot a little to the right or left of the vertical axis, the cue ball really doesn't veer very much off a straight line. If you do the same with a draw shot, however, the cue ball comes back to your right or left, and that makes a big difference in where it ends up. So the draw shot has to be struck more accurately than the follow shot.

Pocket Dictionary

A *draw shot* is striking the cue ball below center so that it spins backward as it goes forward and returns to you after striking the object ball.

Scratch!

After you master the draw and follow strokes, you'll find that they're so much fun, you'll tend to overuse them. The shots look cool and feel good, but try to restrict their use to times when a center ball hit won't accomplish the same thing.

But the big reason why the shot is so tough is that you have to have an excellent stroke and very good follow-through before the ball will spin backward. Be off too much, and you'll scoop under the ball and send it up in the air. Fail to accelerate through the ball with your stroke, and there won't be much reverse spin on the cue ball. Also, it's tougher to get your cue close to level. When you dip the tip to hit the cue ball below center, you usually can't lower the butt of the cue to match; the rail and cushion prevent you from doing that. Now you don't have a level cue, and that adds to the difficulty.

Finally, the draw stroke seems to be especially sensitive to the smoothness and timing of your stroke. If you haven't developed a really good stroke yet, drawing the cue ball will be difficult. Getting to the point at which you can control the draw so that the ball comes back exactly as far as you want it to takes most players many, many weeks of practice to achieve. All in all, it's a very simple but very difficult shot.

If you keep trying to draw the cue ball, but it just hits the OB and sits there (a common experience, so don't feel bad), go over the items in the following checklist:

- ❏ Did you actually hit the cue ball as low as you thought?
- ❏ Did you use a long stroke and complete follow-through?
- ❏ Did you make cue-tip contact with the cue ball when the cue was at the peak of its acceleration?
- ❏ Did you shoot the cue ball with enough speed?
- ❏ Did you chalk up?

Lower your bridge, and try to keep your cue as level as possible as you strike the cue ball below center. A smooth stroke, acceleration into the ball, and complete follow-through are vital to a successful draw shot.

To see how much the cue ball is spinning backward, you could set up the cue ball and an object ball and then take a few shots. I like using the striped ball without a cue ball at first. Set the stripe horizontally again, and hit it so that your tip is centered on the lower edge of the stripe—about halfway down from center ball. Hit the ball gently, and watch the stripe. The ball skids for a brief moment; then the ball starts rotating as though it were rolling toward you instead of away. As the resistance of the cloth gains control, the reverse spin decreases, the ball slides without rolling for a moment, and then the ball starts rolling top over bottom, like normal. The harder you hit the ball, the more distance it covers in each phase. The lower you hit it, the faster it spins backward. The striped ball can give you all that information.

That information is useful for another shot, called the *stop shot*. The stop shot is really just a draw shot, timed so that the cue ball makes contact with the object ball while the cue ball is in its sliding phase. The reason why this shot is so useful is that you can hit the ball fairly hard, but when the balls collide, the cue ball stops dead, because it has no rolling forward spin. Remember that I told you that balls can roll off line if the table is imperfect in some way and the ball is hit very softly (or even if it is hit firmly but hits the imperfection in the table at the end of its roll)? A stop shot allows you to use a firm hit on an area of the table where a rolloff is likely.

You may want to be able to stop the cue ball dead on contact on many other occasions during a game—so many occasions that the draw shot, when used for this purpose, has its own name: the stop shot.

Cue Tips

The ease with which you can play a follow or draw shot depends a great deal on the equipment. Slippery cloth, very low humidity, and polished balls all make it tougher.

Pocket Dictionary

A *stop shot* is when the cue ball hits the object ball and stops dead.

Many novice players say they are able to draw the cue ball when it and the OB are fairly close together, but when the balls are a few feet apart, the cue ball simply hits the object ball and stops dead (an unintentional stop shot). Worse, the cue ball makes contact and then follows the object ball straight into the pocket—cozy, but not a good thing. If this happens to you, the only explanation is that the cue ball was no longer spinning in reverse when it struck the OB (object ball); it was sliding or rolling forward.

This situation is where the striped ball comes in handy. Don't worry about an OB; just shoot the striped ball the length of the table, using a low hit. The ball will slide (scoot) for less than a second and then spin backward (bottom over top) as it moves forward down the table. At some point, depending on how hard you hit it, how well you hit it, and how low you hit it, the ball will stop spinning, slide for a moment, change gears, and then start rolling forward top over bottom. When the reverse spin is gone, the ball no longer draws back when it hits an object ball. If the OB is closer to the cue ball, the cue ball doesn't have time to lose its reverse spin.

As you get better at stroking the draw shot, you'll be able to put it into effect on object balls that are farther and farther away. A top player can shoot the cue ball from one end of the table to an object ball at the far end and still have the cue ball spinning backward when it and the OB collide.

The draw shot is a real divider between people who have developed a stroke and those who haven't. Then again, most people who play recreationally have no idea what it means to have a good stroke. You've got a big advantage over them, and the draw shot will probably come quicker to you than it does to most people. If you practiced and put into place everything that I told you about your stance, grip, and swing, it wouldn't surprise me if you wind up shooting a successful draw shot after only a few weeks of practice, rather than after a few years, like most folks.

Passing It On

A little of the draw effect is passed on to the object ball, especially if it's hit full. Not enough follow seems to be passed on to have much of an effect. The interesting thing about the spin that's passed from the cue ball to the object ball is that it reverses itself. It's the gear effect. You've seen two gears mesh, and when one spins clockwise, it makes the other spin counterclockwise. Turn those gears vertically, and you'll have a good idea of what happens when a cue ball with draw or follow spin hits an object ball. Billiard balls are smooth, of course, so the cue ball doesn't engage the object ball the way that the first gear engages the second gear, but there is a mild gear effect between spinning balls.

The gear effect on a draw shot isn't used a lot, because the effect is modest, but I'll give you an example of when it could come into play. Imagine that two balls are touching each other, and the cue ball is lined up with them. Hitting the first ball transfers energy through the first ball to the second ball, which takes off. The first object ball had equal weights on both sides, so it didn't have any place to go and normally would just sit there. (This information alone is useful for predicting ball behavior when the balls are in line and touching.)

Ewa's Billiard Bits

When the weight of balls on either side of an object ball is equal, energy passes through them. Line up two balls, and hit the cue ball into the first. The second ball takes off, but the first doesn't move. Line up three balls, and the third leaves, but the first and second stay where they were before they were hit.

If you hit the cue ball with draw, however, and it's spinning backward when it hits the first of the two object balls, some of that spin is transferred to the first ball. When the second ball gets out of the way, the first ball rolls forward a little. How far it rolls depends on how much reverse spin you put on the cue ball. This opportunity isn't going to arise too often, of course, but when it does, you'll understand what happens when spinning balls interact, and you can play the shot according to the result that you desire.

This transference of spin and the gear effect come up much more often on shots that use sidespin (English), as I tell you in Chapter 16. If you're reading the chapters in order, the concept will already be familiar to you when you get there.

Following and Drawing with Variables

Keep using the striped ball in place of the cue ball; it'll give you a lot of information about what you're actually doing (as opposed to what you may *think* you're doing) and what the cue ball is doing. If you mentally divide the vertical axis into six equal parts, for example, you'll have five points on the line (see the following illustration). The center point is the center of the ball. Point A is a lot of follow spin, Point B is a little follow, Point C is the center ball hit, Point D is a little draw, and Point E is a lot of draw.

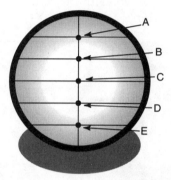

Hitting the cue ball at Point A gives it a lot of follow spin. Point B gives it modest topspin. Point C is the no-spin center ball. D is moderate draw (reverse spin), and Point E is a power draw shot. A and E can be risky; you could miscue.

Hit some balls full in the face while striking your cue ball (or striped substitute cue ball) at these different points. You'll learn what *a lot* of follow and draw are and what *a little* is. Be sure to use the same stroke and same cue-stick speed for all your shots.

Go through the experiment again, but this time, hit the ball harder. Then hit the ball softer. You'll develop a feel for what kind of stroke, combined with what degree of spin, produces what result. Practice enough, and the shots become yours. You'll be able to control the cue ball in a variety of situations, allowing you to make a ball and on the same shot make the cue ball go where the next ball is.

The final variation that you should understand is changing the distance between the cue ball and the object ball. Remember that whether you hit the cue ball with follow (topspin) or draw (bottom, reversing spin), the spin doesn't stay on the ball forever; the friction of the cloth eventually overcomes it. How far does the cue ball have to be from the object ball before you have no more spin left on the cue ball? Try it and find out, varying the degree of spin that you put on the ball (Points A, B, D, and E in the preceding illustration) and using different cue-ball speeds. I can't give you solid figures, because the answer depends on the quality of your stroke, and because I don't know how much you've been practicing what you learned in Chapter 12.

As a general rule, it's best to keep things as standardized as possible. A medium stroke of a center ball hit should be the most common thing that you do; it's the shot that has the fewest side effects. But if that shot doesn't do the job—if it doesn't get the cue ball to a place where you can pocket the next ball—you'll have to add one of the variables. Make the cue ball go farther after the collision with the object ball, or make it come back to you. Knowing how to do those things opens up many places on the pool table that you couldn't reach with a center ball hit.

The Half Step

So far, I've dealt with hitting the object ball (OB) full in the face with the cue ball. You can call that a *full hit* or *straight shot*. I've also talked about how skimming the OB takes very little speed off the cue ball. Now I'll go halfway between those concepts and briefly describe a *half-ball hit*, which is when you aim the center of the cue ball at the edge of the OB (see the following illustration).

The half-ball hit. Aim the center of the cue ball at the edge of the object ball.

I'm showing you this shot just so you'll understand that when you don't hit the OB full or just skim it, but hit it somewhere between, you have two forces working on the cue ball at the same time. Not too many shots are at one extreme or the other; most are partial hits, and the halfway point is the perfect example. It's an easily repeatable shot; keep setting the balls up, and keep aiming the center of the cue ball at the edge of the object ball, and you have exactly the same shot over and over.

I'll use a draw shot as an example. In a full hit, the cue ball stops dead; then draw (reverse spin) takes over completely. But when you just barely skim the ball, draw has very little effect, because the cue ball doesn't run into an obstacle. On a half-ball hit, the reaction of the cue ball is half-and-half—two opposing forces working at the same time. The cue ball ricochets off the OB, but if you have enough reverse spin on it, the spin grabs the cloth as well.

In the following illustration, the cue ball is hitting the right half of the object ball. After the collision, the cue ball wants to go forward and, because of the backspin, come back. The result is that it curves to the side, thereby giving you access to a whole new area of the table for positioning the cue ball for the next shot. Obviously, if you have to use a half-ball hit to pocket the object ball, you can hit the cue ball anywhere on the vertical axis. Where on that axis the ball is hit doesn't affect where the OB ball goes, but it greatly affects where the cue ball goes after the collision.

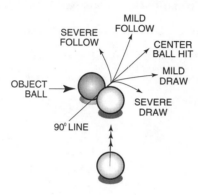

The possibilities of a half-ball hit. The 90-degree line goes through the contact point. The cue ball, hit high goes in the direction of the arrow labeled Severe Follow. This shows that you can hit the object ball in one direction but make the cue ball go in a variety of directions just by choosing where you hit the cue ball with the cue tip.

Learning Draw and Follow

I suggest that you tackle the draw and follow shots by learning what happens to the cue ball first. Use the striped ball in place of the cue ball, and don't bother with an object ball. After you see what's going on by hitting it at various heights and by varying the hardness (speed) of your hit, place an object ball on the table and repeat the process, using a straight, full hit. Only after you master that technique should you move on to the half-ball hit.

Finally, try a quarter-ball hit, a three-quarter hit, a one-third hit, and so on. By that time, you'll have a real feel for draw and follow, and you'll be able to predict where the cue ball will go. After you can predict those things, you'll be able to choose among all the available options for putting the cue ball where you want it to be after you pocket the object ball.

The Least You Need to Know

➤ Use a center ball hit whenever possible.

➤ With a center ball hit, the cue ball bounces off the object ball at a 90-degree angle.

➤ Hitting the cue ball high makes it follow the object ball after the two balls collide.

➤ Hitting the cue ball low makes it come back to you after it hits the object ball.

➤ High and low hits are used to position the cue ball for the next shot.

➤ You can predict the path of the cue ball after it hits the object ball.

English, Anyone?

In This Chapter

➤ How English works

➤ Overcoming missed shots when using English

➤ The positive side of English

➤ The gear effect in billiards

➤ Killing the cue ball

➤ Combining draw or follow with right or left English

➤ The safe zone for English

English was a mystery to me at first. Not the language (although some of the rules *are* pretty strange), but English in billiards. When I hit the cue ball to the left or right of center (doing so applies *sidespin*, commonly called *English*, to the ball), I would frequently miss the shot, especially if I were trying a long shot. And I wasn't alone by any means. Using English complicates both aiming and the behavior of the cue ball, and I don't even start teaching the average student how to apply English until he's reached the point where he can pocket 10 to 15 balls consecutively.

In most cases, a player can position the cue ball for the next shot by sticking to shots on the vertical axis of the cue ball. Even when a student learns sidespin/English, it's better to hit high, center, or low if one of those will do the job.

But in some situations, you have to go to the side of the cue ball, making it spin like a top, to make it go where you want it to go—in other words, to achieve good position. For that reason, you have to know how English works, as well as the pitfalls involved and how to overcome them.

Pocket Dictionary

English is making the cue ball spin like a top by hitting it to the right or left of center. *Sidespin* is a more descriptive but less common word for *English*.

I advise you to have the skills that I taught you in previous chapters down pat before you move to the information in this chapter. You can read and learn a lot of the material after this chapter—most of the drills, most of the bank shots, and most of position play—without mastering sidespin, but not all of it, and it's fair to say that you will be limited in your abilities to win games if you don't know how to use English.

My goal is to give you those skills as painlessly as possible. I've broken the subject into logical, easily digestible sections, and I think that when you're done, you'll have a clear understanding of English.

English: The Reason for the Mystery Miss

When you hit the cue ball to the right or left of the vertical axis, you add sideward force to the forward thrust. Hit the ball on the right side, and it wants to go left; hit it on the left side, and it wants to go right. The main thrust will still be forward, but it will be pushed off to the side of your aiming line. That's the reason why using English makes you miss balls. The cue ball doesn't go where you're aiming because of the sideways pressure.

You can easily see this effect by using the surrogate cue ball. Place the stripe vertically, and strike the ball at one edge of the stripe. Hit the ball slowly, for maximum effect. If you hit it where you meant to, the ball goes forward, spinning like a top, but not exactly where you aimed. If you hit the ball on the right side, it ends up to the left of where you aimed it. The effect is called cue-ball *deflection*.

That's the basic problem with English, but it gets a little more complex when you consider the other features of a hit. In the preceding paragraph, I suggested that you hit the ball slowly (softly), for maximum effect. That was a hint. The speed of the hit

Pocket Dictionary

Deflection pushes the cue ball off the aiming line when the ball is hit to the right or left of center.

affects the degree offline that the cue ball goes. Obviously, the distance from the center axis at which you strike the cue ball also has an effect (more toward the edge = more offline). The distance that the ball travels is a factor. If it starts offline a couple of degrees, this error is magnified by distance, and on a long shot you could miss the object ball completely. It's easy to do.

There is a mitigating factor. The spin on the ball rubs against the cloth as it moves forward, curving the cue ball back in the direction in which you wanted it to go.

In other words, if you hit the cue ball with right English, it goes off to the left, but the spin brings it back to the right. If you hit the ball really hard, all bets are off, but on a medium or soft hit, you can actually see the cue ball curving back toward the aiming line. Unfortunately, the ball doesn't straighten out when it hits the line, but crosses it. If you time the shot right, you can end up making object-ball contact exactly where you aimed. With a whole lot of experience, you can predict how much the cue ball will be thrown offline by the English, and how much and how soon it will curve back. There are times (admittedly, infrequent) when you want this effect to be at its maximum so that you can make a ball that otherwise can't be made.

The best way to get the feel of how far offline the cue ball will go when you use various amounts of English at various stroke speeds is just to hit a lot of balls. There are formulas, but they are a little complex, and in my experience, no one really uses them. Formulas will give you, on paper, an idea of how far offline the ball will go, but until you really see it, feel it, and use your stroke, you won't know much more than when you started.

To get that feel and combine it with the visual result, you have to depend on a billiard basic: consistency. Use a consistent speed, a consistent follow-through, and all the rest. Eliminate the variables for everything except what you're learning. Isolate that, and you can learn quickly. If you have a table at home, great; there's no better place to learn. But do be aware that any other table you play on will give you slightly different results. If you practice in a billiard room, try to stick with one table until you feel that you've got a good handle on aiming with English. Then move to another table (try to find one with cloth that is either newer or older) and practice there for a while.

Although there's some controversy about the issue, many players believe that a very soft hit and a very hard hit cause the most deflection, whereas the medium hit is less of a problem. It just may be that players are more familiar with their medium hit and subconsciously adjust for deflection.

Whatever future tests conclude, the subconscious adjustments that a player makes are everyday things. When you miss a certain type of shot over and over, you find yourself adjusting until you begin to make it over and over. Knowing what is going on will help you make those adjustments faster. There's universal agreement that a hard hit doesn't allow the cue ball to curve back toward the original target. The ball is going too fast for it to grab the cloth, so the spin has no correcting effect.

You can use English on a short shot and not run into too much trouble. The cue ball will still be thrown offline, but because it has just started on that path, it hasn't yet gone too far offline. A short shot may be 18 inches or less. If you use less English—that is, hit the ball just a little to the right or left of center the cue ball won't go too far offline. Stay within the width of a tip (12.75mm, or roughly half an inch) from the vertical axis, and the problems of aiming on short shots almost won't exist. It's when the worst case pops up that you really have to think out what's going to happen. If you have a long shot—say, the length of the table—and have to hit it with a lot of sidespin to achieve your goal, you have a challenge. Practice is the only way to know exactly where the cue ball is going to end up.

Some cues cause more deflection than others do. It's a selling point with some manufacturers, and as is the case with most product claims, some creative license is taken from time to time. If you stick with the recommendations that I made in Chapter 6 about buying a pool cue, you'll possess a tool with the best chance for the least amount of deflection.

Be aware, however, that if you go from cue to cue, you'll have to make those subconscious adjustments, because one cue will deflect more than another. (All cues deflect to some extent. One benefit of having your own cue is (here's that word again) consistency. You'll know how your cue ball is going to curve simply because you've used the cue on so many similar shots. You won't have to figure out that part of the shot, because it will be computed subconsciously.

One trick that you might try is something that pro Jim Mataya showed me years ago. Simply aim as you normally would, as though you were shooting a center ball shot. Then, ever so slightly, move your bridge hand over to the side of the cue ball (right or left) where you're going to apply English. Keep everything else in place. This technique seems to lessen the effect of deflection, even though it breaks a couple of rules of good form. It's not very useful on long shots with sidespin, but it could help on short or medium shots.

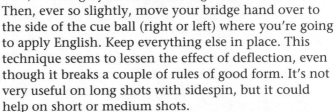

Ewa's Billiard Bits

At least two machines—robot billiard players—have been built to test cues, but the results are mixed at the moment. As testing is refined, it will be possible to definitively determine how each cue performs.

Now that you know what to look for in a shot using English, you can note the results of your stroke at various speeds and degrees of English, and you'll be able to use this new tool with confidence. It's still good, solid advice to use center ball (anywhere on the vertical axis) whenever possible, but when you have to use English, you'll be on top of the action.

Railing Against English

Ewa's Billiard Bits

One mainstay of billiard trick-shot exhibitions is the use of shots with extreme amounts of cue-ball spin. Extreme spin makes the ball behave in a way that surprises the audience and is a real crowd-pleaser.

Although low spin (draw) and high spin (follow) have an effect on the cue ball as soon as it strikes the object ball, English has little effect on the cue ball at that point. It really comes into its own when the spinning cue ball touches a cushion. Billiard balls are relatively smooth. There's some interaction, which I tell you about in the next section, but the most noticeable effect is when the spinning equator of the ball grabs the cloth that covers the nose of the cushion. Then the ball does different things, depending on the angle at which you hit the cushion (at 90 degrees or just glancing it, for example), the speed at which you hit the cushion, and the amount of spinning the ball is doing. It can take off in a new direction or virtually stop dead in its track.

The cool thing, once again, is that whether or not to use sidespin is your decision. Need the ball to stop? Hit it one way. Need it to travel at an oblique angle? Hit it another way. Which way? Ah, that's what you're about to find out.

Here's a step-by-step method of understanding how sidespin affects a ball's rebound angle off a cushion:

1. Place a cue ball somewhere down the center of the table, using the setup that I'm shooting in the following illustration.

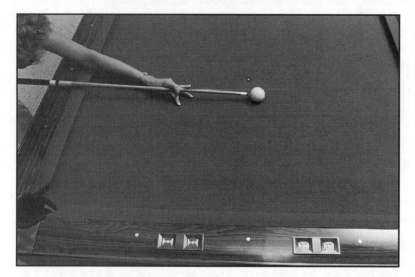

Hit the ball into the cushion with enough force that it just comes back to you. Use center ball first; then various amounts of right and left spin.

2. Aim straight at one of the side cushions, which should be only about 2 feet in front of you.

3. Hit the ball straight into the cushion. Use a hit on the cue ball anywhere on the vertical axis, and the cue ball will come straight back to you.

4. Go to the horizontal axis, and move about a cue tip's width to the right of center.

5. Hit the ball with a medium-soft stroke. Instead of coming back to you, it comes back to your right.

6. Move the cue tip over another cue-tip width, and it comes back even more to the right. The opposite happens—no surprise—when you use left English.

This effect looks kinda neat, but what use is it? It gets the cue ball someplace that a natural (no-spin) hit won't, and sometimes, that someplace is a good place.

When you strike the object ball (OB) with the cue ball and knock it into a pocket, but have to use a fairly soft stroke, the cue ball isn't going to go very far. If, however, the ball is rapidly spinning on its vertical axis (has English) when it touches the cushion, the spin is like an infusion of energy. The force of the spin makes the ball go an extra distance.

201

Heard It in the Poolroom

In casual pool conversation, as I mentioned early in this book, the words *rail* and *cushion* are sometimes used interchangeably. When I defined the terms for you, I told you that the rail is the hard outer frame around the top of the table and that the cushion is the cloth-covered rubber section surrounding the bed of the table. People sometimes say "rail" but really mean "cushion." In the shot pictured in the first illustration in this section, you're facing the cushion, but almost everyone would say that you're facing the long rail or facing the side rail.

The cushions aren't really long. There are six of them, and they're all the same length, although a pair are lined up on the long sides of the table and divided by a side pocket. The rail, however, on most tables, is continuous down the long side. So you can have such a thing as a long rail but not really have a long cushion.

Is that worth knowing? I dunno. Somebody's going to say "the long rail" in conversation someday, and you may be tempted to say "the long cushion." That won't get you banned from your local billiard palace, but you won't sound hip and knowledgeable, either.

Just for fun, shoot the cue ball into the cushion at an angle of, say, 45 degrees. Put a lot of left spin on the first shot, and then repeat the shot with right spin. Either left or right spin (depending on which cushion you hit) will make the cue ball fly off the cushion at an angle less than 45 degrees. (A natural hit leaves the cushion at approximately the same angle at which it entered—something that I show you in Chapter 19.)

Spin in the other direction makes the cue ball *hold up*—a billiard term meaning that the ball resists moving in its natural direction at its natural speed. This effect is also called *shortening the angle* or *coming off (the cushion) short*. More commonly, it's called *killing the cue ball*, which is not as violent as it sounds.

Scratch!

If your cue is not level when you're using English, the cue ball spurts to the side. The ball would no longer be spinning like a top; a downward hit would make it spin lopsided, which would give it a sideways trajectory.

A ball hit very hard does not react like a softly hit ball when it contacts the cushion, because the force of the hit overpowers the spin to a degree. Additionally, the ball is forced deep into the cushion, and the rubber grabs it, exerting a straightening force. The ball does hold up, but because it was hit so hard, it still travels a good distance. It's just that the distance is related more to the hardness of the hit than to the spin on the ball.

These are more variations, I know, but if you remember to reference everything to your basic hit or your basic English hit, you won't have any problems. You can establish your own basic hit that uses sidespin. I suggest you use your foundation hit (medium speed, medium follow-through, and so on) with the addition of one tip of English (meaning that the cue tip hits one cue-tip width to either side of the vertical axis). That's a nice moderate hit, and you go up from there.

The Gear Effect

Although the balls are smooth, they're not perfect. Under a microscope, a billiard ball is rough-looking, with craters and hills. When two balls collide, these craters and hills mesh. Think of the example of two gears that I gave in Chapter 15. Balls are many, many times smoother than gears, of course, but there is a little gear effect in the collision of two balls, and this effect is important enough to have a name: *throw*. When a ball with English (the cue ball) hits an object ball (OB), the OB doesn't follow the same path that it would have followed had it been hit by a cue ball without English. To a tiny degree, the cue ball grabs the OB and throws it slightly offline. This effect can help you make a ball that otherwise was unmakable. It can allow you to put a lot of spin on the cue ball for purposes of position play. And it can make you miss balls that you thought you hit—and *did* hit—on the correct contact point.

If you use a lot of English on a shot—and this is another reason to stick to center ball whenever you can—you have to take throw into consideration when you aim. (And you're already taking deflection and cue-ball curve into consideration.) The nice thing is that if you use what is called outside English or running English, the throw works in the opposite direction from the deflection, and on some shots, these effects come pretty close to canceling each other out.

Inside and *outside* or *running English* are common terms that refer to the direction of spin in relation to the direction in which you want the object ball to go. If you're cutting a ball to the left (making it go left), outside (running) English is right English. Think of outside English as being sidespin that would make the cue ball look, if it were in slow motion, like it was rolling off the side of the object ball.

The effect could have been called *away English*, but it wasn't. *Running* is a bit more descriptive than *outside English* and, therefore, more popular, but I'm going to stick with the word *outside* because it has a relationship with its opposite (*inside*) and is easier to remember.

Ewa's Billiard Bits

A scientist in England superimposed an enlargement of a billiard ball over a picture of the earth and then examined the surfaces. Our planet turned out to be smoother, on average, than the ball!

Inside English, in this example, would be left English, and it's called *inside* because it is in toward the object ball. (The object ball would be to the left side of the cue ball on contact, and you'd be hitting the cue ball on that side.) If you were cutting the ball in the other direction, the definitions would switch: Outside English would be left English, and inside would be right English.

You can throw the ball in either direction, depending on the English that is on the cue ball. I'll use the same example, in which you are cutting the ball to the left to make it go in the left corner pocket. If you use left English, you throw the OB to the right (onto path C in the following illustration), making it go straighter than a natural hit. If you use right English, the slight friction of the two balls lets the spin throw the OB to the left (onto path B), just as though you'd hit a contact point on the OB more to the right of the one that you actually hit.

With a center ball hit, the object ball follows path A. With left (inside) English on the cue, the object ball goes toward point C. With right (outside) English on the cue ball, the object ball goes toward point B. All shots use the same contact point. The effect is exaggerated for the illustration.

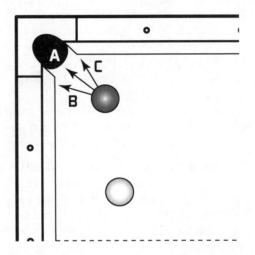

Throw is not something that you use as much as it is something that happens when you want to do something else. You want to spin the cue ball with sidespin (English) to get it to go someplace in particular. Because you're using English, you're getting a side effect: throw. Because the OB is thrown (and the image of the word *thrown* is misleading; it's more like a little nudge offline), you have to hit the OB in a different place to compensate and get the OB to go in the pocket.

In the preceding illustration, left English would make the OB go toward the top cushion (C) and not into the pocket. So if you're going to use left English on this shot, you should aim to hit the OB a little thinner, as though you were trying to make it miss the pocket on the other side (Point B). Then throw will make the ball go in the pocket (Point A).

When you throw an object ball, you also transfer a bit of spin to it. Because of the gear effect, the spin is in the opposite direction. This effect can actually be useful. If the OB is against the left cushion, and you hit it down the cushion into the pocket, but you hit it a little bit off the mark so that it moved away the cushion as it approached the pocket, the right kind of spin could make it go in.

Imagine, for example, that the ball was spinning in a clockwise (left-English) direction. When the ball hit the right side of the corner pocket, the spin would kick it to the left, into the pocket. Knowing that, you could hit the cue ball with right English and have a better chance of pocketing the ball. If the OB was spinning with right English, it might hit the right cushion opening, hold up, be thrown to the left cushion opening, and just bounce back and forth until it stopped. That's called *bobbling (a ball)* or, more commonly, *jawing a ball*—the ball comes to rest in the jaws of the pocket. (The jaws are really called the *mouth* of the pocket, but *mouthing a ball* sounds really dumb, and nobody would think of saying it.)

Pocket Dictionary

Jawing a ball is hitting a ball in such a way that it bounces back and forth at the pocket opening without dropping in.

The transfer of spin can also be used to bank a ball, as I tell you in Chapter 19. Another use is when you can't quite get the cue ball past a blocking ball to properly hit the ball that you want to hit. If the situation is right, you may be able to throw the object ball. In a natural hit, you'd use one contact point, but if you are throwing the ball, you use a different contact point to make it go in the same direction (because you're adding throw). By having a different contact point, you have a slightly different path from the cue ball to the new contact point, and that may be enough to get you by the edge of the blocking ball without touching it. You've then made a ball that didn't look as though it could be pocketed, and you can keep going. (The common reactions of your opponents will be "I didn't think there was room to make that," to which you reply, "There wasn't." A little cat-who-ate-the-canary grin is optional.)

At this point, you're probably saying, "Hey, there's more to this billiards stuff than I imagined. You're sure that this is really basic, must-know stuff?" Yep. You should keep to the simple center ball hit as much as possible, but you have to know about English, deflection, curve, and throw, and also know how to adjust your aiming point, to be able to play the complete game. Otherwise, you'll just be banging balls around, hoping to get another shot after you make a single ball. I'm replacing a dependency on luck (which pales quickly) with an ability to control the balls on the table.

Getting really good at billiards, like getting really good at any sport, takes a long time, but just to increase your enjoyment level substantially, you need to know how to make those spinning spheres do what you tell them to do. Billiards is much like golf, in the sense that you never stop learning, but the knowledge that comes later concerns specific shots and other ways of thinking about situations on the table. That advanced knowledge is all based on the fundamentals that you find in this book. Being able to put together a string of shots—popping in one, two, three, four, five, six, or more balls in a row—not only makes your turn at the table longer (and wins you games), but also makes you feel on top of the world.

Killing the Cue Ball

Remember the stop shot from Chapter 15? If the cue ball was sliding, not spinning top over bottom or bottom over top, when it struck the object ball fully, all forward motion ended. The cue ball stopped dead, and all energy was transferred to the object ball (OB). That's great, if you're straight in. Ah, but suppose that you need to stop the cue ball's movement, and you're cutting the object ball (that is, hitting it other than full in the face)? You do this with English.

If you're cutting the object ball so that it goes to the left, left English on the cue ball slightly retards its movement after it hits the object ball. It's not the 100 percent effective shot that the stop shot is, but it does kill a portion of the cue ball's movement, and you can keep it in the same area where it made contact with the OB.

Don't expect miracles, though. On a thin cut shot, there's not a whole lot that you can do—unless you're very near a cushion. That's where the *kill shot* really shines. The kill shot is a technique that allows you to stop, or at least greatly slow the cue ball after it contacts an object ball.

Pocket Dictionary

A *kill shot* greatly slows the movement of the cue ball after contact with the object ball by using English.

In "The Gear Effect" earlier in this chapter, when I asked you to hit the cue ball against the cushion at a fairly sharp angle to see how a ball with English reacts when it comes off the cushion, the use of *inside* English caused the cue ball to hold up. (In this example, inside is the side toward the cushion.) That resistance slowed it, too. A lot of spin and a softer hit would have caused it to almost stop. You would have killed the cue ball.

If you've figured out which English on a particular shot is inside English, as I showed at the beginning of this section, you'll quickly see that inside English is the type used to kill the cue ball. That applies even when you don't touch a cushion. On a shot with a slight angle (cut), try inside English, and you'll see the spin of the cue ball work against the cloth as the cue ball tries to move away after the hit. It doesn't move easily. You've killed the cue ball.

Before you start going around the pool table like Dirty Harry, realize that as much fun as the kill shot is, you shouldn't use it all the time. When you fight the natural movement of the balls, you're entering a tricky zone. It's better to let them move the way that they want to—and even aid that movement with outside English because it helps the natural roll of the ball. It's much smoother. But on the other hand, don't be like a lot of players (pros included) who just don't like to use inside English. It's the mirror twin of outside English. There's nothing wrong with it, and inside English can be the best way to achieve an object at certain times.

Another shot comes up all the time where inside English is used, but it's not always considered to be a kill shot, because the ball rolls a pretty fair distance. What is being killed is the natural angle of that roll.

If the next ball is located in such a way that instead of coming off the right side of the object ball and heading off in that direction as it is in the illustration, you may want the cue ball to pocket the OB, head toward the cushion at the top of the drawing, and then come straight back. Straight back would be tough, though, so let's say straighter than it would have if you had used center ball or right (outside) sidespin (English). The way to do that is use inside English. The cue ball goes off the OB and hits the top cushion somewhere to the right, and the left spin (inside English) stops it from bouncing off farther to the right. Instead, spin counters the direction of the ball, sort of averaging the opposing forces, and the ball bounces back toward you, relatively straight.

The cue ball and OB are farther apart than in earlier illustrations, so it's hard to see that this, like the others, is a half-ball hit. The cue ball is going to go down the tangent line (remember my second 90-degree rule from Chapter 15) to the cushion, but the inside spin shortens the angle at which it rebounds. You're killing the natural path and making the ball go where you want it to go.

You can apply the kill effect on almost any shot. If a cushion is involved after the cue ball hits the object ball, so much the better. On some shots, the cut is so thin that you may not notice much killing effect, but it's always there when you use inside English. It's a popular effect, but not just because you frequently don't want the cue ball to roll very far after contact with the OB. There's a psychological boost to stopping the cue ball from following its natural path, and that's one of the themes of the last few chapters of this book: getting control of the balls on the table. With a kill shot, you're actively making the balls do things that they wouldn't ordinarily do.

Bring on the Spin Doctor!

This topic could cause you a headache if I'm not careful, so I'll break it to you gently: You can combine low or high with right or left. "Egads!" you say, and I don't blame you. But think about how many more possibilities you open up by being able to hit the cue ball anywhere, by not being restricted to the horizontal and vertical axes. Picture the cue ball as being a clock face. I covered hitting it at noon, 6 o'clock, and points between (follow and draw). Then I told you all about hitting it at 3 o'clock, 9 o'clock, and points between (right and left sidespin). Now you can do 1:45! Seriously, it does give you unlimited options, and what could be better?

Move the cue ball so that it's hitting the OB straight into the corner pocket. Now you have the following illustration.

Scratch!

Using pure extreme follow, or extreme follow combined with English, and hitting the cue ball into a cushion with force makes the ball climb the cushion and jump off the table.

Here, I shoot the 9 ball with a combination of low (draw) and right English. I use the V bridge because I'm using a short bridge to make it easier to see the cue tip and all of the cue ball. Combining follow (top) or bottom (draw) spin with either right or left English is common in pool.

Draw alone would make the cue ball come back after hitting the object ball, making contact with the cushion at point D and bouncing on to point E. Draw with right English makes the cue ball come off point D and head toward point F, from which you can pocket the 2 ball in pocket G.

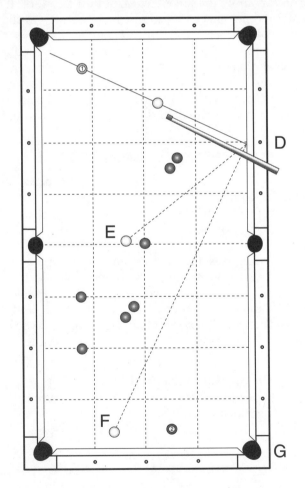

Chapter 16 ➤ English, Anyone?

Suppose that the 1 ball (solid yellow) is positioned on a straight line between the corner pocket and the cue ball, and you have to shoot the 2 ball (solid blue) next, but it's up at the other end of the table. How do you get there? You can draw your cue ball, making it come back to you, but that's more cross-table than up-table. The cue ball would draw back to D and then bounce off naturally along the line marked as E. If you draw and use a little right spin when the cue ball comes back to the cushion, however, it takes off up-table (along the path marked F).

Cue Tips

You can use draw or follow to avoid a natural scratch, too. You don't always have to use these shots to position the cue ball, but if you can do both, you're ahead of the game.

Strike the cue ball at about the 4:30 position, halfway between 3 o'clock (right English) and 6 o'clock (draw). The draw pulls the cue ball back toward you and to the cushion (point D, on the right side of the table); then the spin makes it come off the cushion at an extended angle along line F and to the 2 ball. You can then shoot the ball in pocket G and keep going.

You can do the same thing with follow (topspin). On the same shot, you can combine two different spins with some knowledge that I gave you earlier. Remember the concept of cheating the pocket (Chapter 13)? That's when you don't aim for the center of the pocket, but aim to put the ball in one side of the pocket (which usually is wide enough for two balls). When you cheat the pocket, you no longer have to hit a straight-in shot; you can cut the ball slightly. Therefore, the cue ball, even if it has follow spin, doesn't follow the same line as the OB and doesn't go in the pocket. Instead, it hits the cushion very near the pocket.

Suppose that you decide to cheat the pocket in the shot in the preceding illustration. To make the situation clearer, I'll use the following illustration, showing almost all the balls in the same places; the only thing that I'm moving is the 2 ball.

Now you don't want to go all the way up-table. Instead, because the 2 ball is in a different place, you want the cue ball in a different place. To get there, you cut the object ball to the left side of the pocket (cheating the pocket), and use a combination of follow and left English (called *high-left*). The cue ball, when hit with follow spin, goes to the cushion at the point marked H. As you know, when English makes contact with a cushion, it kicks into effect. So the ball spins off to the left, hitting point J. It then spins off that cushion, still with forward spin, and goes to point K, where you can easily hit the 2 ball into the corner pocket marked L.

How often do the exact shots illustrated in this section come up in your lifetime? Perhaps never. But thousands of shots are very similar and require similar solutions. Combining sidespin and center ball spin is very, very common in billiards. To play the game well, you need to know the principles of off-main axes spin (combining spins). You know the rules and can predict the behavior of the cue ball when it's spinning on either its horizontal or vertical axis. Now all you have to do is add their characteristics together and figure out when the cue ball will touch a cushion.

209

The only ball that has moved from the preceding illustration is the 2 ball, but that's your next ball. To get in position to play it, you have to send the cue ball on a different path but still pocket the 1 ball. See the text for details.

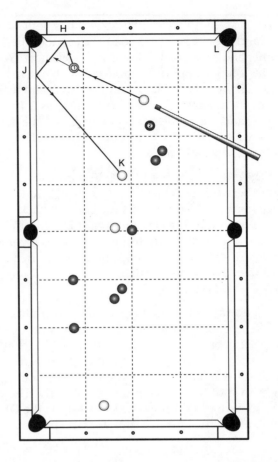

If you hit the cue ball at 1:30, 4:30, 7:30, or 10:30, you're hitting it halfway between the vertical axis and the horizontal axis, and can expect an equal amount of behavior from each side. Should you want a lot of follow but only a little right English, hit the cue ball at the 1 o'clock position. Want a very little follow and a very little right spin? Find the 1:30 position; then move the cue tip halfway toward the center of the cue ball. That technique gives you equal amounts of follow and right English—but tempers both of them.

Any point on the cue ball is now available to you, and you're able to predict what will happen when you pick a particular point. Putting it all together takes practice, but I think that you can now see how you can make the white ball go just about anywhere you want it to go. What power!

In the following illustration, I've shaded the safe zone and left the danger zone white.

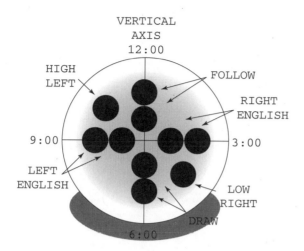

Hitting the cue ball in the white area causes a miscue, but anywhere in the shaded area is safe. Anywhere on the vertical axis causes few problems, but hitting the cue ball to the right or left of that line adds additional considerations, particularly when you're aiming.

Hitting the cue ball close to the edge (white zone) can cause a miscue, although expert players who have years of experience can sometimes bring it off. The dark circles, which represent places where the cue tip strikes the ball, show the basic, pure shots: moderate follow, extreme follow, moderate right English, extreme right English, and so on. The dark circles at the 4:30 and 10:30 positions are there to illustrate the use of follow or draw combined with an equal amount of sidespin (English). But you can use a small amount of left and a lot of follow, for example, by hitting the cue ball at the 11:30 point on the ball. Anywhere in the gray area is acceptable, and you pick your point after you decide where you want the cue ball to go after the hit and the type of spin (if any) that is needed to get it there.

The Least You Need to Know

➤ English is hitting the cue ball to the right or left of the vertical axis.

➤ English makes the cue ball travel off the aiming line.

➤ English is used to increase or decrease the natural distance that the cue ball would travel after striking the object ball.

➤ English is used to alter the natural direction in which the cue ball travels after it strikes a cushion.

➤ English (sidespin) can be combined with either follow or draw to create two effects in one shot.

➤ English can throw the object ball off its natural path.

➤ Don't use English unless you have no other choice.

The Drill Bit

In This Chapter

➤ How drills improve your game

➤ How to practice

➤ Specific drills for specific shot categories

➤ How to make practice more interesting

➤ Where to go for more variety

Coaches spend a lifetime trying to make drills interesting, but I can't think of many sports in which they succeed. Billiard drills are more fun than piano lessons, but they're still drills, and as they say, practice is practice.

To make billiard practice as enjoyable as possible, I'm going to give you some drills that zero in on different skills and techniques, plus give you a chance to measure your rate of improvement. I'm not so blindly optimistic as to think that you're going to spend five or six hours each evening doing the same few drills over and over, no matter how much good that would do your game. But this chapter is a good solid start. When you get burned out on these drills, you can make up your own or get some new drills from the resources in the back of the book (check under "Read Me" and "Video Billiards" in Appendix B). Variety is one of the keys to practice.

In this chapter, you find the Top 10 drills for billiard basics. One drill involves looking at yourself in the mirror; another, a soda bottle; and another, a napkin or sheet of typing paper. All 10 exercises are easy to understand, and it's immediately clear what each drill is trying to get you to focus on. With each one, it will also be easy for you to see how well you're doing and to compare your scoring with the last time you did the drill. In fact, it's not a bad idea to keep a record so that you can chart your progress. If your improvement is flat in one or two of the drills, you can spot the problem quickly and zero in on that area for a while.

I'm going to include some drills for shots that you won't learn until the next couple of chapters, because now is the time when you should get started on drills. But all the drills should be in one chapter; that way, they're easy to find.

Perfect Practice

In music, in other sports, and in other areas, they say that no practice is better than bad practice, and that's also true in billiards. If you find yourself getting careless or starting to just goof around after you've been shooting a particular setup for a while, stop immediately and move on—or find a partner and play a few actual games. Don't practice inattention. Going through a few racks will help you, too. It's just that drills improve your game faster than playing a game with an opponent because they are so focused. One game—it's called Kiss Pool—actually is a drill in game form and a lot of fun. It teaches you carom shots (called *kisses*, in pool talk) and I tell you about those in Chapter 20.

The Top 10 drills in this chapter are mostly on topics that I've talked about up to this point, which are the universal fundamentals of billiards. After the drills, I get into common types of shots (such as the break shot, bank shots, and combinations), in which you put the fundamentals to use when you have to do more than simply hit a ball straight into a pocket.

Ewa's Billiard Bits

Finding a partner to practice with is difficult because you have to find someone at your level of play (and because not a lot of people love practicing). On the pro level it's even tougher. I've lived most of my adult life so far in the very small town of Grand Ledge, Michigan. Amazingly, it's also home to another Top Twenty WPBA (Women's Professional Billiard Association) player named Vicki Paski.

The difference between poor practice and beneficial practice can be revealed in how you're feeling at a particular moment. If you're bored, stop. That's a sure sign that your practice session is about to turn sour. If you're determined to succeed in your drill, keep at it. To keep your interest level up, you might use drills as warmup exercises. Set up a drill and shoot it seriously, paying close attention to what the cue ball's action is telling you. Practice a particular shot—banks, for example—for 10 minutes; then start playing matches. You'll be killer when a bank comes up—guaranteed. Your muscles and brain connect during the drill, and they both have memory, which is put to use when it's called upon. Memory fades, however, and has to be re-enforced. It's the old "two steps forward and one step back" routine. The more you practice, the more you'll move forward.

But now—on to the playing field!

Drilling for Speed

The speed drill is a quickie, and it's simple. It's the same thing that I showed you in Chapter 14 to define soft, medium, and hard hits.

The Basic Speed Drill

1. Hit the cue ball one table length, trying to stop against the far cushion.

2. Hit the ball hard enough so that it goes the length of the table and comes back, stopping as close to the starting cushion as possible.

   This shot is also called a *lag shot* (discussed in Chapter 14), and it's worth some extra practice on its own because it's often used to decide who breaks in the first game. Having the break is an advantage, in most cases.

3. Hit the ball hard enough to make it travel three table lengths: up, back, and up again, stopping against the cushion where the first shot stopped.

Variations on the Basic Drill

You can probably think of a thousand variations on the basic drill, but I'll mention a few just to get you started:

➤ Do the same set of shots across the table, cutting your distance in half. Then try the shots the long way again, but this time, make it your goal to stop the cue ball on the footspot.

➤ Place an object ball a foot in front of the cue ball, and hit it so that it travels the same distances as the cue ball did.

➤ Use the half-ball reference hit, and pick various points for the cue ball to reach.

➤ Place small pieces of paper in a straight line on the table, and go from one to another, both with the cue ball alone and then by hitting an object ball to them.

Cue Tips

If you have a regular playing partner, make a competition out of a drill.

The Paper Speed-Control Drill

Here's a more entertaining method of practicing speed control:

1. Place a sheet of typing paper or a paper napkin on the table.

2. Practice hitting the ball to the center of the paper.

3. Try bouncing the cue ball off a cushion and onto the paper.

Scratch!

Beware of trying too many variations in a short period of time. The goal of practicing speed control is to teach your muscles how to get a certain result (distance), so let them learn by repeating the same exercise as many times as you can. This translates into use in a game by giving you the ability to play better cue-ball position. Simple cue-ball speed, oddly enough, is one of the hardest things to teach and one of the simplest things to understand.

4. Try hitting a ball to that point.

5. Fold the paper in half, place it against a cushion, and get your speed down for that shot.

You can make a contest out of this drill (by yourself or with an opponent). There's even a product on the market that offers a target, set shots, and scoring pads. This product is aimed more at improving your position play (in which the cue ball goes after pocketing a ball), but it's a good speed-control tool as well.

Stroke Drills: Pop 'n' Prop

One of the oldest stroke drills reveals its age by the prop that it uses. It's the soda-pop drill, and it requires a bottle that's the same size that you used to get out of soda machines. One of the smaller plastic versions made today might work, but a can is useless. A commercial guide on the market does the same thing and adds a couple of extra important elements, and you might want to check into that. But in the meantime, try to find a soda bottle.

The Soda-Pop Drill

1. Lay the empty bottle on its side on the table (wash and dry it first, of course).

2. Make a bridge, and stroke about 2 inches into the mouth of the bottle without touching the sides of the opening.

3. When you can make the shot in step 2 consistently, increase your stroke speed and master that stroke.

This drill teaches you how to deliver a straight, consistent stroke and ensures that your movement is level. The commercial device does this drill one better by giving you an adjustable-height tube. You can use this device to practice some of your follow-through, and you can do it at different bridge heights. It's a nice idea, although keeping at it for very long takes some willpower. Start with the soda bottle, and check out the commercial device in a couple of months.

The Mirror Drill

Next to the soda bottle in your stroke-tools closet, you can put a portable mirror. You don't need anything expensive, and something along the lines of 2 by 4 feet will do fine. If the mirror comes on its own adjustable stand, so much the better.

1. Stand on one side of the table, and place the mirror a couple of feet away from the table on the other side.

2. Put a couple of balls on the table, and get down to shoot.

3. As you look from the cue ball to the object ball, keep stroking, and look in the mirror.

4. Ask yourself the following questions:

   ➤ Is my stroke straight?

   ➤ Are all the critical body parts lined up as discussed in Chapters 10 and 12?

   ➤ During the actual stroke, do I wobble, does my elbow waver, or do I twist my rear wrist as the cue tip approaches the cue ball?

You can find the answers to all these questions—and more—while you're actually stroking the ball, just by looking in the mirror.

Ball-Spinning Drills

Although you can spin the cue ball in four major ways—top-spin, bottom spin, right spin, and left spin (plus endless combinations)—I'm going to combine right and left English in one section. What applies to one applies to the other. The same is not true of follow (topspin) or draw (bottom spin) because one is fighting the cloth as it moves, and the other is rapidly slipping over it.

Think of the relationship between follow spin and the cloth as being like a person trying to walk over muddy ground. He slips a little and moves his feet faster and faster, but he doesn't cover any more distance than before he started slipping. Think of draw as a person with a rope around his waist, running one way but losing the battle as a vehicle pulls him the other way. English is the spinning top moving across the tabletop.

Scratch!

Don't be so determined to get better that you burn yourself out on drills. When you get bored with one drill, switch to another.

Drilling the Draw

You know all the variables that affect the efficiency of the draw, from a good follow-through to how low on the cue ball your cue tip is when it hits the ball. In practicing the draw shot, the only thing that should change is how low you hit the cue ball. Try to keep every other aspect of the shot the same from the first time you hit it to the last time.

1. Set up an object ball and a cue ball 8 to 10 inches apart.

2. Off to the side of each ball, mark the spots that they're on so that you can keep putting them back. Try using the gummed area from a sheet of one of those

temporary sticky pads. It was made not to stick too well so that it won't pull up fibers from the cloth when you move it.

3. Mark a few more places in a straight line about a foot apart, beginning on the side of the cue ball opposite the object ball (under you when you bend over, in other words).

4. Practice drawing back to those spots.

Drawing to a specific spot is something that you'll be doing in game situations. It's called *pinpoint position play*. You have to move the cue ball to a very specific and small location to have a shot on the next ball. The opposite of pinpoint position play is *area position play,* which (as you may have guessed by the name) is something that you use when you can land the cue ball anywhere in a fairly large area and still make the next ball.

Draw isn't the only way to get to either an area or a point, but learning to draw to a point gives you the skills that you need when you have no other choice. It even helps in area position play. (I deal more with position play in Chapter 22.)

After you've pretty well mastered the initial drill, move the cue ball 2 feet away from the cue ball and repeat the drill. As you progress (and this is hardly going to be a one-night deal), keep track in a notepad of where the balls are, pick up at that point (or one step earlier, to build confidence), and keep going. When you can place the object ball 7 or 8 feet away and still draw the cue ball back to its starting position, you can say that you're a very skilled player—probably in the top 3 percent of people playing the game.

Cue Tips

Make a drill sheet with boxes for scores after each drill. Fill them in as you do them, and watch for progress. Scores give you a goal to shoot for the next time you practice.

When the cue ball and OB (object ball) are 3 feet apart and you have pretty good control of how far you can draw the cue ball back, change the setup to a half-ball hit, and set up a new series of paper points as targets. Although nothing has really changed in your stroke or in where you hit the cue ball with the cue tip, this variation makes it a little harder. The reason is that any aiming error is more noticeable in the return path of the cue ball.

Following

Topspin is easier to apply and easier to control than draw is, and for that reason, it's the first thing you should consider if the center-ball hit won't get good cue-ball position.

To practice follow, simply move those little pieces of confetti to the opposite side of the object ball. Practice following the cue ball 6 inches, 1 foot, 2 feet, and so on. It's just like the draw drill, but in the reverse direction.

You can do one little shot here that has no counterpart with a draw: replacing the OB. Hit the cue ball with very little follow (maybe half a tip's width up from the center ball) and the correct speed, and the cue ball knocks the object ball away and then rolls gently into the place that the OB occupied. This variation is not easy to do with a high degree of accuracy, but it makes the follow drill more interesting.

Again, as with the draw drill, move on to a half-ball hit after getting comfortable with the full-ball hit that you began with. You can also shoot a shot in which you just skim the object ball (called a fine cut) and try to land on the points that you marked.

An English Drill That's Not About Grammar

Set up a half-ball cut shot, and dig out those little pieces of paper with the almost-glue on them. You're going to use the same half-ball hit for this drill.

1. Start with a center ball hit for reference purposes, and pocket the ball.

2. Set up the shot again, and use half a tip of right English.

3. Keep increasing the distance from the center by half-tip movements, and run through a series of shots with the same-speed hit until you reach the edge of the ball.

Notice where the cue ball ends up. With running English, the cue ball leaves the object ball, hits the cushion, is thrown off the cushion at a wider angle because of the spin, and keeps going. If you hit the ball hard enough that it reaches a second cushion, you'll find that most (but not all) of the spin effect is gone. The ball leaves the rail closer to the angle at which it entered.

An interesting aside: When you use center ball, and the cue ball hits the cushion at an angle, it picks up a little running English from rubbing along the cushion. The more severe the angle at which it entered, the more English is created by friction with the cloth on the cushion.

Repeat all the same shots, using inside English, and place the paper targets at various distances along the path that the cue ball will travel after it hits the rail.

Ewa's Billiard Bits

If you hit the OB straight on with a cue ball that has English on it, the cue ball stops and just sits there, spinning around and around. Remember—English doesn't make the cue ball move until it hits a rail.

Drilling for Position

This is the reason for all that spinning: the position of the cue ball. When you spin the ball backward, forward, and sideways, you do it (in most cases) to get it into position for the next shot. Occasionally, you do it to avoid scratching (when the cue ball goes into a pocket, which is a foul). And every now and then, you won't be making the object ball, but you are caroming the cue ball into a second object ball, which goes in a pocket. Finally, you may be purposely missing the object ball and making the cue ball go to a place where your opponent will be unable to do anything positive. All those things require you to be able to spin the cue ball.

L Drill

The L drill, pictured in the following illustration, gives you a chance to practice returning the cue ball to nearly its starting position. If you check the illustration, you see that the 1 ball is at the top. (The balls are in a reverse L from this angle.)

The L drill is a simple setup that offers you the chance to use a variety of cue-ball positioning techniques.

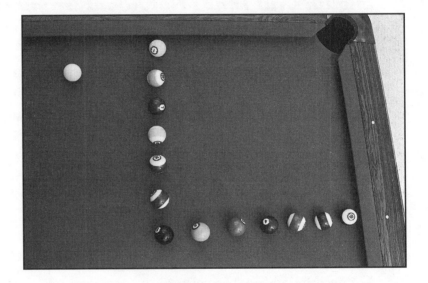

1. Start with cue ball in hand, and hit the 1 ball into the corner pocket. The cue ball (from the pictured starting position) hits the cushion and bounces up along the line of balls. (Apply Ewa's Second 90-Degree Rule of Billiards.)

   That position won't do you much good because you'd be too close to the balls to hit them well. What do you do?

2. Use a little draw (reverse spin, hitting the cue ball low). The 1 ball goes in the pocket, and the cue ball draws back and bounces off the cushion at a different angle from the center ball. Not bad.

3. Try using a little left spin. The 1 ball goes into the pocket, and the cue ball bounces straight into the cushion. The left spin, however, makes it bounce off the cushion in a direction more toward the original starting position of the cue ball.

4. Go on from there, figuring out what's going to happen before you shoot. Mentally experiment with different spin directions and speeds to figure out how to get the cue ball where you want it to go; then work your way around the line of object balls.

Circle Drill

1. Place all or most of the balls in a circle, as shown in the following illustration. This arrangement works best in the center of the table because it allows you to pocket balls in all six pockets without any one of them being too far away. You could set up the circle near one end of the table, but one entire direction would be taken away from you by the end cushion.

The circle drill teaches more than you might suspect. See the text for instructions.

2. Put the cue ball in the center of the circle.

3. Shoot any ball in any pocket—but the cue ball should never leave the circle, and you can never have ball in hand again. If the cue ball nudges a ball after you've pocketed another ball, just let both balls stay where they are, and keep shooting.

Although the focus of this drill is the short draw shot, you also get some practice in shot selection. If you choose the wrong ball to play (to pocket), you'll be in trouble, especially near the end, when only three or four balls are left. You can easily put yourself in a position in which the only way to make a ball is to shoot a cut shot that forces the cue ball to leave the circle. Think ahead.

221

Concentrate...Concentrate...You're Getting...Better!

Concentration is a key element in billiards. Because the sport isn't a reactive game (no one hits a ball to you or runs at you), you can pause and let your mind wander whenever you want to, and then come back to the game. If you do pause, of course, you'll have problems, but the point is that in nonreactive sports, you can come back easily. No ball is going to be rushing at you to make you pay attention. For this reason, a concentration drill is more than a little useful, and this setup is more than just a concentration drill. You can use it in two ways.

To use the setup in the following illustration as a follow drill, take cue ball in hand and place it anywhere on the table. The easiest starting position is about where one of the cue balls is in the picture, or perhaps a little closer to the line of balls.

I've put two cue balls on the table to illustrate the use of this drill as a follow drill. It can also be used as a concentration drill.

1. Hit a ball into the corner pocket, striking the cue ball on the vertical axis but above the equator. It pockets the OB that you hit and follows to the other end of the table.

2. Turn around and hit the second ball back to this end of the table and into the corner pocket. You'll get some exercise because you have to keep changing table ends to shoot, but it teaches you how to follow at just the right speed to leave yourself a good second shot.

To use this setup as a concentration drill, stand at one end, take cue ball in hand, and hit a ball into a corner pocket. All balls have to go into the same corner pocket, so place the last ball in the lineup a bit farther from the cushion, as shown in the left of the preceding illustration. On every shot, you can take cue ball in hand and place it where you want to. The only stipulation is that you make every ball in the same corner pocket.

Easy? After you have your stroke down, this drill is pretty easy, and that's the key. You'll be tempted to lose your focus somewhere along that line of balls. I've seen very good players set up this drill along the headstring, shoot at a corner pocket at the far end of the table, and not make it past eight or nine balls. Every shot is a sitting duck for players at that level, but somehow, they lose it.

Test your ability to concentrate.

The Rail Drill

This drill is something for later; it's tough. There are two versions, and one isn't too bad, but the other—whew.

1. Take a dozen numbered balls, and place one on the cushion in front of each "diamond" (usually circular, as they are on my Gold Crown, pictured in the following illustration) on either side of each pocket. Six pockets, one diamond on each side, equals 12 balls.

Pocketing balls that are against a cushion isn't easy. But this drill zeroes in on the challenge and you'll soon own the shot.

2. Put the cue ball in the center of the table.
3. Make all the balls. You can make them in any order.

One hint: The four toughest balls are the ones on either side of the center pockets. All these balls are frozen against the cushion, which makes them difficult to bank, and the only corner pockets that they will go in are almost half a table away. If you have an opportunity to deal with them early, do so. If you miss and you're having trouble with the drill, let the missed ball stay where it rolled, and shoot it from there at any time during the drill. Later, you can stop when you miss and start over again.

That's a tough drill. The pro-level version is worse; you have to make the balls in numerical order. Former World Champion Irving Crane showed me that version, and it will challenge even the best player. Any time you feel that the drills you're doing are getting boring because they're easy and repetitious, set up this drill, which will test your skills to the max.

The Least You Need to Know

➤ Drills speed your learning curve.

➤ You can make practice more interesting by making it into a competition with a playing partner or by competing against your own previous scores.

➤ There's a drill for every category of shot.

➤ You can create your own drills.

➤ If you get bored or lose concentration while you're practicing, stop.

Part 5
Ewa's Super Shots

At times in life, you've just got to get a little fancy. The occasion seems to require it. You'll run into those occasions in this game, too, and those times are the subject of this part of the book. You're going to get gussied up on the pool table. You may think that all that spinning I told you about in the last part is impressive, but now you're going to get into combination shots, banks, jump shots, and all kinds of other stuff that you didn't know you could do. This part is where I tell you how.

Each shot requires a different technique and is used for special situations (not unlike getting dressed up fancy). When you face those situations, I want you to have the knowledge and skill to pull off a winner. If the position of the balls requires more than just hitting a ball straight into a pocket, you can pick the shot that performs best for you. They're all basic shots in a player's collection, even though some of them look like trick shots.

In fact, I finish this part with some real trick shots that use some of the techniques of the super shots. You'll be able to do some of the trick shots even before you develop good playing skills—after I tell you how to set them up. I also throw in a couple of shots that require significant skill, so that you'll have something to look forward to.

Chapter 18

Getting All the Breaks

In This Chapter

➤ What constitutes a good break shot

➤ Checking the rack before breaking

➤ The fundamentals of break shots

➤ Knowing the goals and how to achieve them

➤ How to break in 8-Ball and 9-Ball

➤ Breaking safe in Straight Pool and One-Pocket

The pool accusation "You break like a girl!" just doesn't have the same impact that it had years ago. You'll find some of the best breakers in the game on the WPBA (Women's Professional Billiard Association) Tour these days. By *best*, I don't mean simply powerful because, as you're about to learn, there's more to the break shot than raw power. Power is certainly a factor, but control is just as important, if not more important. Typically, as one goes up, the other goes down, and the best breaks are those that get the most power only after they achieve perfect control of the path of the ball (aim) and behavior of the cue ball. That's what I'm going to tell you how to do in this chapter.

You'll also find out that there's no such thing as *the* break shot. Different games require different shots, and after a couple of pages, you'll know which shot to use for 9-Ball, which to use for 8-Ball, and so on. That knowledge alone can give you an edge over the average player.

The break shot has become increasingly important in professional pool because the skill of the players has increased to the point where the top echelon is able to *run out* (pocket all the balls on the table without missing) from the first shot of the game. If they make a ball on the break, they get to keep shooting and can win without their opponent ever coming up for a turn. On the amateur level, a good break isn't quite as critical, but it can still give you a head start over the person you're playing against. The more you play, the better you'll become, and the more important the break shot will become.

In the first section, I cover some things that are important in every break shot, no matter what the game. Then I give you information about how to break the balls in the most popular games. Toward the end of the book in Part 6, when I devote entire sections to those and other games, I let you know whether there's anything unique about the break in the less popular games.

Now let's get ready to rumble.

Break Points

Observation is a good teacher, and that's as true in billiards as it is anywhere else. But it helps a whole lot to know what to look for, and that's what I tell you in this section. The break shot happens so fast that it's tough to see a lot of the technique involved. But you can look for something before the shot even starts, and you can look at the way the balls end up when it's all over.

Check the Rack, Jack

All billiard games must start with a tight rack; if they don't, the break shot will be flawed. A *tight rack* is the grouping of the balls at the beginning of the game in such a way that all the balls are touching their neighbors. What makes a tight rack a good rack is proper alignment on the table. As simple as that concept is, it's something that doesn't happen very often. A less-than-scrupulous opponent may actually rack the balls improperly on purpose, although one shudders to think that a person who would do that is loose among the finer members of society. Still, it's best to be on your toes. Check the rack.

Cue Tips

Open break shots are made with a center ball hit, so many players flatten the tip on the break cue, making a center-ball hit easier to execute.

A less-than-proper rack will not break as wide open, which means that there's less chance that one of those zooming balls will find a hole in the table and be pocketed. Traditionally, your opponent racks for you and you for him or her. That arrangement speeds the play, but there's nothing that says you can't agree beforehand that each player racks his own balls. Some pro tournaments do it that way in the early rounds when there's no referee to do the racking. The process takes extra time, but not very much. It also eliminates the awkwardness of looking at the balls after your opponent racks them, finding one or two (or three or four) that aren't touching their neighbors and asking for a rerack.

If there is any ball that you don't want to be *loose* (not touching), it's the very first ball—usually, the 1 ball (solid yellow). The cue ball hits the 1 ball, which in turn hits the two balls behind it. In a tight rack, 100 percent of that energy then spreads to the rack. If the 1 ball is loose, however, it hits the two balls and bounces off them a couple of millimeters, only to hit the cue ball again and be driven into the two balls a second time, by which time those balls have separated and moved away—all in a split second. In short, a lot of energy is wasted bouncing the 1 ball back and forth. The goal is to transfer all the cue ball's energy into the rack.

The front ball is also the one that is most likely to be innocently misracked. The reason is not important to know, but it never hurts to know a little more than other folks do, so I'll tell you what's going on.

First, it's almost impossible to hit the cue ball really hard and have it be flat against the table during its entire journey from the headstring to the rack. If your cue is a fraction out of level—and it will have to be because of the rules concerning cue-ball placement for the break shot—you'll be hitting down on the ball slightly, causing an imperceptible bounce.

The cue ball hits the 1 ball with the cue ball's equator higher, driving the 1 ball down into the cloth a little as it drives it back. The downward driving makes a dimple in the cloth. To check for a dimple, put all the balls in the wooden rack, slide them into place, and take off the rack. If the 1 ball is a fraction of an inch off the mark, it will roll into the dimple, separating from the pack. That's why it's the most likely to be loose (for innocent reasons). If the balls were not placed exactly right and broken when they created the dimple, the 1 ball may even be off the mark, and when you rerack the balls so that the 1 ball doesn't roll into the dimple, the rack itself could be a little to the right or left of dead-center on the table.

The lesson is to always rack correctly, especially on your home table. In a club, you may have to change tables to find one without a dimple (or with the dimple in the correct spot on the footspot).

Scratch!

A wooden rack can warp almost as easily as a cue shaft. If the balls won't rack properly, check the straightness of the rack by sighting down each side. If it's warped, replace it.

Cue Tips

If a table has a dimple in the wrong spot, you can sometimes get rid of it by vigorously rubbing it with your fingertips. Rubbing raises and levels the cloth.

So check the rack of balls (simply called *the rack,* as I told you earlier in the book) to be sure that all the balls are touching one another. Then check the entire rack for alignment. The front ball should be perfectly lined up with the center ball in the third row

Pocket Dictionary

A *short-rack game* is any billiard game that doesn't use all 15 numbered balls.

and the center ball (or the only ball, in a 9-Ball rack) in the last row, and all three should be lined up down the center of the table. A 9-Ball rack is diamond-shaped, with the five rows containing one ball, two balls, three balls, two balls and one ball. 9-Ball is called a *short-rack game* because it doesn't use all 15 numbered balls, as do most other games on the pool table. The 15 balls are racked in a triangle for 8-Ball, so it's easier to check the alignment. Step to the side of the table, and check to see whether the back row is parallel with the back cushion.

The final thing to check in a rack of balls is whether the person who did the racking put certain balls in their proper places. I discuss that subject in Part 6 when I explain each game individually, but as an example, in 8-Ball the 8 must be in the middle of the rack (center ball in the third row). Be sure that it's there before you break. If it should accidentally be put on a back corner, for example, it would be much more likely to go in on the break. In most places, this would mean that you win the game; in others, it would mean that you lose.

Eight-ball, as I warned you earlier, is played by different rules in different places and in different leagues. If you're playing in a place where making the 8 on the break is an automatic win, then when you're racking the balls for your opponent's break, you naturally want to make very sure that the 8 ball is in the middle of the rack, where it has little chance of being pocketed on the break.

The three things to check in a rack of balls are:

➤ All balls are touching their neighbors

➤ The rack is properly aligned on the table

➤ Key balls are in the correct positions

A Rail Break

A *rail break* (off the end rail) won't have the warden and guards coming after you, but maybe it should. It's a bad way to break. Putting the cue stick on the far rail (head rail), placing the cue ball half a dozen inches off the cushion, and then winding up and smashing it to the rack at the other end of the table is nowhere near as effective as a good break with the cue ball on the headstring.

You can legally break from anywhere behind the headstring, so a break off the rail isn't illegal. It's just not an effective way to break the balls.

An end-rail break is tempting when you first learn how to play. The snap of the wrist, the power of the arm and shoulder, and the crack as the cue ball collides with the rack are pretty darned alluring. It makes sense that you could steady the cue better if it were lying on the rail. The problem is that doing it that way is more accurate for only the first 50 or so times that you break—and then only if you don't put a lot of speed into the break. After you develop a solid closed or V bridge (front-hand configuration), you'll get a much better break by using it rather than using the end rail and a rail bridge. The cue tip will be lower, and the cue will be more level.

I keep reminding you to keep your cue as level as possible. If you do that on a rail break, the tip of the cue will be so high on the cue ball that you'll miscue half the time. If, on the other hand, you hit the cue ball in the center (where you get more power), you'll be aiming down, so the cue ball will hop to the rack (hopping really fast, but still hopping) and probably will fly off the table frequently.

But (there's always a *but*) there *is* a rail break that is good. It's not something that I recommend using until you get a lot of practice under your belt, but you can start practicing it as soon as you have the basic bridge, stance, and stroke down solid. This break is a side-rail break, and it's particularly effective in 9-Ball. I've seen people use it in 8-Ball, although it's not the best shot for that game. I tell you about this side-rail break shot in "Diamond Cutting: The 9-Ball Break" later in this chapter. The point to remember here is not to break off the *end* rail.

Cue Tips

To find the headstring, which is sometimes a pencil line on the cloth, count two diamonds down each side rail from the head rail; then connect the diamonds across the table.

Cue Tips

Place the cue ball on the headstring when you break. The ball loses speed as it travels, and the closer you get it to the rack, the faster it will be going when it hits the front ball.

The Body Break

In any game that involves an open break, you can get more power in the cue ball by putting your body behind your stroke. When you do this, you lose a lot of accuracy at first. The technique takes practice. On your final stroke, lower your rear shoulder, and put your body behind the cue. Use more of a throwing motion, getting your shoulder into it and following through much farther than normal. Many pros follow through so far that they have to lift their cues when doing so; otherwise, the cue tips would reach all the way down to the rack and touch a ball (foul!).

Heard It in the Poolroom

Top American pro and former World 9-Ball Champion Johnny Archer has one of the most powerful breaks in the history of the game, even though he weighs no more than 145 pounds. In the finals of the Williard's International 9-Ball Championship, he broke the balls and followed through so hard that the cue flew out of his hands and landed 20 feet away, under the table where the women's final was being played. *That* will break your concentration.

As I told you earlier, though, save this sort of thing until you are really sure of your accuracy. Follow the plan that I presented by concentrating first and foremost on hitting the apex ball accurately. Then increase your speed (power) a small step at a time. When you start to lose accuracy, back off a tad, increase your concentration, and then move up again. Eventually, you can put a little shoulder into the break shot without miscuing or miss-hitting the object ball. Accuracy is the prime consideration, but break at the highest speed possible while still being accurate.

A Word About Your Break Stance

Most players stand up a little straighter for the break shot. I believe that they do so partly because they get some of their bodies behind the shot, even if they're not aware that they're doing it. When you want to stroke the cue hard, you'll find that a low, bent position—typical in shooting an object ball—is just too restrictive. You need to be able to move your body more, or at least feel you have that freedom whether you do or not—and most people do. Too much freedom means a lack of control, however, and above all, you don't want to lose control of your stroke or the cue ball. That can easily happen if you stand too erect or stroke faster than is safe for your skill level.

Scratch!

Never wear slippery-soled shoes when breaking. You could end up flat on your face.

The second thing that many people do for their break stance—and it's something that I do as well—is bend both knees slightly. In your normal stance, your back leg is almost locked (or momentarily locked), but bending both knees a little for the break shot helps you put your body behind the stroke.

In Search of Position

On the break shot in every game, whether it's a game with an open (smash em hard!) or safe (skim one ball gently) break shot, you always play cue-ball position. That means that you always shoot the break shot knowing where you want the cue ball to stop at the end of the shot, and you get it to that place. I know it astounds people to learn that when a really good player just smashes the balls wide open and they fly in every direction, the player has, to a great degree, executed a controlled shot and has maintained control of the cue ball. In fact, letting the cue ball get away from you is one of the most common faults in a break shot.

Sometimes, of course, letting the cue ball get away can't be helped. A couple of the balls bounce off each other, and one of them careens into the cue ball, knocking it somewhere that it shouldn't be (such as into a pocket!). It's not the result of faulty technique; it's just something that happens and can't be predicted or completely controlled. As long as the cue ball was going where it should have gone, you did the best you could.

In almost every game, the position in which you want the cue ball to end up is the center of the table. The center of the table is the place from which you're more likely to have a shot on a ball, and you want that shot to be the shortest average distance. This scenario presupposes that you're going to make a ball on the break. Otherwise, that position would be ideal for your opponent to have when he or she comes to the table after you fail to make a ball on the break.

This may sound like positive thinking ("I want to end up in the center of the table because I know I'm going to be successful and sink a ball on the break"). Rather than being positive thinking, though, putting the cue ball in the center of the table is really just playing the odds. If you break well enough to control the cue ball, it's fair to say that you also break well enough to make a ball on the majority of breaks.

The simplest and easiest way to get the cue ball in the center of the table on a break shot is to put it on the center of the headstring (halfway between the side rails) and break straight ahead, toward the apex ball in the rack. Hit the ball fully, not tremendously hard, and it will bounce back a foot or two and end up in the center of the table.

There's another little trick that allows you to hit the ball harder and get the same result, and you can use it in both 8-Ball and 9-Ball. This trick uses something you already know: a high ball (follow spin). If you hit the apex ball harder, the cue ball would bounce back too far and not be in the center of the table. But if you apply just a little high spin (move the cue tip up the diameter of a tip), the ball will bounce back, catch on the cloth, and roll forward a little to end up just where you want it.

Scratch!

Never use draw (low) on the break shot. The ball will collide with the rack and shoot right back toward you, often landing in the corner pocket for a scratch.

In Straight Pool, as I explain in Chapter 24, you *do* want to get the cue ball to come back to you on the *opening* break shot. (There are many break shots in one game of Straight Pool, and I explain them in Chapter 24.) You want the cue ball to come all the way back and stop against the head rail. But you don't accomplish that with draw (low spin); You use high-right (a combination of follow and right English).

I'm getting a little ahead of myself, though. Right now, I'll just say that you should control the cue ball on the break shot and that in most games, you'll want it to end up in the middle of the table. You best accomplish that task by using a center-ball hit or, on a very hard break shot, with a little high spin. Never use draw on a break shot.

In Search of the 1 Ball

Another surprise: As wild and uncontrolled as the open break looks, you now know that you can play cue-ball position on the shot, controlling the cue ball. But that's not all that you can do. You can also aim to shoot a specific ball into a specific pocket. That may be hard to imagine until I tell you how it works.

The ball that you're trying to pocket is the *apex ball*—the ball at the front point of the rack of balls. The apex ball usually is the 1 ball, but it doesn't matter for this discussion which ball it is. If you use the side-rail break position (which I describe in detail in the 9-Ball section later in this chapter) and hit the apex ball fully—and some people also recommend a touch of inside English—you have a good chance of making it in the opposite side pocket.

Put another way, if you break from the right side rail, the apex ball may go into the left side (center) pocket. How often does that happen on a break shot? Often enough that it's worth going for in some circumstances, especially when you consider the fact that you can't shoot any other ball toward a specific pocket with any reasonable expectation of making it. Billiards is a game of percentages in many ways, especially in the area of shot selection, and this shot may be only a 10 percent or 20 percent possibility. But compared with a 0 percent shot, which any other break shot would be, it doesn't look bad. The best thing about it, of course, is that you're hitting the apex ball full, and you get the maximum amount of *action* (ball movement), whether the 1 ball goes in the side or not. It's a no-lose move, and you can use it on a 9-Ball rack or a full rack of balls.

Pocket Dictionary

Action has a few meanings in billiards: the amount of movement of racked balls on the break shot, the amount of spin on the cue ball, and gambling.

If the 1 ball consistently heads just a little down-cushion or up-cushion from the side pocket, you can adjust your aiming point on the break shot to increase your odds of making the ball. The slight change in aiming and contact points won't affect the power of the break shot enough to make a difference, but it will affect the direction that the 1 ball takes. For some players, a touch of inside or outside English is better than adjusting the aiming point. Try it, and find out which technique works best for you. No matter which method you choose, remember that it takes only a minute adjustment to redirect the 1 ball enough to go in.

Hitting the Highs and Lows in 8-Ball

I'll save the break shots of other games for later in the book, but 8-Ball and 9-Ball are so popular (I imagine that 90 percent or more of the individual games played in billiard clubs are one or the other) that I want to tell you about them early on.

When you're hitting an open break shot, you have to take into consideration the combined weight of the objects that you're attempting to move. In 8-Ball, one ball—the white cue ball—has to move 15 balls. That's tougher than moving just nine balls in 9-Ball, so don't expect to see the balls move as far. On the other hand, there are a lot of balls, so there will be a lot of action (movement). The two back-corner balls are going to move the most. They have nothing to block them, whereas all the other balls are going to run into something behind them or beside them before they take off in some direction.

Few people use the side-rail break shot for 8-Ball, because it doesn't seem to garner enough response from the big pack of balls. Many people come close, however, by placing the cue ball just far enough away from the cushion to allow them to make a bridge on the playing surface. A perfect center-table, straight-on shot is used by quite a few players, but the most common cue position for an 8-Ball break is 5 or 6 inches to either side of the center of the table. You can place your hand firmly on the playing surface (something that you can't do on a side-rail shot) and get the maximum power.

When you're starting out, don't hit the apex ball very hard. The balls can grow wings very easily on a break shot. Keep everything smooth and solid and straight. If you do that—and if the balls were properly racked and you're not playing in ultrahumid conditions—the 15 balls will separate, and you'll be able to play the game as it should be played. Having a solid break—a good thing—means hitting the apex ball dead-center. A solid break produces the most action. A harder break can come later.

Cue Tips

If you're racking 8-Ball for your opponent, make sure that the back-corner balls are not in the same group. If they're both solid colored balls, for example, they may both go in a pocket, and your opponent would have a strong advantage over you from the start.

After you're confident of your straight-on break shot, try a very popular 8-Ball break: hitting the second ball instead of the first. You place the cue ball near the side rail (either one; whichever is most comfortable for you) and aim to hit the second ball (the one behind the apex ball) with inside-low spin. The combination of inside English and draw will keep you from scratching in the corner by pulling the cue ball to the side cushion. (If you're shooting from the right side of the table—toward the right side of the rack—inside English would be hitting the cue ball to the left of the vertical axis. When the cue ball hits the rack, it naturally bounces to the right, and inside English is always against the natural direction of the ball.)

Hitting the second ball is more likely to drive the 8-Ball out of the rack and toward the opposite corner pocket for (usually, depending on the rules) a game-winning break. It also seems to increase the chance that another ball will go into a pocket.

This break is much favored by the better 8-Ball players, but it's more difficult to execute. The first problem is that you don't have a full ball to aim at; part of it is hidden by the apex ball. That requires more accuracy, but working against accuracy is the fact that instead of a center-ball hit, you now have to put a little English on the ball, which is going to throw the cue ball slightly offline. You can see why it's a shot for more experienced hands. Still, it's worth a try and certainly worth learning.

When you're racking the balls for 8-Ball, it's best to have the two balls behind the apex ball be from different groups (a solid and a stripe). It's very important to have the two bottom-corner balls be from different groups. After that, it's moderately important to alternate the balls around the outside of the triangle (solid, stripe, solid, stripe…). Follow all the rules of a good rack: all balls touching their neighbors, the rack properly aligned, and key balls (in this case, the 8 ball) in their proper places.

Because so much 8-Ball is played on small tavern tables (3½ by 7 feet or 4 by 8 feet), which use a heavier-than-normal cue ball, I want to mention how these conditions affect the break. The heavier cue ball is a little harder to hit with high speed, but it decimates the neat rack of balls very effectively at even moderate speeds. Some players prefer using a slightly heavier cue (20 or 21 ounces) when they hit a break shot with this heavier ball.

Scratch!

If, in trying to hit the cue ball hard, you just clip the edge of it with your cue tip, and it slowly rolls toward the rack, you could be in a lot of trouble. If you can, grab the ball! The game doesn't officially start until the cue ball hits the first object ball, and grabbing the ball and putting it back is perfectly legal.

The heavier ball also tends to plow its way through the rack, rather than bouncing back, as a light cue ball would do. This situation can be good or bad. If the ball goes through the rack but doesn't have enough power to get back out, it can end up tied up with (touching) a bunch of object balls, making it impossible to pocket any of them. If you use a strong stroke, the ball usually comes back, having bounced off either the footrail or other balls, and you'll have a better chance at being clear enough to shoot another ball in a pocket (assuming that you make a ball on the break).

Diamond Cutting: The 9–Ball Break

The nine object balls in 9-Ball are racked in a diamond shape, with the 1 ball at the front and the 9 ball in the middle. The rest of the balls can be put anywhere, although you can use certain tricks, as I tell you in Chapter 26. But you can see that the balls, when hit, are much more likely to spread out than are the balls in an 8-Ball rack.

The conventional break for 9-Ball is made from near or off the side rail. If the side-rail position is used, the cue ball is placed 3 or 4 inches from the cushion, on the headstring. A looped (closed) rail bridge is used (see Chapter 11), and the shooter tries to get as close to a center-ball hit as possible, usually settling for one tip or less above center. If a bridge is made on the table, it's as close to the cushion as is comfortable. This angled approach gets the most ball movement and is so effective that at one point, one of the men's tours banned it, placing a limit on how close to the rail the cue ball could be placed. Too many people were making too many balls on the break and then running out the rack, so the games got to be boring for spectators.

I've seen some excellent players place the cue ball 3 or 4 inches from the center of the headstring and break from there with impressive results, but for most people, this type of shot is not as successful as a near-the-cushion break shot.

There is a way to break a 9-Ball rack that increases your chance of making the 9 on the break and winning the game. If the 9 doesn't go in but another ball does, however, the cue ball usually isn't left in a favorable position for you to make a second shot, which makes this style of break risky. Even though the odds of making the 9 ball increase, they're still less than 50–50. More than likely, you'll have to play out the game, and you'll be left in a position in which you can't make, or even hit, the 1 ball, so your opponent will come to the table.

Ewa's Billiard Bits

Every now and then, for some unknown reason, on a particular table the 9 ball goes in the pocket on the break an amazingly high percentage of the time. It happened during one tournament I was in, and the officials finally had to move the footspot (racking point) half an inch back from where it should have been. That solved the problem, but no one knows what caused it.

Scratch!

If a very good player wants to disguise how good she is, she might use the method of breaking to make the 9 ball that I describe in this section. It looks as though they *lucked* or *slopped* the 9 ball in, but they *still* won the game. If you play someone who gets that *lucky,* you're in over your head and should bail out.

If you're still interested in how to increase the odds of making the 9 on the break, I'll tell you how now. If you're shooting from the right side of the table, aim to hit the front ball—the 1 ball—a little to the right of center. Reverse this instruction if you're shooting from the left side. That's all there is to it.

The cue ball, unfortunately, will bounce off the 1 ball toward the side rail, a bit toward the corner pocket, rather than come back to the center of the table. From there, it will come back toward what used to be the back of the rack and is now a cluttered area of moving balls. The 1 ball will have headed toward the side pocket on the opposite side of the table, missed the pocket, and bounced farther up-table. Result: The cue ball and 1 ball are at opposite ends of the table, and another ball (or balls) blocks the path from one to the other.

If you want to take that gamble and increase your odds of making the 9 on the break, that's how you do it. In a friendly game, trying this technique may be worth your while, but I wouldn't do it in any kind of tournament, local or professional.

Breaking Open a Safe

The power break is used in most pool games: 8-Ball, 9-Ball, 6-Ball, 7-Ball, 10-Ball, Rotation, Bank Pool, Kiss Pool, Forty-One, Pea Pool, Cut-Throat, and more. Only a few games use a safety shot for the opening break, and the two best-known are Straight Pool and One-Pocket.

The first game, Straight Pool, is the mother of all pool games—the one played for the world championship during the first two thirds of the 20th century (it's been 9-Ball since then). The second game, One-Pocket, began as strictly a gambling game, but in the 1990s, it became a tournament game as well. It's a game of knowledge and strategy, and is often called *the chess of pool* because it requires creative maneuvering and thinking ahead four or five shots (or more, on occasion).

But I'm thinking ahead four or five chapters. Both games are explained in Chapters 24 and 28, respectively, and right now, I'm talking about break shots.

A safety break is the opposite of an open break. The goal of a safety break is not to make a ball, but to leave the cue ball in a place that prevents your opponent from making a ball on his turn—or, in the best of circumstances, prevents him from even being able to hit a ball in such a way that stops you from making one when you return to the table. Phrased another way, your opponent can't hit a ball and leave the balls so that when you come to the table you won't have a shot.

The best series (for you) goes like this: you break safe; your opponent makes a legal hit but leaves you a shot; then you make a ball and keep making them. Among players of high and equal skill, things are more likely to run this way: you break safe; your opponent makes a legal hit, leaving the balls safe (unpocketable); you make a legal hit, leaving the balls safe; and so on, until someone makes a mistake.

Ewa's Billiard Bits

Players are continually experimenting with different break shots: using spin, banking the cue ball off a cushion and into the rack, and so on. You may see some of these variations and think because a shot is not the standard way of breaking, it's illegal. But the requirements of any break shot are few, and as long as you meet them, you can do almost anything else that you want to do. The traditional approach became the traditional approach simply because it works best.

Breaking Safe in Straight Pool

The requirements for a break in Straight Pool are that the cue ball must contact an object ball and then two or more object balls must touch a cushion. Players quickly worked out the most effective way to do this and leave their opponents safe:

1. Place the cue ball on the headstring, the same distance from the side cushion that the back corner ball is from the cushion at the foot of the table.

2. Hit the cue ball with a moderate to soft stroke, using high-right spin (if you're shooting on the right side of the table).

The ball is aimed to just clip the back-corner ball of the rack. It does so, hits the bottom cushion, spins to the side cushion, and heads back up the table, coming to rest against the top rail. Meanwhile, the clipping hit sent the object ball to the back cushion, where it bounced off and returned to its original place (I hope). The force was transmitted down the back line of balls, and the opposite back-corner ball went straight out to the side cushion on its side of the table, bounced off, and rolled back where it originally was (again, I hope). The result is a neat rack, just like the one you started with, but the cue ball is now frozen against the top cushion a full table's length away. Shooting away from a cushion like that is very difficult at that distance. This is illustrated in Chapter 24.

By the way, the break shot in Snooker, illustrated in Chapter 28, is the same as the first break shot in Straight Pool. The result is different, because Snooker balls are smaller and lighter, and therefore less likely to roll back into their original positions. But aiming, spin, and final cue-ball position are identical. Snooker is played primarily in countries connected with Great Britain.

Breaking Safe in One-Pocket

One-Pocket, because it started as a gambling game, isn't as codified, but you also break safe. Sometimes, the requirements are the same as the ones for Straight Pool, but more often now, you're required to drive only one object ball to a cushion.

The object of the game is different from that of Straight Pool. Each player can make balls in only one pocket (hence, the name of the game). I explain One-Pocket in Chapter 28, but you need to know that basic fact now to understand the One-Pocket break. As you do in 8-Ball, you hit the second ball in the triangular rack. This time, you hit softly, using inside English. The cue ball bumps the balls toward one pocket; the balls don't bounce around because you hit them softly. The cue ball bounces off the rack and hits the bottom rail, where the inside (also called *reverse*) English fights its natural roll. The ball holds up, rolls to the side rail about two diamonds up, and stops there. That's the safe break in One-Pocket.

The Straight Pool and One-Pocket breaks are totally different from anything that you'll see in the open break games. The shooting technique that you use is the same one you use on any normal shot. You don't stand straighter, or put your body into it, or use any of the other tricks used in the open break. You shoot normally. The lack of power and frantic ball movement give both these games a more subdued and respectable image (although One-Pocket is just becoming respectable). Both games, probably not coincidentally, are more popular with mature, experienced players, but there's absolutely no reason why everyone can't play them. If you're the cerebral type, you should check out games that start with a safety break.

The Least You Need to Know

➤ The open break shot is different from all other shots in billiards.

➤ A good break should be, above all, accurate.

➤ Check the rack before breaking.

➤ On a break shot (and all shots), keep your cue as level as possible.

➤ You can alter your stance and form on a break shot.

➤ You can (and should) play cue-ball position on a break shot.

➤ The best method of breaking the balls in each game has been worked out over time.

Chapter 19

Bank Deposits

In This Chapter

➤ Why you should avoid the bank shot, if possible

➤ Systems for banking

➤ The effects of spin, speed, and angle on a banked ball

➤ When to use special effects on a bank shot

➤ Cue-ball position on a bank shot

The bank shot is widely known even among people who don't play pool. Although they may not be 100 percent sure what it is, they are still familiar with the term. Best-selling author Donald E. Westlake used it as the title of one of his books, *The Bank Shot* (about a bank robbery), and the book was later made into a movie with Robert Redford and George C. Scott, so it must be part of general public knowledge. But if you watch professional billiards on television, you may realize that you rarely see a bank shot. Something must be going on here.

I can tell you that I would rather cut a ball in than bank a ball in any day. But I also know that bank shots come up sometimes and that I'd better know how to handle them. That's the subject of this chapter.

In the world of theory, a ball that hits a cushion at a 45-degree angle bounces off the cushion at a 45-degree angle. If only that were so. Thinking that—and players who don't know what I'm about to tell you probably do believe it—is one sure way to miss a lot of banks.

A bank shot looks simple, and it can be defined simply enough. A *bank shot* is hitting an object ball into a cushion, from which it bounces off and goes where you want it to go: in the pocket, into another ball, or into a safe place where your opponent won't be able to hit it. Shoot the ball into a cushion, and watch it bounce back. You've just hit a bank shot. What could be easier? Not much—until you try to do it and send that object ball to a specific place while sending the cue ball to another specific place. Then you have to know some things.

Pocket Dictionary

A *bank shot* is hitting an object ball into a cushion; a *kick shot* is hitting the cue ball into a cushion.

When you shoot the cue ball into the cushion and it then hits an object ball, you've made a *kick shot*. In a bank shot, you shoot the object ball into the cushion; in a kick shot, you shoot the cue ball into the cushion. The shots are very different, and I reveal the mysteries of the kick shot in Chapter 22, but for now, let's go to the bank.

Plane Talk

Plane geometry, as you may remember from school, deals with angles and flat surfaces. Solid geometry deals with solid objects. Billiards deals with balls, but we're actually more concerned with plane geometry than with solid.

The easiest way to look at angles in billiards is to imagine yourself above the table, looking down, and seeing everything as a flat surface—including the balls, which you now see as circles. The diagrams in this book are two-dimensional (length, width) rather than three-dimensional (length, width, depth). Presenting balls as balls instead of flat circles would just clutter things, and my goal is to make a complex sport simple.

Ewa's Billiard Bits

No official record exists for the number of consecutively banked balls, because bank pool was not a tournament game until recently. Unofficially, however, the greatest bank player who ever lived—BCA Hall of Famer Eddie Taylor of Knoxville, Tennessee—holds the record by banking 28 balls in a row. To the uninitiated, that number may sound small, but believe me, it's astounding. I don't know anyone, anywhere who has come close to matching Taylor's feat.

In explaining the bank shot, I'll be using the phrases the *angle in* and the *angle out*.

Take a cue ball, and place it 6 or 7 inches off one of the long rail cushions. Hit it to the cushion on the other side of the table, but don't hit it straight into the cushion. Aim it down-table a foot or so. The ball hits the cushion and bounces back to your side of the table, although it ends up a couple of feet from you.

If you measure the angle between the cushion and the approaching path of the cue ball, that is the *angle in* or the *approach angle*. Measure the angle from the cushion to the line where the ball left the cushion; that is the *angle out* or *departing angle*. If you use a center ball hit at medium speed—and if you have good-quality cushions, good but not new cloth, and not too much humidity—the angles will be very close to each other.

Over the years, the first thing taught to new students has been *angle in equals angle out.* This effect is sometimes called the *mirror system*, meaning that the angles are mirror images of each other. Actually, this is true only under very specific conditions, but it's close enough to accurate for use when you play.

Later in this chapter in the section "Change at the Banks," I'll tell you how to change the angle out without changing the angle in; but for now, I'll deal with the basic shot, in which the angles are virtually equal. I always like to have a reference shot, and in banking, this is it: Medium stroke, center-ball hit, and perfect conditions equal a set of matching angles. In real life, you don't run into perfect conditions very often, and I'll show you how to find out what the conditions are doing to your angles.

The angle in and angle out can be anywhere from near 0 degrees to 90 degrees. Actually, 0 degrees wouldn't be a bank; you'd just be rolling the ball down the cushion edge. (The edge, by the way, is called the *nose* of the cushion.) At a 90-degree angle, of course, you're aiming straight into the cushion, and the cue ball is coming straight back at you. A 45-degree angle is one of the easiest to picture, so I'll use that in some of the examples in this chapter.

Pocket Dictionary

The *angle in* is the angle at which a ball approaches the cushion. The two sides of the angle are the cushion and the approach line. The *angle out* is the angle at which a ball leaves the cushion. The two sides of the angle are the cushion and the departure line.

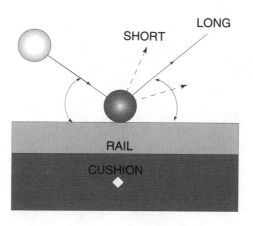

Angle in (A) equals angle out (B). The normal path of the cue ball is along the solid line. If the ball comes off long, it goes more in the direction of the top dashed line. If it comes off short, it goes along the bottom dashed line (marked short*).*

Two other terms that I use—and that you'll run into when you're talking about, thinking about, or figuring angles in pool—are *shortening the angle* and *lengthening the angle*. A ball is said to *come off short* if the angle out is bigger than the angle in. This is also called *straightening the ball*, although that phrase can be misleading, and I'd rather not see it used. To help you picture the effect, suppose that you hit a ball into a cushion at a 45-degree angle, but it comes off the cushion at an angle of 75 degrees. In other words, the ball came off straighter (more toward the center of the table) than it went in. *Coming off long* is, of course, the opposite. The next illustration makes things clear.

243

Using the reference system of angle in equals angle out, you can see how it would be relatively easy to figure out most bank shots. Many players, up to the pro level, get a mental picture of the bank and where to strike the cushion to get the object ball (OB) where they want it by walking around the table and viewing the shot from the other side (the side with the cushion that's going to be struck). In the following illustration, that side is the one where the photographer was standing. You'd stand close to the table and view the shot. It's easy to pick the spot on the cushion that will be where you want the OB to hit (or at least a narrow area that looks about right). Shoot the ball, and see how close you were.

Finding an aiming point on a cushion rather than a pocket takes some practice. Try walking around the table (to the side where the photographer isstanding to take this picture). It will help you visualize the angles.

That system is one of many. Others give you the exact point where the OB needs to contact the cushion. Exactly why there are so many systems for banking is difficult to say. It could be just that an individual's personality gravitates toward the look and feel of a particular system. For some people, the ghost table works best; for others, the parallel-line system is better. Every system has its advocates, and I'm sure that as you look over the choices in this chapter, one of them will appeal to you more than the others—each to his own.

Scratch!

Not all cushions are the same. The shapes may differ on off-brand tables, but the biggest difference is in the rubber used for the cushion. Some types give you a truer rebound than others. If your banks are consistently off, but conditions are good, the cushions are suspect.

You Can Bank On It

Before I get into banking systems, you need to know a few more terms. I try to keep the jargon to a minimum, but these are basic billiard terms, and if I didn't use them, my explanation of the systems—and things in future chapters—would get really long-winded. So add these terms to your vocabulary.

A *cross-table bank* is one that you shoot across the table. It can go in either the side pocket or a corner pocket and still be a cross-table bank, but if it is aimed at the corner pocket it's called a cross-corner bank. If you're shooting the length of the table and banking back into the corner pocket, the shot is called just a long bank. If a ball is near a cushion and you clip it, driving it into the cushion, and the ball then bounces off and into a pocket on the opposite side of the table, you are said to have *crossed* or *cross-banked the ball*.

The Ghost Table

You had the ghost ball for aiming, and now you have the ghost table for aiming banks. Very simply, you imagine another table, set parallel to your table, with the closest cushions overlapping the real table and the pockets fitting in the real pockets. To use the ghost table, imagine that the two tables are hinged along the cushion and open up like a clamshell. Find the same pocket on the ghost table that you want to bank the ball into on the real table. (Hint: That pocket will be on the far side of the ghost table.) Just aim your OB to that pocket. That's all there is to it.

The tricky part is seeing something that isn't there and aiming at it. With a ghost ball, the trick was easy; an entire table is a little tougher for most people. But if you're able to visualize the ghost table, it's probably the simplest banking system going (see the following illustration).

Suppose that you're going to bank a ball across the table (called, oddly enough, a cross-table bank), into the center (side) pocket. (The pockets in the middle of the long rail are called side pockets because they're in the side of the table, as opposed to the end or the corner. In snooker, they're called the middle or center pocket.)

Pocket Dictionary

A *cross-table bank* is a bank across the table, as opposed to a bank the length of the table. *Crossing a ball* is hitting the edge of an object ball so that it goes into a cushion and then bounces back, crossing the path of the cue ball. *Cross-banking* is banking a ball by crossing it.

Cue Tips

It's hard to use the ghost-table system at home, because most home billiard rooms aren't large enough. In a billiard club, there's usually a table next to yours, and when you pick out the ghost pocket, it will probably fall somewhere in the middle of the next table. Use that real spot as your aiming point.

Stand on the cue-ball side of the real table—the side you'll be shooting from—and picture the hinge and the ghost table opening up. Picture the far side pocket of the ghost table; then get down and hit the object ball to it. The ball will, of course, hit the real cushion and bounce back into the side pocket on your side of the table.

You can do the same thing with the corner pocket (also a cross-table bank). If you have a long bank (length of the table rather than across it), you can put your ghost table end to end with the real table, once again with the pockets overlapping. The system works just as well this way as it did on the cross-table bank shot.

The ghost table. The text tells you how to aim by using the pockets on the ghost table to bank balls on the real table. Some people can imagine a point in midair better than others can, so see whether this system works for you.

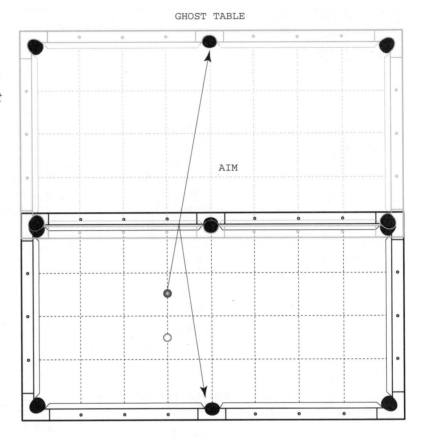

GHOST TABLE

AIM

The First National Bank of the Parallels

Figuring out parallel-lines banking is easy and works pretty well.

The following illustration helps explain the concept, but you need words, too, and I've got a few of those. This system is easiest to use if you suspend your cue over the line and then move the cue to the object ball. That technique also makes it easy to spot someone who is using the system, because he'll be holding his cue above the table and carefully moving it sideways—something you don't do in any other system. You can visualize the line without using your cue, but why make it hard on yourself?

In the illustration, the goal is to hit a ball cross-table and bank it into the center pocket near you. I'll call that pocket B, and the center pocket directly across from it is pocket A. Draw an imaginary line (see, you really have to be creative to play pool!) from the object ball to the pocket that you want it to go in (B). Find the halfway point. Suspend the butt of your cue at that point (a few inches over the point), and hold the shaft end over the opposite pocket (A).

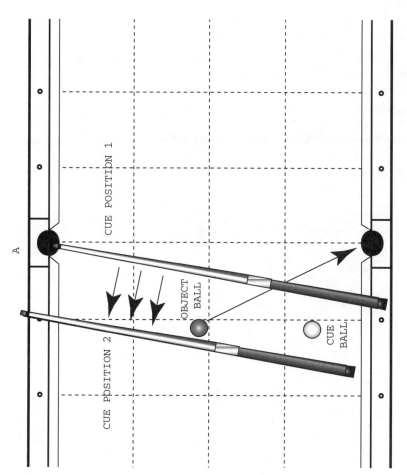

This is the parallel-lines banking system. Like a couple of other systems, it uses the pocket that's across the table (A) from the pocket that the ball will go in (B). Also like some other systems, it requires a bit of imagination, because you have to draw an imaginary line and find its halfway point.

Now move your cue to the object ball, but make sure that you keep the cue oriented in exactly the same direction. The result: Cue position 2 (in the illustration) is parallel to cue position 1. That's why the system is called the parallel-lines banking system. The point where your cue crosses the cushion is where you want the object ball to hit if you want it to go into pocket B. That point is marked in the illustration with a little *X*.

System X

The X system (see the following illustration) is fairly easy, and some people believe that it's a little more accurate than the preceding two, because it looks a tad more complicated. It's similar to the

Scratch!

Many of these banking systems are best visualized by using a cue, but be careful not to touch a ball with any part of the cue or your hand. That can be a foul, which will cost you your turn.

parallel-lines system, but you don't have to depend on your ability to keep a cue aiming in the right direction as you move it.

Draw a line from the object ball to the middle of the opening in pocket B, which is the pocket across the table from where you expect to make the object ball (pocket A). Draw a second imaginary line straight to the cushion from the object ball (line 2). From that point on the cushion, draw a line to the center of the opening in pocket A (line 3). The *X* where the two lines cross may be hard to find, because the lines are invisible. I find that it's easier to use my cue to make line 1 (the one to pocket A). I keep the cue there, as line 1, with the tip in the pocket; then I can more easily visualize the other lines. After I find the *X*, I draw a final line straight to the cushion. That point is where I aim the object ball to make it in pocket B.

This diagram belongs in your X file. The text explains how to draw these imaginary lines for the X system of banking. This is one of the most accurate systems around.

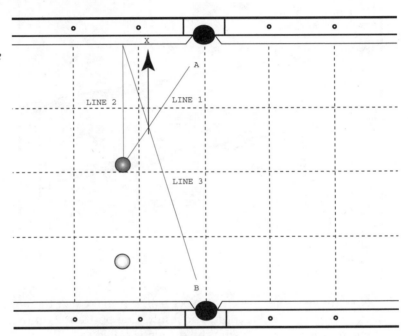

Feeling from a Bank

In the game called Bank Pool, every ball pocketed must be banked in. No straight-in shots, combinations, or luck are allowed; you have to bank a ball for it to count. It's rarely a tournament game, although there have been sporadic Bank Pool events. The game is played heavily in Kentucky and the surrounding area, but not often elsewhere. When I've talked to the nation's best bank players, they've told me that all the systems they've tried work well, but that when a person has banked as many balls as they have, every bank is really shot by feel. They call on their experience, because they just know where to aim the object ball so that it banks into a pocket. They don't use systems, and even when they started, they rarely depended on a system to know where to hit the ball.

Banking by feel is a legitimate way to bank a ball—if you have that experience behind you and know what varying spins and speeds do to make the ball come off at an unnatural angle. Beginners bank by guesstimate, which is not the same thing (although it may look like it). Guesstimating gets you there some of the time, but don't let it mislead you into thinking that it's a high-percentage approach. Banking by feel also gets you there, but it takes a storehouse of banking experience to be successful.

The best approach is to try the systems described in the preceding sections, find the one that you're the most successful with, and use it over and over. The more experience you gain with a system, the faster, more easily, and more accurately you'll be able to use it. At a certain point, you'll discover that you're no longer depending on the system, because you've developed a feel for banking.

The Easiest Banking System

Here's a final word on the angle-in-equals-angle-out system. This simple formula works for a medium stroke, center ball, level cue, and good conditions and equipment. If any of those factors varies, the formula gives you the reference point that you need to figure out how far off normal the variable takes the ball. And if you don't vary anything too much, the formula still takes your object ball very close to the pocket (often close enough to go into the pocket). To turn it into a simple banking system, you just need to be able to guess.

Look back at the first photograph in this chapter. You can see that if I hit the object ball full, it would hit the cushion closest to the camera and bank toward the side pocket where I'm standing. But the OB wouldn't go in, because it would be too far to the right (the right as you look at the picture).

Mentally make a little *X* where the object ball would hit the cushion on this straight shot. Now move that *X* a little to the left, and use the angle-in-equals-angle-out equation. Ignore the cue ball; its only purpose is to hit the object ball where you mentally place the *X*, and it doesn't otherwise figure into the angles or the formula.

Now that you've moved the *X* to the left, figure out the new path of the object ball. It should be closer to the pocket—and if you moved the *X* to the right spot, the ball will go in the pocket. Adjust as needed until you have the right spot.

That's the estimated-angle-in-equals-angle-out banking system. No system is easier, although a couple of the others are a little more precise. Chances are, however, that you'll have a lot of success with this simple little gem.

Cue Tips

Here's a tip that will help you picture your banking angles. Walk around to the other side of the table, and look at the balls and pocket from that perspective. You'd be amazed by how a change in perspective makes everything obvious.

Multiple-Cushion Banks

On rare occasions, the only way to get the object ball into the pocket (or to put it somewhere that your opponent can't hit it) is to bank the ball two or three cushions. For a close estimate of where the ball will end up, you can double the systems described in the preceding sections—one for each cushion. But you also need to take into consideration an additional factor: what happens when the object ball comes off the first cushion. Because it approached from an angle, the ball rubs against the cushion nose, which adds sidespin (English) to the ball.

Remember that English has little effect on the path of the ball until the ball touches a cushion. (It curves out slightly and spins back in, as I tell you in Chapter 16.) In a multiple-rail bank, the ball picks up English on the first cushion (*outside English*, also known as *running English*) and is spinning when it hits the second rail, so it comes off the rail long. That situation messes up the figures in the banking systems, and you have to estimate a correction factor. If the angles in and out are fairly steep (closer to straight into the cushion), there will be less added spin than if the angle is slight (closer to parallel with the cushion). This situation also comes up when you're kicking a ball, as I explain in Chapter 22.

Trying to compensate for that added English—by going into the first cushion with a little inside spin, for example— makes the ball come off the first cushion at an unnatural angle, either long or short (short, in the case of inside spin). That, too, makes any system inaccurate. The only way to deal with this added spin is to add it into your computations as a rough estimate based on experience, knowing that the ball will come off the second angle long.

Change at the Bank

Now that you know the effect of English (sidespin), draw (bottom spin), and follow (topspin) on a cue ball, and you also know about the gear effect, I can put them together in telling you how to bank a ball into a cushion. You can use all these effects to make the ball come off the cushion at an unnatural angle—and you choose the angle.

You can also play around with two more factors that affect the rebound angle: the speed (hardness) of the hit and the angle (shallow or sharp) at which the ball approaches the cushion. The following sections take these factors one at a time.

The Gear Effect and Banking

In "Multiple-Cushion Banks" earlier in this chapter, you saw how sidespin can shorten or lengthen the way that a ball comes off a cushion in a bank shot. Inside sidespin makes the ball hold up (come off the cushion at a sharper angle), whereas outside spin makes a ball come off the cushion long (at a smaller angle than the one at which it went into the cushion).

Well, draw and follow can have similar effects. Draw tends to shorten the rebound, and follow tends to lengthen it, just as outside English lengthens it and inside English shortens it. The key to hitting a bank with sidespin (English) is to remember to figure in the gear effect. If you put left spin on the cue ball, it translates into right spin on the object ball, and it's that right spin that hits the cushion.

Speed Shortens

Hitting a ball hard makes it go deeper into the cushion, which tends to straighten the rebound angle. What happens is that the ball is grabbed by the cushion, which tries to kick it straight out. The front face of the ball (as the ball enters the cushion on its approach angle) runs into a wall of resistance in front and to the side when it presses into the cushion.

Picture a ball hit into a cushion at a shallow angle, and I think you'll be able to understand that the cushion force against the ball is more in front and on the side than at the rear of the ball. The shallower the angle, the more pronounced the wall of resistance, and the more straightening effect it has on the object ball. This effect makes a firm shot rebound short. A shot hit at medium speed shows a little of this effect, but not much, and a slow shot shows no straightening effect at all. Speed, then, is a very important factor when you bank a ball, because it can seriously affect the rebound angle.

Scratch!

If the object ball is close to the cushion, it's tougher to bank. It bounces back so fast that it often collides with the cue ball a second time, and neither ball goes where it's supposed to go.

Cue Tips

If the cue ball is close to the cushion and you're going to bank it, try using inside English. This technique often scoots the cue ball to the side after it hits the object ball, getting it out of the way.

Slow! Wet Bank Ahead

High humidity also acts as a straightening element on a bank shot. A damp cloth stretched over a damp cushion deadens the response of the cushion, and it loses some of its bounce. Less bounce means that the ball comes off the cushion short. The ball also slows down. That doesn't have any direct effect on the angles, but it may mean that you have to hit the ball harder to get it where you want to go, and as you now know, the speed of the ball *does* affect the angles.

The Long Line at the Bank

Banking from one end of the table to the other simply magnifies any error in your bank. You'd think that this fact would automatically make long banks very low-percentage shots, but a good number of players actually find them to be easier than cross-table banks. The difference is probably just psychological—but hey, this game is mostly mental anyway, and any psychological boost should be appreciated.

My guess is that it has something to do with the fact that a lot of cross-table banks (into the side pockets) seem to put you out in the middle of nowhere, whereas the long cushion walls of the table-length bank seem to give you reference points that stay within your line of vision while you aim your bank. Then again, maybe not.

Whatever the reason, one thing is definite: There's no reason to fear a table-length bank shot. You can use all the same systems, and all the rules of the variations apply. Like everything else I'm teaching you, if you practice it, you can do it.

When to Use the Variables

When I showed you how the variables—spin, speed, and so on—affect the angle at which the ball leaves the cushion, I did it for a reason. At times, you can't shoot an angle-in-equals-angle-out bank and make the object ball go in the pocket—there may be a *blocking ball* (a ball that is in the path of the cue ball or object ball). If so, simply reach into your new bag of billiard knowledge, choose your weapon (spin, speed, and so on), and adjust your shot accordingly.

Go back to the first photograph in this chapter. Picture the path that the cue ball would take on it's way to the object ball. Now put an imaginary ball just over the edge of that path, so I can still hit the object ball, but can't hit it at the angle needed to bank it into the pocket near me. I'd see where the object ball would go with the hit that I can put on it. If it's long, I put outside spin on the cue ball (remember the gear effect). That puts inside spin on the object ball which makes it come off the cushion shorter than it normally would. Or I hit it hard and let the speed shorten the rebound angle. If I have a lot of shortening to do, I might use both spin and speed.

The other times when you may need to alter the angles is when you want the cue ball to go somewhere in particular. You can put spin on the cue ball, because you now know how to get the cue ball to go somewhere with spin. But if you do so, the cue ball transfers the opposite spin to the object ball (gear effect) and changes the rebound angle. To compensate, you have to aim the object ball at a different point on the cushion. That way, the effects cancel each other out, and the object ball goes where it originally was going to go: in the pocket. The result for the object ball is the same, but the cue ball now goes in a direction that is different from the original shot, because you added spin to it and because you're hitting the object ball at a different angle.

Pocket Dictionary

A *blocking ball* is any ball that blocks (or partially blocks) the path from the cue ball to the object ball or from the object ball to the pocket.

You may want to read that paragraph again. The thing to take away from it is that you can use something other than center ball and medium speed to change the path (but not the ultimate destination) of the object ball and to end up with the cue ball in different positions. The concept is, admittedly, a little complex. and a bit difficult to execute successfully until you've been playing and practicing for at least six months. But I'd rather explain it to you, and show you how you can do it to achieve a goal, than have you do it accidentally and not understand how or why you missed a bank shot that you thought should have gone into the pocket.

This knowledge also lets you reverse-engineer missed shots. Notice what the ball did. You now know what caused it to do that, so you can figure out what you must have done (hit it with sidespin when you thought you were hitting center ball, for example).

Back-Cutting a Ball

In the following illustration, I'm back-cutting a ball (also called *shooting a reverse cut*). When you back-cut a ball, you're not necessarily banking it, although in the picture, that's what I'm doing on this shot.

Defining a back cut briefly is not the easiest thing in the world, but the definition requires an explanation, and I'm to keep things as easy and as quick as possible. So here goes: A *back cut* is shooting a ball from inside its natural angle. You can back-cut a bank or a regular shot, but it's easier to understand the concept of a back cut when you think of a bank shot (at least, I think it is). Let's see.

Set up a cross-table bank shot as I have in the illustration below, but take away the cue ball. Draw an imaginary *V* that takes the object ball neatly into the cushion closest to the camera and then into the opposite pocket. Any time the cue ball position is within that *V*, you're back-cutting the object ball. Any time the cue ball is outside the *V*, you're simply cutting the object ball. If the cue ball is on the line of the *V*, you're shooting a straight (full in the face) shot.

> **Cue Tips**
>
> This technique is illegal in a game, but when you're practicing your bank shots at home or at the club, place a piece of chalk on the cushion to mark the spot that you want the object ball to hit.

Now move the object ball so that it and the cue ball are in line with the pocket. If you shoot straight, the object ball goes in. If you move the cue ball to the right of the picture frame, you are shooting a back cut (reverse cut), and if you move it to the left in the picture, you're shooting a regular cut shot.

The reason why back cuts are important to know is that when players start to play, they sometimes fail to think of shooting a back cut or think that's there's something mysterious about it. *Au contraire*. A back cut follows all the rules of any other cut shot, and as I've said before, the exactly straight-in shot is so rare that you can say that almost every shot is a cut shot.

The cue ball is inside the natural V (see text), which makes this shot a back cut (also known as a reverse cut) instead of a regular cut. Not every player notices back cuts.

Figuring the angle for the reverse bank shot in the illustration is the same as figuring the angle on any bank shot. The same systems are used, the same contact point/aiming point figuring is used, and the same stroke is used. Extreme back cuts are a trifle more difficult, because when you're down on the shot, you're looking a little away from the pocket, rather than finding what falls naturally within your view. But don't let that fact intimidate you in any way. A back cut is just as easy as a cut shot.

The Least You Need to Know

➤ You should avoid banks, if possible, because they leave room for error.

➤ You can bank a ball across the table, into the side or corner pocket, or the length of the table into a corner pocket.

➤ Banks are not limited to hitting just one cushion on a shot.

➤ There are various systems for figuring out how to hit a successful bank shot.

➤ The speed of the balls, spin on the cue ball or object ball, and angle of the bank all affect the way that a ball rebounds.

➤ You can use the preceding variations to make difficult banks or achieve cue-ball positioning.

Chapter 20

Combos, Caroms, Kisses, Clusters, and the Two-Way Shot

In This Chapter

➤ How to play a combination

➤ All about carom shots

➤ There's kissing in billiards

➤ Throwing a ball without ever touching it

➤ Eliminating clusters of balls

➤ Why you should smile when you see a two-way shot

This next level of shots puts together many of the basics that you've learned in the past few chapters. Up to now, you've been able to use your knowledge of spin and speed to make shots and get position with the cue ball after the shot. That still applies in this chapter; making shots and getting position are how you win. But in this chapter, you get the chance to use your imagination and creativity in a new, more exciting way.

I give you the fundamentals of the shots, and just knowing that they exist will take the walls out of your billiard thinking. Your friends will look at the balls on the table and think that you're in a hopeless position. Then you'll pull one of these gems from left field and watch their jaws drop. Shots like these open opportunities when there don't appear to be any, and they very often make the difference between winning a set and losing it. You'll see one (or more) in virtually every professional tournament match. They are basic shots that every player should have in his or her arsenal. The same opportunities come up in nontournament games, too, and you need to know how to recognize and handle them.

I once talked with the late, legendary Willie Mosconi, who was World Champion 15 times, and during the conversation, I asked what he did when he didn't have a shot. Without hesitation, he said, "You always have a shot." What he meant was that if you're knowledgeable enough and creative enough, you can always come up with something that puts you at an advantage. It may be a clever safety (I tell you about safeties in Chapter 22), but more often, it's an aggressive shot.

The best players, like Willie Mosconi, can always be counted on to produce magic out of a mess. More likely than not, these shots are the ones that they pull out of their little black bag. Most of them involve a third ball; you use the cue ball, the object ball (OB), and a second OB. That means that you have to be very accurate when you shoot one of these gems, but it doesn't change any of the fundamental rules of ball behavior that I told you about in previous chapters. The laws of physics still apply.

Pocket Dictionary

A *combination shot* (usually called simply a *combination*) is hitting one object ball into a second object ball, almost always with the goal of pocketing the second OB.

Breaking the Combination

Hit one object ball into another, and you've hit a *combination* shot. As far as definitions go, that's all there is to it. The goal of a combination shot is simple: to pocket the second ball. The reasons to shoot a combination are just as simple: if the first ball won't go in a pocket or if the second ball is a game-winning ball. But if everything is so simple, why do players avoid the combination shot unless it's a sitting duck?

What makes a combination a difficult shot is the fact that any error in aiming is magnified by the time the first object ball gets to the second object ball. Naturally, the farther apart the balls are, the more the error gets magnified. This is illustrated in the following diagrams.

When the object balls are close to each other and close to the pocket, you have a large margin for error. Hitting either of the marked contact points still pockets the second ball of the combination.

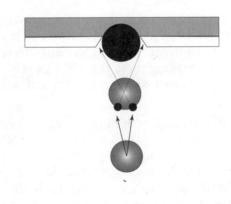

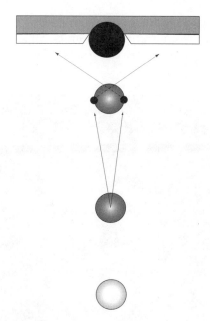

This illustration shows the same errors in hitting the first object ball as in the preceding illustration, but the result, because of the increased distance between the balls, is a total miss.

You have a fairly large margin for error when you're hitting a ball into a pocket, because the pocket is twice the width of the ball. If you're a millimeter or two off in your aim, and if the pocket is only a couple of feet away, no problem. If the OB travels at a 45-degree angle instead of a 48-degree angle, it still goes in the hole. If the object ball (OB) is really close to the hole, the margin is even greater. But 1 or 2 degrees or more on the angle—and that means missing the contact point by only a millimeter— can be a problem over the length of the table. By the time the OB gets to the pocket, it can be many inches off.

Square the Error

Now let's put that knowledge to work on a combination. With a combination shot, there is space between the first OB and the second OB, so if your hit on the first OB is off by a couple of degrees, that error is greater by the time it hits the second OB (meaning that you miss the contact point by more). Instead of being 1 or 2 millimeters off the correct contact point, you could be 5 or 10 millimeters off. The second OB might not go anywhere near the pocket.

The three most common conditions that are favorable to a combination are when all three balls—the cue ball and both object balls—are within the total distance of 1 foot, when the second OB ball is very close to a pocket opening, or when the two OBs are very close to each other. You can see what this looks like in the photo below. In the first situation,

Scratch!

The worst combination, bar none, occurs when both object balls are against a cushion. The second OB may be close to the corner pocket, but that doesn't matter. The shot leaves zero margin for error.

there's not much distance for any error in aiming to be magnified. In the second situation, a small error doesn't matter, because the second ball can be off and still go in the pocket. In the third situation, the key distance (between the two OBs) is so small that an aiming error can't be magnified.

A typical combination. The balls are close together, they are fairly well lined up, and the last ball is close to the pocket. This is a game of 9-Ball, and I'm about to hit the 1 ball into the 9 ball, which will then go into the pocket and win the game. Knowing how to win sure is fun!

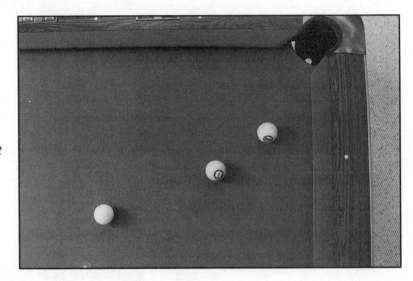

So not all combinations are the same. Some are high percentage and some are low percentage, and now that you can recognize the characteristics of each, you can decide which are playable and which are too tough to give you a good chance of success. The ability to judge the difficulty of shots—the percentage of times you'll make it against the percentage of times you'll miss—is something that you'll carry throughout your billiard-playing lifetime. Many times, the smart thing to do is shoot a safety (see Chapter 22) rather than go for the shot. To know when to do that, you have to know your own abilities, as well as know what shots are tougher or easier than they look.

In the chapter on trick shots (Chapter 23), I show you a shot in which two object balls placed at one end of the table, touching each other. The shooter stands at the other end of the table with the cue ball and shoots at the front ball. If the balls are set up correctly, no matter where the shooter hits the front ball, both balls go in (one in the bottom-left corner pocket and the other in the bottom-right corner pocket). The margin of error is huge, because the object balls are touching and can go in only one direction each, no matter what the contact point is. Shots don't get any higher-percentage than that, and seeing that same opportunity on the pool table has to bring a smile to your face.

Aiming a Combination Shot

If you're faced with a combination that looks promising, there's a good way to figure out how to aim it:

1. Go to the second OB (the one that will go in the pocket), and aim it as though it were a cue ball. That's the way to find the spot on the second OB that the first OB needs to hit.

2. After you find that spot, do the same thing with the first OB: Aim it at the spot on the second OB that you want it to hit. By doing that, you've found the contact point on the first OB, and all you need to do is hit that point with the cue ball.

Naturally, you want to use center ball, because any sidespin (English) will only complicate matters. Remember, too, that any cut shot adds a little spin to the object ball. If you're cutting the first OB to the right, it will have a little left spin when it hits the second OB—not a lot, and it won't matter much over a short distance. But if the balls are worn or dirty, the effect could amount to enough to negatively affect the shot.

Following are a few things to consider before doing the combo mambo:

➤ Combos are easiest when all the balls are close together.

➤ If the second OB is right in front of the pocket, one ball can be a good distance from the other.

➤ A combo is easier if the two object balls are close to each other.

➤ Always try to shoot a combo using center ball, a medium or soft stroke, and a level cue.

➤ Any original aiming error is magnified by the time that the second OB is hit.

The magnification of error is the toughest thing about a combination shot. Overcoming this factor takes a lot of concentration and very precise aiming, which probably is why so many people forget all about playing position. Unless you're knocking the game-winning ball in the pocket (more combinations are played to sink the 9 ball in the game of 9-Ball than at any other time), you'll have another shot after you make the combo. As with any shot, if you don't move the cue ball into position for a follow-up shot, making the combo doesn't do you much good. So remember to *play position for the cue ball when you shoot a combo.*

Cue Tips

If you're having trouble with combination shots, try pretending that the second object ball is a pocket and that you're aiming at a particular part of the pocket (as I explain in the discussion of cheating the pocket in Chapter 13).

Pocket Dictionary

When a ball spinning on its vertical axis (sidespin) touches another ball and lightly grabs it, it is said to be *throwing* it off its natural line. Also, when two balls that are touching are hit by a moving ball (better thought of as *push*) the second ball is *thrown* off line.

Throwing a Ball into a Pocket

One combination shot is a little different from the normal combo, and it requires you to bring an additional bit of information to the table. I mentioned a trick shot a couple of paragraphs ago and said I'll tell you more about it in Chapter 23. But it introduces something that you need to know about in this chapter: the concept of *throw*. You know about one kind of throw. When the cue ball is hit with sidespin, it throws the object ball a little offline when it hits it, especially if the balls are old or dirty. The other type of throw comes into play in a combination shot when the first and second OB are touching. I think of this force as a push, but the common term in pool is throw, so I'll use that term (but keep the push concept in your mind).

The quickest way to see throw in action is to set up the trick shot that I mentioned. Put an object ball on the footspot. Freeze a second object ball to it, and sight down the table to make sure that the balls are perfectly lined up toward the center of the corner pocket. If you took a cue and hit the ball in back, the one in front would head exactly toward the pocket.

Now take the cue ball and go to the other (head) end of the table. Aim anywhere on the front ball (the one on the footspot), and hit it. I'll bet that you missed the pocket. The ball hit the bottom rail near the pocket, but it didn't go in. The reason was throw (or push). The front ball did, indeed, transfer energy to the second ball and drive it forward, but because the balls were touching, the hit also exerted some force in the direction away from the cue ball's path. That pushed it forward a little and made you miss, even though the two balls were lined up to hit the center of the pocket.

When you run into a combination in which the balls are touching (or within $1/8$ of an inch of each other), take this phenomenon into consideration. You can decrease the effect slightly by using outside English on the hit, but it still shows up.

On rare occasions, three balls are touching, and you have to hit one of the end balls. (The game has an endless number of possibilities—all of which seem to come up eventually—and you'll never get bored, no matter how long you play.) All the same rules apply, of course. You just have to figure out the double push (throw) from the first object ball to the second, and from the second to the third. Then you have to look at two contact points and establish two 90-degree lines to figure out where all three balls are going.

Theoretically, you could do this computing of multiple contact points and articles with 9 balls or 15 balls—a full rack, in other words. But the huge number of contact points, recontact points, angles, and interactions makes it impossible. Still, it's not outside the realm of consideration. In Part 6, I show you how to rack the balls with certain balls in certain places because the probability of the balls in specific places going in specific directions is high. I figured this out by observing rack after rack, though, and not by making careful calculations involving the almost-instantaneous interactions of the balls on the break shot. The breaking of a rack of balls could be thought of as one huge combination shot, but that's a pretty scary concept.

The Carom Corner

You can make a ball other than the first object ball, as I showed you in the preceding sections on the combination shot. Another way to do that is to use a carom. A *carom* (pronounced care-um) is a shot in which the cue ball hits the first object ball, bounces off, and hits a second object ball, which goes into a pocket. In an earlier chapter, I gave you an example as a way of illustrating Ewa's Second 90-Degree Rule of Billiards, so the concept should be vaguely familiar to you already.

To nail down the concept, shoot a Carom, as follows:

1. Place two balls together, as though they were frozen at the moment of impact.

2. Draw an imaginary line from the center of one ball to the center of the other.

3. Draw another line, at a 90-degree angle to the first, at the halfway point of the first line (the contact point).

4. Shoot one of the balls. The moving ball (the cue ball, in a simple shot) hits the object ball (OB) and bounces off along this line (to the right if it approached from the left, and vice versa).

As I showed you with draw and follow, you can change this natural center ball direction, making it more or less than 90 degrees.

Let's deal with the simple center ball. The situation on the table in the following illustration is that the ball you must hit won't go in a pocket, because another ball is sitting right in front of the pocket, blocking its path. Because of the positioning, a combination is too tough. Guess at a point on the first OB, and see where the natural 90-degree path of the cue ball will take the white ball. If that path will send the cue ball into the second OB and knock that ball in the pocket, you've found your contact point. If not, pick another contact point on the first OB and see what that does. When you eventually find the right point, you can use a center-ball hit and easily pocket the second OB.

Pocket Dictionary

A *carom* is making the cue ball hit an object ball and then bounce off and hit another object ball (usually, in pool.) into a pocket.

Ewa's Billiard Bits

One way that people create new trick shots is to start with the basic principles and shots in this chapter. They twist concepts slightly or combine a couple of shots into one shot. You can make up your own tricks the same way.

A typical carom opportunity. The 1 ball can't be pocketed, but by hitting the 1 in the correct place, I can carom the cue ball off it and into the 9 ball, which will go in the pocket. This is so much fun!

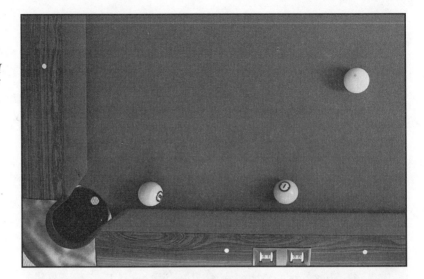

Uh-oh. Yes, it's a Carom opportunity, but it's tough. Notice the difference in angles (the cue ball off the 1 ball) and the increased distances between the balls. Also notice that the 9 ball is a little farther from the pocket than in the preceding illustration. All those factors add up to a very tough shot.

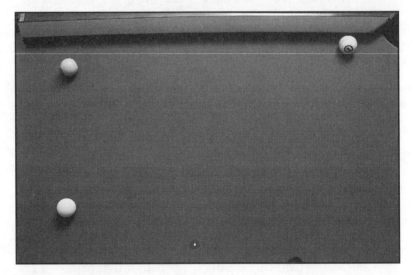

Caroms with Draw and Follow

If no point that you can hit will make the cue ball go off the first OB the way that you need it to, you can start thinking about hitting the cue ball with a little draw or follow to alter its path. This, as you know, complicates things a little bit, but if the balls are close together, you shouldn't have much of a problem. On rare occasions, you'll have to use sidespin (usually, combined with draw) to get to the object ball.

After you've opened up to the idea that you don't have to pocket the ball that you hit first, caroms, like combinations, pop up more frequently than you might have thought. The ability to see and execute them broadens your range of possible shots, gives you opportunities where there don't appear to be any, and gets the problem-solving part of your billiard brain working.

Like combinations, caroms require a little figuring and a very accurate hit. Also like combos, caroms often cause cause players to ignore what will happen to the cue ball and first object ball after the carom has successfully pocketed the second OB. Take a minute to figure out the paths and distances that the cue ball and first object ball will travel. Remember—unless the game-winning ball was pocketed, you'll have to shoot the same object ball on your next shot, and you want it and the cue ball to end up in places where that's possible (and easy!).

Scratch!

You don't have a shot, and you're tempted to just smash the balls to see what happens. Resist. Many more bad things can happen than good things. Trust me on this one.

A Pair of Special Caroms

A couple of caroms are especially neat, and they're worth talking about. One is called a tickie, and the other is a carom with draw. I'll discuss the second one first, because it needs little preliminary explanation.

You know how to draw your cue ball, and you know what a carom is, so simply combine the two. Hit the object ball fairly full, drawing the cue ball back into another ball, which you'll hit into a pocket. The shot usually comes up at one end of the table or the other. You have to hit a ball (say, the 2 ball). The cue ball is near corner pocket A, and the 2 ball is along the cushion, halfway to corner pocket B. Trouble is, two or three awkwardly placed balls are in the way. And sitting right in front of pocket A, not far from your cue ball, is the game-winning 9 ball. The draw-carom is the obvious shot if you know about it, and now you do.

This shot is really just a draw shot. But because the first object ball isn't the one that's supposed to go into a pocket, and because the cue ball does come off it and knock in a second object ball, it is a carom shot as well. You don't have to restrict its use to a game-winning ball; you can use it on any ball.

You can do the same thing with a lot of follow, but generally, wherever you can get following the object ball, the object ball itself could go, and you could shoot a combination instead. Putting a huge amount of follow on the cue ball makes knowing where it's going after it hits the object ball a little tricky. The combination usually is the better choice.

There is a game called Carom (see Chapter 28), played with three balls (four in Korea) on a table

Pocket Dictionary

Tickie (also spelled *ticky*) is when the cue ball hits the cushion and then the back side of an object ball near the cushion, and continues on.

Ewa's Billiard Bits

The world record for the number of
consecutive caroms scored in Three-
Cushion Billiards is 28. A Japanese
player and a Flemish player are co-
holders of the record.

without pockets. The object is to make a carom on the
first ball and send your cue ball into the second ball,
scoring a point. I mention the game here because that
game uses a shot called a *tickie* (also spelled *ticky*). In the
most popular variation of the Carom game, called Three-
Cushion Billiards, you have an additional requirement
to score a point: Your cue ball must touch a cushion or
cushions three times before hitting the second ball. The
tickie shot is very useful in accomplishing this feat
under certain circumstances, and it has proved to be
useful enough to adapt to the pool games.

To execute a tickie, the first OB that you hit has to be
near a cushion but far enough away for another ball to
be able to pass behind it. The perfect distance is about 3
inches from the cushion. Aim the cue ball at the cushion in such a way that it bounces
off, hits the back side (the side nearest the cushion) of the object ball, and then either
goes back to the cushion or continues on a straight line down the cushion. That's
simple enough. In fact, it's almost *too* easy. On shots in which players come from
behind an OB like this, they often scratch in the pocket down the cushion. But if you
have the right circumstances, the shot can be great.

The two most common situations are when a second OB is located down the cushion,
near a corner pocket, and the ball just out from the cushion is the ball that you have to
hit. A tickie turns out to be easier to shoot than many combos, especially if the two
object balls have some distance between them. Instead, try to hit the first OB into the
second OB. Shoot a tickie. The cue ball bounces off the back of the first OB and heads
right toward the pocket, knocking the corner ball in.

A tickie tends to be easy because two things correct each other: the angle at which you
approach the first OB and the angle at which the cue ball leaves the first OB. If you
aim a little off in one direction, the cue ball hits the OB in a different place, which
turns out to be about right to send the cue ball toward the pocket. If you aim a little off
in the other direction, you hit the cue ball in a different place, which turns out to do
the same thing. If your aim is substantially off, of course, the tickie won't be successful.
When you see the opportunity for a tickie, take advantage of it.

A variation is a combination–tickie. Instead of shooting the cue ball into the cushion
and having it hit the back of the first OB, try shooting an OB along that path. The OB
performs a tickie, and then knocks the ball near the pocket into the pocket. This
sounds a whole lot more difficult than it is. You still have to aim carefully, but it's not
even as precise as aiming a simple combo at those distances.

Kiss the Balls Goodbye

A *kiss shot* is similar to a carom. Actually, the shot includes a carom, but the first OB is
the one doing the 90- degree thing—not the cue ball. When you shoot an OB into

another object ball with the idea that it (the first OB) will bounce off and go into a pocket, you have executed a kiss shot. The balls react with results that you can predict, after you give it a little thought. When it looks like you don't have a shot, a kiss shot is one more possibility to consider. A sample kiss shot is shown in the next photo.

Try the same aiming method I advised you use when lining up a combination. Pick out the place on the second object ball that is at a 90-degree angle to the pocket. Then use your cue stick on the first object ball as though it were the cue ball. Where your cue tip would need to hit the first object ball is the contact point for the cue ball. Working backward like this is much easier than estimating where the cue ball should hit the first OB, figuring where it would go, deciding whether that's exactly where you want it to go (and, if not, how to adjust)…. Work it backward, though, and it's a snap.

Again, don't forget to pay attention to where the balls will go after they collide. This situation is different from the carom shot and combination shot. In a kiss shot, your first object ball is the one that goes in the pocket. The second OB may or may not be the ball that you have to shoot next, but even if it's not, it may roll into other balls, disturbing and rearranging them. So you have to figure out where the second OB will go and what it will do.

The cue ball is something that you always have to know about, and in a kiss shot, you should think ahead to the next ball that you want to shoot, to make sure that the cue ball ends up in a good position for you to do that. I've advised you to use the softest shot possible to accomplish your goal, and this situation is a good illustration of why that's important. When your object ball hits the second OB, it's usually to your advantage to have it move as little as possible. (Sometimes, however, it's not, as I explain in the following section.) A hard hit can rearrange things drastically, and there's no telling what you may end up with. Keep control by keeping it slow.

When you're shooting the cue ball into a cluster, try to hit a particular ball in a particular spot—the spot that will do you the most good, of course. Be aware, too, that too light a hit opens the possibility that the balls won't roll far enough and that the cue ball will end up in a cluster. That's the worst thing that could happen. If you can break up a cluster by contacting an outside ball on its outside edge, you're in good shape. But whatever works best in a particular situation, know what's going to happen before you take that final stroke with your cue.

Pocket Dictionary

A *kiss shot* is hitting an object ball into another ball so that it bounces off the other ball and goes into a pocket.

Ewa's Billiard Bits

The term *kiss shot* is so appealing that it was used as a title of a 1992 movie starring Whoopi Goldberg. She played a single mom who beat all the guys playing 9-Ball and decided to support her family by entering a big tournament.

Pucker up for a simple kiss. Hit the 1 ball into the 2 ball, just to the left of straight on, and the 1 is guaranteed to drop in the pocket. Remember Ewa's Second 90-Degree Rule of Billiards, and tell me where the 2 ball would go. Also, would you put spin of any kind on the cue ball?

General Clusters

You're on the horns of a dilemma (could be little horns, could be big horns, could be both). Two shots are available, but you really can't see how one is any better than another. You're shooting the 2 ball, but you notice that the 5 ball and 7 ball are frozen together, sitting full on the side cushion, and are impossible to shoot into a pocket. If you shoot the 2 ball with one kind of spin, it will go into the two frozen balls and knock them apart. But that shot will leave the cue ball in a position that makes pocketing the 3 ball difficult. On the other hand, you could spin off the 2 ball into a place that makes the 3 ball easy, but still leaves the 5 and 7 unplayable. What do you do?

Separating frozen balls, whether it's just two or a *cluster* of three or four, is almost always something that you want to do as early in the game as possible. For one thing, you may get out of position and not be able to do it later. For another thing, the balls may bounce into other balls and end up frozen to something else, meaning that one or more of them will have to be broken out again. Finally, breaking up a cluster removes a distraction. There is a rule—more of a guideline, really—in billiards that says, "Don't move balls unnecessarily." The reason this saying exists is that moving balls around haphazardly complicates things, constantly changing the layout of the table and possibly adding trouble. Multiple bumping-around causes the game to get out of your control. But when trouble already exists, as in clusters of balls (whether they're frozen together or not), you should generally take care of it as soon as possible. The photo shows a typical cluster buster shot.

An experienced player comes to the table after the break and immediately looks for clusters of balls. Clusters are trouble, and it would be unfortunate to make (*run,* in

Pocket Dictionary

A *cluster* is the same in pool as in English: a group of items (in this case, balls).

266

pool talk) four or five balls, only to discover that the next two are so close together as to be unmakable in any pocket. The result would be a shot in which you couldn't make a ball, so you'd be turning over a table that is half-cleared. Your opponent would like the situation, but you wouldn't.

Trying to break up clusters at the beginning of the rack matters less when you're learning to play, because the cue ball is more likely to get out of your control and accidentally bump into balls—perhaps balls in a cluster. But as you practice more, it's good to keep the pointers in this section in mind.

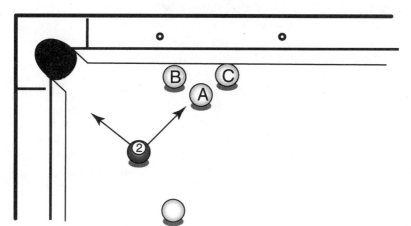

You played position on the 2 ball so that you could shoot it into the corner pocket, and the cue ball would naturally go into the cluster of balls (A, B, and C), breaking the balls apart so that you could pocket them later. With draw or follow, you can modify the path of the cue ball if your position is a tad off. Use a firm stroke.

If you do have a cluster that you have to break up, the best thing to do is check the balls that you'll play before the cluster and see which one is easiest to use. If a ball is close to a pocket and also close to the cluster, and if you can get the cue ball into position to pocket the ball and naturally roll into the cluster, that's the ball you want to use. Always make things as easy and natural as possible.

The Two-Way Shot

Everyone likes the two-way shot, because it's a win–win shot. The shot is tough to create, but learn to recognize it when you come across it. The shot frees you to take a low-percentage shot—one that, at your current skill level, you make a low percentage of the time—that you normally wouldn't shoot.

The "two" in the phrase two-way shot refers to making a ball and playing a safety with the cue ball at the same time. That way, if you miss the shot

Pocket Dictionary

A *two-way shot* is a shot that can be made but that, if you miss it, results in favorable (to you) positions of the balls.

you will have left the cue ball in a place where your opponent cannot hit the ball he or she is required to hit. Of course, the position that the cue ball goes to has to be one where, if you *do* make the shot, you can shoot a second ball.

The requirements for a two-way shot are:

1. You have a shot that is makeable.

2. The cue ball can be placed in a spot that will give you a shot on the next ball.

3. If you miss the shot, the very same place the cue ball goes in requirement #2 will be one which will not allow your opponent to make a ball. (In a rotation game the ball he or she would have to hit would be the same one you failed to pocket. In 8-Ball the ball she or he would have to hit would be one from his or her group—either the solid colored balls or the striped balls.)

The preceding paragraph sounds like an unreasonable pile of demands for any single shot, but the two-way shot comes up more often than the list of features would lead you to believe—my guess is maybe 1 shot out of 50. That's a very unscientific guess, but I can tell you flat out that it's nothing like 1 in 1,000 or anything like that, so you *will* come across it. The key is to recognize it. Psychologically, playing a two-way shot is a boost to some people, because they don't have to worry about missing, so they play the shot with more confidence and less worry. The irony is that that makes it more likely that they'll make the shot and not have to deal with missing.

The Least You Need to Know

➤ All the shots in this chapter are fundamental to the game and follow the basic rules, even though they may look difficult at first.

➤ A combination shot is tough because the margin for error is so tiny.

➤ A Carom shot pockets the second ball that the cue ball hits.

➤ A kiss shot uses a second object ball to change the direction of the first object ball.

➤ Clusters of balls (two or more) present a problem that should be solved early.

➤ The two-way shot is a win–win situation. If you fail to pocket the ball, you've left the cue ball in a safe place.

Chapter 21

The Flying Cue Ball and Other Weird Tales

In This Chapter

➤ The how and why of the jump shot

➤ Shooting the massé

➤ How making the cue ball curve can get you out of a jam

➤ The dangers of shots in which the cue is not level

➤ Thinking about where the cue ball will end up on a jump, massé, or curve shot

The jump shot has been very controversial in professional billiards. During the 1986–87 season, it really became a hot topic; new cues had been developed that made jumping the cue ball over other balls much easier than doing it with your regular playing cue. Was this development good? Bad? Should jumping be allowed, but not jump cues? How would the average player react to suddenly seeing pros jumping balls all over the place? Would billiard-room proprietors, who had spent a lifetime banning the jump shot in their clubs, go ballistic if the pros started jumping balls on TV?

Everyone had a point of view.

Among the players, there were two groups. One group believed that the game should not change because changing the rules or changing the equipment made it a different game—one that could no longer be compared with the games of the past two centuries. The other group believed that the equipment and rules in other sports had changed as demands on those sports changed, and now that television was requesting more excitement and action, the jump shot gave it to them. Also, the audiences loved it.

If you've watched a match on television lately, you know which school won out. When the color commentator says, "Looks like she's going over to her seat to get her jump cue," you can feel the tension rise in the audience. People in the stands lean forward, and I can only assume that people at home are doing the same thing. The jump shot offers the potential for real disaster or spectacular success. There's not much in between. And now that the shot is legal in most places, I'll tell you all about it, as well as its cousins, the massé and curve.

You shouldn't attempt any of these shots until you've mastered all the previous material, however. The shots are tempting because they're so adventuresome, but they're also difficult and can severely damage your cue, the table cloth, and the slate itself.

Get Over It, Already

Jumping the cue ball over another ball isn't legal in all places or in all tournaments, but since the early 1990s, the presumption going in is that it is legal, whereas the presumption before that was that it was illegal. Unless the tournament director or club owner tells you that jump shots are not permitted, you can assume that you can use them. There's still no generally accepted position, however, on *jump cues* (cues that are especially designed for this shot). Some tournaments, some leagues, and some billiard rooms allow them; others don't.

Pocket Dictionary

A *jump cue* is a cue that is shorter than normal, making it easier to jump the cue ball over the other balls.

You know how I keep reminding you to keep your cue as level as possible? Well, in this case, don't. All the special shots in this chapter require you to elevate the butt of your cue. Normally, you want to avoid making the cue ball curve, so you'd keep your cue level. Normally, you want to keep your cue ball on the table, which means a level cue. Curves and jumps would just complicate a normal shot. But this chapter is about the times when normalcy won't do the job. You're going to curve the cue ball on purpose, and you're going to make it take flight.

How to Jump

There are two ways to get a cue ball airborne: illegal and legal. Even when a jump shot is permitted in a game, it still must be done according to certain rules. The main rule is that you cannot dig under the ball and scoop it into the air. That is a foul in many venues, and even if it's not, a scoop often results in such a weak hit (if any) that no ball touches a cushion after contact, which *is* a foul. It happens accidentally among beginners who are trying a draw shot (they haven't had the advantage of the information in this book), and it can happen to you after you've been playing for a while if you lose your concentration while trying to draw the cue ball. It's not a foul under those circumstances.

Exactly where the line is drawn between the shot's being a foul and not being a foul is hard to say. It centers on intent, and from the position of the balls, you can generally determine whether the intent was to draw the cue ball or scoop it into the air. Scooping is a no-no, whether or not it's a foul in your venue.

The legitimate way to get the ball to jump over a blocking ball is to hit down on it. The slate is as hard as…well…a rock, and the cloth is thin, but somehow, if the ball is hit with a downward stroke, it bounces into the air. Where the compression comes from, I'm not sure. The cue shaft bends into a mild *S* shape, but I don't think the bend accounts for the cue ball's jumping up. Well, no matter—the point is that it does work. In this chapter, I tell you the technique for jumping, what happens to the cue ball and object ball, when to use a jump shot, and when not to jump a ball.

The following illustration shows the classic jump-shot stance. Notice that everything is in line, just like in a normal shot. Eyes, elbow, shoulder, back hand—they all form a straight line. The V bridge will get your hand higher than a closed bridge, and it's the best one to use for a jump shot. This position is a little awkward, and you have to get really balanced and solid to execute a smooth stroke. The stroke itself changes because of the inability to follow through. Also, a throwing or tossing motion works better than a regular stroking motion. Notice, too, that I'm not going to jump over the center of the 5 ball; I'm going to jump over the edge, which means that I don't have to get the cue ball as high in the air.

This is the form to use when jumping a ball. Here, I'm going to jump over the edge of the 5 ball to hit the 9 ball. Everything is lined up, just as in a normal shot, and I'm using a very elevated V bridge. The big difference, of course, is that my cue is at about a 45-degree angle to the tabletop.

The jump-shot stroke involves more wrist action because it is a darting or tossing stroke. You don't want to have a death grip on the cue because it's going to run up against a brick wall, and you could sprain your wrist. Rather than follow through, you have to stop the cue before it hits the cloth and let the cue tip follow the path that it

Ewa's Billiard Bits

There was a period during the 20th century when a lot of billiard knowledge was kept secret and died with its possessors. The jump shot is one of those things, and it had to be reinvented. No one used the jump shot for a long, long time, but records have been found testifying to its use a hundred years ago or more.

wants to take, up from the table and off the cue ball. So there's not a lot of arm movement in a jump shot stroke/toss/throw.

The height of your jump is determined by the hardness of your hit and, even more, by the angle of your stroke. The higher you lift the butt of your cue, the higher the ball jumps. The higher you lift your cue butt, of course, the more awkward and difficult it becomes to deliver an accurate stroke. About seven people in America can jump a ball by delivering a stroke that is very, very close to a 90-degree angle to the table. The cue ball jumps up and lands $2\frac{1}{2}$ to 3 inches from where it started. These players can jump a ball that is almost touching the cue ball. (Needless to say, don't try this at home—or at a billiard club, either!) So jumping with a very elevated cue is possible. I told you about these few experts just to let you know that there's no physical limit (up to 90 degrees) on cue elevation for a jump shot.

When to Jump

In most cases, you won't have to get the ball very high off the table. A blocking ball will more likely be partly off the line to the object ball than it will be exactly dead-center on the line. You'll be jumping over the side of the ball. Jumping over the center is possible, and a jump-shot expert can clear the ball with a couple of inches to spare. But generally, when you evaluate whether to jump a ball, you prefer not to have to jump over its center. If that's what is necessary, try very hard to find another shot.

There is a safer, easier, and more accurate way to get around a blocking ball: You can go to a cushion with the cue ball and have it bounce off to hit your object ball. This technique is called kicking at the ball, and I give you the inside scoop on it near the end of Chapter 22. Always consider a kick shot first; then resort to a jump shot if you (a) can't get a clear path for a kick and (b) have confidence in your jumping ability.

You can jump a ball only when the object ball (the ball you're aiming to hit) is going to be hit pretty much full in the face. If it's not a straight-on hit, the cue ball (still hopping) glances off it and bounces right off the table. You *could* jump it on a cut shot, but that would be very unwise. Disaster is certain.

The final consideration is the distance of the ball being jumped from the cue ball. A foot is ideal, and 18 inches isn't bad. If the distance is less than a foot, you'll have to elevate your cue butt quite a bit for the ball to reach its maximum height quickly. If the distance is more than 18 inches, the shot creates a ball with a lot of forward power. It had better hit the object ball very squarely, or it will keep going—and it may do so anyway.

The ideal jump shot hits the object ball and the table at the same time and stops dead. It's fine if the contact happens on the first, second, third, and tenth bounce, as long as the cue ball hits the object ball and the table at the same time. This not only inhibits the cue ball from bouncing after contact, but also keeps the object ball from bouncing. If the cue ball hit the OB while the cue ball was on its way down or way up, it would make the OB bounce instead of roll. You can get lucky and land it in the pocket, but you might also get unlucky. The ball may be in the middle of a bounce when it hits the pocket, and it might go off the table or hit the back of the pocket (a piece of iron, usually wrapped leather) and ricochet back onto the tabletop. So distance is a factor in two ways: the distance to the ball and the bounce point of the cue ball.

The best conditions for a jump shot are when:

➤ You don't have to jump over the center of the blocking ball.

➤ The shot is a straight one, not a cut.

➤ The ball being jumped is a foot to 18 inches away from the cue ball.

Drawing a Jump

Some people say that they can put sidespin (English) on a cue ball during a jump shot, but if they can, the effect is minimal at best. Hitting the cue ball anywhere but on its vertical axis sends it off-course. You can, however, put draw and follow on the cue ball, and draw is an especially good thing for this type of shot. Draw stops the cue ball at contact (a stop shot, jump-style) and makes it hop backward after contact, or at least reduces its forward motion after contact. That gives you control of a potentially runaway shot, and control of the cue ball is good.

The technique for applying draw to a jump shot is something that you probably won't believe the first time I tell you, so read this paragraph again at a later date. The first thing that you do is figure out (from experience) how high to elevate the butt of your cue and how hard to hit the cue ball to get the desired height and distance to the first bounce point. Realize that even though you're aiming way up on the ball, you are shooting at the equator of the center ball. The equator has moved in relation to your cue approach line. As you know, the way to get draw (reverse spin) on the cue ball is to hit it below center. So *without moving your back hand,* drop the cue tip slightly. Now you're hitting below the new equator, and you'll put reverse spin (draw) on the cue ball when you jump it over the blocking ball.

If you don't believe it, you're in the majority. Maybe 1 of every 50 people I tell about this technique grasps it right away. But get fairly good with your jump shot and then try it. You'll like it.

Ewa's Bank Jump

Here's a sneaky shot that no one will see coming. It combines your knowledge of banking (see Chapter 19) with your new knowledge of jumping. I use it as a trick shot in some of my corporate exhibitions and at new club openings. I'll grant you that the situation doesn't come up more than once every thousand hours of pool that you play, if that, but it *will* come up, and you'll be the only person who knows what to do. The shot also teaches you something about the cushions and how they react when balls don't hit them at a normal angle.

Place the cue ball a few inches off the end cushion, about a foot from the corner pocket. Enclose the ball by running a quarter-circle of balls around it, from cushion to cushion. Place an object ball—let's say an 8 ball—right in front of the corner pocket on the other side of the table. The challenge is to hit the 8 ball into the pocket. Because you're surrounded, there seems to be no way to do it.

Well, buckaroo, there is. Hit the cue ball straight into the long cushion by the corner pocket, but elevate the butt of your cue a little when you do it. That makes the cue ball leave the surface of the table just a little, and it catches the top of the cushion point. The cushion compresses and kicks the ball back toward you, over the quarter-circle of balls, where it lands, knocking the 8 ball cleanly into the hole.

A variation that I sometimes use is to put three balls in a row as though I were going to hit a combination into a corner pocket. But before I shoot, I put a spare cue stick on the table between the two object balls. You know that you can jump with the cue ball. But how do you get the object ball across the cue stick? Two methods are available:

➤ Use a moderate jump shot, and when the cue ball hits the first object ball, it will be a little off the table. That means a downward hit on the object ball (just like a cue makes a downward hit on the jump shot), causing the first object ball to jump over the cue stick and knock the second object ball in the pocket.

➤ Elevate the cue stick more, so that the cue ball just grazes the top of the first object ball, goes on over the cue stick, and pockets the second object ball.

Can you play these shots in real games? They're all legal, but even putting the props aside, you won't have many opportunities to put them into practice. What I want to get across is that when a cue ball leaves the surface of the table, different rules apply, and different things happen. Every jump shot that you shoot requires you to do some extra thinking before you pull the trigger.

Pocket Dictionary

A *massé shot* is shooting down on the cue ball to make it curve in a half-circle.

The Mighty Massé

When you can't hit the ball that you need to hit because a ball is blocking the path, you can't use a kick shot, and you don't want to use a jump shot, two options are still open to you. One option is the curve (which I'll show you in the next section), and the other is the super curve, or *massé*. It, too, requires an elevated cue.

The massé is a neat little shot. I call it "little" because in most cases you're not going too far with the cue ball. It's the way that it gets from point A to point B that's unique. You apply a large amount of spin to the cue ball, but you do it from directly above. The cue stick is at a 90-degree angle to the table in a pure massé and close to that in other massé shots. When the angle of the cue in relation to the playing surface starts to drop down to 60 or 70 degrees or less, you're moving toward a curve shot. Check the following photo as you read.

Because the cue is in the air, one of the worst problems with a massé is keeping your aim and stroke rock-steady. If you can keep your arm against your body, it will be a big help. See the text for details.

The characteristics of a massé stroke are similar to those of a jump-shot stroke. You want to keep as steady as possible because the cue butt is up in the air and likely to wiggle around. Shooting a massé when the cue ball is in the center of the table is difficult almost to the point of being impossible. The closer to the cushion the cue ball is, the more chance you have to brace your hand and arm against your body and create a steady bridge.

Your backhand, meanwhile, can grip the cue in either of two ways. Neither is better than the other, except for you. Different body configurations make one grip more natural and more comfortable for some people, but a strain for others. I use a grip that is roughly the same as my normal shooting grip. Other people use a grip that's more like someone throwing a spear. Perhaps the best way to describe it is to imagine someone raising his hand in class, and someone else slipping a cue into it. Or take a golf-swing grip and raise it over your head.

Heard It in the Poolroom

W. C. Fields used a billiard skit in his vaudeville act. He drilled a hole through the table and cloth, where the audience couldn't see it, and then pretended to shoot a massé so hard that the cue went all the way through to the floor. He revived the scene for the movies.

Picture the cue ball as a clock face. Now you're looking down on a clock face. The only place where you shouldn't hit the cue ball is dead-center because that will cause no movement in the cue ball and may damage your cue. But you'll rarely hit it above the equator (the new equator, on a sphere seen from above), because that would make the ball scoot toward you. The question is what happens when you hit the ball somewhere below the equator.

You can put draw, left English, right English, or a combination on the cue ball when you hit it from above. The ball acts a bit differently, but you should recognize the general character of the movement. When you use center-axis draw, the cue ball squirts out, the spin catches, and the cue ball comes back to you without ever having touched another ball or a cushion. No way can you put that much draw on a shot with a level cue. When you put horizontal-axis right English on the ball, it squirts out to the left, the spin catches, and the ball comes back to you.

The real use of the massé, though, is when you hit the cue ball with low-right or low-left. The ball makes a half-circle—perfect for going around a ball that's in the way. Vary the degrees of draw and sidespin (sidespin from above, remember) with different stroke forces, and the cue ball can go out to the side a foot and then suddenly take a right turn just in time to contact the object ball.

You can use this shot when you don't have a lot of distance to cover but need to get around a blocking ball. Although you can actually get a lot of distance out of a massé, the curving effect is soon lost, and only the hardness of the hit and the running English make it travel so far. The important characteristic of the shot is the fact that the cue ball curves a lot. It won't be a characteristic that you'll need very often, but when you're in a certain fix, nothing else will get you out of trouble.

Curves Ahead

You may have noticed the flow of this chapter, from the most severe and dramatic shot to the curve, a gentle but practical shot. The curve is moderate, and its goal is modest. It strives only to leave the straight line between the object ball and the cue ball so that it can go around the edge of a semi-blocking ball and then return to its normal path. The shot is nothing flashy, and it's unlikely to get out of control and embarrass the player, either. It's a useful shot, and you'll need it a little more often than you will the impressive shots described earlier in this chapter. The curve is well worth practicing, and you don't have to worry about smashing the slate, splintering your cue shaft, or having balls bounce merrily all over the floor.

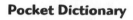

Pocket Dictionary

A *curve shot* makes the cue ball arc to the left or right of the aiming line and then come back to it.

To shoot a curve—and this is going to come as no surprise—you elevate the butt of your cue slightly. You don't need much elevation, and you don't want to get into the area of the massé or jump shot. All you need is maybe 10 to 30 degrees from the playing surface. You may want to use an elevated V bridge as I show you in the illustration in "How to Jump" earlier in this chapter—not that elevated, of course, but still elevated.

All the rules that apply to a normal stroke also apply to the curve shot: keeping all the parts in line, following through, and so on. The degree of elevation, as always, affects the degree of curve, and that elevation, combined with the speed of the shot and how much sidespin you apply, determine how much the ball is going to curve and how soon it will curve. At one extreme, you may shoot from one end of the table to the other, and the cue ball may curve offline 10 inches before the spin starts it back toward its target. Before the ball gets there, it will have lost its sidespin and will be rolling normally. At the other extreme, you're approaching a massé type of ball reaction.

The curve is used because it's so easy to control and because it changes the path of the cue ball from a straight line, giving it the power to go around blocking balls. Not every blocking ball is exactly on the line that you want to go on, though; sometimes, only the edge of a ball is in the way. In that situation, you could jump, or you could curve. Given a choice, always shoot a curve shot. It's less likely to get out of control, and the person who owns the table will nod approvingly at your prudent choice.

How Did We End Up Here?

Getting cue-ball position with a jump shot, massé shot, or curve shot is tough. There's no way around it. When you start spinning the cue ball in odd ways, getting it to leave the table and making it follow an abnormal path, you're giving up a lot of control. All these shots are hard to shoot with real precision—much harder than straight-on shots or normal cut shots—and harder still to shoot in such a way that you can move the cue ball to the right position after you pocket a ball. So added to the riskiness of the shot is the danger that even if you make the ball, it won't do you any good because the cue ball will end up someplace where you can't hit the next ball. The odds of a mishap like this are greatest on the jump shot, greater on the massé shot and great on the curve shot.

Does that unpredictability factor make these shots more potential trouble than they're worth? No, because they are extreme shots and shots of last resort. When nothing else will do, these are the shots that you call on. They are risky on many levels, but you could end up in good shape if you execute them well. Without them, you wouldn't have any chance. When other, more prudent, options are not available, take on the risk of a jump, massé, or curve. You know that sooner or later, you're going to be in a situation that's tough, so learn these shots (starting with the curve) so that you'll be able to use them when you need them.

It's easier to predict where the cue ball will end up if you hit it softly. This is true of any shot, but it's even more important for these three shots because the cue ball can get away from you so easily. Shoot softly when possible (and carry a big cue stick, of course).

Another thing that helps you predict the final resting place of the cue ball is to try to accomplish your goal with moderation. Don't curve a lot if you can curve a little. Don't jump high if you can jump low. Don't massé around a ball with a big patterned circle when a smaller pattern will do. The spin, which you used previously to control the position and path of the cue ball after contact with the object ball, is used on the massé and curve to control the path of the cue ball *before* contact with the object ball. You can't use it for playing cue-ball position, but from what I've shown you in previous chapters, you should be able to figure out where the cue ball will end up. You can control that position, to some extent, by the speed (hardness) of the hit. But sometimes, even that is determined by how you want the cue ball to move before it contacts the OB. Bottom line: Cue-ball position is very often out of your control when you play these shots.

The Least You Need to Know

➤ The jump, massé, and curve shots are shots of last resort.

➤ The jump shot may not be legal in all circumstances.

➤ Many of the regular rules of stance and stroke apply, but follow-through is not one of them.

➤ Using a hard (powerful) stroke when you play one of these three shots can lead to disaster.

➤ Although you can control the shots to some extent, the cue ball tends to run wild after it hits the object ball.

Position and Safety Play

Now we get back to ground zero and some of the more everyday parts of the game. No more flash—this chapter is about intelligence, common sense, finesse, and nondesperate measures. In the next few pages, I'm going to tell you about the importance of playing position and about the basic goals and strategies of *position play*—that is, of putting the cue ball in the best place to make the next ball. I'm also going to tell you about *safety play*, which is what you do when you don't have a shot. I'll be using the fundamentals of center-ball hits, follow, draw, and sidespin (English) that you've already read about, and I'll be telling you what constitutes good position and a good safety shot.

The idea behind position play is to make it as easy on yourself as possible. Move the cue ball to a spot where the next shot is easy. If you can keep doing that, you can keep shooting and eventually win the game. When you make an error and find that you can't make the next ball, you turn to the safety shot. This is another place to exercise your creativity.

Many of the previous chapters discussed basic physical techniques for billiards. This chapter is about thinking. What position do I want the cue ball to end up in after I pocket this ball? Would something else be better but not as obvious? Is it better to

Pocket Dictionary

Safety play is putting one or more balls (especially the cue ball) in such a position that your opponent is in trouble when he comes to the table. *Position play* is controlling the balls (especially the cue ball) so that when they come to rest after you've pocketed a ball, they're in position for you to pocket another ball.

Scratch!

In 8-Ball, you don't necessarily want to pocket every ball that you can pocket. Leaving just one or two in your group puts you in a worse position than not making any of them (see Chapter 25).

make this ball or to play a safety and make my opponent shoot a difficult or impossible shot, and maybe get ball in hand? What position can I leave the cue ball in that would make it hard for my opponent to hit the object ball?

These questions are very common, and unless the correct action is very obvious, you'll run over them in your mind before you make a decision and bend over the table (at least, I hope you will). When you get done with this chapter, you'll understand how to evaluate a table layout and how to make the best decision. I'm going to give you some simple, general principles and tell you some things to look for when you approach the table. When you get the general idea of how to think in billiard terms, you'll be able to go to a table and make the right decision quickly. You'll be a billiard brain!

You Get What You Play For

If making (pocketing) one ball is fun, it's a good guess to say that pocketing two or three is more fun. Pocketing a whole table full of balls without missing is the most fun of all. You not only get a sense of personal accomplishment—you met every challenge and conquered it—but also win the game, and winning can be a very pleasant thing.

To make all the balls, however, you have to have a clear shot at each of them, and that means that the cue ball has to be in a certain area (or sometimes a very specific place) for each shot. It also means that the object ball must have a clear path to the pocket (or be a part of a makable combination shot). After the balls are broken open and you look at the layout, you'll frequently find that not all balls have clear paths to a pocket. (In billiardese, this situation is abbreviated as "He/she doesn't have a pocket" or "The *X* ball has no pocket.") What's a player to do? Read on.

Look At What You've Gone and Done

You broke the balls. Suppose that one went in—or your opponent broke the balls and one didn't go in. Either way, it's your turn at the table, and you're faced with chaos. There are balls all over the place (you broke them well), and you know that it's up to you to figure out what to do about it. For simplicity's sake, suppose that the game is 9-Ball. The rules are that you must strike the lowest-numbered ball on the table first. You can make a combination and another ball can go in, but you must hit the lowest-numbered ball first. Also, whoever makes the 9 ball wins.

That's one objection that purists have to the game, by the way. Player A can make eight balls, but Player B can make only one ball (the 9) and win. But be that as it may, both players are playing under the same rules, with the same odds, so it evens out in the end.

So you're playing 9-Ball, and you pocketed one ball (let's say the 5) on the break. Now you should look at what you've done.

First, look for clusters (two or more balls very close to each other) that might present a problem. Then look for the 9 ball (the only striped ball on the table; it has a yellow stripe up its back), and see whether it is hanging out near a pocket opening. If so, check to see whether another ball can be used as the first object ball in a combination on the 9 ball.

Next, check to see where the 1 ball is in relation to the cue ball. Can you hit the 1 directly? If not, how are you going to hit it? (Will you bounce the cue ball off one cushion? Or will you use two cushions for a kick shot—which I'll get to near the end of this chapter.)

Finally, check to see which balls don't have an open path to a pocket and whether the blocking ball is a lower number than the ball without a path (it will be cleared first if it is).

When you were little, you probably got some advice that went like this, "Don't go out looking for trouble." Forget about it. This is the time when you want to spot anything on the table that might be trouble. You look for opportunities, too, but your first priority is to see whether any balls are going to present problems and begin thinking about how to solve those problems. The 6 ball has no pocket? That's not really a problem if the 2 ball is blocking its path because you'll pocket the 2 before the 6. If the 6 is blocking the 2, however, you need to see whether you can shoot the 2 ball into the pocket at the other end of the table by getting the cue ball between the 6 and 2. If you can, you backtrack to the 1 ball and see what you have to do with the cue ball to get it to that spot after it pockets the 1.

Ewa's Billiard Bits

A *runout* is making a ball on the break and then making all the rest of the balls, earning the right to break the next rack. The record for consecutive runouts in a 9-ball tournament is nine, established in the early 1990s by Denver's Danny Medina. His opponent didn't even get to come to the table until the score was 9–0!

Scratch!

If you don't think you'll be able to make one ball after another until all of them (or all in your group plus the 8 if you're playing 8-ball) have been pocketed, the balls in clusters and the balls that are blocked by other balls from going into a pocket probably shouldn't be disturbed—at least, not right away.

How to Make a Plan

When you're playing by yourself (this exercise takes far too much time to do in a real game), stop to take a long look at the layout after the break shot. Start with the highest-number ball (the 9) and figure out the ideal position for the cue ball to make that shot. Then find the next-highest-number ball (the 8, unless it went down on the break), and see how you would get to that position from the 8. To end up in a position shooting the 8 that is perfect for getting to the 9, you have to figure out how to come off the 7 in a natural and easy way to get to the right position on the 8...and so on, down to the 1 ball.

In short, you play the rack backward in your mind, from the last ball to the first. You have a connect-the-dots line for the cue ball from start to finish because you planned it from finish to start. In pool talk, the whole thing isn't exactly called "a line," but when a player makes a ball and the cue ball doesn't go to the right place for the next shot, it's called "getting out of line." You'll hear that expression a lot because it happens a lot. This game takes more skill than appearances indicate. Your goal is to stay online.

If some balls will present a problem, thinking about them before you shoot your first shot will pay. Figure out which shot is the best one for sending the cue ball into a cluster, for example. Or think about nudging a blocking ball out of the way on a certain shot. Or consider shooting a ball in a less-obvious pocket if the closest pocket is blocked. Under the best circumstances, try to create two opportunities to take care of trouble balls. If the first opportunity doesn't work, you're not left in a fix.

Pocket Dictionary

Getting out of line (or, sometimes, *getting off line*) is rolling the cue ball, after a shot, to a bad position for making the next ball.

It's always good to have a plan, but if something goes wrong, don't hesitate to regroup and come up with a new approach. If you get out of line, for example, you may have to play a safety shot instead of pocketing the next ball. Or you may have to shoot it into a different pocket than the one called for in the original plan. Or you may have to bank it instead of shooting it straight in. Whatever the new circumstances are, never be a slave to your original plan. Adjust and alter as needed.

Sew Up the Balls with a Pattern

Patterns, in billiards, refers to the plan that you create when you decide how you're going to play the balls—in other words, when you decide what position you want the cue ball to be in for each shot. If you think of it as a pattern instead of a plan (unless you're good at picturing schematics), you'll be able to visualize it more easily. A pattern doesn't have to include every ball on the table.

To see a pattern, you should reverse-engineer the layout, but you can do that in a general way (even a somewhat vague way) the farther you get up the list. Nail down the ball that you're going to shoot, the ball after that, and the third ball. Spotting trouble in the layout, getting a general idea of your approaches, and having a firm plan for the next three balls is the typical approach of a player who has it all together and is going to advance rapidly. If you have a pattern in your mind, you'll have a much greater chance of success.

When you're just starting, all you need to concentrate on is making one ball at a time. Then, if you don't have a shot, you can try a safety. As you get better, you can make a plan to get the cue ball in position after your shot to make the next shot. Keep adding balls to your plan/pattern as your skill level increases.

When a break shot leaves the balls widely scattered, with some near pockets, you may think that you have an "easy layout" or "(obvious pattern)," but if you want to talk real pool talk, you would say, "It's a *road map*" or "It's a *Cosmo*," or you'd say, "*It's connect the dots.*" All these terms mean the same thing: This is a snap.

When you've played long enough, you'll begin to realize that certain patterns repeat. You'll shoot a couple of balls, and it will suddenly dawn on you that you've done something similar a couple of times before. These, too, are called patterns. There's no word in pool talk to differentiate between the new pattern that you devise for each layout as opposed to the common, repeated patterns (such as standard patterns versus fresh patterns), but there probably should be. As is true of almost everything else in life, if you feel that what you're dealing with is familiar territory, you'll have more confidence, and the odds that you'll succeed will be high. So keep an eye out for repeating patterns. They make life easy.

Pocket Dictionary

A *pattern* is a logical and simple plan to get the cue ball from one object ball to another, although you may hear some people divide it into a *difficult pattern* or *easy pattern*. A *road map* is pool slang for a layout of balls that presents no problem. *Connect the dots* is pool slang for the preceding terms. A *cosmo* is the same thing. It's named after a billiard comedian and trick-shot artist who performed under the name Tom Cosmo.

Get On the Right Side of the Ball

The title of this section doesn't refer to complimenting the ball (something that would do you no good at all) but to positioning the cue ball on the side of the ball that allows it to pocket the ball and move to the next desired position with a natural roll. The best example is a shot into the side pocket. The cue ball can be up-table or down-table from there and still cut the object ball into the pocket. But if the next ball is up-table, the *right* (correct) side of the object ball to be on, for that shot, is down-table.

I can't use the more associative words *right* and *left* in talking about the sides because right and left depend on which side pocket you want to pocket the ball in. If it was one side then left would be up-table, but if you shoot it into the other side pocket rolling to the right would be up-table. I hope that what I'm getting at is clear: You want to be on the correct side of each ball you shoot, and the correct side is the one that allows the cue ball to roll naturally forward into position for the next shot. The following diagram illustrates what I'm talking about. It's one of those pictures that's worth a thousand words.

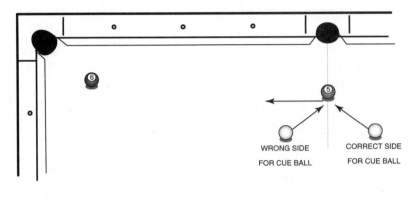

Getting on the correct side of the object ball makes life much easier. The cue ball then naturally rolls in the general direction in which you need it to go for position on the next shot (the 6 ball). Getting cue-ball position on the wrong side means you'll have to bounce around the table to get back where you need to be to shoot the next ball.

Heard It in the Poolroom

One of the most famous pool anecdotes involves a fan who brought a friend to see the famous Willie Mosconi. After watching a match, the fan asked his friend what he thought. "He's not so good," the friend said. "He never had a difficult shot." The best players don't because they have such superb control of the cue ball that they never get out of perfect position.

A natural roll is better, psychologically, but it's also better physically. You want to avoid doing anything fancy with the cue ball. Remember that every hit other than dead-center opens the door for slight errors and imprecise cue-ball roll. When you're positioning the cue ball on the correct side, you're striving to make the shot as simple, as controllable, and as predictable as possible. If you're on the wrong side of the ball, chances are that you'll have to use some fancy sidespin, some extreme draw, or enough follow and power to make the cue ball travel three cushions to get back to the end of the table where the next balls sits. This type of shot may look fancy, but it adds a ton of risk. Your goal is to become good enough to be able to eliminate risk.

Area Position Play and Pinpoint Position Play

From their names, you can probably guess what the terms *area position play* and *pinpoint precision play* mean. When you play area position on a shot, your goal is simply to put the cue ball in a certain area. That area may be 6 inches square, or it may be 12 inches by 25 inches. It may be—and often is—fan-shape. Whatever the size and shape, you can still think of it as an area. If the cue ball stops anywhere in that space, you'll have a reasonably good shot.

The opposite of area position play, of course, is pinpoint position. As the name suggests, the shot requires you to position the cue ball on a specific spot; otherwise, you won't be able to make the next ball. There are many reasons for pinpoint precision play to come up, chief among them being the fact that other balls are situated in the area and would block a shot. Only a small pathway to the object ball is available, and the cue ball must come to a stop exactly on that pathway. That's pinpoint position play.

Pocket Dictionary

Area position play is putting the cue ball in a general area from which you can pocket the next ball. *Pinpoint position play* is putting the cue ball on a specific spot, because that's the only place from which you can pocket the next ball.

Full-rack games (all 15 balls) and nonrotational games (you can hit balls out of numerical order) with closed (safety) breaks usually require pinpoint position play. Straight Pool and One-Pocket are the most common. 9-Ball is the most common area-position game, but on some shots, you'll have to play pinpoint position, or close to it. (There's no exact dividing line between the two types of position play.) 8-Ball is a game that starts with a lot of pinpoint position play because so many balls are on the table and you can hit only half of them—either the solids or the stripes. (Your opponent has the group that you don't have.) But it can be more an area-position game toward the end. The diagrams and captions on the next page should give you a solid idea of when to play area position and when to play pinpoint position.

It's easier to get more lax than it is to get more precise. For that reason, I advise you to get good at pinpoint position play. Practice it, and when you have to execute it, you'll be able to do it. It's cue-ball control at its finest. If you just practice area-position play, you'll get sloppy, with a sort of "Hey, if it ends up anywhere on the table, I'm OK" attitude. Even during a match, on a shot that requires only area position, try for pinpoint position in that area. It sharpens your skills.

One caveat: If pinpoint requires you to do something fancy with the cue ball and you really need to shoot only area position for that particular shot, forget trying for pinpoint; go with area. I don't want you adding complications. If you're tempted, remember the old Tulvanese admonition, K.I.S.S. (_Kewa Islap, Samani Su_, or "Spin that white ball, pal, and you're asking for trouble").

On this shot, you can play area position. Make the 5 ball and put the cue ball anywhere in the shaded area, and you can not only make the 6 ball, but also get position off the 6 to the 7 ball.

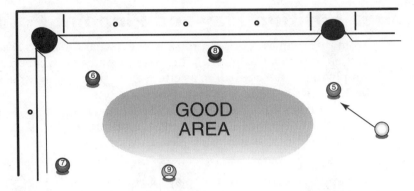

GOOD AREA

Area position won't do now. You have to be in a very specific place to have a good shot on the 2 ball because of all the clutter. The more balls on a table, obviously, the more often pinpoint position shots are needed. Having to shoot one particular ball, as you do in any rotation game (such as 9-Ball), also makes pinpoint position come up frequently.

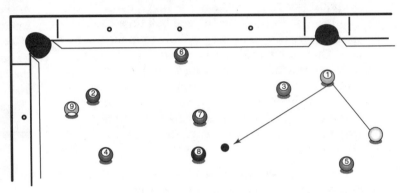

Playing It Safe

Whoever first called it "dirty pool" had no understanding of the game. Not trying to make a ball, but instead rolling the balls where your opponent cannot execute a successful shot takes skill and knowledge and is just as legitimate as pocketing a ball. It's the defensive strategy in a game that is generally one of offense. Not playing a safety is the same as giving up. It also usually costs you the game and perhaps the match. Safety shots are so important that experienced players practice getting out of safeties, and returning safeties, on a regular basis.

A *safe shot*, or *safety*, is simply positioning the ball(s) in such a way that your opponent has no opportunity to make (pocket) a ball. A *good safety* is one in which your opponent can't pocket a ball or even hit a return safety. A *very good safety* is one in which your opponent can't even hit the ball that he or she has to hit. Shoot a very good safety, and you receive ball in hand—that is, your opponent will have failed to hit the ball that he or she needed to hit, which is a foul, and you get to put the cue ball anywhere on the table you want. That's a huge advantage.

Playing the Odds

When do you shoot a safety? The reward for good safeties is so great (cue ball in hand when your opponent fouls) that after you learn about them, it's tempting to shoot them all the time. On a practical level, however, this approach turns out to be a poor one. Continually shooting safeties means that you'll struggle to play one when the opportunity really isn't there. Playing a safety often means putting spin on the cue ball, and that opens the door for inaccuracy in ball placement. A safety is a shot, and you can miss it just like any other shot. If you do, you could be in deep trouble.

Besides not being a winning strategy, constant safeties are boring for most people. There is the belief—and it has some merit—that a good safety is in fact an aggressive tactic toward getting an advantage (ball in hand). But that's a single, solid safety, not a recommendation to play safeties for the entire game.

Another punishment that can result from safety play is loss of game. The rules for the vast majority of games on the pool table say that three consecutive fouls by a player results in loss of game, no matter how many balls remain on the table. This rule doesn't apply to three fouls in three consecutive innings (turns) at the table, but to three consecutive shots. In other words, if my opponent plays a safety, and I fail to hit the proper ball, it is a foul. He then has ball in hand and plays another safety. I again fail to hit the proper ball, and it is the second foul. My opponent plays a third safety. I hit the ball and make it. Then I scratch, fail to hit the next ball, or foul in some other way. Although I've just made my third foul in three consecutive turns at the table, I didn't make three consecutive fouls because, on the third turn, I made a legal shot before the third foul.

So even though the penalty for a foul is substantial, you shouldn't continually try to make your opponent foul by shooting safety shots because you can get into trouble on your own and accidentally give your opponent the advantage.

When, then, do you shoot a safety? The answer involves the percentages (the odds) and the layout of the table. If you don't have a shot (can't pocket a ball), you should immediately consider a safety. If you have a shot that is a very low-percentage shot (you don't figure to make it very often), you should immediately consider a safety. If the shot is borderline but missing it could lose you the game and making it won't necessarily let you win the game,

Scratch!

Under some sets of rules, you must warn your opponent when he has committed a second consecutive foul by telling him, "You're on two." Failing to do so means that he can commit a third consecutive foul and not suffer the loss-of-game penalty.

seriously look at the possibility of shooting a safety. If the shot is makable (whether it's easy or hard) but it would be impossible to get position on the next ball, consider a safety. In this case, you may want to make the ball and get the cue ball in a position to play a very good safety off the next ball, or you may want to play a safety instead of making the first ball. Your strategy depends on the layout, and you'll have to judge each case of this type on its own.

When do you *not* shoot a safety? When you have a reasonable chance of making the ball and a reasonable chance of getting position on the next ball. When you're just beginning to play, neither the shot nor the position is likely to be successful—but then a safety probably wouldn't be successful, either. So don't shoot a safety when you're learning how to play; go for the shot, and get the experience of trying to make balls. Making balls is where the fun is and what you need to learn first. Save the safety play for later.

Besides, getting ball in hand is less an advantage for a beginner than for an experienced player. It allows a beginner to make one ball, but that may be all. Giving up ball in hand isn't that serious a loss, either, because your opponent probably is also a beginner and won't be able to use his advantage to run (pocket) all the balls left on the table. Safeties require you to control the cue ball tightly, and until you reach a level at which you can do that with confidence, I suggest that you forego the idea of shooting safeties.

Following are some situations in which you want to shoot a safety:

➤ When you reach a level of play at which you have good cue-ball control.

➤ When the shot is makable, but getting position on the next ball is impossible.

➤ When you can't pocket the object ball.

➤ When the shot is very difficult, and you don't expect to make it more than 60 percent of the time.

➤ When the shot is tough, and you know that your opponent's ability to get out of a safety is weak.

How to Play a Good Safety

You can hide the cue ball, hide the object ball, or hide both of them. By *hide,* I mean put them behind a blocking ball (or behind the corner of a cushion at a pocket opening—rare and difficult, but not unheard of). I can't say that one of the three choices is more effective than the others because some hiding is better than other hiding, but I can tell you that the best approach usually is to hide the cue ball. Hiding just the object ball generally leaves a path for the cue ball to hit a cushion and approach it from the back, thereby easily scoring a hit (a legal shot). The safety was effective insofar as it prevented the other player from pocketing the object ball, but it didn't result in the valuable penalty of ball in hand because the player didn't commit a foul by failing to hit the ball and then contact a cushion.

Hiding both the object ball and cue ball has the potential of being the best safety, of course, but it's usually very hard to do because you're playing pinpoint position for the cue ball *and* the object ball.

With two out of three options shot down, it won't surprise you to learn that the only remaining choice—hiding the cue ball—is the one that's used most often. It's just cue-ball control, and any player who's ready to shoot a safety has already learned to control the cue ball with speed and spin.

Hiding the cue ball is the main part of a good safety, but other factors can add to it. If, for example, you hide the cue ball behind another ball that is fairly close to a cushion, you are eliminating the number of angles that your opponent can use in bouncing from cushion to cushion to end up striking the object ball. If you snuggle your cue ball behind another ball and come to rest against it, you're also eliminating a lot of angles that your opponent could have used to reach the object ball. If you hide the cue ball behind a ball in such a way that the only path (hitting another cushion with the cue ball) to the object ball is blocked by a third ball, it will be a better safety. In short, any factor that blocks or limits the exit paths of a hidden cue ball makes a safety stronger because your opponent has far less chance of hitting the OB.

When you hide the object ball, but not the cue ball, you've left many possibilities open to the incoming player (your opponent). She can shoot the cue ball in any direction and bounce off one cushion—or two, or three, or more cushions—to get at the object ball. She can put sidespin on the cue ball and create a new, unnatural angle off a cushion that allows her to hit the object ball (OB). She can use curve, massé, or a jump shot (which you learned about in Chapter 21). Simply hiding the OB probably will prevent your opponent from making the ball, but it's not very likely that it will stop her from hitting it. So just hiding the OB is a safety, but not a particularly strong safety.

You can imagine that hiding both balls would be difficult. On rare occasions, the balls are placed so that you can do this without a dangerous amount of spin, but by and large, it doesn't come up often. Look for the opportunity, but don't expect to find it. If the layout makes it possible, concentrate on hiding the cue ball and putting less stress on shooting to hide the object ball. I've seen many players fail to hide either ball by trying too hard to hide both.

Corner-hooking a ball is dangerous but can be an effective safety shot under rare conditions. Each of the six pockets has two corners where the line of the cushions take sharp turns into the hole. Those are the corners of the pocket. As you so often find in billiards, a word can refer to two different things. There are corner pockets (four of them) and corners for each pocket, so you can say "the corner of the corner pocket" and be making sense. To avoid that type of sentence, you can also call the corners *points*.

Pocket Dictionary

A *corner hook* is placing a ball (usually, the cue ball) on the edge of a pocket, against the inside edge of the cushion.

As far as safeties go, the corners can be useful. Because the hole is round, there is a spot just inside the edge of each pocket that allows the ball to stay on the table but be partially hidden. Most of the table is cut off, and a corner-hooked ball can be shot in only one or two directions. The trouble is that placing a ball so that it's corner-hooked is a very delicate operation. You're liable to pocket the ball by mistake. You shouldn't try purposely corner-hooking someone (although it happens often enough by accident) until you're pretty advanced in your skills, but I want you to know about the shot so that when it comes up, you won't be caught off-guard.

Kicking Your Way Out of a Safe

A *kick shot* is like a bank shot, except that you hit the cue ball into the cushion first, and it comes off and hits the object ball. In a bank shot (see Chapter 19), you hit the object ball into a cushion, and it comes off and goes into a pocket. Virtually the only time you would ever shoot a kick shot is when you can't hit the object ball directly—because someone played a safety on you and hid either the cue ball or the object ball or because your opponent missed a shot and that's how the balls ended up. It can also happen that after the break, you can't see the first ball that you have to hit, but in most cases, you're allowed to push out.

It pays to become good at kick shots because this skill will stop people from playing effective safeties against you. If you take away (or strongly limit) your opponent's use of safety shots, you are in a much more advantageous position. As your skill level, and the skill level of your playing partners goes up, you'll find that the skills of safety play and kicking balance themselves out, to some degree. A very good safety will take a very good kick to overcome it. A lesser safety won't even be worth playing at that point.

This is one reason why playing a lot of safeties, as powerful as they are, isn't a practical way to win games. Under the right conditions, the safety is the best shot. You'll use it, and people will use it against you. That's why developing good kicking skills is so important.

Although it's not a kick shot, the pushout is something that eliminates the need to make a kick shot. It's very common in tournament billiards and club billiards. A *pushout* is simply this: If you break and make a ball but cannot see the next ball that you have to hit (or choose not to hit it because of its position), you can elect to call pushout and hit the cue ball anywhere. It doesn't have to contact another ball, and nothing has to contact a cushion. The incoming player can then look at the position of the balls and either take a shot or reject it and make you shoot from the pushout position. Without this rule, you would have had no choice but to kick at the ball that you couldn't see, which would in effect be a penalty for doing something good (making a ball

Pocket Dictionary

A *kick shot* is hitting the cue ball into the cushion so it bounces off and hits the object ball. A *pushout* is when, on the first shot after the break, the player at the table may elect to roll the cue ball anywhere, rather than shoot the shot before him. The incoming player then has the option of shooting the cue ball from the new position or rejecting the shot and making the original player shoot from there.

on a break). Giving a penalty for something good didn't make sense, so the rulemakers came up with the pushout.

Kick Start

The same rules that apply to banking apply to kicking, so you can start trying kick shots right away. You can alter the angle out (see Chapter 19 for a refresher on terms) by the force of the hit and by spinning the ball. When you shoot the cue ball into the cushion, rather than hit an object ball into the cushion, you can put a lot more spin on the ball. That means you can make it twist and turn at some severe, unnatural angles without a great deal of trouble while still being able to predict its path.

Shooting the cue ball into the cushion gives you more accuracy, too, because you don't multiply the error. Remember that the problem in a combination shot (Chapter 20) is multiplying error because three balls are involved. The fewer balls, the less multiplied error. When you're down to one ball, as you are in a kick shot, you have the potential for the most accurate shot of all. A tickie shot (which I cover in Chapter 20) is really a kick shot because the cue ball hits the cushion first.

One thing to keep in mind when you're kicking is that the cue ball must have enough power to hit the cushion (where it loses some power), bounce off, hit the object ball, and still drive one ball (itself or a numbered ball) to a cushion. Otherwise, it's a hit, but not a legal hit, and you'll suffer the same penalty that you'd have received if you hadn't hit it at all. Think about the fact that the cue ball is going to travel a certain distance; hit a cushion; lose some speed; hit a ball; and probably drive that ball toward the center of the table or into other balls, which will decrease its speed. A kick shot, therefore, is generally hit with a medium-hard stroke.

As you practice and play more and more, you'll hit some kick shots that result in safeties. That's nice, because you successfully got out of a safety by kicking and turned the tables by shooting a safety. What if you could do this on purpose? Well, you can, with practice. Think first about which side of the object ball you want to hit (rather than just thinking about making some kind of contact). If you kick off a cushion and make contact with the left side of the object ball, where will the OB and cue ball go? Would hitting it on the right side produce a better result? Is one or the other more likely to drive the OB toward a pocket or toward a cluster of balls, where it could hide? Or could you bounce the cue ball off the OB (remember Ewa's Second 90-Degree Rule of Billiards) and hide it?

I'll be the first to confess that a kick-safety shot isn't an easy thing to do. But if you think about it, make a decision, and try to hit one side or the other, you give yourself the possibility of a really good result. If you hit the OB in the center, you're still fine; you got out of the safety. Learning the angles, learning ball behavior off a cushion, and executing with good form pay off in all types of situations, the kick shot not the least among them. One almost-accidentally-successful kick that ends up in a return safety can intimidate the daylights out of an opponent, who will probably think that you did it exactly as you intended and without struggling. It may be a long time before that player tries to shoot safe against you again.

I like to get a feel for the angles by pointing my cue toward the cushion while looking at the object ball in the far-right corner of the table. This process lets you visualize the correct path of the cue ball for the kick shot.

The object ball is a big ball, and I have figured out where to hit the cushion with the cue ball so that it will bounce into (and probably pocket) the object ball. Fixing the cushion aiming spot is difficult. It's illegal to mark the cushion with a piece of chalk (or anything else), so you really have to fix the spot in your mind before you bend over to shoot.

Before I show you my favorite kicking system, I want to point out something that relates to the photos above. In this example, I can't directly shoot at the ball in the right corner—the ball that I have to hit next—but I can kick one cushion and hit it. In Carom games, that object ball would be called a *big* ball. The reason is that it is near a cushion. In fact, the ball in the picture is near two cushions (and a corner pocket, although Carom tables have no pockets). The ball might as well be three times the size it is, because it's that easy to hit. If I figure angle a little incorrectly, aim a little bit off the point on the cushion I want to hit, or accidentally put some sidespin (English) on the cue ball and send it long or short, I will still hit the object ball. The cue ball can hit a second cushion (near the OB), missing the object ball, and bounce off and still hit it.

In other words, an object ball near a cushion (or cushions) presents a much larger target than an object ball in the middle of the table. When you have to kick at a ball near a cushion, you have a large margin of error and are almost guaranteed to make contact. This is reassuring when you're kicking, but leaving the OB near a cushion is something that you want to avoid if you're the one shooting the safety. Good or bad, it all depends on which side of the fence you're on.

Ewa's Favorite Kicking System

This kicking system is a snap—and it's accurate. Check out the following illustrations.

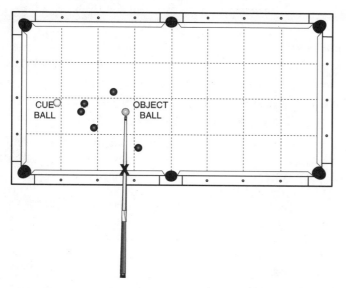

This is the easiest kicking system of all. Place the cue at a 90-degree angle to the rail, with the tip almost touching the object ball. Mark the place (X) where the cue crosses the edge of the cushion.

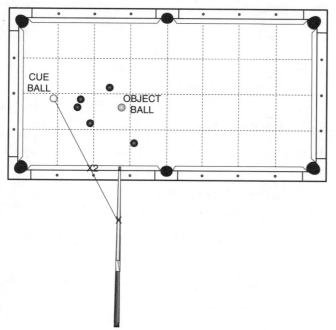

Move the cue back until the tip is touching the edge of the rail. Create an imaginary line from your X on the cue to the cue ball. The spot where that line crosses the edge of the cushion (X2) is your aiming point for a successful kick shot.

293

This technique is simple, accurate, and easy to remember. Try it!

1. Walk around to the other side of the table where the cue ball will hit the cushion.

2. Put your cue tip close to the object ball, and rest it on the rail and cushion at a 90-degree angle to the cushion line.

3. With a thumb and a finger (or any other digits), grab the cue where it crosses the beginning of the cushion (marked "X" in the first of the preceding illustrations), and draw the cue back, still on the straight line, until the cue tip is at that point (X) on the cushion.

4. Draw an imaginary straight line from the place where you're holding the cue to the cue ball that you want to hit. Where that line crosses the cushion (X2) is your aiming point. Make a mental note of that point.

5. Go back around the table and aim the cue ball at the aiming point (X2). The ball hits the cushion, kicks off, and goes right into the object ball.

If you want to hit the object ball on one side or the other (to make it go in one direction or the other when it's hit), you start with the cue tip on that side of the ball rather than in the center. Using this easy system, you have a good chance of driving the object ball directly toward a pocket, or of driving it to one end of the table and the cue ball to the other end with the hope of achieving a return safety. With a little practice, you'll be amazed at how accurate you can become and how often you can pocket an object ball at which you kicked. Because you're aiming in the other direction (toward the cushion, not the OB), pocketing a ball this way looks almost unbelievable, and most people think it was just luck. Let them.

Now, you may be wondering, "If that works for kicks, and a bank is like a kick, can I use it for banks?" Sure, you can. Begin with the pocket where you want to object ball to end up, pretending that it's the object ball. Then measure to the actual object ball as though it were the cue ball. You'll have the point on the cushion where you want the object ball to hit when you bank it. You'll have adapted my favorite kicking system to banking, and you'll have another arrow in your quiver.

The Least You Need to Know

➤ Getting good cue-ball position is vital to being able to make (pocket) one ball after another.

➤ You can get good cue–ball position by using speed and spin.

➤ Analyze the ball layout by planning backward, from the last ball to the first.

➤ If you don't have a good chance of pocketing a ball, play a safety shot instead.

➤ The penalty for failing to hit the ball that you have to hit is severe.

➤ Kicking (hitting the cushion first with the cue ball) gets you out of most safeties.

Chapter 23

Tricks of the Trade

In This Chapter

➤ Trick shots you can do right now

➤ The difference between setup shots and skill shots

➤ How to apply the basic rules of billiards to trick shots

➤ Six balls in one shot

➤ Trick balls for trick shots

Watching a billiard match can be interesting and entertaining, even if you have no idea what's going on. But the interest may not get you past a couple of matches unless you have a basic knowledge of the game you're watching. If you really understand what's happening on the table, you can watch quality billiards for hours. And if you've read this far (presuming that you started at the beginning and didn't arrive here by fanning through the pages), you'll now be a sophisticated viewer. Shots that look easy, or even shots that look like mistakes, will be fraught with meaning for you. You don't even have to pick up your first cue to get a whole lot more enjoyment out of a tele-vised tournament or even a local competition.

Trick shots are similar. The more you know about billiards, the more you'll be able to appreciate and enjoy a professional trick-shot exhibition. The unversed may "Ooh" and "Aah" at the magical display, but you'll be impressed by the player's skill and knowledge, and just like when you watch a magician, you'll try to figure out how he or she does it. Well, I'm going to show you. (Actually, I gave away all the secrets when I showed you how balls behave and how you can alter and control that behavior. Now I'm simply going to show you how to put those secrets to use under unusual circumstances.)

Types of Tricks

Trick shots are separated into two groups. The player who is doing the exhibition may not tell the audience about these groups, but you'll be able to figure out which is which.

Setup Shots

The first group of trick shots is called *setup shots*. The success of these shots depends on the performer's knowing exactly how to place the balls on the table. When the setup is done, shooting the shot successfully is almost automatic.

A setup shot can be missed, however, especially during the early part of the exhibition. One possibility is that the room humidity, cloth, and cushions are behaving slightly out of the norm. Another possibility is that the performer didn't set the balls up exactly right; some setup shots have to be very precisely positioned. It's also possible that the performer accidentally put a touch of spin on the cue ball, and the spin transferred to the object ball (the gear effect), making it go off line—although this occurs far less often than the first possibility. Knowing the characteristics of ball behavior (as you now do) gives you a good start in predicting what's going to happen before the performer actually shoots.

Pocket Dictionary

A *setup shot* is a trick shot that depends on proper positioning of the balls before the shot.

I do a lot of setup shots for corporate appearances, and on one or two shots (after the shot is properly set up), I let someone from the audience do the actual shooting. These are also the kinds of shots that I use on television-talk-show appearances. When David Letterman, Regis Philbin, or Dennis Miller makes a shot that I've set up, the audience loves it. (This type of statement, by the way, is called *name-dropping*, and it's lots of fun, too.)

Skill Shots

The second type of shot is called the *skill shot* or *stroke shot*. The balls are still set up in certain positions, but even then not everyone can make the shots. In fact, only someone at a very high skill level can achieve any degree of success with these shots, and they're best appreciated by an audience that has some billiard knowledge. The shots still have to be set up correctly, but that's no guarantee that they will be made. In a skill shot, it's more common for a single ball to be pocketed, whereas many setup shots pocket multiple balls. That's not part of the definition or a requirement, and you'll see multiple balls pocketed in skill shots and a single ball pocketed in a setup shot, but a skill shot more often focuses on one ball.

Pocket Dictionary

A *skill shot* (also called a *stroke shot*) is a trick shot that depends on both the proper positioning of the balls and the playing skill of the performer.

In the following sections, I describe some of the shots that I use in my exhibitions. You'll be able to execute most of them as soon as you're able to hit the cue ball in a straight line—and maybe even before then. A couple of others are more difficult, and you should hold off on trying them until you have good control of the cue ball. I'm including those shots, and the skill shots, to give you an idea of what a difficult trick shot is like.

It's a Setup!

The following illustration shows the basic two-balls-on-one-stroke (shot) that I set up for inexperienced people—plus two more balls. (I sometimes set up the four-ball version for beginners, though, and they almost always make the shot.)

This shot is called Four on the Floor, and it's a breeze—when the balls are set up correctly. See the text for that information.

Now I'll take the trick apart and show you how it works. For the moment, ignore the two balls that are touching the cue ball. Although it's a little difficult to see from the angle in the photo, the striped ball is sitting on the footspot, and the solid-colored ball to its left is touching the striped ball. At first glance, it looks as though the stripe and solid are lined up toward the center of the far-left corner pocket. It would seem logical to align them like that, but you know about throw (push) now, so you know that if two touching balls lined up toward the pocket are hit from the direction of the cue ball, the solid ball will be pushed a little off line and hit the end cushion near the pocket. The solid ball won't go in the pocket.

One of the secrets of making this shot is that the two balls are lined up a little bit to the left of the pocket (a couple of inches up the left cushion, on most equipment, in typical humidity). On contact, the solid ball is pushed off that line and onto the line directly into the pocket.

Pocket Dictionary

Frozen means touching, as when two or more balls are frozen or a ball is frozen to the cushion.

Ewa's Billiard Bits

Many of today's trick shots started as *proposition* shots. One player proposed to shoot a shot and bet that he could make it. Others would look at it, deem it impossible, and wager accordingly. The public is more sophisticated today, and just the suggestion of a proposition makes people clutch their wallets.

That takes care of positioning the solid ball. For the striped ball, just recall Ewa's Second 90-Degree Rule of Billiards. Place the front ball so that the 90-degree line is directly toward the center of the pocket in the far-right corner.

When the cue ball hits the front ball, the stripe zooms to the pocket on the right, and the solid zooms to the pocket on the left. It helps to hit the front ball dead-center, but it's not necessary. The forces and direction are decided by the relationship between the striped ball and the solid ball. Although this shot is a trick shot, when you run into a situation in a game in which two balls are touching, you can use the same rule to figure out where they are going.

As for the balls on either side of the cue ball, they, too, are touching (*frozen,* in billiard parlance). If you aim them directly toward the side pockets, they won't go in because of the throw involved with frozen balls. Aim them at the closest corner of the side pocket or even a tad up the cushion. Then, when you stroke the cue ball toward the balls at the far end of the table, you'll send the first set into the side pockets. When this shot is done quickly, all four object balls fly into the pockets within a split second.

I probably shouldn't tell you this, but there's a trick within the trick. If you want to fool a friend (in a nice way, of course), you can set up the shot (or just the far two balls) and shoot it successfully. Then invite your friend to set it up. She, knowing nothing about push (throw), will aim the balls at the pockets, and one ball won't go in. Show the setup a second time, successfully pocketing both balls, and then let your friend shoot it a second time. She'll line up the two balls really, really carefully this time—and again, one ball won't go in. What you do at this point depends on what kind of person you are. I'll let you decide whether or not to tell your friend about throw (push).

The Butterfly Shot

Are four balls in one shot not enough for you? In the Butterfly shot, you make six at once—and each ball goes in a different pocket! This shot is a lot of fun, but it's a little tricky to set up. If you misplace one ball, as many as three will miss their pockets. If you don't shoot straight down the center, you could miss all six. When you see a performer setting up this shot, don't expect him or her to make it on the first try (although that can happen). With trick shots, it's common to give the performer three tries.

You can think of this shot as being two lines of three balls each, with the center ball pushed in a little, or as a sort of *X* shape (see the following illustration).

Six balls in one shot! If only this situation would come up during a championship tournament!

To understand the setup, draw two imaginary lines: the long center line and the cross-table line. The *long center line* runs from the center of one end rail to the center of the far end rail. The *cross-table line* runs from the center of one side pocket to the center of the other side pocket. The end of the table where the cue ball is placed is the *cue-ball end*. Now that you've got some terms to work with, I'll explain how to set up the balls.

Place the two center balls about three quarters of a ball's width apart (1.6 inches), equal distances on each side of the long center line. The balls should be about 8 inches from the cross-table line. When these two balls are in place, you can place the other four balls rather easily. Remember throw, and also remember that the two balls on the ends of the rows (on the cue-ball end of the rows) will be forced back toward the shooter, so figure throw from the direction of the center balls.

To make that concept a little clearer, I'll describe it again, using only the three balls on one side of the table. The center ball goes into the side pocket. The far ball goes into the far corner pocket on the same side of the table. The ball on the near end comes back to the corner pocket near the shooter on the same side of the table. (The center ball sends it there when the center ball is hit by the cue ball.) Because the force on this ball is from the end of the table opposite the shooter, toward the end near the shooter, you have to account for throw (push) by going to the other end and viewing the placement

Cue Tips

If you get the urge to try the Butterfly shot, you can invest in a special rack made exclusively for this shot; it sets all six balls in perfect position. Not surprisingly, it's called a Butterfly rack.

of the ball. Repeat this process with the three balls on the other side of the long center line. The three balls on each side must be frozen.

Place the cue ball on the spot, on the long center line, and shoot directly down the center of the table. A small bit of draw usually is helpful. Use a medium but firm stroke. Shoot straight, and all six balls will go into different pockets.

The first few times you try this shot, it's very likely that some balls will miss their pockets. Notice whether they miss on the left side or right side, and adjust accordingly the next time you set up the shot. The condition of the cloth, the room humidity, and other factors that I keep telling you about can play havoc with this shot, so don't be discouraged if you aren't completely successful at first.

The Football Shot

This shot is called the Football shot because with a little imagination (all right, a lot of imagination), the 8 ball could be like a quarterback running the ball up the middle while the linemen scatter the opposing players. The result is a scored touchdown (the ball goes in the pocket). The theory that you use while setting up the Football shot (see the following illustration) is Ewa's Second 90-Degree Rule of Billiards.

The Football shot. The problem is getting everything out of the way so that the 8 ball can score a "touchdown" in the side pocket. The solution is in the setup.

Near the cue ball, just to the right in the picture, is the 8 ball. That's your quarterback. Although it may be difficult to see the numbers, the ball closest to the cue ball is the 7 ball, and the one in line with that is the 1 ball. These balls are touching (frozen), as are the 8 and the ball to the right of it. The balls in pairs are also frozen.

Hit the 7 and, because of the Second 90-Degree Rule, it goes off to the left (left and right as you view the picture, not from my point of view). The 1 ball goes straight into the first pair of balls and then also goes off the left. That starts a chain reaction, with the left ball of each pair going to the left and the right ball going to the right. The result is that the path to the pocket is cleared.

When the cue ball bounces off the 7 (the first ball hit), it goes into the 8 ball. Because the 8 and the ball with it are frozen, the 8 goes off at a 90-degree angle, which is directly toward the pocket. The path is cleared a fraction of a second before the 8 rolls to any spot previously occupied by a pair of balls. Then the 8 ball rolls into the side pocket while all the other balls are scattered.

The setup on this shot requires more patience because 14 object balls are used, but the result is impressive. If the presenter tells a little story with the shot, the story makes it even more interesting. Knowing the final goal (making the 8 in the side pocket) helps tremendously, and an audience—whether at an exhibition or at your home—will be more interested and more impressed if they know what to look for.

Although the Football shot involves more balls than the Butterfly shot, there's a little more room for error in this setup. The balls don't have to travel such a long distance and arrive at such a precise point; all they have to do is get out of the way so that the 8 ball can go through.

Cue Tips

If you don't have any football fans among your audience members (friends and neighbors), you can call this shot Moses Parting the Waters.

Ewa's Billiard Bits

I used the Football trick shot in an exhibition in Italy. I began the program by making two balls on one shot, then three on another, and so on. I then explained to the translator I was going to make the 8 ball go through the defense in the Football shot, and he told the audience. It went perfectly on the first try and I was very pleased with myself when I turned to the audience—and was met with dead silence. I questioned the translator who, it seemed, had misunderstood and told everyone I was going to make eight balls in one shot and they were embarrassed for me! Not only that, but they don't play football in Italy!

The Pick-a-Pocket Shot

The Pick-a-Pocket shot (see the following two illustrations) is eerie. It looks innocent enough—just seven balls in a circle. In the photo, I put two cue balls on the table to illustrate something, but before I get to that, let me ask you to guess in which of the four closer pockets the center ball (in this case, an 8 ball) will end up. Take a moment. Don't show me your card. Got it? Now, without even knowing which pocket you chose, I can say that you're absolutely correct! Then I can prove it by shooting into the circle, and the 8 ball will go in the pocket you guessed.

The Pick-a-Pocket shot. I've put two cue balls on the table to show you where to start. Use either spot, shoot straight into the circle at the 8 in the center, and see where it goes. Then try the other position. It works equally well, of course, if you place the cue ball on the other side of the table.

Here's a closeup of the circle of balls. The cue ball shown here is the one at the top left in the preceding illustration. The spaces between the two sets of three balls each are on the long center line of the table. The 8 ball, in the center, is centered on that line.

The trick is that the 8 will go in any of the four pockets near the balls: the two corner pockets or either side pocket, depending on where you place the cue ball before you hit the cluster.

Set up the shot, and try it yourself:

1. Shoot from the top cue-ball position in the photo. Aim directly into the far corner pocket, and you'll see that there's a ball directly on that line.

2. Play as though you're shooting that ball into the corner. The result is that the ball in the middle of the circle goes directly into the other corner pocket (the one on the same side of the table on which you're standing).

3. Move the cue ball to the bottom position in the photo, in a straight line from the bottom-left corner pocket to the far side pocket. There's also a ball on that line.

4. Aim the cue ball toward the far side pocket and shoot. The ball in the middle goes in the other side pocket—the one near where you were standing for the first shot.

5. Switch sides and move the cue-ball positions to the other side of the table, to make the shot work in reverse. So without changing the position of the seven balls in the center of the table, you can make the surrounded ball in your choice of four pockets.

The balls do have to be set up carefully; aiming is straight forward. Leave a slight space at both sides of the circle along the long center line. That leaves three balls frozen (touching) on each side. Just place the cue ball at various points around the circle of balls. Many players like to shoot this shot with a little draw (reverse spin) to get the cue ball out of the way.

The Coin-Wrapper Shot

You don't see paper coin-wrappers as often as you used to, but if you come across some and you want to shoot the Coin-Wrapper shot, grab them. Today, wrappers are usually clear, pliable plastic, and those don't work at all. Wrappers for quarters work the best. One of them has to be cut to the proper length. A ball is 2.25 inches in diameter, and the cue ball has to pass under both balls suspended on the wrappers, but the lower ball has to be a bit under the top ball.

Shooting the shot is fairly straightforward. Some performers use follow on the cue ball, and others hit the object ball that's in front of the pocket (the 9 ball in the following illustration) as a cut shot.

In the former case, the cue ball goes under the suspended balls, knocking the wrappers away, and continues on to hit the 9 ball, following it into the pocket. In the latter case, the cue ball hits the 9 ball into the pocket and goes off at a 90-degree angle, into the cushion and away from the action. In either case, when the wrappers are knocked away, the suspended balls come straight down. Because one ball is a little bit under the other, the top ball hits the bottom ball, and the balls go in opposite directions. One follows the cue ball's path and goes into the same pocket as the 9 ball; the other moves in the opposite direction, going into the pocket near me in the illustration. The shot is neat, simple, and fun.

The Coin-Wrapper shot is a real crowd-pleaser. Seeing balls up in the air like this is enough to grab almost anyone's attention. For those whose curiosity hasn't been piqued, the sound of two balls dropping on a slate bed is startling.

You have to be very careful about setting up the suspended balls in a straight line between the two side pockets. You also have to be very careful about cutting the second wrapper to the correct length; otherwise, someone standing on the opposite side of the table from you could get hit by a flying ball. A low miscue could have the same dangerous consequences because it would scoop the cue ball into the low ball, which would go into the high ball, which in turn would act as though it were being shot out of a cannon. Not good.

Try this shot cautiously, and when you're sure that it's right, you can use a full (but moderate) stroke.

How Did She Do That?

Following are two tricks to try when you feel that you've made good progress in playing the game, have mastered some of the setup trick shots, and want to stretch the envelope. Both shots involve draw (reverse spin), which audiences seem to like because the cue ball switches directions unexpectedly. Both also require a prop, but unlike coin wrappers, these props are items that come with a table and are close at hand. Finally, both shots require considerable skill and practice.

The Over-and-Under-the-Bridge Shot

Place a mechanical bridge across the table about half a diamond up the side rail, as you see in the following illustration. This is high enough for a ball to pass under it, yet not too high for a ball to jump over it. You'll do both in this shot. The placement of the three balls—the 1 ball, the cue ball, and the 9 ball—is simple, and you can use the photo as a guide. Place the balls in a straight line (although it helps if the 9 is very close to the edge of the pocket so that any contact taps it in). Place the cue ball close enough to the bottom cushion that you can use the rail to bridge on. The cue ball and 1 ball should be lined up for the far corner pocket.

The Over-and-Under-the-Bridge shot. The text explains how to get the cue ball to pocket the 1 ball, jump the bridge, come back under it, and then pocket the 9 ball. This shot will make the neighbors sit up and take notice.

What you intend to do in this shot is make the cue ball go airborne, hit the 1 ball straight on, and propel it into the far corner pocket. Because you hit the top of the 1 ball with the airborne cue ball, it jumps over the bridge. So unlike a regular jump shot, which requires you to jump over the ball, this shot requires you to jump the cue ball so that it hits the top of the 1 ball. You have to elevate the butt of your cue to make the cue ball jump, of course. Because the cue ball is going forward and just hits the top of the 1 ball, it keeps going forward and up, over the bridge handle. By the time it lands, the 1 is out of the way, on a path to the far corner pocket.

But that's just half the shot. You hit the cue ball below center, at the 6 o'clock mark, so that it has reverse spin (draw) on it. After it jumps over the bridge handle, the cue ball hits the cloth and the draw catches. Then the cue ball comes back under the bridge, toward you, and knocks the 9 ball in the pocket. Two balls in one shot and a spectacular jump—what more could one ask for?

The technique is a draw-jump shot. You know how to perform both elements from previous chapters (see Chapter 15 and 21), and you know how to combine them. But executing this shot is tough. If you jump too high, the cue ball just skims the top of the 1 ball, which then just dribbles forward a foot or two. If you fail to get enough elevation, the cue ball hits the 1 too fully and won't have the angle to be deflected upward and over the bridge. Without draw, of course, the ball jumps the bridge, lands, and goes forward, leaving the 9 ball untouched.

I'm always telling you to keep your cue as level as possible, but as I explained in the section on jumping balls, the only way to get the cue ball airborne is to elevate the butt of your cue. You aim low on the cue ball to put reverse spin (draw) on it, and you have a jump-draw shot. Remember to stay in the vertical axis and to hit the ball at 6 o'clock. This shot takes a good stroke and a very precise hit on the cue ball, coupled with proper cue-stroke speed.

The Steady-Jump-Draw Shot

Look at the figure in the preceding section to see the setup to use for the Steady-Jump-Draw shot. Half the trick is to get the rack balanced on the two balls! Hold one ball on top of the other with one hand, and place the rack on top with the other (see the following illustration). The weight of the rack helps steady the two balls. Then you get to the shot itself, which requires a significant amount of skill. You've done the "steady." Now, it's on to the jump.

After going to all the trouble of balancing a shiny, slick ball on top of another, I'm going to knock them down—but in the process, I'm going to pocket all three balls. Can you figure out how?

The first part of the trick is similar to the Over-and-Under shot: You must hit a jump shot that is the perfect height. The cue ball has to be high enough to hit the top of the bottom ball in the stack, at about the same point you hit the 1 ball in the Over-and-Under the-Bridge shot, but not so high as to hit the top ball either first or at the same time. Hit the bottom ball first, and it starts toward the corner pocket in the bottom-right corner of the picture. The top ball is hit next (almost simultaneously) and follows the bottom ball. Meanwhile, when you shoot the jump, you also have to put draw on the cue ball, hitting it at 6 o'clock just like in the Over-and-Under-the-Bridge shot, so that when it lands back on the table, it spins in reverse, catches the cloth, comes back toward you, and pockets the 9 ball in the corner (under my hand in the illustration).

Scratch!

Don't try this shot with a heavy stainless–steel rack. The edges, though rounded, can damage the cloth.

A lot goes on in a very short time during the Steady-Jump-Draw shot. You elevate the butt of your cue so that the cue ball is airborne when it hits the bottom ball in the stack. That ball (the bottom ball) immediately starts toward the corner pocket on the right. The cue ball immediately is deflected upward into the top ball in the stack, sending it (the top ball) on the same path as the bottom ball. Then the cue ball falls back to the table, where the draw that you put on the cue ball takes effect. Then the ball comes back toward you to pocket the 9 ball in the left corner pocket. All this happens in an instant.

This shot is a little noisy (because of the falling rack), exciting, and unusual—and it takes a good measure of skill. Wait until you possess a really good stroke and a successful jump shot before trying this one.

Crazy 8s

Manufacturers have made trick balls for billiards that are readily available at billiard supply stores, at some billiard room pro shops, and through magazine mail-order. The two most common are the off-balance 8 ball and an 8 ball and 9 ball that are glued together. You'll even see the latter in some professional trick shows.

To use the 8-9 ball, holding it as though you had two loose balls in your hand, and put it down a foot in front of the side pocket. Place it at a 45-degree angle (roughly) to the cushion, and explain to your neighbors that you can win by making the 9 ball, but you have to hit the 8 ball first, and if you hit the 8 ball first, the 8 will go in one direction, the 9 will go off at a 90-degree angle (just like the first trick shot in this chapter), and neither one will go in. But add that if a really skillful player puts Cockney English on the cue ball, instead of regular English, both balls will go in! Hit the 8 hard and fast so that the audience won't notice that the balls are glued together. Bingo!

The off-balance 8 ball rolls in a straight line if you slam it. Any soft or medium hit causes it to wobble in all directions as it rolls. It looks like a real 8 ball, so you can put it in the rack when you start a game of 8-Ball. Better still, challenge your playing partner to make a certain shot. Place the 8 ball along the long cushion, about two diamonds ($2^1/_2$ feet or so) from the corner pocket. Give him cue ball in hand, and tell him to pocket the 8 in the corner. It won't go in. You have to be standing close by to grab the 8 when it misses so that the other person won't see it start to wobble. But shooting it normally will do no good. Hitting it very hard might make the ball go in, but even that's iffy. In any case, novelty balls are fun—once.

The Least You Need to Know

➤ There are two kinds of trick shots: setup and skill.

➤ Anyone can make a setup shot that's been set up properly.

➤ Beginners should not attempt skill shots.

➤ The basic laws of billiards apply to every trick shot.

➤ Trick balls can be used in trick shots.

Part 6
The Games People Play

Now that you know how to pocket balls under almost every circumstance imaginable, it's time to learn the games of billiards. 9-Ball, 8-Ball, and Straight Pool are the most popular cue games in the world—the stuff of championships and casual games between friends. In this part, I walk you through the object of each game, the rules, and how to win. I also show you how to handicap the game so that you and a friend (or stranger), if you're at different skill levels, can still play competitively.

Straight Pool is as basic a game as possible. Simple, enjoyable, and classic, this game presents billiards in its purest form. 8-Ball is the next-most-basic game, and it's the one that most people play when they don't know a lot about pool. One person (or couple) has the solid colored balls, and the other has the striped balls. Simple? Maybe. But I think that after you read Chapter 25, you'll think of 8-Ball in a different way.

Want speed, excitement, action? Then 9-Ball is your game. It's the one that you see on TV, and it's rapidly gaining on 8-Ball in popularity. In Chapter 26, you learn what it's all about: what makes it exciting, how to play, what its special rules are, how to win, and how to handicap for players of different skill levels.

But those three games aren't the only ones that are available to you. In this part, I also tell you about games designed for an odd number of people, games for couples, and a bunch of special games that appeal to a lot of folks. Some are simple and others are advanced, but this second tier of games offers a lot for the player. I think that the games have different characters. Look them over, and see whether one makes the hair on the back of your neck stand up.

Chapter 24

Playing It Straight

In This Chapter

➤ Why Straight Pool is a great learning game

➤ The rules and how to keep score

➤ The importance and technique of the opening break shot

➤ How to make lots of balls

➤ How to handle trouble balls

➤ How to level the field for players at different skill levels

I'm going to start this part of the book with the game that many people think of as being pure pool. It's called Straight Pool, or 14.1. It has simple rules; it uses the full rack of 15 numbered balls; you can shoot any ball you want to; and each ball counts as 1 point, no matter what number is printed on it. Players can set the game for any number of points—the first person to make a total of 25 balls or the first person to make 150 balls, for example. There's no jarring break shot (you break safe), and Straight Pool has an elegance that many other games don't have. The game also has the advantage of being an excellent learning tool, primarily because almost every shot is short, the player can shoot any ball on the table, cue-ball control is critical, and the rules are simple.

Straight Pool (often called just *Straight*) is a relatively recent name—maybe 60 years old. The game is still called by an earlier name: 14.l (spoken as either "fourteen-one" or "fourteen-point-one"), which came from the fact that 14 of the 15 object balls are pocketed, and 1 is left on the table while the first 14 are reracked so that the game can keep going.

Straight Pool is the game I grew up on, and it is definitely a game that I encourage people to learn. To me, it is basic pool, and no matter what your favorite game ends up being, the knowledge that you'll gain from Straight Pool will help you for the rest of your billiard-playing life.

The game is most popular in the Northeast, and it's a shame that it has never been more popular in the South and West. For most of the 20th century (until the mid-'60s), Straight Pool was the game that determined the world champion. From the mid-'60s on, 9-Ball became the more popular game for championships, and Straight Pool tournaments waned. Today, a player can be world Straight Pool champion and/or world 9-Ball champion (if a Straight Pool world championship is staged—something that's no longer the case every year).

Don't let the diminished popularity of Straight Pool deter you, however; it's still pure pool, and it's an excellent game to learn, especially when you're beginning to play. In this chapter, I tell you what the game is all about.

What It's All About

The object of Straight Pool is to pocket a lot of balls. It doesn't matter which ones they are (as long they're not solid white—the cue ball) because each ball is worth 1 point. If you're very good, you can start off pocketing balls and go until only one object ball is left on the table, at which point you pause. The 14 balls that you pocketed are brought up and racked, with the front position left vacant. When the rack (the triangular device) is removed from the rack (the balls organized in form for breaking), you resume playing. No rule says that you have to hit the lone ball, but that's almost always the best ball to play, because it's loose and the others are not.

You continue shooting until you miss, at which time your opponent comes to the table and begins shooting. Play continues until 14 of the balls are pocketed (either by you alone or by you and your opponent), leaving the 15th ball on the table and reracking the 14 pocketed balls. The first person to reach a predetermined number of balls pocketed (typically, 50, 75, or 100, but either 125 or 150 in tournaments) wins, and the game is over.

You could play a *race* (also known as *best out of X number of games*) to two games or three games, but races are generally reserved for other games, because it's easy to make a Straight Pool game last as long as you want. Just increase the predetermined number to which you're playing.

While you are new to the game, you could break the balls open instead of breaking safe, as is traditional. This practice gives you some free balls (not near other balls) at which to shoot. After you can make two balls in a row with some consistency, however, switch to the real Straight Pool break.

Pocket Dictionary

A *race* is the number of games to win. A race to 8, for example, is another way of saying *the best out of 15 games*. Whoever wins 8 games first wins the contest. A *race* is also the act of getting to the winning point, as in "We're racing to five [games]."

Straight Pool is a game of short shots. The rack is broken open in such a way (without hitting it as hard as in 8-Ball or 9-Ball) that the balls stay on the bottom half of the table. At least 80 percent are pocketed in the two bottom corner pockets. Perhaps 15 percent are pocketed in the side pockets, and just 2 percent or so go in the far corner pockets (the ones at the end where you stood to break the first rack—the head of the table).

The abundance of short shots makes Straight Pool a good game for the beginner, but I don't want to mislead you into thinking that the game is easy. If your opponent shot you safe, if you failed to get position, or if the balls are in clusters (as they often are in Straight Pool), you can have a dozen balls within 2 feet of the corner pockets at the end of the table and not have a shot.

Straight Pool is also a game of finesse and pinpoint position play. With so many balls in such a small area, you have to play a lot of soft shots that are very accurate. Otherwise, you'll be in the middle of a mess with nothing to shoot at, and you'll end up playing a safety. You'll get to use all the spinning techniques, but none of them is used on power shots, so you'll find it much easier to learn control of the cue ball. In fact, there's probably no better game to play for practice and for learning cue-ball control. After you get pinpoint position on short shots, it's easy to extend that skill to getting area position on long shots for games such as 9-Ball. Learning the other way around is much tougher.

The final thing that Straight is about is keeping a *run* (a consecutive series of pocketed balls without a miss) going, and the key to doing this is knowing what makes a good break shot. For example, say you've pocketed the first 14 balls, and you pause to get them reracked so that you can continue shooting. If you then pocket the lone ball, you'll have nothing else to shoot at; all the balls will be in a solid pack, and none of them can be aimed into a pocket. Your run will be over. To keep going, you must pocket the lone ball *and* drive the cue ball into the *stack* (another name for the rack of balls) so that balls are driven loose. It's your goal to drive one of the balls someplace where you can shoot it in and keep your run going.

The break shot (not the opening break, which is a safety, but every break after that) is the place where everyone runs into trouble. Players get out of line, and although they can pocket the lone ball, they don't have a way of getting the cue ball to break up

Scratch!

Some players younger than 25 grew up playing only 9–Ball, and they may tell you that learning Straight Pool is a waste of time. Pay no attention. Straight will make you a better player in all games.

Pocket Dictionary

Stack is another name for balls in the shape of the rack. The term is used mostly in Straight Pool but occasionally in other games.

the rack. Or they try too hard to break up the rack and let their concentration on making the ball slip, so they miss the shot. There's nothing worse than breaking up the rack and missing the object ball. Your opponent gets to come to the table and probably has a plethora of shots available—not a good thing. So Straight Pool is very much about the break shot.

Special Rules

All the fundamental rules of pool apply, of course. You must touch a rail with a ball after the cue ball makes contact with the object ball, and so on. You do not have to hit the lowest-numbered ball first or stick to the solids or the stripes, but you do have to meet the basic rules.

Special rules involve the penalty for committing a foul. I mentioned this in an earlier chapter, but it's worth repeating here about the game so that you'll have all the material in one place. Your first foul deducts 1 point from your score; it's as though you didn't make one of the balls that you previously made. If you shoot a ball into a pocket and foul, that ball comes out and is placed on the footspot, and 1 point is deducted from the score you had before you pocketed that ball. If you commit two consecutive fouls, a second point is deducted. If you commit a third consecutive foul, you are penalized *16* points! (The penalty is figured as 1 point for the foul and 15 additional points because it's a third consecutive foul.)

Remember, though, that this is a third consecutive foul measured in shots, not in turns at the table. In other words, you can commit a foul, your opponent can shoot, you commit a second foul, your opponent shoots, you make a ball, and on your second shot you commit a foul. That's three consecutive fouls in three consecutive turns at the table, but it's not three consecutive fouls on shots because you made a legal shot before the third foul (which now becomes a first foul). If you do lose 18 points, however (1 + 1 + 16) and commit a foul on your fourth shot, it counts as a first foul, not a fourth. In other words, after three consecutive fouls, you start your count of fouls from zero again (Whew! At that rate of increase, you were probably worried that a fourth foul would get a penalty of 88 points or something).

Pocket Dictionary

A *call shot* means verbally indicating the object ball that you are going to hit and the pocket it will go in—"5 in the corner," for example.

Both the break shot and regular shots have some unique requirements that, if not met, result in a foul being called on the player. On the break shot, you must drive at least two object balls and the cue ball to a cushion or cushions. Failing to do so is a foul. Other games have other rules for the break.

Straight Pool is also almost always played as a call-shot game, and in the old days, pool jargon included "*call shot*" as an alternative name for Straight Pool. Calling your shot means naming the ball that you are going to shoot and the pocket you are going to make that ball in—"5 ball in the side," for example. You've probably heard that expression in a movie or a TV show. It's a very common rule for Straight Pool (although not in all recreation versions) but fairly rare for the other games. But nothing says that the officials and/or players can't decide to play under that rule.

In most situations, you are not obligated to call a very obvious shot, such as a short straight-in shot. Banks, combos, and caroms, however obvious they may seem to be, are not considered to be obvious and have to called. In a professional tournament, an old-time referee (and some younger ones who emulate the famous referees of old) might call every ball for the player (usually not mentioning the pocket). If he calls the wrong ball, the player is supposed to say so before shooting.

What happens if you correctly call the pocket, but the ball doesn't go in? No penalty, other than losing your turn because you missed a shot. What if the ball goes in another pocket? No penalty, but no count either. The ball is spotted on the headspot, and you lose your turn. And what if the ball goes in the correct pocket and another object ball goes in that pocket (or some other pocket)? Both balls count, and you shoot again. On a combination shot, you generally just need to call the ball that is going in the pocket, not the first ball that you hit. (You also have to name the pocket, of course.) In other words, if you shoot a combination of the 6 ball into the 3 ball and you name the pocket, all you need to do is say "3 in the side," not "6 into the 3 and the 3 in the side."

Heard It in the Poolroom

During the late 1980s, I set the women's world record for consecutive balls pocketed (Straight Pool) in a tournament: 54. In 1992, at the U.S. Open in the Roosevelt Hotel in New York City, I was playing Cathy Petrowski on one table. Next to me, former U.S. Open Champion Loree Jon Jones was playing Vicki Paski. I noticed a murmuring in the room. I was in the middle of a run—somewhere around 20 or 25 balls—and realized that Loree Jon was on a high run. Someone told me she was approaching my record, and suddenly, the crowd burst into a standing ovation. She had made her 55th ball in a row!

When the room calmed down, we both continued shooting on our adjoining tables. Moments later, there was another burst of applause as Loree Jon ended her run at 64 balls. By then, my total was in the 50s and still going, and the murmuring started again as the attention (and tension) in the room shifted. Moments later, there was still another standing ovation as I ended my run at 68, reclaiming a world record that had been out of my possession for less than 10 minutes!

The final set of rules that are peculiar to Straight Pool involve the 15th ball. After 14 have been pocketed, remember, the player pauses before shooting the 15th ball while the 14 pocketed balls are reracked. But suppose that the 15th ball is in the area where the balls have to be racked. It is picked up and put in the rack, and the rack is set up just like it was for the opening break—that is, all 15 balls in a triangle. The cue ball is then moved to its opening position—anywhere behind the headstring (or *line,* as it's usually called; sometimes it is also called *the kitchen*).

You might think that we've covered just about every situation, but there's more. Suppose that the cue ball, rather than the 15th object ball, is in the area where the balls have to be racked. Then the cue ball goes behind the line, but the 15th ball stays where it is. Think that does it?

Suppose that the cue ball is in the rack area, but the 15th ball is already up behind the headstring. Then the 15 goes back on the spot at the point of the rack, and the cue ball goes anywhere behind the headstring.

That should about cover any possible situation that will ever arise in any game of Straight Pool—except, of course, the possibility that when the player pocketed the 14th ball, he or she also accidentally pocketed the 15th ball. In that case, all 15 object balls go in the rack, and the cue ball goes behind the headstring.

And here's another possibility: Suppose that the cue ball comes to rest on the headspot, and the 15th ball is in the rack area, too. Both balls can't be put on the headspot, so the cue ball stays there, and the 15th ball is placed somewhere you've never heard of before: the center spot. This spot, which is in the center of the table, is never marked on a table and is seldom used for anything in pool (it's where the 5 ball goes in snooker), but it does exist.

Now I've covered just about all the possibilities. This little oddity with the racking is the only thing about Straight Pool that is the least bit difficult to learn, and it doesn't come up often. When it does, refer to the rulebook or the preceding paragraphs. Don't bother trying to memorize the rule. The only two situations that come up with any frequency are either when the cue ball or the 15th ball is in the rack and the other ball is not; you might memorize those two rules. As for the rest—forget about them.

How to Win

The break shot is so important that most Straight Pool strategy is broken down into two categories: (1) the break shot and (2) everything else. Although Straight is a simple game, strategy is still involved. Some strategy involves safety play, and some involves pattern play. A critical item is where the last ball (the 15th ball) is left in relation to the cue ball.

The Winning Opening Break

Breaks are divided into two types: the opening break and all others. The opening break is a safety shot because you can't reliably call any ball on the break, and this is a call-shot game. A good break, as I mentioned in Chapter 18, meets the requirements of driving two object balls and the cue ball to the rails, and not leaving your opponent a shot. To do this, place the cue ball on the headstring (you have to break from on or behind the headstring) almost the same distance from the side cushion as the corner ball in the rack is positioned. The perspective is a little off, but if you measured from the cue ball to the right cushion, from the right rear corner ball in the rack to the cushion, the second measurement would be $2^1/_4$ inches longer. That just happens to be the width of a ball.

The cue ball position is important to a good break shot in Straight Pool.

With high-right spin, send the cue ball down to just clip the right edge of the rear object ball in the rack. The cue ball bounces off to the right, and the right spin takes effect when the ball hits the cushion causing it to hit the long rail a foot or so from the corner pocket, coming back up and across the table to the same point (about a foot from the corner pocket) at the head of the table on the other side. It then bounces gently off that cushion and ends up frozen to the top rail.

This is another case in which pictures speak louder than words, so check the preceding illustration again, and I'll use that perspective to describe the safety break in Straight Pool again. The cue ball hits the far-right corner ball. It bounces off the far rail, a foot to the left of the pocket. Spin brings it about a foot from the far-right corner on the long rail. It crosses the picture from far right to near left (actually a little out of the picture) and hits just about a foot short of the top-left corner pocket (out of the picture), from which it rolls to a stop at the point that you see in the following illustration.

This result of a break shot—a safety—leaves your opponent with few shot options.

In the best of all worlds, the right-rear corner object ball would go to the bottom rail; it's frozen against the ball to its left and has to obey Ewa's Second 90-Degree Rule of Billiards. From there, it would bounce back to where it started. The force of its being hit would be transmitted down the back row, and the last ball in the row (the left-rear corner ball) would go straight to the left side rail and bounce back where it started.

You rarely see the best of all worlds, however. More likely, the rack ends up looking something like the preceding illustration. But that's great. You shot a wonderful safety! Now imagine how your opponent feels coming to the table and seeing this setup. What problems does he have, and if you were in his shoes, what would you do in reply?

There are three problems in the preceding illustration, and you'll run into them in the opening break in Straight Pool fairly often, so you've got to learn to deal with them. These problems are:

➤ The cue ball is frozen to the top cushion. You can't hit it dead-center; you have to use follow. Worse, you have to elevate the butt of your cue to even do that, which opens the possibility of hitting a curve shot when you don't want to do anything but hit the ball straight.

➤ The nearest object ball is all the way down at the other end of the table, making the shot tough even if you could hit the cue ball properly.

➤ The only ball that can reasonably be said to present a possible opportunity is the front ball. You can cut it in the corner pocket, but if you do, the Second 90-Degree Rule will send your cue ball straight into the left corner pocket.

The solution is to play a return safety—something that frequently happens in Straight Pool. It's almost as though the game takes a little while to get warmed up. A safety break is followed by an exchange of safeties until one player makes a mistake and leaves a good shot. One trick is to leave a very difficult but makable shot in the hope that your opponent will decide to take a fling at it and miss. That's not always possible, however, and the safest route is to indulge in a battle of safeties.

The break shot, by the way, isn't all that easy either. If the balls aren't racked perfectly and you don't skim the corner ball perfectly, you probably won't end up in the attractive position shown in the preceding photo. Chances are that the cue ball won't be perfectly frozen on the top rail, and chances are that a stray ball at the other end of the table won't be all that far from a corner pocket. The person coming in—your opponent—is more than likely going to have some kind of shot or some kind of easy return safety. Breaking with a result like the figure on the opposite page happens to experienced players, but it doesn't happen every time. Straight Pool is the only game in which breaking is such a disadvantage that the person who wins the *lag* (the roll of the balls to decide who breaks) always makes the loser of the lag do the breaking.

If you do face the shot in the figure, I advise that you use a shot similar to the break shot, in which you skim one ball and return to the head of the table with the cue ball, or else a soft shot in which you hit a ball and leave the cue ball frozen on the balls at the front of the rack. The first is the better choice as far as results go, but it is more difficult to pull off.

The Winning Break After the Opening Break

Check out the next illustration, and you'll see what many people feel is the perfect break shot. You have made the 14th ball, and the 3 ball is the 15th. The 14 were reracked, and now you're ready to resume. With no spin at all, you can pocket the 2 ball into the bottom-right corner pocket (out of the picture but close by), and the cue ball will hit the second ball in the stack full on.

This is the perfect position for a Straight Pool break.

It's better to go into the stack with the cue ball by hitting a numbered ball full in the face, because there's less chance of burrowing the cue ball into the mass of balls and being left in a touch position, which could happen more easily if the cue ball hit the stack between two balls. This way, it hits the second ball (the light-colored striped ball) from the front full in the face and bounces back. All the force is directed into that ball and then into the group, and all the balls spread.

You don't have to slam the daylights out of the stack to get it to spread, which is a common mistake among beginning Straight Pool players. Sometimes, force helps, but it's not a good idea to use it without thinking. If you take a second, you can see (using the Second 90-Degree Rule) where the balls will go when the cue ball hits the stack. Your goal is to separate them as much as possible, and if you slam them too hard, the outer balls will hit the cushions and bounce back toward the stack area. A medium stroke will separate them neatly, giving you shots.

Play position off the ball in the stack that you want to hit so that you can control the final location of the cue ball. You do that with speed and spin, as you know, and you want to end up about where you started from. That position is above most of the balls, giving you a nice vantage point to each corner pocket, and it's close enough to make whatever shot pops up easy to make. So do this successfully and you can keep running balls forever. (Theoretically.)

A second break position favored by some players is behind the rack. Leave the 15th ball where the number 12 ball is in the following figure. When the balls are reracked, you'll have the arrangement shown in the figure. Pop the striped 12 ball into the right corner pocket (out of the picture), and the cue ball goes naturally into the base of the triangle, scattering the balls.

A break from behind the rack is popular with some players in Straight Pool.

On any break shot (after the opening safety break), there's a chance of scratching by bouncing off the rack and into a pocket. Use your knowledge of the Second 90-Degree Rule to figure out where the cue ball will hit the stack and where it will go when it leaves the stack. If that place is a pocket, alter the path with low or high spin (draw or follow).

Special Safeties for Straight Pool

I've already covered one special safety that is used in Straight Pool: the distance safety. Because all the object balls tend to stay close together at the far end of the table, a good safety (if no OBs are near a pocket opening) is simply to place the cue ball at the far end of the table. Freezing the ball to the cushion is best, and I showed you a moment ago.

Scratch!

Hitting the stack hard opens the opportunity for one of the object balls to hit a cushion and then collide with the cue ball, driving it into a pocket for a scratch. Control your speed.

Another strategy used in Straight Pool is to call a "safety" and pocket a ball. This is a call-shot game, remember, so if you say that a shot is a safety and then pocket a ball, the ball is simply spotted on the footspot, and your opponent comes to the table. This can be good when, for example, one ball has ended up at the head of the table near the cue ball, but the layout is such that you couldn't shoot a second ball successfully. Call a safety, pocket the ball, and leave the cue ball frozen on the top rail. You've given up a turn, but your opponent is in a world of hurt. Whatever she or he does probably will be to your advantage.

On occasion, you may want to foul on purpose. If, for example, the rack of balls is still tight together and you're at the head of the table, you have two shots at your disposal. These shots, although they are fouls, can tilt the game in your favor. One shot is to softly hit the cue ball between the two front balls in the rack. Actually, you aim slightly toward one or the other and use a little inside English (sidespin). The shot freezes the cue ball and the two front balls in their own mini triangle, while the impact goes through the rack and knocks the two back corner balls free. If you tap them hard enough, one of the corner balls will hit the back cushion, and the shot will even be legal. Now your opponent has to shoot away from the rack, but no matter where she leaves the cue ball up-table, you have a shot at one of the separated corner balls. That can get you started.

The other on-purpose foul is hitting the cue ball against the cushion behind the stack making it rebound into the balls. Some of the outside balls come loose and separate from the stack, and the cue ball is frozen at the back of the stack. Again, if you hit hard enough, this shot can even result in a legal hit by driving one of the object balls to a cushion, but that normally is too hard a hit; it loosens too many balls, including balls in the back row. In this case, it's better to hit lighter, take a foul, and leave your opponent in a terrible jam.

Picking Your Break Ball

The *break ball* is the name for the 15th object ball—the one that you use as a target for the cue ball to bounce off and break up the stack. Obviously, having a well-placed break ball makes the break shot easier. Balls like those in the preceding two illustrations are ideal. When you approach the table, look for balls that are already in those positions; then try to pocket them last. Figure out a pattern, working backward (as I showed you in the pattern/position section of Chapter 22).

Pocket Dictionary

A *break ball*, in Straight Pool, means the ball that is used to send the cue ball into the stack, breaking up the triangle of balls.

Pattern play is critical to Straight Pool because you must have a plan to get to the final two balls in a rack. The ball just before the last ball is called the *key ball* because it is the key to your getting position on your break ball and opening the stack. Pick your break ball and then your key ball, and keep working backward to the last ball on the table (which will be the first one that you shoot). If, along the way, you get out of line, make whatever adjustments are necessary. Just try to never disturb your key ball and break ball until it's time to hit them.

Pocket Dictionary

A *key ball*, in Straight Pool, means the ball that is used to get position on the break ball.

In some cases, you or your opponent will have spread the stack, and you'll see that there simply isn't any ball that would be a good break ball. What should you do? Manufacture a break ball by nudging a likely candidate into place during another shot. Normally, I'd tell you not to disturb any balls that weren't trouble balls—that you should try to play (in Straight and other billiard games) without touching another ball unnecessarily. But if you don't have a break ball, you're not going to be able to continue running (pocketing) balls. Your only choice is to create a break ball by moving one of the object balls into place, and the only time you'll be able to do that is when you're pocketing another object ball. This involves delicate cue-ball control—one reason why the word *finesse* is so often applied to Straight Pool.

More Straight Strategy

As you would in any billiard game (other than Carom), the first thing you should do when you approach a table is look for trouble. Trouble—situations that might prevent you from pocketing some of the balls on the table—includes the following:

➤ Clusters

➤ Balls frozen against the cushion (they're tougher to shoot)

➤ Balls that block other balls from going into a pocket

➤ Any ball that is way up at the head of the table (the end where you stood to break)

You should take care of these situations as soon as possible. Much of your pattern design centers on turning trouble balls into makable balls.

Balls that are frozen against the cushion are more difficult to pocket because your margin for error is less than half what it would be if the ball were away from the cushion. Any error in aiming or contacting the ball that would drive it toward the cushion will make you miss the shot because the spring of the cushion pushes the ball away from the straight line to the pocket. That cuts your margin for error in half.

But you can also hit the object ball so that it goes on a line away from the cushion. It doesn't seem possible at first. How can you cut a ball on an angle so that it goes away when the cue ball can't hit that side of the object ball because the cushion is in the way? Well, the cue ball is moving. It has force. And that force pushes the cushion in so that it can actually contact the ball on the "inside" and hit it on a line that is away from the cushion. Finally, when you hit a ball down the cushion to the pocket, the target area is much smaller than if you hit an object ball into the pocket from the middle of the table. All those factors combine to make pocketing a ball that's frozen to the cushion more difficult than the average cut shot.

Cue Tips

Pocketing a ball frozen on the rail is easier if you use a touch of inside English (sidespin). If the rail and object ball are to your right, for example, use a little left spin.

323

You already know that it's better to break up clusters early, but in Straight Pool it sometimes seems that all you have is clusters. The balls are not broken hard or generally hit hard, so they tend to gather around the rack area. With that many balls on the table confined to such a small space, it's impossible not to have clusters. When you see a cluster, don't automatically think that you have to break it up by running the cue ball into it while making a ball that's not in the cluster. Often, clusters present *dead balls*—that is, balls that are frozen like the first trick shot in Chapter 23 and almost can't be missed. See if that's the case before you try to break up the cluster.

If there's no dead ball and you do have to break up the group, try to do so gently. If you hit with any kind of power, chances are—with so many other balls close by—that one or two of them will simply roll into other balls and form new clusters. Especially in Straight Pool but in all billiard games, it's a good general rule not to move balls unnecessarily. It can only create potential problems.

Blocking balls are sometimes difficult to hit. If a ball won't go in a pocket because another ball is in the way, you should, obviously, shoot the blocking ball in first. But sometimes, you can't. The object ball and the blocking ball may be too close together, or the angles may not allow you to get between the balls to shoot the blocking ball. When this happens, you have to treat the balls like a cluster and move one or the other. Blocking balls are always a problem, and you should try to clear them first; but if that's not possible, try to nudge the blocking ball or the other ball into a slightly different position, in which one of them can be pocketed. Generally, with a little finesse and good cue-ball control, you can get a shot at a blocking ball and clear the path to the pocket for the other balls.

The opposite situation arises sometimes: a ball that is hanging on the edge of a pocket, ready to drop in, but needing a little tap. If you leave this ball and attack other balls, you may get into trouble. Should you miss one of the other balls, your opponent comes to the table with a sure shot available, and that can start her on a run that adds up to a big score.

On the other hand, it's sometimes wise to leave a *hanger* (a ball close to the lip of the pocket) as an *insurance ball* (a ball that can be made easily if you get out of position while you're shooting more difficult shots). Should you accidentally snooker yourself (place the cue ball behind a blocking ball), you can shoot your insurance ball and get back in the swing of the pattern. So when do you shoot a hanger, and when do you leave it hanging? That's something you have to figure out by looking at the placement of all the other balls. When you are beginning to play Straight Pool, it's probably a good idea to shoot all hangers right away. As you get more experience and are able to make 8 or 10 balls in a row, you can evaluate hangers on an individual basis.

For various reasons, one or two balls may be at the opposite end of the table from the big group around the

Pocket Dictionary

Hangers are balls on the edge of a pocket opening. The meaning is often expanded to indicate any very easy shot. An *insurance ball* is an easy shot that isn't taken right away but is saved, in case you get into trouble on a more difficult shot.

rack. One player may have put it there on purpose during a safety or to prevent his or her opponent from being able to put the cue ball at that end of the table, thinking it was a safe shot. (If all the balls are around the rack, a good safety is to put the cue ball near the head of the table, but if a ball there can be pocketed and used to get the cue ball back down to the group at the foot of the table, that safety option is taken away.) Dealing with that solitary ball usually is best done early. If you wait until you're close to the end of the rack (all but a few balls have been pocketed), you may find it difficult to get up to the ball, make it, and get good pinpoint position a table length away. On occasion, it's best to wait to shoot it, but that's rare.

You must take all these problem situations into account when you plan your attack. Making a pattern includes trouble balls. Even when the balls are spread open, with none close to another, strategy is still involved. This gets more into the expert level of play, but you should know that the order in which you shoot the balls is often a deciding factor in whether you succeed in running the rack (making all 14 balls, or all balls remaining after your opponent shoots). Complete books deal with little else but making correct choices in Straight Pool pattern play. See Appendix B for some good selections.

Handicapping

Players of unequal skill levels frequently want to play each other. In many sports, making the game fair and interesting for two players like this is fairly difficult. Not so in billiards.

I often play my daughter, Nikki, and I can even the playing field by doing many different things. I can play one-handed, left-handed, or give her a spot, for example. A *spot* is an unevening of final goals of the two players. You can do that by saying that one player has to win X number of games to win the match, whereas the other player has to win $2X$ games. Straight Pool is the easiest game to handicap because each ball is 1 point, and the stronger player can give the newer player a certain number of points on the wire. The phrase *on the wire* comes from the days when Straight was the main game in billiard rooms, and each table had a wire suspended over it. There were sliding wooden beads for each player, and that was how you kept score. Giving someone 30 points on the wire on a game to 50 meant that you moved 30 beads on that player's side of the wire before the game started. The new player had to get only 20 more points to have 50, whereas the experienced player had to get all 50.

As you'll see in the rest of this part of the book, other games have different handicapping schemes, but they all serve the same purpose: to level the playing field when two people of different skill levels are competing. The point spot in Straight Pool is the simplest, which is only fitting because the game itself is basically simple. The strategy, as I

Pocket Dictionary

A *spot* is the giving of points, games, or some other advantage to a player at a lower skill level so as to level the playing field.

showed you in this chapter, can become a little advanced (especially when you're dealing with the break shot), but fundamentally, it's a matter of creating patterns and following through on them without error. Shots are short; control of the cue ball is paramount; the cue ball rarely touches more than one cushion during a shot (and frequently doesn't touch a cushion at all); and there's no need to hit the cue ball hard, possibly losing control of it and also losing the game. With a full rack of balls on the table, you often have to break up clusters and use a lot of the other techniques that I've taught you, but that's the challenge and fun of the game.

The Least You Need to Know

➤ Straight Pool has special rules.

➤ You use softer shots in Straight Pool because you cover shorter distances.

➤ Look for trouble balls before you begin to shoot.

➤ Eliminate trouble balls early.

➤ Find a potential key ball and break ball when you first examine the layout.

➤ Devise a pattern that will logically take you from one ball to another ball.

➤ Each ball counts as 1 point, regardless of the number printed on it.

Eight Is Enough

8-Ball is, unquestionably, the most popular pool game in the United States, played in amateur leagues and billiard clubs across the country. In a way, 8-Ball has gotten a bad rap. Because it is the game that nonplayers are most familiar with, and because it is the game that works best on small coin-operated amusement pool tables, and because it is the game of choice for socially oriented pool leagues, it is thought of as being a frivolous, entry-level game. Not so. 8-Ball can be played at a fairly high level. You don't see it often in professional tournaments, because top players prefer the challenges of 9-Ball (or even Straight Pool and One-Pocket), but also because it can have some extended periods of safety play, which are less interesting to nonbilliard-knowledgeable audiences.

Because it's not a tournament game, and because leagues control the rules that their members play under, the rules for 8-Ball are all over the road. I mentioned before that in the same billiard club, one league may play one evening, another league may play the next evening, and individuals may be playing games of 8-Ball elsewhere in the room—and no two groups are using the same rules. That aside, I can tell you about some basic principles and common rules that will give you a head start in learning 8-Ball. I'll even try to make the rules section as simple as possible.

So many people play 8-Ball that I strongly recommend that you learn the game. It's different from other pool games and adds more interest to your time at the table. It lends itself well to play by two couples, which can't be said of all billiard games, most of which are best played head to head. It's more difficult to practice by yourself than other games, because you have to switch your brain from being the person with the solids to being the person with the stripes after every miss. So 8-Ball has advantages and disadvantages compared with other pool games, and whether you make it your main game depends on what you want to get out of playing pool. Besides, no one ever said that you have to be good at only one game!

What It's All About

Whoever makes the 8 ball wins. But before you can pocket the 8, you have to pocket all the balls in your group. You can't combination the 8 ball into a pocket early in the game, as you can in 9-Ball. If you do that in 8-Ball, you lose, instead of win.

The two groups of balls are the solids (1–7) and the stripes (9–15). There is absolutely no difference between the solids and stripes (same weight, size, and so on) other than their markings. You can also think of the groups as being the low balls and the high balls. In some places, 8-Ball is called *Stripes and Solids*; in others, *Highs and Lows*. But everyone recognizes the term *8-Ball*.

After you determine which group is yours (see "Special Rules" later in this chapter), you have to pocket either all the stripes or all the solids and then pocket the 8 ball to win.

The 8-Ball Rack

All 15 numbered balls are used in 8-Ball, and they are racked in the familiar triangle shape, as you see in the following illustration.

The 1 ball doesn't necessarily have to be in front, but that placement is traditional. Try to have the other balls alternate. The arrangement in the preceding illustration is a rack that gives the player who breaks less of an advantage than she would normally have, as I'll explain in a second. The breaker has an advantage because she:

➤ Is likely to make a ball on the break

➤ Gets to pick (under some rules) whether she wants to have the solids or the stripes

➤ Gets to keep shooting (if a ball was made on the break).

The full set of balls is used in 8-Ball. The 8 always goes in the middle, and the other balls can go anywhere (but see the text for the secrets of a winning racking pattern).

Making a ball on the break can be a serious factor in this game. If the balls were racked randomly, there's a great probability that some solids are grouped and some stripes are grouped. If two or three balls are made on the break, the breaker probably would sink balls that were all in one group.

When you rack for your opponent, use the model in the preceding illustration, and alternate stripes and solids. The only rule of racking is that the 8 ball must be in the middle of the rack. The wise options that you should follow are to make each ball come from a different group than the balls on each side of it. The two balls behind the 8 ball should also be from different groups (one solid and one striped).

Notice that the back two corner balls are stripes—the natural result of alternating groups. This isn't the most perfect result, because those two balls have the best chance of going in on the break. Nothing blocks them from shooting out and covering a good distance, whereas all the other balls are constrained to some degree. But if you make one a solid, you no longer have alternating balls. Still, it's better to change the pattern on the back row, making one of the corner balls a solid and one of them a stripe. This arrangement forces you to have two balls of the same group in the middle of the back row, but it's a better option than having two corner balls of the same group. In other words, reading across the back row, you might have solid, stripe, solid, stripe, stripe. At least the critical corner balls are different, and that's important.

Scratch!

Warning—8-Ball played on a coin-operated tavern table is a totally different game from 8-Ball played on a regular pool table. On the coin-op table, all pocketed balls (except the cue ball) must stay pocketed, the playing surface is smaller and more crowded, and the cue ball is bigger than the other balls.

The 8-Ball Break

The 8-Ball break (as I mentioned in Chapter 18 on break shots) is an open break, and the more powerful it is, the better off you are. The goals of your break shot are to separate the balls as widely as possible, give them enough momentum to roll around a lot and find a pocket, and to pocket at least one ball (preferably, two or three). To help you do this, the rack must be as tight as possible (all balls touching their neighbors), and your break shot must be as strong and as accurate as you can make it.

The best break shot in 8-Ball is to hit the second ball in the rack. (See the following illustrations for cue-ball position.) This shot causes the most *action* (spreading of the balls) and may push the 8 ball into the corner pocket.

Probably the most effective cue-ball position for the break. It's a rail break, and some people prefer to move the ball away from the cushion just a little so that they can get their hand on the table. You wouldn't want the cue ball to be closer to the cushion than this for your break shot in 8-Ball. A little reverse spin will keep you from scratching in the right corner pocket.

This is a fairly good position for breaking in 8-Ball, but not quite as strong as the one in the preceding illustration. Don't move the cue ball any closer to the center of the table than this breaking position.

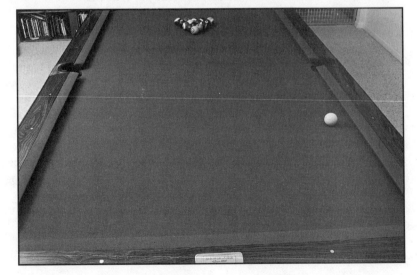

This break is not an easy one, because you have to aim carefully and still deliver a lot of power (which you can do through the speed of your stroke). When you are just starting in billiards, use a center ball hit on the front ball, and switch to hitting the second ball in the rack on your break shots only after you master the stroke and know to aim and execute accurately.

As you do in all games, you must break from behind the headstring, and I suggest that you place the cue ball on the headstring and break off the side rail if you feel confident doing so. It's the most effective angle for an 8-Ball break, but as I told you in the chapter on breaks, a rail break is a little more difficult to execute. Until you've practiced it, you may want to move the ball away from the cushion just enough to get your hand on the table.

The following figure shows the result of a good 8-Ball break. The balls are widely scattered, and except for the three balls near the left cushion, they don't present any problems. Those three balls are in one another's way and may have to banked, nudged around, or shot into the left corner pocket nearest the camera. This is the time to make your plan and work out a pattern.

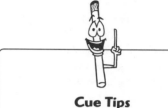

Cue Tips

Waxed balls break apart easier than unwaxed balls do.

A good 8-Ball break leaves the balls widely scattered on the table.

The Rest of the Game

8-Ball can be a defensive game, and you rarely see even very experienced players break and run out (make all the balls in their group and the 8 ball). The other player's balls

Ewa's Billiard Bits

In England, Australia, Hong Kong, parts of Canada, and a few other places, 8-Ball is played with a set of balls that consists of seven yellows, seven reds, and the black 8 ball. This game is called *Yellows and Reds*. It's a very defensive game, which stretches out the playing time—a positive thing on a coin-operated table, on which you're charged by the game, not by the time that you're playing.

frequently block pockets, so that you can't shoot a ball in them, or are in clusters and can't be pocketed. So somewhere along the line, a player will play defense by shooting a safety. As in Straight Pool, there can be an exchange of safeties (sometimes extended) until one player makes a mistake. This can happen two or three times in a single game.

8-Ball is a good game for learning to manipulate the cue ball. With seven of your opponent's balls in the way, you have to become good at zipping in, out, and around those balls to get a shot at yours. You can't turn the cue ball loose (hit it hard and that hope something goes in), because:

➤ If you accidentally pocket the 8 before you've pocketed your balls, you lose (under most rules).

➤ If you accidentally pocket an opponent's ball, it counts for her or him.

Special Rules

If you're playing in a league or tournament, some kind of printed list of rules should be available. If you're just playing among friends or with someone you met at your favorite billiard room, you must decide on a few options before you start playing. If you'd rather not make these decisions, you can go to the BCA (Billiard Congress of America) rulebook. The BCA rules are used for that league, but they're also the default set of rules for most games, because the rulebook is available in every billiard room in the United States (and in many overseas).

All the basic rules of billiards apply in 8-Ball, of course, and the variations exist where the unique circumstances of 8-Ball call for a rule. I'll go over the major rules in the following sections; then you can make your own decisions.

Break Rules

BCA rules are that to be legal, the break shot must drive at least four numbered balls to the cushions or pocket a ball. Most leagues have a similar rule. Failure to do one or the other is a foul. The object of this rule is to prevent someone from breaking safe, as you do in Straight Pool. A safety break would make the game last a long time unless the incoming player smashed the balls wide open. If the rules also included making the game a call-shot game (more on that in a second), it's unlikely that anyone playing after the opening break would smash the balls open. So without the first stipulations (four balls to the cushions or a ball pocketed), the contest would turn very defensive and last forever.

Things will happen on the break that may stop you cold. Here are some common break-rule situations that may generate questions:

➤ Player A breaks and nothing goes in.

➤ Player B comes to the table and has his choice of solids or stripes.

This situation is fairly universal. But suppose that player A makes a stripe, looks at the table layout, and sees that it would be to his advantage to have the solids. One school of thought says that player A made a stripe and has to take the stripes as his group. Another school says that player A shouldn't be penalized by having to take the less-advantageous group of balls when he did something good (made a ball on the break); therefore, regardless of which group the pocketed ball belongs to, if any ball (other than the cue ball, of course) was made on the break, the breaker has his choice of groups. So there are two rules. Take your pick.

Suppose that nothing is made on the break. Player B comes to the table, sees a nice straight-in shot on a striped ball, and bends over to shoot. Just as he enters his final stroke, however, he hiccups and misses the shot. Because player A chose stripes but didn't pocket the ball, is player B forced to accept solids? Not under most rules. Again, the logic is that a player who makes an error shouldn't get an advantage by doing so. Player B shouldn't suffer and can choose either solids or stripes at this point.

Cue Tips

The BCA and many other leagues sell (or will send free) a set of their rules for 8-Ball. See Appendix B for the addresses.

Scratch!

If someone tells you that an 8-Ball rule (or a rule for any billiard game) rewards a bad play or favors luck over skill, it very likely is a rule that this person just made up for the situation he's in.

Suppose that player A scratches on the break. What do you do? The incoming player usually is awarded cue ball in hand behind the headstring—not anywhere on the table, as in 9-Ball. But suppose that player A also made a ball *and* scratched on the break. On a coin-operated table, there's no way to get the balls (other than the cue ball) back out without putting in more money, so the practical rule is that the ball stays down (it has to), and the cue ball goes to player B.

But letting the ball count on a scratch is like rewarding a player for a foul, and when you're playing at home or on a full-size table in a club, there's no reason to follow this rule. Most people bring the ball back up and spot it on the footspot. That way, player A isn't rewarded by keeping the ball pocketed on a shot that was a foul. The same reasoning applies not only on the break shot, but also on any shot that is a foul at any time during the game.

Traditionally, making the 8 ball on the break shot wins you the game, but few sets of 8-Ball rules today actually contain that rule. The rule was always used more by people who were playing 8-Ball socially than it was used in any structured setting.

Official 8-Ball rules vary, so here are some options for you to choose among for your nonleague game of 8-Ball:

➤ If you're not playing on a little coin-operated table, you have the option of spotting the 8 ball and letting player A go on with the game. Making the 8 ball on the break is pretty much luck, and this option makes the game less haphazard and more skill-oriented.

➤ You could spot the 8, and if no other ball was pocketed on the break, player A could lose his turn. The rationale is that player A didn't pocket a ball that stays pocketed and, therefore, didn't really pocket a ball.

➤ The BCA offers an interesting option. If the player A so opts, she could have the balls reracked, and she could rebreak.

➤ You could make the 8 on the break a game-winner. If you're playing on a coin-operated table and can't get the ball back out of the pocket, you may as well make it a winning shot.

Stripes or Solids?

In this section, I'll tell you why you may want to choose one group of balls over the other. Whether you have solids or stripes as your group is almost always determined on the break shot. The final determination varies, and I gave you those options earlier in the chapter.

I need to mention one more thing first, though. After you determine which player has solids and which player has stripes, you must hit a ball from your group first. It's like hitting the lowest-numbered ball on the table first in 9-Ball and Rotation. If, for example, you have solids, you must hit a solid as your first object ball. That ball can then hit a stripe, and the stripe can go in the pocket. Why anyone would want to make one of his opponent's balls is beyond me (but in very, very rare situations, it would be a good thing to do, strategywise). What is *not* legal is hitting a striped ball into a solid with the goal of pocketing the solid ball (your group). A three-ball combination—your solid, a stripe, and a second solid that you're trying to put in the pocket—is fine, however. Difficult, but legal.

The 8 Ball

Under some rules, the 8 ball is neutral until another ball has been pocketed. Under other rules, the 8 ball is neutral throughout the entire game. Under still other rules, the 8 ball is never neutral. *Neutral*, in this context, means that you can hit the ball first and not commit a foul.

Suppose that no ball is made on the break. Player B comes to the table and sees a neat combination of the 8 ball into the 6 ball. He can play that combination, hitting the 8 first and pocketing the 6, legally, even though the 8 is not in his group. If the 8 is neutral throughout the game (not a common rule), you can use it to combination one of your balls into a pocket at any time.

If you pocket the 8 ball before all the balls in your group, the result is almost always loss of game. The same is true if you knock the 8 ball off the table or pocket it on the same stroke that you use to pocket the last ball in your group (even if you call both balls and the 8 ball is the last to drop into a pocket).

Another variation of the game—one that makes it a little tougher—is Last Pocket 8-Ball. The one rule that is different from regular 8-Ball is that you must pocket the 8 ball in the same pocket in which you pocketed your last ball. Shoot six stripes in a corner pocket and the last stripe in a side pocket, and you have to make the 8 ball in that side pocket, too. If the 8 ball goes in any of the other five pockets, you lose. This version of the game is simple, but it opens the way for different strategies. Your opponent, knowing that you must pocket the 8 in a specific pocket, can then attempt to block that pocket with one of her balls or just combination the 8 into a place that makes getting to that one pocket very tough or impossible. This one little rule adds a lot of strategy (and sometimes, a lot of time) to a game of 8-Ball.

Pocket Dictionary

In 8-Ball, *neutral* means that you can legally hit the 8 ball first, whether you have solids or stripes.

Scratch!

Some leagues have rules against talking over a shot with anyone who is not on your team (such as a friend who's watching). Doing so can result in a foul.

Call-Shot 8 Ball

Some rules specify that 8-Ball is a *call-shot game*, meaning that you have to call the ball and pocket on every shot. Under other league rules, you have to call the pocket only for the 8 ball. One league requires that you not only call the ball and the pocket, but also call anything else that the object ball will touch. Therefore, if you are shooting at a corner pocket, and the object ball skims a cushion before going in (as is likely to happen if the object ball and cue ball both start out near or against a cushion), you must call that. If there is a possibility that the object ball will touch another ball before going into the pocket (because another object ball is partly blocking the pocket, or because you're shooting a kiss shot), you must call that. If you call something and it doesn't happen (you don't skim the cushion, for example), but you successfully pocket the ball, you lose your turn (on a coin-op table) or lose your turn and see the ball taken out of the pocket and placed on the footspot. If you don't call something and it *does* happen, you also lose your turn.

The object of making any game a call-shot game, 8-Ball included, is to eliminate slop and luck. Hit enough balls hard enough, and something will eventually go into a pocket. But that's not pool. To be sure that skill is rewarded, the call shot was intro- duced. How far it should be taken is a matter of debate. When you start playing, don't bother with call shots at all. At that point, you should be concentrating on making a ball. When you get into position play (controlling the cue ball), you may want to start silently calling the ball and pocket as a way to aid your focusing. After that point, you can pick the call-shot rules that you like best—or none at all.

How to Win

Knowing how to win can be a psychological problem. I've seen players who somehow didn't feel that they deserved to be the champion, so when they came to the finals in a tournament, they placed second time after time. After they got over that hurdle, however, they were able to win again and again.

But knowing how to win also involves knowing the strategies and characteristics of each game. It's a mistake to take all your experience of one game into a different game when only certain aspects apply. The following sections describe some of the unique features of 8-Ball.

The Most Important Thing to Know About Winning 8-Ball

The most important thing that you need to know about how to win a game of 8-Ball is which group—the solids or the stripes— gives you the best opportunity. Sometimes, you don't have a choice; your opponent gets first pick. But when you can make that decision, choose carefully. Approach the table, and look over the layout carefully. Isolate the two sets of balls (solids and stripes) in your mind. Look for trouble balls— clusters or balls with no pocket (that is, balls that are blocked by other balls from going into a pocket or are otherwise impossible or difficult to pocket). Then consider the possible solutions. Work out a pattern for each set, and only then decide which group you want.

At first, this process could take a couple minutes or more, but as you get familiar with the game and the way that the balls typically break open, you'll usually be able to do this in 30 seconds.

After you selected a group, you have to be sure that you have a shot to start off the pattern. It does you no good to pick a certain group and find that you can't get things going, because from the cue ball's starting position, no ball in that group can be pocketed. If you run into that situation, you can use a clever solution.

Suppose that the solids all look nice and easy, but you can't make a solid from your starting point. Play a

Cue Tips

Knowledge of the character of each billiard game is more important than people realize. Technical skill helps you pocket the balls, but knowledge tells you which ball to pocket.

safety. You can do it in such a way as to leave your opponent a very tough, but makable, shot on a stripe. You can even play a safety by using a striped ball, even though you want solids, because at this point, no one has laid a legal claim to either group. Call *nine in the side* or whatever, and use the 9 ball to bounce off of to get proper position for your cue ball. You don't make the ball, but you're not obligated to stripes at that point, either, because no ball has been made. Calling a group on your first shot doesn't make it your group if you don't sink the ball. Your opponent will come to the table, see no shot on a solid ball, see the bait that you left on the difficult striped ball, and have almost no choice but to shoot it.

The Second-Most-Important Thing to Know About Winning 8-Ball

Not making a ball can sometimes be better than making it. That's the second-most-important thing about winning 8-Ball, and it derives from the fact that half the balls on the table aren't balls that you can hit.

I'll give you a worst-case scenario as an example. Player A breaks, and a solid ball goes into the pocket. She looks over the table and likes the looks of the solids, except for one that's a bit of a potential problem. With one down, there are six to go until the 8 ball, and she begins popping them into pockets. The last ball is the trouble ball, and there's still no way to deal with it, so she taps it to another position where she can make it on her next turn. When player B comes to the table, she sees that almost half the balls have been cleared out of her way, and she has no trouble finding a pocket for every stripe that she has. Player A's decision to pocket almost all the solids removed any blocking balls to player B's stripes, and it's clear sailing for player A to the 8 ball and victory.

Now, if your opponent is a newer player who can't run all seven balls and then make the 8-Ball, there's no reason not to do what player A did in the preceding example. You know that you'll get another shot sooner or later. It becomes a bad move only as you become a better player. When you're figuring out your playing strategies, you have to take into consideration not only your skill level, but also your opponent's skill level. Early in your experience, the best thing to do is pocket everything you can. You'll be playing with other people who are also just starting, and pocketing balls is more fun and gives you more good experiences for your memory bank. But when you get good at controlling the cue ball, you need to know the things that I've told you in this section.

Ultra-Defensive 8-Ball

Roll one of your balls in front of each pocket opening, and your opponent can never make a ball. Rolling a ball that precisely is harder to do than it appears, and this technique certainly takes the fun out of the game. It could win you a game, but it isn't very likely.

You'll see the defensive style played (maybe not to block every pocket, but rolling balls in front of two or three pockets) on coin-operated tables, because it makes the game last a long time, and coin-ops charge by the game, not by the hour. But it turns out not to be a game-winning strategy, because your opponent sees what you're doing with the first ball that you roll in front of a pocket. He then does the same thing with one of his balls in front of a different pocket, or he rolls one of his balls up against yours so that any attempt to make your ball results in one of his going in, too.

Some of these games tended to go on for so long that the BCA created a rule for stalemated games—those in which the 8 ball had been accidentally rolled in front of the pocket and a numbered ball was behind it but touching it. Hitting the numbered ball would make the 8 go in, resulting in loss of game, so no one can make the 8. In this situation, a stalemate can be called, and the game can be restarted.

The strategy of rolling a ball in front of a single pocket can be effective on rare occasions; so can the use of safeties at the appropriate time. But if you play an ultra-defensive game of 8-Ball, it won't be long before other players either figure out a way to beat the strategy or simply refuse to play you.

Not Shooting the Easy Shot

In 8-Ball, it's often wise not to shoot a very easy shot. If a ball from your group is right in front of one of the six pockets, you're usually better off ignoring it. Use it as an insurance ball instead.

Pocket Dictionary

An *insurance ball*, in 8-Ball and Straight Pool, is a ball that is very easy to make, but is left unmade. If the player gets out of line and is without another shot, she can then turn to the easy (insurance) ball and knock it in.

An *insurance ball* is a very easy shot that you can always shoot, should you get out of position during your pattern for the other balls; it's always there and always easy to make. Beginners are tempted to hit an insurance ball in first, only to find that what remains is much more difficult. It's better to have the insurance ball hanging around. If your cue-ball positioning on another ball is bad, you can always shoot the insurance ball.

A general guideline is to shoot the more difficult shot first and the easier shot second, unless the easier shot gives you better position on the difficult shot.

Handicapping 8-Ball

Making the game an even contest for players of different skill levels is more difficult in 8-Ball than in other games. At first, it might seem to be logical to give the weaker player fewer balls to shoot. That player may, for example, get to pick up two balls in his group and take them off the table after the break. But as I told you in the preceding section, unless you are sure of making all the remaining balls, the only thing you accomplish is making a clearer table for your opponent, so it's almost a negative for the weaker player to remove balls.

The most common 8-Ball handicap is to have a race to a certain number of games (first player to win three games wins the match, for example) and to make the winning number different for each player. The newer player has to win only one game to win the match; the experienced player has to win three games. That's called *two games on the wire*, if you remember Straight Pool terms from Chapter 24.

You can also handicap by technique, as I mentioned. One player may have to shoot opposite-handed (left-handed, if she is right-handed, for example), or may have to shoot standing on one foot, hold the cue with only one hand, and so on. But handicaps of that type tend to be gimmicky. Instead, you might let the lesser player always be the one who chooses which group of balls (stripes or solids) he will have, always have the break, and always get to shoot the first shot (or reject the shot and make his opponent shoot the first shot).

Various leagues employ different handicapping methods, some of which are a bit complex. Other methods simply amount to something like a golf handicapping system, in which you keep track of your success over a certain period to establish your rating. But for casual play between friends and billiard-room players, the easiest and most common method is simply to spot the lesser player a certain number of games on the wire.

The Least You Need to Know

➤ You must make all your balls (the solids or stripes) before you can make the 8 ball.

➤ Legally pocket the 8 ball, and you win.

➤ Rules vary from billiard room to billiard room and from league to league, but for friendly competition, you can choose the rules that you like.

➤ The way that the balls are racked can influence who wins.

➤ Choosing the best group (stripes or solids) is the key to winning 8-Ball.

➤ Making almost all the balls in your group can help you lose, not win.

➤ 8-Ball can be played by two or four players—or teams.

➤ 8-Ball can be handicapped for players of unequal skills.

Chapter 26

The TV Game: 9-Ball

In This Chapter

➤ Why 9–Ball is the TV game

➤ Why the break is so important in 9–Ball

➤ How to rack the balls to make the break less important

➤ The strategy and character of 9–Ball

➤ The way to win

➤ How to handicap the game

The discipline I like most is 9-Ball, which is the game that the pros play on TV. In most other games, you have a choice of which ball you'll shoot. Not in this one. 9-Ball is a rotation game, meaning that you have to shoot the lowest-numbered ball on the table. That ball can be used in a combination, and another ball can be the one that is finally pocketed, but you always have to hit a certain ball first. This rule can create many exciting and irritating situations. You'll be forced to hit bank shots, kick shots, combinations, jump shots, curve shots, dunks, alley-oops, lobs, chips, sand shots...well, perhaps not all those, but you get the idea. 9-Ball is a game for the adventurous.

As demanding as 9-Ball is, the game also involves an element of luck. In most billiard games, the layout after the break is a matter of luck to some degree, but luck is even more of a factor in 9-Ball. There are only 9 object balls on the table instead of 15, and only 1 of those 9 needs to go into a pocket to end the game. The ball can go in on the break, or you can make a spectacular break, sinking four, five, or even six balls, and end up not having a clear path to the first ball that you have to hit. Conversely, you can widely scatter the balls and have nothing go in, although the 9 may be sitting in a pocket opening and the 1 ball and cue ball could end up a foot away, in a direct line to the pocket, so that your opponent has an easy win on her first shot. Little wonder that pros put so much emphasis on the break shot, studying it, practicing it, and experimenting with it.

To mitigate the luck factor, some rules have been instituted for professional play, and almost all those rules have been picked up by amateur players. In this chapter, I'll go over the generally accepted rules of the game.

9-Ball isn't a bad game for the beginner to play. It allows you to try a lot of shots with spin (but the less often you spin the cue ball, the better off you are). It also allows players to move the cue ball around the table for position (there are fewer balls to bump into). But the game is also more difficult for beginners, because you have to hit one certain ball on each shot, no matter how easy a shot on another ball might be. Try some 9-Ball, but play more Straight Pool (and even 8-Ball) at first. Having a large number of balls to choose among for each shot makes life a whole lot easier.

Cue Tips

If you're ever in a hurry but just have to stop for a minute and play a quick game of pool, choose 9-Ball. No game can be over faster (you can make the 9 ball on the break), and even at normal length, the game usually lasts only about 10 minutes.

What It's All About

Whoever makes the 9 ball wins. If the shot is legal, the game is over when the 9 drops in a pocket. All the basic rules of billiards apply, with the additional requirement that you must strike the lowest-numbered ball on the table first. Balls are worth nothing, as opposed to being worth a point apiece in Straight Pool. As they are in 8-Ball, the other balls are just a means of getting at the winning ball. Only the balls numbered 1 through 9 are used in this game.

The 9-Ball Rack and Break

The 9-Ball rack is diamond-shaped, with the 1 ball in front and the 9 ball in the middle. The other seven balls can be racked anywhere, but earlier in the book, I promised to give you a little inside information about the rack, and I'm going to do that now.

On a powerful but typical 9-Ball break, the two balls behind the 1 ball go up-table, toward where you stood when you were breaking. The very back ball (at the end of the diamond closest to the end cushion) goes to the end rail and usually (if it doesn't run into anything) bounces almost all the way up-table. The two balls in front of the back ball stay down-table. The balls on either side of the 9 ball tend to head toward the corner pockets, too, but are also likely to get kicked to the center of the table or end up at the foot of the table.

Why is any of that information important—or even interesting? Because careful placement of the balls numbered 2 through 8 increases the chance that your opponent (for whom you are racking, and who you expect to sink a ball on the break) will have to go up-table for the 1 ball, all the way back down-table for the 2 ball, all the way back up for the 3, and so on. That situation increases your opponent's chance of eventually missing. It's a small edge, but in a game in which the break shot is so critical, you want every edge you can get.

This racking technique is good only for a player who you figure can run the table. If your opponent typically makes two or three balls and misses, you'll want to rack balls 2 through 8 in a totally different way. You figure to come to the table after a couple of balls have been made, and you want the layout to be as easy as possible, not as difficult as possible. Under those conditions, you rack the balls so that the 1, 2, and 3 balls are in positions that send them up-table; the 4, 5, and 6 balls are in positions that put them in the middle or middle end of the table; and the last balls in positions that put all of them at the end of the table. Nice and neat—and something that not many people know about.

In earlier chapters, I described a tight rack, a loose rack, and a misaligned rack. The following three photos show you what to look out for in a 9-Ball rack.

The first photo shows a rack that has two problems. The 1 ball isn't on the footspot, as it needs to be; and if you look carefully, you can see that not all the balls are touching their neighbors. The last ball and the one next to it are not touching, and the 9 ball is not touching the one to the left of it (left in the photo). If you break open a rack like this one, you'll be at a disadvantage, because it's less likely that any ball will go in a pocket on the break.

A bad rack in 9-Ball. The 1 ball must be resting in the center of the footspot for the rack to be any good. The balls must also be touching their neighbors, and in this rack, they're not.

In the next photo, the rack has been moved forward so that the 1 ball is on the footspot, which is the correct position. Great, but the 1 isn't touching the balls behind it, and this is the worst possible thing that could exist in a rack—for the person who's breaking. But it's not bad for his opponent, who's doing the racking. That space kills the power of the break shot by letting the 1 bounce off the balls behind it, rather than directly transferring the cue ball's power into the rack and making the balls fly apart. Never break a rack that looks like this.

Now the rack is in place as far as the 1 ball is concerned. But the 1 isn't touching the balls behind it! This is the worst thing that could happen in racking for 9-Ball.

The last photo corrects those elements but adds a different error: The rack is not straight on the table. Check the picture and the caption for things to look for in rack alignment. The 1 ball, the 9 ball, and the last ball should be lined up straight down the table. The center diamond on the top and bottom rails is dead in the center and will help you line up these balls. If necessary, place a piece of chalk on the diamond (actually, circular instead of diamond-shape on most modern tables, but still called a diamond) at the center of the far rail (the head rail, where you stand to break); then sight from the diamond at the foot rail. (By the way, in the picture, the two rectangles on either side of the diamond on the foot rail are counters for keeping score for up to four people.)

344

The 1 ball is on the spot, and all the balls are touching. The problem is that the rack is misaligned. If you draw a straight line from the cue ball, which I've placed in the center of the table, and the circle (called a diamond) *on the rail, you'll see that the 9 ball is on the line, but the 1 ball and the last ball are not.*

Here's a bit of inside info on the outside balls in the rack, which are sometimes called the *wing* balls. The outside corner balls (the ones on either side of the 9 ball) tend to go toward the corner pockets on the break but to hit the long cushion around 3 to 6 inches above the pocket—that is, unless you force them to go elsewhere. By breaking from a headstring position as close to one cushion as possible, by using a rail bridge, by hitting the 1 ball perfectly full in the face, and by hitting with a lot of force, you can sort of push the far wing ball toward the end of the table which just happens to be where the corner pocket is. The other wing ball won't go anywhere near its pocket, but as long as you make a ball, who cares?

Speaking of the 1 ball, if you break from that same position (off the rail) or a tad farther from the cushion and hit the 1 ball just right, it has a fair chance of going into the opposite side pocket on the break shot. See the photo on the next page for the range of cue ball positions.

These are shots that the professionals discovered when the break became important in 9-Ball matches, but you don't have to be a professional to make them; you just have to hear how to do that, which is what you're doing right now. When you hit the 1 ball as I've just described, you have a good chance of actually being able to predict that two balls—the 1 ball and the wing ball on the opposite side of where you're breaking from—will go very close to specific pockets. You've still got seven other balls rolling around, and they may go in somewhere, too.

Ewa's Billiard Bits

Can you make all nine balls on the break? Doing so is physically possible, and I've heard rumors of its being done, but to my knowledge, it's never been done in a national tournament.

The odds that you'll make a ball on the break just went up dramatically. Now all you have to do is practice everything that I've told you up to now and bring yourself to the level at which you figure to run out (pocket all the balls on the table) if the layout is open after your successful break.

The range for a typical 9-Ball break is illustrated by these two cue balls, but it is perfectly legal to place your cue ball anywhere behind the headstring.

The Rest of the Game

Although a runout is the most positive thing that you can do, not all 9-Ball games are strictly offensive. Defense plays a big part. It can even win you a game on the three-foul rule, which I'll explain in the following section.

Safety play is common in 9-Ball, because in many situations, you won't be able to hit the single ball that you must hit, or because the ball has no pocket, or because the shot that you do have is a very low percentage shot. Safety play, in a way, is easier, because you only have to prevent your opponent from being able to hit a single ball. Sometimes, safety play is also more difficult, because there are fewer balls on the table to hide behind. So a single game can be played with offense, defense, or both.

Overall, though, 9-Ball is regarded as being a game of offense and aggression. Because it's not usually a call-shot game (even though it can be), it is a game in which players are tempted to take a fling and smash the balls all over the table in the hope that something (especially the 9 ball) will go into a pocket. This method isn't the most sophisticated way to play, but alas, it's sometimes effective.

Special Rules

There aren't too many special rules for 9-Ball, and odd situations rarely occur. In that sense, it's a simple game. The break shot in 9-Ball, as in 8-Ball, requires you to drive at least four object balls to cushions or to pocket a ball. That requirement eliminates the possibility of breaking safe. As in all games, you must break from behind the headstring. As in almost all other games, if the cue ball or any other ball goes off the table during the break (the most likely time) or at any time during the game, the player has committed a foul and loses his or her turn. If a ball is pocketed on this foul or any other, it stays in the pocket, because a pocketed ball doesn't add to or detract from anyone's score. The exception, of course, is the 9 ball itself. If it is pocketed on a foul, it is brought out of the pocket and placed on the footspot.

After a foul, the incoming player receives cue ball in hand, and he or she can put the ball anywhere on the table.

Three Consecutive Fouls

This rule is defined the same way that it is in Straight Pool: three fouls in three consecutive *shots*, not three consecutive *turns* at the table. The difference is in the penalty phase. In Straight Pool, the penalty increases steeply on the third consecutive foul, but in 9-Ball, it gets as severe as possible: the player loses the game. It doesn't matter what the score is or how many balls are left on the table; everything stops, and the game is over.

The Pushout Rule

The pushout rule applies only to the first shot after the break shot, no matter which player is taking the shot. Suppose that player A (her again?) breaks the balls and knocks five of the nine balls into pockets. This would be a spectacular and rare feat, but it is still possible to end up with no shot when all the balls come to a standstill. The ball that player A needs to hit could be hidden behind two other balls, or the cue ball could be hidden. Player A might have a tough or impossible kick. If player A failed,, player B could come to the table and take advantage of player A's bad luck by running the few remaining balls and winning the game.

Would a spectacular break be punished? That didn't seem right, so the rules were changed to include the pushout. Player A, finding herself in the unfortunate position described in the

Ewa's Billiard Bits

BCA Hall of Famer Eddie Taylor is now retired, but he *is* the greatest banker that ever lived. Eddie loved the pushout rule, because he could always push out to a nearly impossible bank shot. The incoming player knew that he couldn't make the shot, but he was terrified of giving it back to Eddie to shoot. Taylor would just sit in his chair, smiling, as his opponent wrestled with the impossible problem.

347

preceding paragraph, could call pushout and then hit the cue ball with the cue tip, making it go anywhere she wants it to go.

Other rules are suspended during a pushout. In other words, player A does not have to make contact with a certain ball or to drive a ball to a cushion after contact. There doesn't even need to be any contact. She simply hits the ball where she wants to. At this point, player B comes to the table and looks at the shot. If he thinks that the new position of the cue ball is untenable, he will reject the opportunity to play the shot, and player A must play from the new position. If player B thinks that he can do something positive, he can elect to shoot, and player A sits down and watches. The result is that a player is less likely to be punished for doing something well (making balls on the break), and an element of skill and knowledge is applied to the game instead.

How to Win

To win, make the 9 ball. Seriously. There's not a great deal of strategy in 9-Ball—at least, not the type that you see in 8-Ball and One-Pocket. It's a straightforward game. Developing a good, accurate vision of your abilities will take you a long way. If you know that you can run out, do so, but if you're doubtful, find a point at which you can play an effective safety. If you're beginning to play and are playing with another beginner, take a fling at every shot and forget safety play. As you get some experience, you can add the other elements.

Breaking up clusters, getting position, and playing safeties have been covered in previous chapters, and they apply as much to 9-Ball as to any other game.

By saying that 9-Ball doesn't involve a great deal of strategy, I'm not saying that the game is easy or that it involves *no* strategy; I'm just saying that the strategies will become obvious as you go along. You don't have somebody else's group of balls to be concerned about (as you do in 8-Ball), and you don't have to create or find a break ball and key ball (as you do in Straight Pool). You just have to make the 9 ball.

The strategy in this game revolves mainly around shot selection—that is, determining the best angle at which to approach each shot so that the cue ball can get to the next-highest-numbered ball. The real tester in 9-Ball is the ability to execute the pattern that you decided was the best for the situation. (*Tester*, by the way, is also billiard jargon for a very difficult shot, whether the difficulty is to pocket the ball or to get position on the next after you pocket the ball.)

Pocket Dictionary

Tester is pool talk for a very difficult shot. The difficulty may be in pocketing the ball or in getting position on the next ball.

You may have long shots, shots that call for a lot of spin on the ball, cut shots that are so thin (almost cutting a ball 90 degrees into a pocket) that pool jargon calls it *cutting the paint off the ball*, and shots in which you have to bounce the cue ball off two, three, or even four cushions to get into position for the next ball. Often, there won't seem to be any way to get the cue ball from the shot that you're making to the next ball on your list. Figuring out a way and then executing the shot is the core of most 9-Ball strategy. Finding the *easiest* way and executing the shot is the core of most winning 9-Ball strategy.

Sometimes, of course, there really is no reasonable way to get from one ball to the next ball, so part of the strategy of the game is knowing when to play a safety. If you see no way to get from the 4 ball to the 5 ball, for example, it might be a better move to play a safety on the 3 ball instead or wait to get to the 4. That's the kind of thinking that you need to do in 9-Ball, and you can't easily figure it out when you start playing billiards. That's why I suggest that you begin by trying to hit the lowest-numbered ball into a pocket (or at least make it roll somewhere), rather than try to fool with safeties, shot selection, and difficult position plays. Make balls. If you can't hit a ball into a pocket, hit it into the 9 ball, and make the 9 move. (Maybe the 9 will go into a pocket, and you'll win.)

Cue Tips

A good way to practice thinking about 9-Ball patterns is to put just the 7, 8, and 9 balls on the table, and put the cue ball wherever you want. Think about the three-ball pattern. When you get good, add the 6 ball.

Practice your break shot, paying particular attention to hitting the 1 ball into the side pocket and the far wing ball into the corner pocket, and leaving the cue ball in the center of the table. Learn to make patterns from the balls on the table. Unlike 8-Ball and Straight Pool, 9-Ball doesn't allow for a huge number of optional patterns, because you know the order in which the balls will be pocketed (barring a combination, kiss, or carom shot—three possibilities that you should look for when you examine the layout).

The mental game may be a bit more important in 9-Ball than in other games. It's fairly common for a player to get down to the 9 and suddenly choke, making a bad shot and missing the ball. The pressure of knowing that all the balls before the 9 counted as chaff, and that the kernel of truth is before you in the form of a white ball with a yellow stripe, is enough to make you mentally retreat. Learn to get over that situation and win games. You can do it, now that you have this book in your hands.

Handicapping

9-Ball is an easy game to handicap, with options beyond giving games on the wire (you have to win three games to win, and I have to win five games to win) and giving someone the break every time (instead of alternating breaks or playing winner breaks). One option is to give the lesser player two winning balls—the 9 and the 6, for example. The stronger player has to make the 9 ball to win, but the newer player can win by making either the 6 or the 9. If there's a larger difference between players, you can

Pocket Dictionary

Winner breaks means that the winner of one game gets the opening break shot in the next game. *Alternate breaks* means that the players take turns breaking. *Breakabout*, which means alternating breaks, is a slang term used by very knowledgeable players.

change the spot to the 9 and the 4, or you can add to the spot by using the 9, the 7, and the 5 (or any other combination that will put the players on a level playing field).

Another option is to give up the last two, which is a small spot (handicap). *The last two* means that the lesser player can win by pocketing either of the last two balls on the table. The last two always includes the 9 ball, but not always the 8 ball. (The 8 could get pocketed on a combination using the 7, for example, and the last two balls would then be the 7 and 9.) If you use the last two as a spot instead of the 9 and a specific ball, the lesser player is denied the opportunity to hit that other specifically named ball into a pocket early in the game, because it hasn't yet been determined what that ball is.

If there is a lot of difference between players, they can agree on a spot (handicap) that requires the stronger player to bank each ball into a pocket, whereas the lesser player can shoot normally, banking only if he or she chooses to. Alternatively, the stronger player could *make two and stop*, which means that she could pocket two balls but then have to play a safety, taking away the possibility of her running the table. A good player, however, would be a good safety player, too. So although this spot sounds impressive, it isn't that much of a giveaway.

The fact that there are so many ways to handicap 9-Ball helps make it a popular game. When you start to play, you'll probably team up with someone of similar experience, and handicapping won't really be an issue. Natural talent may zoom one of you ahead of the other, however, and a spot will keep the competition interesting, forcing both of you to play at your peaks if you want to win the match.

One of the skills of billiards is judging the abilities of another player at your local billiard room and figuring out what kind of spot would give you an equal chance of winning. You'll develop this skill with experience. Play some strangers (the counter person can tell you who is at a similar skill level and can introduce you). After a few games, you can establish a handicap that will give each of you an equal chance of winning.

The Least You Need to Know

➤ The break is the most important shot in 9-Ball.

➤ Placing the balls in the rack in certain places reduces the advantage of having the break.

➤ The only goal of the game is to make the 9 ball.

➤ You can aim to make certain balls in certain pockets on the break shot.

➤ Position play can be difficult in 9-Ball.

➤ This is the game in which the cue ball spins the most and in which you'll see the most spectacular shots.

➤ Pattern play is different from that in other games, but no less important.

➤ 9-Ball is easy to handicap so that players of unequal skill can play each other.

Chapter 27

Games for Threesomes, Foursomes, and Moresomes

In This Chapter

➤ Games made for an odd number of players

➤ Games for two couples

➤ 8-Ball as a team game

➤ How to turn any billiard game into a game for two couples

Billiards is primarily a one-on-one sport, but it's a versatile game and can be played solo, by three people (in a limited way), by two couples, and by teams. Not many sports can satisfy so many situations. The only drawback in having more than two players is the fact that only one person at a time can occupy the table—and if that person is good, that time can be long. For groups of three or four, it's actually better if nobody knows what he or she is doing. In tennis, if players are real beginners, they spend a lot of time running around the fence to get the ball. In golf, if the players are real beginners, they spend a lot of time doing landscape repair. But in billiards, if the players are real beginners, they get to play more!

Only two billiard games are really suitable for three or five people: Cut-Throat and Golf, which is played on a snooker table. The name alone gives you a pretty good clue about the character of Cut-Throat, and I tell you more in this chapter. Golf is almost exclusively a gambling game.

Some very obscure games that can be played by an odd number of people, but finding three (or five) people who know the rules is more trouble than it's worth. If you are a party of two or four, however, you can enjoy just about any billiard game. A foursome can simply use the simple expedient of switching turns to turn a standard game into a couples' game.

Leagues field teams to play pool, and the most common game is 8-Ball. Fundamentally, the teams just take turns playing. The interest is kept high during the long waits by team enthusiasm and the opportunity to socialize with players on the other team or their fans. There are a few 9-Ball leagues, and the competition is team-oriented, but basically, it's just taking turns. In football, soccer, baseball, hockey, and other team sports, your teammates can somehow work together or assist one another in achieving a goal. It doesn't work that way in billiards unless the format is trading shots rather than turns, as I explain in the pages that follow. The bottom line is that pool is a one-on-one sport that can be successfully adapted for play by three, four, or more people.

Adapting 8-Ball for Foursome or Team Play

The easiest way to adapt 8-Ball for a group of four or more players is to have each player take alternate innings. Player A-1 shoots until he misses; then player B-1 shoots until she misses; then it's back to team one and player A-2, and from there to team two and player B-2. This method is simple, but it creates a long time between opportunities at the table. A better variation is to switch after every shot. Player A-1 shoots and makes a ball; player A-2 shoots the next shot and makes a ball; player A-1 shoots again and misses. Then the other team starts. This variation actually makes a game take longer because of the continual switching of players within a team's turn, but that's OK. You just play fewer games.

Cue Tips

Some leagues take their 8-Ball so seriously that they appoint team captains and even have a designated coach for discussions about strategy and shot selection.

Teams can do the same thing, although with five team members, switching individual shots can get to be a real problem. This arrangement does even out the skill level more, however, because a really good player or really poor player doesn't dominate the team. If you're playing in a club setting rather than at home, you can hold one-on-one round-robin matches. In a round robin, each player gets to play every player on the other team. For two five-person teams, you would need five tables, and there would be a little waiting while people who finished fast stood around until a table was open, but the waiting time would be short, and there would be a lot of action.

Cut-Throat

The game with the strange name depends on honesty to work—at least, the 9-Ball version of it does. Actually, Cut-Throat, although it's a specific game, has become almost a generic word for any billiard game someone can devise in which an odd number of players can play. The most popular versions are 9-Ball and the original Cut-Throat, a game that uses 15 balls (each player has 5). Other sports and games have their versions of Cut-Throat, too, so the concept should be familiar to some of the players before the game starts.

When three people are playing 9-Ball, it's easy for two players to gang up on the third. The player before the victim always shoots a safety, and the player after the victim always goes for a shot, no matter how unlikely. The victim doesn't have a chance. So Cut-Throat, despite its name, really depends on honesty; everyone has to put forth an honest effort to make the ball. In fact, that element is so critical that players sometimes refer to the game as *Honest Effort*. Everyone takes a turn, everyone tries his or her best, and whoever makes the 9 ball wins.

Pocket Dictionary

Honest effort is pool talk for a game with three or more players in which each player must make a serious attempt to pocket a ball when it is his turn.

The original Cut-Throat is played with all 15 numbered balls. If three people are playing, one player has balls 1 through 5, the next player has balls 6 through 10, and the third player has balls 11 through 15. If five people are playing, each of them is assigned three balls in consecutive order (1–3, 4–6, and so on).

In this game, you don't pocket your own balls; you aim to eliminate your competitors by pocketing all of *their* balls. The last person who has a ball or balls remaining on the table wins the game. All the standard rules of billiards apply, and no really deep strategies are involved. You simply try to pocket a lot of balls that belong to the other players.

You can make the game more demanding by making it a call-shot game, but that sort of defeats the purpose. Keeping it easy, positive, and slightly aggressive is more the ticket. With a full rack of 15 balls on the table, players always seem to have relatively simple shots, especially during the first half of the game. Cut-Throat is simple, quick, and fun.

Pill Pool

Pill Pool can also be played by an odd number of players and is effective even when players of different skills want to get involved. The only thing that you need to do is visit your local billiard supply store or pro shop, or call a mail-order supplier, and get a pill bottle and a set of pills. The *pill bottle* is a plastic container (it used to be leather) that is shaped roughly like a narrow-neck soft-drink bottle. The *pills* are beads with numbers that match the 15 numbered balls.

Pill Pool (also called Pea Pool, because the little pills resemble peas, or Kelly Pool) is a fun game, because everyone has a secret. At the beginning, all

Pocket Dictionary

A *pill bottle* is a small, opaque plastic bottle used in Pill Pool to hold 15 small, numbered plastic beads, each with a number on it. The bottle and beads can also be used to determine the placement of people at the beginning of a tournament. *Pills* are the small plastic beads, numbered 1 through 15, used in Pill Pool.

the pills go into the bottle, the bottle is shaken, and everyone gets a pill with a number on it. You don't show the number to anyone, but that numbered ball becomes your ball. If you're the first to pocket the ball whose number you have, you win. Technically, you could play with 15 people, but the game would be over when the first ball was pocketed. Three to five people works best.

Although playing skill is certainly involved in Pill Pool, the most important thing is whether you get a high number or a low number—and how good you are at not letting other people know what you got. The objective is to pocket your own ball before any of the other players pockets his or her ball. When the first person pockets his ball, he shows the matching pill to the other players and is declared the winner.

This game is like 9-Ball in that you have to contact the lowest-numbered ball on the table first, but you can then make a combination, kiss, or carom. The way that you let the cat out of the bag about what number you have is when you have an easy shot on

Scratch!

It's cheating to buy a set of pills and take the number 1 pill with you when you go to play Pill Pool.

a ball and instead try a combo, kiss, or carom to make a different ball. The other players may then try to go after your ball and put it in a pocket (especially if it is a low-numbered ball), depriving you of a chance to win and increasing your opponents' chances.

You can get a little tricky and go after a different ball, but that strategy doesn't always work out. The cleverest thing to do is get lucky and draw a low-numbered pill from the pill bottle. That's basically all there is to it. Pill Pool is fun and easy, and any number of people can play.

Mr. and Mrs. Pool

This game is a variation on Rotation, and you play with all 15 balls. In Rotation (which I explain in Chapter 28), each ball counts the same amount as the number printed on it. The game goes to a total 120 points (add up all the ball numbers), so whoever is first to score 61 points or more wins.

In Mr. and Mrs. Pool, you divide the number of players into 120. That means that 2 to 6 people, 8 people, or even 10 people can play—not 7 or 9, which are numbers that don't go into 120 evenly. Five players, for example, equals 24 points. Add one point to get 25. The first player to score 25 points wins the game.

The balls are racked in the standard triangle shape, with the 1 ball in front, the 2 ball and 3 ball on the other corners, the 15 ball in the center, and the 14 and 13 balls just behind the 15. Other than the ball placement in the rack, all other standard rules apply. Mr. and Mrs. Pool is another game that is simple and fairly fast, and that can be played by more than two people.

The Least You Need to Know

➤ Billiard games for groups are high on fun, but not necessarily on skill.

➤ Cut-Throat is a game for an odd number of players.

➤ 8-Ball can be a team game, suitable for league play.

➤ Pill Pool can be played by any number of players.

➤ Mr. and Mrs. Pool can be played by any number of players, as long as that number can be evenly divided into 120.

A Slate of Other Popular Games

The orderliness, the precision, the predictability, and the mathematical certainty of billiards appeal to millions of people. Others like the action, the surprises, the luck of the break, and the color of the game. For some people, it's a test of skill, focus, and determination that they can undertake alone or against friendly competitors. Others find the social possibilities of billiards to be immensely attractive. Still others find it to be the right atmosphere for conducting business. And a big group simply likes a sport in which they don't sweat. Billiards is all things to all people.

Still, billiards—like cards, music, and computer software—is based on math, and that fact means that it can be manipulated. The result is that hundreds of billiard games have been invented. The most popular games—the ones that I covered in previous chapters—have risen to the top because they work best for large groups of people in certain circumstances. As you get more and more into the sport, you'll want to experiment with other games, and in this chapter, I discuss with you the second tier. These games are well known among people who play regularly, but not among the most casual players.

Each of the games in this chapter has a certain appeal. One may be just the game for you. Although each of these games has a coterie of devoted followers who do some proselytizing on its behalf, but the games never seem to have the massive appeal of

9-Ball and 8-Ball. That doesn't mean that they're not good games. Some of them are excellent, and all of them tackle balls on green cloth in a way that seems to emphasize particular skills. A couple of games are cerebral; some require exceptional shot-making skills; some require unending patience; and some are combinations of all those things.

If you get the opportunity, I suggest that you fool around with these games. If one appeals to you, look into it further and find someone who plays the game. As I said, fans of less-popular games are always looking for converts.

Ewa's Billiard Bits

You may have seen star pro 9-Ball player Allison Fisher on television. Did you know that she's English and an 11-time Ladies' World Snooker Champion?

Snookered!

Snooker is a good game, much like Straight Pool with a little 9-Ball thrown in at the end, but not very popular in the United States. It's the 9-Ball of Great Britain—the most popular game and the TV game there—but pool is currently making strong inroads.

Snooker requires serious attention because it's so difficult to pocket a ball (called *potting* a ball in British-influenced Snooker circles). That's also one of the reasons why it's slowly losing favor to the faster, flashier, and (frankly) more accessible pool games.

What It's All About

Snooker, like Straight Pool, is a game of points. Fifteen balls, all solid red and worth 1 point apiece, are racked in a triangle at the footspot. But there are also 6 other balls on the table, at various spots found only on Snooker tables. A black ball, rated at 7 points, is placed behind the rack, near the center ball in the last row. A pink ball, rated at 6 points, is placed in front of the apex (front) red ball. A blue ball, worth 5 points, is placed on a spot in the center of the table. A yellow ball (2 points), brown ball (4 points), and green ball (3 points) are placed in a row on spots along the headstring. A half-circle, known as the *D*, is drawn from the yellow ball to the green ball. When a player breaks (or *breaks off*, in Snookerese) or gets ball in hand, he must place the cue ball within the D. There is no cue ball in hand anywhere on the table, as there is in pool.

Pocket Dictionary

Being *snookered* means being hooked. The cue ball does not have a clear path to the object ball.

The break (breakoff) shot is identical to that of Straight Pool, but sometimes, instead of letting the cue ball cross the table on the way back, players prefer to let it come straight back. Freezing the cue ball on the headrail is very good. (In international Snooker, however, the headrail is called the footrail, and the footrail is called the top rail.) But an easier (and, therefore, more common) tactic is to let the cue ball bounce off the headrail and roll up behind the green, brown, or yellow ball. If it does, the opposing player finds that he has been *snookered*. He can't shoot directly at his ball. It's similar to "being behind the 8 ball" and is the standard safe opening break.

Scoring Points

A total of 147 points are available, although if all the balls are made, the total can turn out to be less than that number, as I explain in the following paragraphs. Scoring 147, then, is logically known as

Pocket Dictionary

Maximum, in Snooker, means a score of 147 points. *Century*, in Straight Pool and Snooker, means a score of 100 points.

a *maximum*. Scoring 100 points in a single turn at the table is known as a *century* and is usually applauded, whether or not the player has finished his run.

You score points by pocketing (potting) a red ball (1 point), which then gives you the right to try to pocket any of the numbered balls. The red stays down, but the numbered ball, if pocketed, is respotted. You can reach the score of 147 by pocketing a red (1 point), then a black (7), then another red, then the black again, and so on, followed by all the colors in order (2 through 7). You get a lower score if you pocket a red, then a blue (5 points), then a red, then a pink (6), and so on, but all the balls will still have been pocketed.

When all the reds are gone (they stay in the pocket when they're made) and nothing but numbered balls are left (they, remember, are respotted after they are made), the balls, as in 9-Ball, have to be pocketed in numerical order. A maximum score on what is known as *the colors* (the numbered balls alone) is 27 (2 plus 3 plus 4, and so on). If two players have scores before they begin pocketing the colors that are more than 27 points apart, the player with the lesser score knows that he must snooker his opponent *and* make all the colors. If a person is snookered (played safe) and fails to hit the ball that she has to hit (the lowest-numbered ball on the table), she has fouled and is penalized a certain number of points. In The United States, all fouls are 7 points (some old-timers use four points), but in international (British) Snooker, the system is more complex and is based partly on the value of the ball that needed to be struck. If you tried to hit a blue ball (5 points) and missed it, for example, the foul would be 5 points.

Snooker Tables and Balls

In the United States, Snooker is played primarily on 5- by 10-foot tables, but you can still find some 6- by 12-foot tables, mostly in metro markets in the Midwest and Northeast, around the Canadian border, and in Oklahoma. It's fairly difficult to locate a 12-foot snooker table in the States, because they take up a lot of room and because the game is not that popular here. The 12-foot Snooker table used to be the standard table in every billiard room in Canada, but in the mid-'90s, the game started fading and pool began growing, so there are fewer and fewer all the time.

The pockets on Snooker tables are not cut to sharp points at the cushion, like pool tables; rather, they are rounded. That means that you can shoot into a side pocket

Ewa's Billiard Bits

Snooker is so popular in England (top players make more than a million dollars a year) that champions are the subjects of exposès in tabloid newspapers.

(called a center pocket in Snooker) from a more obtuse angle, but if you hit the ball hard enough to strike the round portion on the opposite side of the pocket, the ball kicks back to you. On a pool table, a ball hit the same way would ricochet into the pocket. Shooting into the side pocket in Snooker, then, requires a softer hit if the angle is sharp (*sharp* meaning from closer to the cushion than from the middle of the table). The figure below shows ball positions and the opening shot in Snooker.

Snooker balls—and pockets—are smaller than Pool or Carom balls and pockets. Smaller means lighter, too, so it takes less power to hit a Snooker ball a long distance than it does a pool or Carom ball. That's helpful, because the table is larger. A larger table coupled with smaller balls and pockets, however, means that a player's shot-making skills (aiming and execution) must be greater. This fact discourages many beginners, but on the pro level, Snooker players seem to have as easy a time making balls as pool players do on a pool table—at least, when the balls are gathered on one half of the table. Long shots on a Snooker table are *really* long, and pros often miss them.

This is how all the balls are positioned at the beginning of a game of Snooker. The cue ball can be placed anywhere in the D at the head of the table, but this position is the best. The break shot (called a breakoff in International Snooker) is very similar to the break shot in Straight Pool.

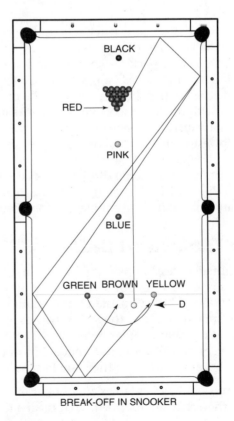

BREAK-OFF IN SNOOKER

362

Variations on the Game

Snooker was played in The United States during the 1930s, '40s. and '50s as a gambling game, and to speed the exchange of money, many of the red balls were taken off the table. Thus, we have Three-Ball Snooker, which is played with just three red balls and all the colors, and Six-Ball Snooker, which is played with six reds and the colors. Naturally, the scores are lower and the games are shorter than a game played with the full complement of 15 red balls and the colors. This is not a bad idea for beginners (using fewer balls, not gambling!).

Special Rules

In the United States, all standard billiard rules apply to Snooker, but in the international game, there is one very critical exception: After contact between the cue ball and object ball, a ball does *not* have to touch a cushion. Oddly, this situation doesn't come into play very often in the men's professional game, because it's not a tremendous advantage in safety play. One reasons is that the pros tend to keep all the balls gathered in a limited area, and they usually have a shot or a better type of safety available. On an amateur level, there is much more occasion to avoid a shot and simply roll the cue ball up against the object ball for an easy safety. On a 12-foot table, the cushion-after-contact rule might be too difficult for players to handle, but on the smaller 10-foot version used in the United States, it is reasonable.

Changes are made in the international rules from time to time, especially for the purpose of refining existing wording. At some points, the rules get as complex and esoteric as PGA rules, but the simplified American version is more straightforward.

If you're interested in Snooker, I suggest that you keep an eye out for a 12-foot table, and when you find one, try your hand at the game. At first, you'll probably feel that it's an impossibly big playing area (72 square feet versus a pool table's 40.5 square feet) for such small balls and small pockets. But as you get used to it, you'll discover that most of the game is played at the foot of the table (called the *top of the table*, in international Snooker) with relatively short shots of 1 to 4 feet. Part of the end game—playing the 2, 3, and 4 balls—is done at the top of the table, over short distances (when you're up there). After the 2, 3, and 4 are made, the next ball is, of course, the 5 ball. The 5 ball is spotted in the center of the table—sort of a halfway point to get back to the other end for the 6 and 7 balls.

Golf on a Snooker Table

In the United States, many Snooker tables are for a game called Golf, rather than Snooker. Only the numbered balls are used, and only as many of them as there are players. A game with three players, for example, would assign the 2 ball to one player (there is no 1 ball), the 3 to the second player, and the 4 to the third player. As many as seven people can play (a red ball becomes the 1 ball), and a Golf game can last a very long time among defense-minded players.

Cue Tips

You can improve your shot-making abilities by playing 9-Ball with pool balls on a snooker table; its small pockets require exact aim.

The object is simple: Pocket your ball in all six holes, in order. The difficulty comes when your ball is in position to be pocketed, but six other players want to pocket their balls and move yours to a position where you can't pocket it. By the time your turn comes around, it's unlikely that you'll have a shot. That's why a game with more than two or three players can seem to last an eternity. Golf is most often played by men over 50, and especially by retired players.

One-Pocket: Billiard Chess

One-Pocket is one of the games that was been invented for the pool table during the 20th century. Its origins are a little murky, but it appears to have begun during the 1920s, probably in Oklahoma City. Before that, people played a game called *Side Apiece*, in which each of two players could pocket balls only in the three pockets on his side of the table. That game was still being played up to World War II. One-Pocket has also been known as *Pocket Apiece* because each player has only one pocket in which he can legally make balls.

What It's All About

One-Pocket is about patience, banking, tight cue-ball control, and knowledge of recurrent One-Pocket shots. The object is to make 8 balls (1 more than half of the 15) in your pocket before your opponent makes 8 balls in his. What could be easier? Answer: anything! In a game of One-Pocket, an exchange of safeties can go on for two hours. Then again, it's possible for the game to be over in five minutes.

Ewa's Billiard Bits

In a recent national-championship One-Pocket tournament in North Carolina, the two world-class players in the finals were both defense-minded. The match was to go to the first player who won five games, but one game took two hours, and another took a little over three hours. Finally, both players and the tournament director agreed to make the winner the first player to win *three* games. The crowd breathed a sigh of relief.

The two pockets chosen by the players are always the two corner pockets at the foot of the table, by the rack. They're the most likely, by far, to be easier targets than the side pockets or the corner pockets at the other end. The player who breaks picks his pocket, and it's assumed that the other player will take the other corner. The breaker hits a safe break, trying to nudge balls toward his pocket and to leave the cue ball on the side rail, a foot or so from his opponent's pocket. Then the battle begins.

One-Pocket is regarded as being a defensive game, because you spend more time knocking your opponent's balls out of pocketable positions than you do pocketing balls in your own pocket. One-Pocket players regard those shots as being offensive shots, because they create opportunities to win. Whatever the case, it's fair to say that when two players of equal skill play the game, the one who has more patience will win. That player won't take a fling at a very difficult shot, but will play another safety instead.

Playing a very good safety that doesn't allow your opponent to shoot a ball at his pocket, bank a ball toward his pocket, kick a ball toward his pocket, or otherwise move a ball toward his pocket is very difficult. Any balls between the cue ball and the player's pocket can likely be moved closer to the pocket or even pocketed. When the cue ball is between the pocket and the object balls, it's not uncommon for one or more of them to be banked or kicked into (or at least near) the player's pocket. While doing that, of course, the player must also leave the cue ball in such a position that his opponent cannot shoot, bank, kick, or nudge a ball toward his own pocket. You can see that the concept of the game is simple, but the play is usually very complex.

By the way, I was gender-specific in the preceding paragraph, because women rarely play One-Pocket. Theories abound as to why this is so, but as they say, let's not go there. I did think that you might be interested to know that, however.

Special Rules

If a ball is pocketed in a pocket other than one of the two corners claimed by the two players, it is spotted on the footspot. There is no penalty for such a shot, which is why it's occasionally used as a strategic shot. If you accidentally pocket a ball in your opponent's pocket, it counts for him, and you lose your turn. If you're not playing on a table with ball returns (tunnels under the table that gather the balls in a tray at one end of the table), and if your pocket fills to the point at which you shoot a ball in and it bounces back out, the ball stays where it lands. You don't get to count it, and you lose your turn.

Any foul in One-Pocket is punished by a loss of 1 point and a loss of turn. Losing 1 point means losing one ball, so if you foul, you must place one of the balls that you've pocketed back on the table, on the footspot. There is no three-consecutive-fouls rule in most One-Pocket games, but one ball is lost on each foul. It could happen that you commit a foul when you have no balls to put on the table (at the beginning of the game, for example). In that case, you owe a ball, and after the next inning (turn at the table) in which you make a ball, you have to take a ball and put it on the spot. In other words, when you have no balls and you foul, you then owe one. The other player then shoots. On your next turn, you make a ball, then another, then a third, and finally miss. At *that* point, you take one of the three balls that you made in your pocket and put it on the spot, so you have only two balls to your credit.

One-Pocket has other rules, but they get too detailed to go into here. If you're interested in looking further into the rules, check out a book on the game, such as *Winning One-Pocket* or the *BCA Official Rules and Records* book. Other books and videos listed in Appendix B give you more information about, and examples of, the game.

How to Win and How to Handicap

The strategy of the game is also far too complex to handle here. Entire books have been written about One-Pocket strategy, including *Winning One-Pocket* mentioned in the preceding paragraph, which is part of a two-volume set. That'll give you an idea of what you're letting yourself in for if you decide that One-Pocket sounds interesting. The game takes patience to play, and it also takes patience to learn. If you go for chess over checkers, Straight Pool over 9-Ball, and thick books over thin ones; if you would rather read a story than see one; and if you like outwitting an opponent as well as outplaying him, it's possible that after you become a pretty fair billiards player, you should investigate the intricacies of One-Pocket. Surprisingly (to some people), the game has gotten more popular lately, and there is even a mini-tour of One-Pocket tournaments held in the United States. The game has yet to catch on overseas in any significant way, however.

As long and as complex as the game can be, handicapping it is a snap. The break is very important, and giving up the break when it's your turn (the game is normally played with alternate players breaking) is a big handicap. Instead of playing that the first player to sink eight balls (the majority) in his pocket wins the game, the numbers can be adjusted. If the better player has to pocket 9 balls before the other player pockets 7, for example, that may make the contest even. If the better player still easily wins, the handicap can be increased: the better player would have to pocket 10 balls before his opponent pockets 6 balls. Each step is a large one, because there's an increase on one side and a decreased demand for the other side.

Carom

The Carom games are played on tables that have no pockets, and although there are several variations, scoring is always done in points. You make a point by hitting two other balls with your cue ball. I say *your* cue ball, because there are two cue balls on the table at all times—yours and your opponent's. One is marked with a small black dot or is pale yellow instead of white. The third ball (in the most popular versions of the game) is red. In Korea and a few other places, Carom games use four balls: two cue balls, a red ball, and a yellow ball. In that version, you use your cue ball to hit the red ball and the other white ball, but if you hit the yellow ball, you lose your turn.

The most popular version of Carom is called Three-Cushion Billiards. In this game, you must shoot your cue ball and it must hit both the other balls, but before it hits the last of them, it must touch a cushion or cushions three or more times. That's the heart of the game—and about the only rule.

Here are a few examples of legal shots:

➤ Your cue ball hits a cushion, then the red ball, then two more cushions, and then the other cue ball.

➤ Your cue ball hits cushion A, then cushion B, then comes back to cushion A, and then hits the red and white ball.

➤ Your ball hits either the white or red ball, then hits all four cushions and then two of them again, and then the remaining ball.

➤ Your cue ball hits two cushions, then one of the balls, then the same two cushions, and then the remaining ball.

➤ Your cue ball hits the red ball, then a cushion, then the red ball again, then two cushions, and finally the other cue ball.

All these shots meet the requirements of a legal shot. Your cue ball hits three cushions and both of the other balls, the last of which was hit sometime after your cue ball hit at least three cushions. Each successful shot counts as 1 point. A game can be played to any predetermined number of points. Championship games are usually to 50 or 60 points, but officials are currently playing with that format in an attempt to make the game more interesting for spectators.

A less complex version (also an easier one) is Straight-Rail Billiards, which eliminates all the requirements for hitting cushions. You simply must drive your cue ball so that it hits the other two balls; it can hit cushions on the way, or not. For someone who wants to learn the Carom games, especially Three-Cushion Billiards, Straight-Rail Billiards is a good way to start.

Other versions of the Carom game have come and gone in popularity over the past 100 years. Usually, the top players got so good at scoring points that restrictions had to be added to make the games interesting. Three-Cushion Billiards has suffered few changes, but the other games, called—as a group—Balkline, have had fairly drastic changes and are not frequently played today.

Scratch!

When you hear someone refer to "the black ball" in a Carom game, but you see only two white balls and a red ball, don't worry. The white ball with the small black dot on it is called *the black ball* to distinguish it from the other cue ball: *the white ball*, which has no dot.

Ewa's Billiard Bits

I've known World Champion Three-Cushion Billiard star Torbjorn Blomdahl since the mid-1980s, although he lived in the south of Sweden, where Three-Cushion is popular. In the northern part of the country, where I grew up, that game is rarely played; there, it's all pool.

Rotation

Even if you've never played it, you've probably heard of this game, either as Rotation or 61. The game has been around a long time and used to be very popular. It's still the most popular game in the Philippines but has faded elsewhere in favor of the shorter version, called 9-Ball (which you already know about from Chapter 26).

Heard It in the Poolroom

In the Philippines, the most popular game is Rotation, and the best player in the world is a Filipino named Efren Reyes. He and I were defending champions at a 9-Ball tournament and appeared on TV together. I should explain that for world-class players, running out (making all balls from the 1 to the 15 without missing) is extremely rare in Rotation. The host of the show asked Efren about Rotation and then asked for an example. Efren tossed 15 balls on the table and ran out perfectly the very first time. The host asked whether he could do it again. He did—and then he did it a third time. It was an astounding performance—especially for a 7 a.m. show!

Rotation is…well, a rotation game, which means that you have to hit the lowest-numbered ball on the table first. In 9-Ball, the goal is to get to the 9, which is the winning ball. But in Rotation, the numbers on the balls count as points, and the first player to reach 61 points or more (half the available 120-point total of all balls, plus 1 point) wins the game. Combinations, kisses, and caroms are allowed, so it's possible to use the 1 ball to sink the 15 ball and get 15 points on the first shot, rather than get just 1 point by making the 1.

Rotation is usually played as a call-shot game, but it doesn't have to be; the choice is up to the players involved. Without call shots, however, it's common to see someone whack the 1 ball into any other ball around, in the hope that something from the larger-numbered end of the group will go into a pocket. That, as they say, is fun, but it isn't pool, and it's fun that soon wears thin. Try a call-shot game instead.

Cue Tips

With the numbers on the balls being so important in Rotation (an older game than 9-Ball), and not in other games, you might think that pool was originally Rotation. Not so. The numbers serve to identify the balls in any call-shot game—especially Straight Pool which predates Rotation.

A game of Rotation usually is not brief, unless it's played by expert players who have years of experience. If you feel that the requirement to hit the lowest-numbered ball first is tough in 9-Ball, just imagine what it's like when you have a rush-hour traffic jam of 15 balls on the table. The game typically heats up and speeds up later, when half the balls have been pocketed and the big numbers are left. Still, it's not a game that I recommend for beginners, because the first half of the game is frequently difficult and slow. Do the shortened version—9-Ball—until you get good at that; then try some Rotation.

Bank Pool

Bank Pool has been around for a long time, and it's easy to describe. You play it like regular billiards, but you have to bank every ball into a pocket for it to count. Each ball counts as 1 point. The first player to score 8 points wins the game.

Describing and playing are two different things, of course. In Chapter 19, I told you that I'd rather shoot a severe cut shot than shoot a bank shot; then I explained all the things that could happen during a bank shot (a little spin can make the object ball bank off the cushion at an odd angle, and so on) Now imagine a game in which every shot is a bank shot. Well, not every shot—the break is simply an open break, as in 8-Ball and 9-Ball. Any ball made (pocketed) on the break gets spotted and doesn't count as a point. All banked balls must go into the pocket without touching another ball, so combinations, Caroms, and kisses that include a bank don't count. Bank Pool is also almost always played as a call-shot game.

There have been a few national Bank Pool tournaments, most often in Kentucky, southern Ohio, and western Tennessee, where the game is very popular. One-Pocket includes a lot of bank shots, so One-Pocket players and Bank Pool players are often the same people. As in One-Pocket, the first player to get the majority of the balls (8 of 15) wins the game. Also as in One-Pocket, if a player fouls, he must return one of his pocketed balls to the table and put it on the spot (losing a point). He also loses his turn.

Cue Tips

When you're watching a Bank Pool match, you'll hear a lot of strange terms, which are shorthand for common call shots in the game. *Back*, for example, means "I'm banking this ball the long way, back to the corner where I'm standing." Opponents respect the call.

Equal Offense and Internet Equal Offense

Equal Offense is a game invented by BCA Master Instructor Jerry Briseth, who holds the copyright on it but places no restrictions on its use at this time. The Internet version allows players from different parts of the world to play one another via computer.

Equal Offense is similar to Straight Pool but can be played by any number of players. Internet Equal Offense is commonly played by teams from various countries. As in Straight Pool, all 15 numbered balls are used, and the game is played to a predetermined number of points, with each ball counting as 1 point. The main scoring difference between Equal Offense and Straight Pool is that a maximum number of points can be scored in a single turn (inning) at the table. Typically, the limit is 20 points.

This game is a call-shot game, but you don't lose points if you foul while attempting a shot. You simply end your turn at the table. That rule makes the game offensive (hence, the name) rather than both offensive and defensive. The game appeals to beginners who don't want to be bogged down or distracted by complex rules about fouling.

To play the Internet version of the game, you have to have a computer and be online, but you also need to have the computer located near a pool table. For more information about getting involved, see the BCA address in Appendix B.

Same Table, More Games

Before you rush out and invent your own game to play on a billiard table, you should probably know that somebody may have already thought of it. Check out the BCA rulebook in Appendix D for more popular variations of billiards. Beyond that, there's no good single source for the more obscure billiard games, many of which have come and gone. Players may remember them, but no one plays them anymore. Others are popular only in a small geographical area.

There are also obscure rules for existing games. In 9-Ball, for example, the pushout rule used to apply to every shot—not just to the first shot after the break, as is common today. In fact, the game wasn't even called 9-Ball by most players; they called it Pushout instead. Those rules are seldom used now, but any player who was active during the 1960s or before is very familiar with that version of 9-Ball.

All the unusual and less-popular games are pretty useless if you don't have someone—and preferably a lot of someones—with whom to play the game. That's what makes less-popular games fade away and what makes the key games even more popular. 8-Ball and 9-Ball rule the roost today. One-Pocket is probably the third-most-popular game, but it's often used as a gambling game, is difficult to learn, isn't temperamentally suited to everyone—and is a distant third in any case. Straight Pool is probably fourth in popularity. After that, the dip is fairly steep.

If you plan to spend a lot of time in a country that was (or still is) associated with England, try your hand at Snooker before you go, although you'll probably find that people also play pool there. If you plan to spend time in a country associated with France or Spain, you'll find some people still playing Three-Cushion Billiards or another variation of caroms, as well as pool and possibly a local variation of Snooker. I advise you to take up the games in which you'll find the most competition—9-Ball and 8-Ball—and then add Straight Pool for its purity and ability to develop your skills. These games have proved to be both fun and challenging, and they let you develop your abilities among a group that includes millions and millions of players in the United States alone. Enjoy!

The Least You Need to Know

➤ Playing games other than the three or four most popular versions of pool can improve your skills.

➤ Carom is played on a table that has no pockets.

➤ Snooker is played with different balls, on a table with rounded pocket corners.

➤ Rotation is the 15-ball version of 9-Ball.

➤ One-Pocket is a game of tactical skills.

➤ Bank Pool is a great way to learn to bank balls.

➤ You can play pool on the Internet.

Pocket Dictionary

Billiards is full of jargon, which isn't surprising, because all sports (like almost all endeavors) have their own terms, official and unofficial. British Snooker terms describe the same things that pool terms describe, but almost all the terms are different. Some are a little more descriptive. When a Snooker player scratches, it's not called a scratch; it's called an *in–off*, meaning that the cue ball went in the pocket and off the table. More descriptive, but not quite as snappy as *scratch*. Instead of *stop shot* (the pool term), they call the same shot a *stun shot*. The pool term is a little clearer, and the Snooker term has some flair. It would be interesting, but probably impossible, to find out the historical who, where, and when of all the words in cue sports.

In this glossary, you'll find a couple hundred of the most common words in billiards. Learn these terms, and you'll sound as though you've been playing all your life.

Action   1. The amount of movement resulting from an open break shot or a shot designed to break up a cluster of balls. 2. The movement of the cue ball caused by spin. 3. Gambling.

Aiming point   The point on the object ball where you aim the center of the cue ball.

Alternate breaks   At the beginning of each game, taking turns shooting the opening break shot.

Angle in   The angle at which a ball, bounced into a cushion, approaches that cushion.

Angle out   The angle at which a ball, bounced into a cushion, leaves that cushion.

Area position play   Rolling the cue ball, after it pockets an object ball, to a general area when that is sufficient to pocket the next ball. *See also* **Pinpoint position**.

Backstroke   The portion of your stroke in which you are drawing the cue tip away from the cue ball.

Balance point   On a cue, the point at which the weight of the front (shaft) equals the weight of the rear (butt).

Ball in hand   The reward to the incoming player after another player fouls. Ball in hand allows the incoming player to place the cue ball anywhere on the table and to begin shooting from there.

Ball returns   Tubes, troughs, gullies, or channels (depending on the manufacturer) arranged under the table so that pocketed balls end up in a tray at one end of the table.

Bank   Drive an object ball into a cushion firmly enough that it bounces back out.

Banks   A game in which every shot must be a bank shot.

Bar box   Slang for a coin-operated pool table (usually 7 feet long), most often found in taverns and teen centers.

Bed   The flat playing area of a billiard table.

Billiard supply stores   Stores that sell billiard tables and other equipment. These stores usually also sell other home rec-room items—everything from jukeboxes to barstools.

Billiards   The name that is now used for all cue sports. *Billiards* used to refer only to games played on a table without pockets. (Those games are now in the billiard subsection called *Carom*.)

Blocking ball   A ball between the object ball and the pocket.

Bottom   Short for *bottom spin*; another term for *draw* or *reverse English*.

Bottom rail   The short rail at the end of the table where the balls are racked.

Bottom spin   *See* **Draw**.

Breakabout   Slang for *alternate breaks*.

Break ball   In Straight Pool, the last ball in a rack, used to send the cue ball into the new rack of balls after the reracking.

Breaking safe   The act of breaking the balls in a fresh rack in such a way that no ball is pocketed and your opponent is unable to pocket a ball.

Bridge   1. The configuration of your front hand when stroking. 2. The device used for shots that are out of reach. *See* **Mechanical bridge**. 3. The distance between your front hand and the cue ball.

Butt   The thick, heavy end of the cue stick.

Butt plate   The plastic collar at the heavy end of the cue, which usually has the cuemaker's logo carved in it.

Call shot   The requirement that you name the ball that you intend to pocket and the pocket that it will go in before you make the shot.

Carom   1. The group of games played on a pocketless table. 2. A shot in which the cue ball hits the first object ball and bounces off it. The aim of the shot is to make a second object ball rather than the first.

Century   In Straight Pool and Snooker, the 100-point mark, if reached in a single turn at the table.

Cheating the pocket   Hitting the object ball so that it goes into one side of the pocket.

Cheese, the   The 9 ball, in a game of 9-Ball.

Choke   Misperform under pressure.

Closed bridge   A bridge that involves wrapping a finger over the cue.

Club   A billiard room. No membership is required in rooms in the United States.

Combination   A shot in which the first object ball goes into a second object ball, which then goes where you want it to go (usually in a pocket).

Connect the dots   Slang for an easy runout.

Contact point   The point at which the cue ball actually hits the object ball (different from the aiming point, except on straight shots).

Corner-hooked   When the cue ball is on the edge of the pocket but up against the inside of the cushion, so that a player must shoot the ball in a limited direction.

Cosmo   Slang for an easy runout.

Crossing a ball   Hitting an object ball on its edge when it is near a cushion, so that it bounces off the cushion and goes where you want it to go.

Cross-banking   Crossing an object ball and banking it into a pocket.

Cross-table banking   Banking a ball across the table the short way, from side cushion to side cushion (or pocket).

Cue   1. The piece of equipment that you use to strike the cue ball. 2. Slang for the act of hitting the cue ball. ("Cue the ball low" means hit it below center.)

Cue ball   The white ball.

Cue tip   The piece of leather at the pointed end of the cue.

Curve shot   A shot made by elevating the butt of your cue and hitting down on the cue ball, causing it to curve as it goes forward.

Cushion   The cloth-covered rubber outer boundary of the table bed.

Cut shot   Any shot that isn't a straight shot.

D   On a Snooker table, a marked area in which you must place the cue ball for the break shot. The cue ball is also placed in the D when you get ball in hand.

Dead ball   A ball that cannot be missed—usually, one that is frozen to another ball and aimed at a pocket.

Deadstroke   An emotional and psychological state during which every shot you make is perfect, yet you have a decreased sense of time and of your surroundings.

Deflection   The amount off the intended line that the cue ball goes when it is struck with either right or left English (sidespin).

Diamonds   Markings along the rail of the table, usually circular but sometimes diamond-shape.

Directional cloth   Cloth with fibers that lie in one direction. This type of cloth affects the paths of the balls, because you can be going against the nap (the fibers), with it, or at an angle across it, so that the resistance is different. *See also* **Nap**.

Dogging it   Losing concentration and missing a shot, or simply not trying hard enough because you took the shot for granted. *Dogging it* can be the same thing as *choking*.

Draw   Hit the cue ball below center so that when it hits an object ball it returns toward you.

Drop pockets   Pockets that retain the balls hit into them, rather than return them under the table to a central location. *See also* **Ball returns**.

8-Ball   A billiard game played with 15 object balls and a cue ball. The winner is the player who pockets all the balls in his group (solids or stripes) and the 8 ball.

English   An effect in which the cue ball is hit to the right or left of the vertical axis.

Exhibition   A performance by a professional billiard player, not involving tournament play.

Felt   The misnomer for billiard cloth, which is always wool or a wool blend.

Ferrule   The white plastic material around the tenon at the small end of the cue, just behind the cue tip.

Follow   Short for *follow spin*, meaning that the cue ball was struck above the equator.

Follow-through   Driving the cue tip past the point when it hit the cue ball.

Footrail   The short rail at the end of the table where the balls are racked.

Foul   Any violation of the rules.

14.1   *See* **Straight Pool**.

Frozen   Touching. Balls can be frozen together, but a ball can also be frozen to the cushion.

Full-size table   In pool games, a 4-1/2- by 9-foot table; in International Snooker, a 6- by 12-foot table; in carom games, a 5- by 10-foot table.

Furniture-style billiard table   A table that looks more like fine furniture than utilitarian sports or recreational equipment.

Getting out of line   Not being able to stick to the pattern that you need to follow to make one ball after another.

Grip   The configuration of your hands on the cue.

Handicapping   Altering what it takes to win a match so that players of unequal skill have the same opportunity.

Hanger   1. A ball that is easy to pocket. 2. A ball on the edge of the pocket. 3. Pool slang for anything easy.

Head of the table   The end of the table from which you break.

Headrail   The short rail at the end of the table from which you break.

Headstring   A line at the head of the table. You find the headstring by going down two diamonds on each side rail; the line connecting the diamonds across the table is the headstring.

Hill   One game from winning a match. In a race to seven games, the player with six games is said to be *"on the hill"* A match that is tied six games to six, in a race to seven, is said to be a *hill–hill* match. *See also* **TV game** and **TV match**.

Hit   1. A good hit occurs when the cue ball strikes the object ball where it was supposed to, and the cue ball hits the right object ball. 2. The feel of a cue hitting the cue ball and the appropriateness of the ball's reaction. (There also can be a good-hitting or a bad-hitting cue.) 3. Striking the cue ball where you tried to contact it (*hitting it good*) or not doing so (*hitting it bad*).

Honest effort   Trying to make a ball when it is your turn. This term is mostly used in games of 9-Ball and Cut-Throat among three or more players.

Hooked   Being unable to directly hit the object ball with the cue ball because another ball is in the way.

Hustler   A person who uses spin and other forms of deception to get your money. The term is associated with billiards because of the 1961 movie *The Hustler*, but it is applicable to all of life's situations.

In-house league   A league with teams that play all their games in one location.

In stroke   Playing very well. *Being in stroke* is not like being in deadstroke, but it's getting close. *See also* **Deadstroke**.

Inning   A turn at the table (a player's inning) or set of turns (you and your opponent).

Inside English   Left cue-ball sidespin when cutting a ball to the left, and right cue-ball sidespin when cutting a ball to the right.

Insurance ball   An easy shot that is left untouched until (and unless) a player makes a position error and cannot make another shot that he planned to make.

Jawing a ball   Hitting a ball into a corner pocket, but hitting the sides of the pocket so that the ball bounces back and forth in front of the hole but does not drop in.

Joint   The section at which the two pieces of a cue attach.

Judy   The cue ball. *See also* **Rock** and **Whitey**.

Jump cue   A shorter cue made specifically for jump shots.

Key ball   In Straight Pool, the ball just before the break ball. The key ball allows you to get proper position on the break ball.

Kick shot   A shot in which the cue ball is hit into a cushion so that it bounces out and then hits the object ball.

Kill shot   A shot that puts spin on a cue ball so any lateral motion stops (or almost stops) as soon as the cue ball strikes the object ball.

Kiss   Bounce an object ball off another object ball, usually with the intention of making the first object ball go in a pocket.

Lagging   Rolling a ball up and down the length of a table to determine who gets the first break in a match.

Line of sight   The line from a player's eyes through the cue ball to the nearest wall.

Massé   A shot that involves striking down on the cue ball, causing it to curve sharply as it squirts out from under the cue tip.

Maximum   In Snooker, a score of 147 points.

Mechanical bridge   A device that looks like a cue with a doodad on the end, used to reach shots that could otherwise not be easily reached.

Miscue   Hit too close to the edge of the cue ball with the cue tip.

Mouth of the pocket   The opening of a pocket before the hole.

Nap   The fibers of the cloth. *See also* **Directional cloth**.

Neutral 8 ball   Designation of the 8 ball in a game of 8-Ball meaning that any player can hit the 8 first, rather than a ball from her group (stripes or solids) if she so chooses. If the 8 ball is not designated neutral, that shot would be illegal.

9-Ball   A billiard game played with nine object balls and a cue ball. The winner is the person who pockets the 9 ball.

Nuts, the   A term meaning that there is no way you can lose. If a player of equal skill gives you a big handicap, for example, you can say that you *have the nuts*. Minnesota Fats said he had the *Hungarian Nuts* on certain games, because he normally had *the nuts* on all games. The Hungarian Nuts was a situation so astronomically lopsided that it surpassed the nuts.

Object ball (OB)   The first ball that the cue ball hits. Any ball to be hit after the OB can be called a second object ball.

One-Pocket   A game in which each player can pocket balls only in his own pocket. Making the majority of the balls (8) means that you win the game.

Open break   A break shot that breaks the rack of balls so hard that they open up and go in all directions.

Open bridge   A bridge for your front hand, in which the cue rests in a *V* created by the end of your thumb and your first finger.

Outside English   Left sidespin on the cue ball when cutting a ball toward the right, and right sidespin (English) on the cue ball when cutting a ball to the left.

Owning a player   Slang for your attitude toward a player who can't win, but keeps coming back because he's sure that he's better than you.

Owning a shot   Having total confidence that you have mastered a shot.

Pattern   The plan that you've made when you come to the table, perhaps dictated by the balls, if they are in a common layout (pattern) of their own. Otherwise, the player creates the pattern.

Pea Pool   *See* **Pill Pool**.

Pill bottle   The plastic container that holds the numbered beads for a game of Pill Pool.

Pill Pool   A game that uses a pill bottle and *pills* (small beads with numbers on them) to determine which numbered ball is your ball. Pocketing your ball before an opponent does wins you the game.

Pinpoint position   Playing the position of the cue ball after it pockets a ball so that the cue ball stops in a specific place, giving you a clear view of the next ball to be pocketed. *See also* **Area position play**.

Pocket speed   An effect in which the object ball is hit only hard enough to reach the pocket opening and drop in.

Position play   The act of hitting the cue ball with the correct speed and, if needed, spin while pocketing a ball, so that the cue ball bounces off that ball and goes to a place where the next ball can be pocketed. *See also* **Area position play** and **Pinpoint position**.

Pot   Pocket (a ball). British Snooker players laugh at the American term *shotmaking* but don't feel the least bit embarrassed about saying, "He potted the pink [ball]."

Push   1. The act of contacting the cue ball with a pushing motion rather than a striking motion (an illegal hit). 2. Short for *pushout*. 3. When two balls are touching and one is struck by the cue ball, pushing the second ball offline (more commonly, but less descriptively, called *throw*).

379

Race   A contest in which the first person to win a predetermined number of games wins the match.

Rack   1. The wood, plastic, or metal device used to arrange the balls for the beginning of a game. 2. Those balls in that position. 3. Slang for a complete game. 4. To rack, meaning to gather the balls in the device in definition 1. 5. Pool slang for losing a game (*going to the rack*).

Rail   1. The hard outside perimeter of a billiard table. The cloth-covered cushion is attached to the rail. 2. Slang for the cushion/rail unit (as in "I hit the cue ball three rails").

Rail bridge   The configuration of your front hand when it is on the rail and/or cushion.

Reverse   Short for reverse spin (*draw*).

Road map   Slang for an arrangement of balls that is easy to pocket.

Rock   The cue ball. "He can't draw his rock" is a negative comment about the abilities of a player, meaning that he doesn't have enough skill to execute a draw shot. *See also* **Judy** and **Whitey**.

Rolloff   An effect in which a slow-moving ball doesn't go in a straight line for reasons other than spin (nonlevel table, foreign matter on the cloth, and so on).

Rotation   A game that uses all 15 numbered balls. You get the number of points printed on the ball when you pocket it. The game is also known as 61 because that is the winning total. (The balls total 120 points.)

Running English   *See* **Outside English**.

Runout   Poolese for pocketing all the remaining balls on the table.

Safety   A shot that prevents your opponent from being able to pocket a ball.

Safety break   The opening shot of the game, made in such a way that nothing is pocketed and the cue ball ends up in a position where your opponent cannot pocket a ball.

Scratch   The act of shooting the cue ball into a pocket, either intentionally or unintentionally. A scratch is always a foul, but a foul is not always a scratch.

Screw, Screw back, and **Deep screw**   British Snooker term for *draw* (reverse spin). The first two terms are interchangeable; the second simply means a lot of draw (power draw) shot.

Setup shot   A trick shot that, when the balls are properly placed, is very difficult to miss.

Shaft   The narrow end of the cue.

Shaft papers   Very fine sandpaper or plastic sheets with miniature grids, used to smooth and clean a cue shaft.

Shaper   A device that shapes a cue tip.

Short-rack game   Any pool game using fewer than 15 numbered balls.

Shot-making   Pocketing a ball. Players who are known as good shotmakers excel at making extremely difficult shots but usually are weak on position play. *See also* **Pot**.

Sidespin   An effect in which the cue ball is hit to the left or right of the vertical axis. *See also* **English**.

Skill shot   A trick shot that not only requires that the balls be properly set up, but also requires that the performer be an expert player.

Slate   The stone beneath the cloth of a billiard table.

Slice   *See* **Cut shot**.

Snooker   A game played with 15 red balls and 6 colored balls on a table with rounded pocket openings. Snooker is most popular in England and countries that have British influence.

Snookered   Not having a straight shot at the object ball because another object ball is in the way. *See also* **Blocking ball**.

Solids   The 1 ball through the 7 ball, in the game of 8-Ball.

Spectator chairs   Special-purpose billiard chairs that resemble barstools.

Spot   A circular tab placed on the cloth in the center of the foot-half (rack end) of the table. Other spots may go on the corresponding spot at the head end of the table and in the middle of the table, but they are rare.

Spot a ball   Take a ball out of a pocket and place it on the spot (technically, the footspot).

Spot shot   A shot in which there is a ball on the spot and the player has ball in hand behind the headstring.

Stack   Slang for the rack of balls or any large cluster of balls in the area of the rack.

Stance   The proper body position in which to shoot a shot.

Straight Pool   A game in which each ball counts as 1 point, and you can play to any number of points. You do the latter by leaving the last ball in a rack unpocketed until the preceding 14 balls are reracked.

Stripes   The 9 ball through 15 ball, in a game of 8-Ball.

Stroke   The swing in pool. The stroke encompasses the grip, the position of the body and all its parts (especially the eyes and back arm), the rate of acceleration of the cue, the timing of the contact with the cue ball, and the follow-through.

381

Stroke shot   *See* **Skill shot.**

Sweat   Watch a game, rooting for a particular player. The term is often shortened, in pool talk, to "I sweated Jane's match," meaning that I watched Jane's match. "I sweated Jane and Bill's match," on the other hand, means that you watched it but weren't rooting for one over the other.

Sweater   Someone watching a pool match.

Tester   A difficult shot.

Tickie or **ticky**   A shot in which the cue ball goes into a cushion (*see* **Kick shot**) and then strikes the back of an object ball near the cushion, so that the object ball goes toward the real target, which is a second object ball.

Tip tool   Any device used to shape or roughen the cue tip.

Top   Short for *topspin.*

Topspin   An effect that makes the cue ball spin forward at a greater rate of spin than if it were rolling naturally.

Traveling league   A league that has teams in different locations. One team travels each week to play an opposing team on its home court, and that team later travels to the other team's home court.

Triangle   Another name for the device used to shape the balls before the game starts. *See also* **Rack.**

Trimmer   A tool that trims the edges of a cue tip.

TV game   The deciding game in a *TV match.*

TV match   A match that is tied one game short of the winning number. *See also* **Hill.**

Two-way shot   A win–win shot that, if missed, leaves the cue ball in a position from which the object ball cannot be pocketed or sometimes even hit.

V bridge   *See* **Open bridge.**

Whitey   The cue ball. *See also* **Judy** and **Rock.**

Winner breaks   An arrangement in which the player who won the preceding game shoots the break shot in the following game.

Wrap   The material, on most cues, wrapped around the cue butt where your back hand grips the cue.

Resources

In this appendix, you'll find all kinds of resources for information about pool and billiards:

➤ Books

➤ Videotapes

➤ Web sites

Books

The first book on billiards was published in 1674, and there has been a steady stream ever since. Of the hundreds of billiards books published in English, I've picked some recent ones that might interest you. Unfortunately, if you want to know more about Snooker or carom games, not much material is available in the United States. Snooker books are available in abundance in Great Britain, and a few are available in Canada. Some carom books have been published in the United States, but they're not easy to find and tend to be a little advanced.

The following three books are the ones that I suggest you get first. If you can't find them in bookstores (and you probably won't), check "The Worldwide Billiard Web" later in this appendix, or contact pool and billiard periodicals.

Byrne, Robert. *Byrne's New Standard Book of Pool and Billiards.* Orlando: Harvest/ Harcourt Brace & Co., 1978, 1998.

Capelle, Phil. *Play Your Best Pool.* Midway City, CA: Billiards Press, 1995.

Koehler, Jack. *The Science of Pocket Billiards.* Laguna Hills, CA: Sportology Publications, 1989.

Following are a few others that are worth checking into:

Byrne, Robert. *Byrne's Wonderful World of Pool and Billiards.* Orlando: Harvest/ Harcourt Brace & Co.,1996.

Davis, Joe. *How I Play Snooker.* London: Country Life Ltd., 1949.

Fats, Minnesota. *The Bank Shot and Other Great Robberies.* Cleveland: World Publishing, 1966.

Fels, George. *Advanced Pool.* Chicago: Contemporary Books, 1995.

Fels, George. *Mastering Pool.* Chicago: Contemporary Books, 1997.

Henning, Bob. *The Pro Book.* Livonia, MI: BeBob Publishing, 1997.

Hoppe, Willie. *Billiards...As It Should Be Played.* Chicago: Contemporary Books, 1941.

Koehler, Jack. *Upscale One-Pocket.* Laguna Hills, CA: Sportology Publishing, 1995.

Martin, Ray. *99 Critical Shots of Pool.* New York: Times Books, 1977.

Mataya, Ewa and Bob Brown. *The Ewa Mataya Pool Guide.* New York: Avon Books, 1995.

Mizerak, Steve and Michael Panozzo. *Steve Mizerak's Complete Book of Pool.* Chicago: Contemporary Books, 1990.

Monk, The. *Point the Way.* Orange, MA: Samsara Publishing, 1990.

Robin, Eddie. *Position Play in Three-Cushion Billiards.* Las Vegas, NV: Billiard World Publishing, 1979.

Robin, Eddie, ed. *Shots, Moves and Strategies in One-Pocket As Taught by the Game's Greatest Players.* Las Vegas, NV: Billiard World Publishing, 1996.

Robin, Eddie, ed. *Winning One-Pocket As Taught by the Game's Greatest Players.* Las Vegas, NV: Billiard World Publishing, 1993.

Spencer, John. *Teach Yourself Snooker.* London and New York: NTC Publishing, 1986.

Here are a few other books that will give you more information on the billiard world, from tournaments to hustlers, from toy tables to priceless antiques, and a lot more. They're not books on how to play the game, but they're very interesting nonetheless.

Mosconi, Willie and Stanley Cohen. *Willie's Game.* New York: Macmillan, 1993.

Shamos, Mike. *Illustrated Encyclopedia of Billiards.* New York: Lyons & Burford, 1993.

Shamos, Mike. *Pool.* New York: Mallard Press/BDD Promotional Book Company, 1991.

Shamos, Mike and George Bennett. *Shooting Pool.* New York: Artisan, 1998.

Simpson, Brad. *Blue Book of Pool Cues.* Minneapolis, MN: Blue Book Publications, 1996.

Stein, Victor and Paul Rubino. *Billiard Encyclopedia.* Minneapolis, MN: Blue Book Publications, 1994.

Billiards on Video

Watching pool on TV is a great way to learn. Hundreds of instructional tapes are on the market, ranging from general introductions for beginners to pretty advanced stuff. There are even a dozen or so tapes just on trick shots.

But a tape doesn't have to be straight instruction for you to learn from it. A company called Accu-Stats videotapes almost all the major tournaments each year, making them available on home VHS versions. One of the best parts about the tapes is the fact that each has an expert commentator and guest player who talk knowledgeably about the action. Watching these tapes is like having a top-class player tell you the choices that a player faces, the options, and what the player ends up doing and why. It's real analysis, because the tapes are aimed at a pool-savvy audience, and there's no need for commercial interruptions. On the other hand, the commentary is a little more...shall we say, unstructured and conversational.

In any case, these tapes are well worth looking into. You'll find them through Web sites or through ads in pool and billiard publications. Tournament tapes (and a few instructional tapes) are produced by Accu-Stats Video Productions, Bloomingdale, New Jersey. Instructional tapes are available at local billiard supply stores and through ads in pool and billiard publications.

> [Host]. *Chef Anton's Magical Menu of Pool Ball Wizardry.*
>
> [Host]. *Cue Up with the WPBA Pros.*
>
> Briseth, Jerry. *How to Play Pool Right.*
>
> Byrne, Robert. *Byrne's Standard Video of Pool & Billiards.*
>
> Byrne, Robert. *Byrne's Standard Video of Pool & Billiards,* Vol. 2.
>
> Doss, Bob and Bert Kinister. *Basic Jump Shot Tape.*
>
> Feeney, Don ("The Preacher"). *Sighting and Aiming.*
>
> Fels, George. *George Fels' Winning 8-Ball.*
>
> Hall, Buddy. *Buddy Hall's Clock System.*
>
> Hall, Buddy. *Focus on Position Play.*
>
> Hopkins, Allen. *Secrets of a Champion.*
>
> Hopkins, Allen. *Secrets of One-Pocket.*
>
> Jopling, Willie. *Ultimate Trick Shot Tape.*
>
> Kinister, Bert. *Advanced Fundamentals.*
>
> Kinister, Bert. *Bert's 10 Best Hustles.*
>
> Kinister, Bert. *Run Out 9-Ball.*
>
> Kinister, Bert. *The Shotmaker's Workout.*
>
> Kinister, Bert. *The 60-Minute Workout.*

Massey, Mike. *Massey Shots* (trick shots).

Mathews, Grady. *The Finer Points of Banking.*

Mathews, Grady. *The Finer Points of Pool.*

Mathews, Grady. *The Finer Points of One-Pocket.*

Mathews, Grady. *The Finer Points of Straight Pool.*

Meucci staff members. *Pool School.*

Sigel, Mike. *Mike Sigel's Winning 8-Ball, 9-Ball and Straight Pool.*

Varner, Nick. *Championship 8-Ball.*

The Worldwide Billiard Web

According to Karin Kaltofen, who compiled the long Web list below for *Pool & Billiard Magazine*, there are more than 5,000 billiard-related addresses on the Web (as of this writing), with dozens more joining every day.

The two best places to start (because they have links to all the other major sources, which have links to every other source) are:

http://www.poolmag.com

http://bca-pool.com

The following sections list some other sites that are worth visiting.

Accessories

Dead Stroke Designs
http://www.turnpike.net/~deadstroke/

R.C. Designs International
http://www.bca-pool.com/rcdesigns/

Ride the Nine Designs
http://www.ridethe9.com/

Winning Garb
http://www.poolhall.com/winninggarb/Default.htm

Associations/Leagues

Asia

Asian Pocket Billiard Union
http://www.bca-pool.com/associations/wpa/wpa_apbu.htm

Japan Billiards Home Page
http://www2s.biglobe.ne.jp/~jbhp/

Australia

Australasian Pool Association
http://www.bca-pool.com/associations/wpa/wpa_apa.htm

Australian Billiards & Snooker
http://www.ausport.gov.au/bilsp.html

Heatherton Shooters 8-Ball Pool
http://www.users.bigpond.com/tomatz/

Snooker Australia
http://www.billsnook.com.au/

Canada

Aactive 8-Ball and 9-Ball Leagues
http://www.pool-leagues.com/

Ontario Billiards & Snooker Association
http://www.obsa.on.ca/

Europe

Austrian Snooker
http://unet.univie.ac.at/~a9400049/ashp/

Carombolage Billiard Home Page
http://www.truro.nscc.ns.ca/uhl/carambolage.html

Dutch Pool Billiards
http://www.noord.bart.nl/~quintus/

English Pool Association
http://www.epa.org.uk/

European Pocket Billiard Federation
http://www.bca-pool.com/associations/wpa/wpa_epbf.htm

International

World Confederation of Billiard Sports
http://www.worldsport.com/sports/billiards_sports/home.html

World Pool-Billiard Association
http://www.bca-pool.com/associations/wpa/

South Africa

Pegasus Pool League
http://www.pool.co.za/

United States

American Cuemakers Association
http://www.cuemakers.org/

American Poolplayers Association
http://www.poolplayers.com/

Billiard Congress of America
http://www.bca-pool.com/

Billiard Education Foundation
http://www.bca-pool.com/bef/

National Wheelchair Billiards Association
http://www.bca-pool.com/nwba/

Pot O' Gold Pool Leagues
http://www.potogoldleagues.com/

Pro Billiards Tour
http://www.propool.com

Professional CueSports Association
http://www.cuesports.com

United States Snooker Association
http://www.tourboard.com/uusa

Women's Professional Billiard Association
http://www.wpba.com

Billiard Supply Stores

Canada

Dufferin Game Room Store
http://www.gameroom.sk.ca/

Mr. Billiard Supply
http://www.valuenetwork.com/business/mrbill.htm

United States

California

AAA Billiards of Beverly Hills
http://emoon.com/vendor/la/AAABilliards/

Alco International Internet Discount Superstore
http://www.alcobilliards.com

Billiards & Barstools
http://www.pooltbls.com/

The Gameroom Gallery
http://www.gameroomgallery.com/

The Poker Store
http://www.4-1-1.com/poker

Triangle Billiards
http://www.tribilliards.com

Colorado

Backyards & Billiards
http://www.backyardsandbilliards.com/

Quality Table Games
http://www.qualitytablegames.com/

Connecticut

The Billiard Zone
http://www.billiard-zone.com/

Florida

Life of Luxury Billiards
http://www.lifeofluxury.com/billiards.html

Hawaii

50th State Coin-Op
http://aloha.com/~50coinop/

Louisiana

Billiards, Inc.
http://www.neworleans.com/billiards/

Money Machines
http://www.moneymachines.com/

Maryland

Cues-N-Things
http://www.cuesnthings.com/

Michigan

Saffron Billiards
http://www.saffrons.com/

Mississippi

The Panther Den Game Room
http://www.angelfire.com/ms/bigtathome/

Missouri

Jeffco Billiards
http://www.tetranet.net/users/billiards/

New Hampshire

Ac-Cue-Rate Billiard Supply
http://www.q-ball.com/

New Jersey

A GameRoom Store
http://www.bca-pool.com/gameroom/

Billiard Towne
http://www.bca-pool.com/billiardtowne

New York

Gates Billiards
http://www.gatesbilliards.com/

North Carolina

H.E.A.D.S.
http://www.netpath.net/heads/

Ohio

Billiards-Plus
http://www.billiards-plus.com/

Danny Vegh's Recreation Supply
http://www.dannyveghs.com/

Oregon

The Pool Table Shop
http://www.teleport.com/~poolshop/

Pennsylvania

Monarch Billiards
http://www.monarchbilliards.com/

Royal Billiard & Recreation
http://www.royalbilliard.com/

South Carolina

Carolina Gameroom
http://www.scbilliard.com/

Tennessee

Billiard Pro Shop
http://www.billiardpro.com

Texas

Billiards of Texas
http://www.billiardsoftexas.com/

Fort Worth Billiard Supply
http://www.dfwbilliards.com/

Hawley's Billiards
http://www.hawleys.com/

Utah

Best Billiards Sales & Service
http://www.bestbilliard.com/

Virginia

Billiard Express
http://www.ontheline.com/long/

PKSpas
http://www.crownmall.com/pkspas/

West Virginia

House of Billiards
http://www.ianet.net/~billiard/

Books (see also Instructional Material)

Blue Book of Pool Cues
http://www.cuebook.com/

Chalk Holders

Pocket Chalkers
http://www.poolhall.com/pocketchalkers/default.htm

Cues

Billiard Pro Shop, Inc.
http://www.billiardpro.com

Billiardcue.com
http://www.billiardcue.com

Bludworth Originals
http://www.billiardcues.com/

Blue Grass Cues
http://www.bright.net/~poolcues/

BourQues Custom Cues
http://www.bourques.com/

Capone Custom Cues
http://www.voicenet.com/~caponejr/

Chesapeake Cues, Ltd.
http://www.finecues.com/

Clawson Custom Cues Inc.
http://earthpages.com/clawsoncues

Competition Sports Corp.
http://www.adamcues.com/

Cousin's Custom Cues
http://www.traknet.com/ccc/

The Cue Gallery
http://www.CueGallery.com/

Cues-N-Things
http://www.cuesnthings.com/

Cuetec Cues
http://www.bca-pool.com/cuetec/

DeRoo Cues
http://www.freeyellow.com/members/deroo/

Dufferin Cues
http://www.bca-pool.com/dufferin/

1st Class Billiards/Shooters
http://www.shootersbilliards.com

Greg Hearn Custom Cues
http://www.winwin-ent.com/hearn/

The Kinetic Cue
http://www.kineticq.com/

Longoni Cues
http://www.bca-pool.com/longoni/

McDermott Cues
http://www.mcdermottcue.com

Meucci Originals
http://www.meuccicues.com/

Paul Mottey Custom Cues
http://www.motteycues.com/

Prather Cues
http://www.prathercue.com/

Ray Schuler Custom Cues
http://www.schulercue.com/

Richard Black Custom Cues
http://www.neosoft.com/~blackq/

Robinson Cues
http://www.virtualbilliards.com/rcue/

Viking Cue Manufacturing
http://www.vikingcue.com/

Vogel Titanium Cues
http://www.vogelcue.com/

Cue Cases

Billiard Pro Shop
http://www.billiardpro.com

Eagle Custom Wood & Leather
http://www.eaglecustom.com/

1st Class Billiards/Shooters
http://www.shootersbilliards.com

Instroke Cue Cases
http://instroke.com/

Justis Cases
http://members.aol.com/JJustis4/

Cue Gloves

Sir Joseph Cue Gloves
http://www.bca-pool.com/sirjoseph/

Cue Stands

Bay State Billiards Enterprises
http://members.aol.com/sidepokket/mule.htm

Qkaddy
http://www.beakem.com/qkaddy/

Cue Tips

Future Cue Tips
http://www.flash.net/~jlowery/home.htm

Device Aids

Billiard Pro Shop
http://www.billiardpro.com

Easy Shot Promotions
http://www.ozemail.com.au/~conw/easyshot.html

Elephant Balls
http://www.bca-pool.com/elephantballs

The Kinetic Cue
http://www.kineticq.com/

Rodriguez Enterprises, LLC
http://www.bca-pool.com/cueguide

Sterling Billiards
http://www.bca-pool.com/easyshot

Strokemaster International
http://www.bca-pool.com/strokemaster

Distributors

Atlas Billiard Supply
http://www.cuestik.com/

Best Billiard Sales & Service
http://www.bestbilliard.com

Billiard Pro Shop
http://www.billiardpro.com

1st Class Billiards/Shooters
http://www.shootersbilliards.com

Imperial International
http://www.imperialusa.com/

North American Billiards
http://www.mainerec.com/billiar4.html

Ride the Nine Designs
http://www.ridethe9.com/

Rodriguez Enterprises, LLC
http://www.bca-pool.com/cueguide

Saffron Billiards
http://www.saffrons.com

Snooker, Billiard & Pool Tables
http://www.knowledge.co.uk/xxx/access/snooker/

Trusty Online
http://www.victorycue.com/

Worldwide Billiards, Inc.
http://www.worldwidebilliards.com/

Furniture

Mikhail Darafeev
http://www.darafeev.com/

Instructional Materials

BCA Instructional Products
http://www.bca-pool.com/products/ip.htm

A Billiard Atlas on Systems & Techniques
http://www.billiardsatlas.com/

Eight Ball Data
http://www.bca-pool.com/8balldata/

40 Ways to Improve Your Game
http://www.pool-hq.com/

Gambler's Bookstore of America
http://www.gamblersbooks.com/gbacatbd.html

Master Stroke 1
http://www.bsintl.com/mstroke1.html

The Monk Billiard Academy
http://www.themonk.com/

Play Your Best Pool
http://www.billiardspress.com/

Pool Instruction Book by Desmond Allen
http://www.harborside.com/home/a/allen/poolbook.htm

The Science of Pocket Billiards
http://www.bca-pool.com/koehler/

Secrets of 3-C Billiards
http://205.179.24.1/billiards/welcome.html

Travesty's Guide to Billiards
http://www.mylink.net/~yugosoft/index.html

Upscale One Pocket
http://www.bca-pool.com/koehler/

Magazines/Publications

All About Pool
http://www.bca-pool.com/allaboutpool

American Cueist Magazine
http://cust.iamerica.net/cueist/

Billiard & Dart News
http://idt.net/~amayes/

Billiard News
http://www3.sympatico.ca/bullit

Billiard World Online Magazine
http://www.billiardworld.com/

Billiards Digest
http://www.billiardsdigest.com

News & Cues
http://www.aracnet.net:80/~newscues/

Player's Choice Magazine
http://www.amd-inc.com/playersmag/

Pool & Billiard Magazine
http://www.poolmag.com

Snooker Scene Magazine
http://www.ejriley.com/sscene.htm

Women & Billiards Online Magazine
http://www.webhostmall.com/women&billiards

Mail Order

All Seasons Pool*Patio*Spa
http://www.sisna.com/all_seasons/

Atlas Billiard Supply
http://www.cuestik.com/

Best Billiards Sales & Service
http://www.bestbilliard.com/

Billiard Pro Shop
http://www.billiardpro.com

The Billiard Zone
http://www.billiard-zone.com/

Challenger Snooker/Pool Supplies
http://www.billiardsupply.com/

Champion Billiard Supply, Inc.
http://www.championbilliards.com

Compleat Gamester
http://www.compgames.com/

Cue & Case Connection
http://www.gnutec.com/ccc/ccc.html

Discount Cues & Cases
http://members.aol.com/cues4you/

1st Class Billiards/Shooters
http://www.shootersbilliards.com

The Gameroom Gallery
http://www.gameroomgallery.com

Gates Billiards
http://www.gatesbilliards.com/

Internet Cue Store
http://www.cuestore.com/

McAlarney Pools, Spas & Billiards
http://www.mcalarney.com/

Mueller Sporting Goods
http://www.mueller-sporting-goods.com/

The Pool Table Shop
http://www.teleport.com/~poolshop/

Purewater Pools/Spas/Darts/Blrds
http://www.cyberus.ca/purewater/

Rack 'M Up Billiards
http://www.flinet.com/~jeffg/

Saffron Billiards
http://www.saffrons.com

Scioto Valley
http://www.sciotovalley.com/

Tom's Qstix
http://www.tomsqstix.com/

Triangle Billiards
http://www.tribilliards.com

V-Que Billiard's Supply Company
http://www.vque.com/

Virtual Billiards
http://www.virtualbilliards.com/

Watertown Billiards
http://www.execpc.com/~wttnbill

Maintenance

Billiard Maintenance Products
http://WWW.geminitec.com/pool.html

Miscellaneous

ISU: Property and Liability Insurance for the Billiard Industry
http://www.isusf.com

PAOLO ARATA & C. S.p.A: Slate (Billiard table slate)
http://www.arata.it/

Players

Accu-Stats Picture Gallery
http://www.accu-stats.com/as-pics2.htm

BCA Hall of Fame
http://www.bca-pool.com/hof/

Billiard World Pro Player Photos
http://www.billiardworld.com/pros.html

D&D Billiards Pro Page
http://www.voicenet.com/~mpool/thepros.html

PBT Pro Pictures
http://www.propool.com/pros.htm

PCA Player Profiles
http://www.cuesports.com/players/players.html

World Registry (rankings)
http://www.world-registry.com/

WPBA Player Profiles
http://www.wpba.com/players/playlist.html

Pockets

Cin-Caro Manufacturing
http://www.cin-caro.com/

R.C. Designs International
http://www.bca-pool.com/rcdesigns/pockets.htm

Pro Shops/Clubs

Canada

Black Dog Billiard Café
http://www.blackdogcafe.com/

Bo'Diddlys Pub & Billiards
http://www.boco.com

Cachet Club
http://www.cachetclub.com/

Pins & Cues
http://www.discoveredmonton.com/pinscues

Q-Ball Billiards Club
http://www.islandnet.com/~lars/Q-BALL/qball.html

The Shot Pool Pub
http://www.theshot.com/

Spain

Copenhagen Pool & Snooker Club/Pool Pub
http://diana.cps.unizar.es/isc/personales/fju/billarfju.html

United States

Arizona

Clicks Billiards
http://www.billiards.com/

California

Blue Fin Cafe and Billiards
http://www.bluefin-billiards.com

Chalkers Billiard Clubs
http://www.citysearch7.com/E/V/SFOCA/0002/44/33/

Dome Billiards CafT
http://www.hollywoodwired.com/domebilliards/

First Place Billiards
http://www.geocities.com/Colosseum/3868/firstplace.htm

The Great Entertainer
http://www.geocities.com/Colosseum/3868/greatentertainer.htm

Hollywood Billiards
http://www.geocities.com/Colosseum/3868/hollywood.htm

Hot Shots
http://www.centralcoast.com/hotshots/

Players Billiard & Volleyball Club
http://www.americandreams.com/players/

The Polo Club
http://www.thepoloclub.com/

Rack'N-Cue
http://www.geocities.com/Colosseum/3868/rackhome.htm

South Beach Billiards
http://www.pbilliards.com

Florida

Clicks Billiards
http://www.billiards.com/

Georgia

Barley's Billiards
http://www.barleys-billiards.com/

Side Pokket Billiards & Sports
http://wjimages.com/SidePokket

Illinois

Breakers Billiards
http://www.apci.net/~cueball/

Shark City Billiards & Sports Bar
http://www.sharkcity.com/

Indiana

Nick's Billiards CafT
http://www.qklink.com/nicks/

Kansas

Side Pockets
http://www.ies.lafayette.in.us/knickerbocker/nicks/

Louisiana

Clicks Billiards
http://www.billiards.com/

Maryland

Champion Billiards, Inc.
http://championbilliards.com/

Edgar's Billiards Club
http://www.edgarsclub.com/

Massachusetts

Boston Billiard Club
http://bostonbilliardclub.com/

Michigan

Golden 8 Ball Billiards
http://www.golden8ball.com

Minnesota

City Billiards Bar & CafT
http://www.citybilliards.com/

The Club Billiards & Arcade
http://www.4theclub.com/

Mississippi

The Panther Den Game Room
http://www.angelfire.com/ms/bigtathome/

401

New Hampshire

Legends Billiards & Tavern
http://www.legend.qpg.com/

New Jersey

The Break
http://www.americaninternet.com/thebreak/index.htm

Jack's Racks Family Billiards
http://www.nealcomm.com/racks/index.htm

New Mexico

Billy Aardd's Club
http://www.nmt.edu/~billiard/

New York

Corner Billiards of New York
http://www.cornerbilliards.com

Hippos: The House of Billiards
http://www.hipposbilliards.com/

Hollies' Billiards Pool Hall
http://www.rotw.com/rockland/hollies.htm

North Carolina

Cue 'N Spirits
http://www.poolcues.com/

Ohio

Ohio Billiards of Belden
http://www.starcom2.com/ohbilliards/

Pennsylvania

D&D Family Billiards
http://www.voicenet.com/~mpool/

Texas

Austin Billiard Rooms
http://206.251.18.60/features/pool/players.htm

Bostock's Billiards and Bar
http://www.our-town.com/~bostock/

Clicks Billiards
http://www.billiards.com/

Hawleys Billiards & Pool Supplies
http://www.billiardstore.com/

Virginia

Champion Billiards, Inc.
http://championbilliards.com/

Q-Ball Billiards
http://www.wizard.net/business/qball/

Schools

Billiard Seminars International
http://www.bsintl.com/bsi.html

Cue-Tech Instruction
http://www.poolschool.com/

The Monk Billiard Academy
http://www.themonk.com/

Pool Instruction by Desmond Allen
http://www.harborside.com/home/a/allen/poolclinic.htm

The Pool School
http://www.bca-pool.com/poolschool

Scuffers

Porcupine Tapper
http://www.rackem.com/

TIP-PIC
http://www.ontheline.com/long/tippic.html

Software

Billiard Management

Bauer Electronics, Inc.
http://www.bauer-electron.com/

Carambolage Administrative System
http://www.worldcity.nl/~clarijs/billiard.html

Georgia's Billiard Network Software
http://www.gabn.org/software.htm

Snooker Manager
http://www.servcare.demon.co.uk/snooker/

Tournament Bracket Software
http://www.sound.net/~jimbarr/pplofkc/sharware.html

Home-Computer Games

Championship Pool
http://www.wizworks.com/v_cpool.htm

Eight Ball Data
http://www.bca-pool.com/8balldata

Free Stroke Pool
http://www.rotw.com/cdroms/pool/

Peter Grogono: Snooker Simulator
http://www.cs.concordia.ca/~faculty/grogono/snooker.html

Pool Master
http://www.bestbilliard.com/download/download.cfm

Ultimate Pool for the Mac
http://www.cs.princeton.edu/~jhs/shareware/Pool/pool.html

Virtual Pool from Macplay
http://www.macplay.com/website/titles/vpool.html

Virtual Pool/Virtual Pool 2/Virtual Snooker
http://www.interplay.com

Interactive Games

Billiards Live
http://www.cybercanarias.com/pool/

Cyber-Pool
http://www.cybercanarias.com/pool

Internet Equal Offense
http://www.tourboard.com/ieo

9-Ball Challenge
http://www.soton.ac.uk/~micf/pool/index.html

Virtual International Pool Ladder
http://www.caj.net/~deilerin/vpool

Tables

AAA Pool Tables and Games
http://www.accessrex.com/Pool.html

Altamonte Billiard Factory/Proline Billiard Tables
http://proline-billiard.com/

AMF Playmaster
http://www.bca-pool.com/amf/

Antique Billiard Tables/Accessories
http://home1.gte.net/schwing/

Australian Billiards
http://www.australianbilliards.com.au/

Avante Sales, Ltd.
http://www.avante.co.uk/

Bar Billiards, Ltd.
http://www.bar-billiards.co.uk/

Betson Imperial
http://www.betson.com

Billares Sam
http://www.billaressam.com

Billiard Pro Shop
http://www.billiardpro.com

Brunswick Billiards
http://www.brunswick-billiards.com/

CalSpas and Camelot Billiards
http://www.calspas.com/

Classic Billiards Antique Tables
http://members.aol.com/cbilliards/billiards.htm

Dynamo, Ltd.
http://www.dynamo-ltd.com

E.J. Riley, Ltd.
http://www.ejriley.com

1st Class Billiards/Shooters
http://www.shootersbilliards.com

Gandy Pool Tables
http://www.gandys.com/

Golden West Billiard Manufacturing
http://www.billiardmfg.com/

Indoor Outdoor Pool Tables
http://www.conroy1.com/tristate/inout.htm

Kasson Manufacturing
http://www.bca-pool.com/kasson/

Mikhail Darafeev, Inc.
http://www.darafeev.com/

Mitchell Custom Pool & Billiard Tables
http://www.thefrontpage.com/mall/pooltables/

Murrey International
http://www.billiardtables.com/

North American Billiards
http://www.mainerec.com/billiar4.html

Paolo Arata & Co. Slate
http://www.arata.it/

Playcraft Industries
http://www.playcraft.com/

Pool Tables by Adler
http://www.accessrex.com/AAA008.html

Pro Line Billiard Tables
http://proline-billiard.com/

Royal Astro Billiards
http://www.csiworld.com/royal/

Sir William Bentley Antique
http://www.billiards.co.uk

Steepleton Billiard Tables
http://www.iglou.com/steepleton/

Unique Pool Tables
http://www.flash.net/~jsa/pool/

Vitalie Manufacturing
http://www.vitalie-manufacturing.com/

Willie Holt Ireland, Ltd.
http://www.willieholt.com

Vertical Blinds

Vertiscapes
http://www.vertiscapes.com/8ball.htm

Videos

Accu-Stats
http://www.accu-stats.com/

Buddy Hall Video
http://www.bca-pool.com/cueguide/cg-bnv.htm

Gilligan's Game of Billiards
http://www.awod.com/gallery/business/gilligan/

House of Billiards Table Repair Video
http://www.ianet.net/~billiard/video.html

Pool Players Video Bible
http://www.savenet702.com/pool.html

Paul Gerni: Live & On Cue
http://www.bca-pool.com/gerni/video.htm

Who's Who

Billiard Congress of America Hall of Fame

The Billiard Congress of America Hall of Fame has enshrined 37 people over the years. Not all are players. Some, such as John Brunswick and Herman Rambow, simply had a very significant impact on the sport and were inducted in a special category called Meritorious Service. The vast majority of the Hall of Fame members, however, are, quite properly, great players. Most won world championships and a few won multiple world titles.

The list does not include the greatest Snooker or Carom players because the association is American and those games have never reached a broad audience in the United States. These are the world's greatest pool players. Current tournament players, with a few exceptions, have not been inducted into the Hall of Fame. The thinking of the committee concerning current players and the Meritorious Service category changes from time to time. When one of the co-authors of this book was on the committee, he proposed separating the Meritorious Service category and creating a Billiard Business Hall of Fame award. No action was taken, but nominations tend to be almost exclusively for the greatest players in the sport's history. One, two, and on rare occasions three, people are added each year during an induction ceremony at the annual BCA International Trade Expo.

Mini-bios, composed by the BCA, accompany each sketch and will give you an idea of the achievements of Hall of Fame members.

Special thanks to Jason Akst and the BCA for permission to reprint the player illustrations and bios. Players are listed in alphabetical order.

Joe Balsis, who was born in Minnersville, Pennsylvania, never could resist knocking the balls around one of the pool tables in his father's recreation room. By the time he was 11, Balsis was playing exhibitions against the likes of Andrew Ponzi and Erwin Rudolph. He won junior titles four consecutive years. During pool's doldrum years, Balsis left the game, and it wasn't until 1944 that Balsis, a boat machinist in the Coast

Guard, won his next title: Armed Services Champ. In 1964 "the Meatman," as Balsis is known because of his family's meat business, returned to competitive pool. Between 1965 and 1975, Balsis competed in the finals of the U.S. Open five times, winning twice (1968 and 1974). He won the prestigious Billiard Room Proprietor's Association tournament in 1965, then captured the World All-Around championship in Johnston City, Illinois, in 1966. He won the Jansco brothers' Stardust Open All-Around title back-to-back in 1968 and 1969.

Jean Balukas is the second woman inducted into the BCA Hall of Fame. She was born in Brooklyn, New York, and is the Hall's youngest member. An excellent all-around athlete, Jean competed in her first BCA U.S. Open when she was 9 years old, finishing seventh. She won her first BCA crown when she was 12. Since then, Jean has collected seven BCA U.S. Open 14.1 titles, six World Open titles, and countless 9-ball and straight pool crowns. She has been named Player of the Year five times.

John Brunswick was a Swiss immigrant woodworker who founded what has become the Brunswick Corporation, the largest pool-table manufacturer in this country. Producing his first billiard table in 1845, Brunswick went on to develop an American market for billiard equipment. He is credited with the rapid growth of billiards in the late 19th century.

Lou Butera was born in Pittston, Pennsylvania. He learned to play at his father's pool room in the small coal-mining town. After watching BCA Hall of Famer Erwin Rudolph in an exhibition, 14-year-old Lou decided to devote his life to pool. He was runner-up to Irving Crane in the 1972 World Championship in Los Angeles. In 1973, he defeated Crane in the finals of the same event to win his first World Championship. Nicknamed "Machine Gun Lou" for his rapid-fire style, Lou recorded a 150-ball run against Allen Hopkins in just 21 minutes in 1973. Butera has since won numerous titles.

Jimmy Caras was born in Scranton, Pennsylvania, and is the second living person to be elected to the Hall of Fame. Jimmy started playing billiards at the age of 5. At 17, he defeated Ralph Greenleaf in an exhibition match to become known as the Boy Wonder of The World. Nine years later, in 1936, he won his first world championship. He won again in 1938, 1939, and 1949. Eighteen years later, in 1967, he won the U.S. Open in a field of 48 players. His record of "most balls," "most games won," and "fewest innings by a champion" still stand in the record book for that size field.

Welker Cochran, a champion who trained for his billiard matches with the same intensity as a professional boxer, won his first of two 18.2 Balkline titles in 1927. He later went on to become the Three-Cushion champion five times in the 1930s and '40s. Like many stars of the sport, Cochran learned the game in his father's billiard establishment, and he became the protégé of Frank Gotch, the wrestler, who sent young Cochran to Chicago to hone his playing talents.

Irving Crane was born in Livonia, New York. His love for the game started as a child, when he was given a toy billiard table. Although he played steadily as a teenager, he did not enter tournament play until the age of 23. He won his first world title in 1942. Since then, he has won almost two dozen major championships, including the world crown in 1946, 1955, 1966, 1968, 1970, and 1972, plus the International Round-Robin championship in 1968. Crane was the victor in the 1978 World Series of Billiards (a combination of 14.1 and 9-Ball) against a strong field of outstanding competitors. His greatest triumph, however, was his victory in the 1966 U.S. Open, when he won the championship in a never-to-be-excelled record run of 150 and out.

Arthur "Babe" Cranfield, the only person ever to win the National Junior, National Amateur, and World Professional pocket billiard titles, was born in 1916 to a Syracuse, New York room owner. He was giving exhibitions by the age of 10, when it was predicted he would eventually beat Ralph Greenleaf. He won the New York City and National Junior titles at age 15, breaking previous high-run records, and was the National Amateur champion in 1938 and 1940. He traveled frequently to give exhibitions for the National Billiard Program. He interrupted his promising career to enlist in the Army Air Corps in 1942. After the war, Babe appeared frequently in World Tournament ranks. He took the world straight pool title from Luther Lassiter in 1964, making him the first left-handed champion since Alfredo DeOro. Always known for being a gentleman, Babe spent his professional life as a music executive but always found time to promote the game of pocket billiards.

The career of distinguished Spanish champion **Alfredo DeOro** encompassed both Three-Cushion and Pocket Billiards and spanned the closing of the 19th century and the opening of the 20th. DeOro, who served in his country's diplomatic corps, first gained the Pocket Billiard crown in 1887. He was to repeat the achievement 16 times in the next 25 years. DeOro held the Three-Cushion title 10 times from 1908 through 1919. In 1934, at the age of 71, DeOro came out of retirement for a Championship Tournament, winning two dramatic victories from defending champion Welker Cochran and the ultimate winner of the tournament, Johnny Layton.

411

Fourteen-time World Pocket Billiard Champion **Ralph Greenleaf** possessed all the flash and flair of a natural showman. With his beautiful actress wife, Princess Nai Tai Tai, the handsome Greenleaf put together a sparkling trick-shot performance and toured the Vaudeville circuit in the 1920s and '30s. The audiences watched him perform his spectacular shots by looking at a huge mirror suspended on stage over the playing table. Greenleaf won his first Pocket Billiard championship in 1919 and his last one in 1937.

Willie Hoppe, whose brilliant career was one of the longest in the annals of the sport, is considered by many to be the greatest All-Around billiard player of any era. In 1906, at the tender age of 18, Hoppe won his first world's title by defeating the renowned French champion, Maurice Vignaux, at 18.1 Balkline in a memorable match in Paris. He went on to win the 18.2 Balkline and Cushion Carom titles, and years later, between 1936 and 1952, he held the Three-Cushion title 11 times.

John Wesley Hyatt, known as the father of the American plastic industry, was an inventor rather than a player, but his invention of the celluloid plastic billiard ball in 1868 revolutionized the billiard industry. Hyatt began his search for a suitable synthetic billiard ball material when a New York billiards firm offered a $10,000 prize for a substitute for ivory. Hyatt's earlier attempts involved shellacking a paper pulp sphere and a ball made of layers of cloth.

Considered by many to be the finest 9-ball player ever, **Luther Lassiter** was born in Elizabeth City, North Carolina. Lassiter earned his nickname "Wimpy," for all the hot dogs and Orange Crushes he could pack away as a youngster hanging around the local pool hall. By the time he was 17, "Wimpy" was packing away his share of opponents. Lassiter's biggest years in tournament play came in the 1960s. In the 11 years of the Jansco brothers' All-Around Championships in Johnston City, Illinois (1962–72), Lassiter won the straight pool title five times, the 9-Ball title four times, and the One Pocket title once. On three occasions Lassiter went on to capture the All-Around title (1962, 1963, 1967). He also won the BCA U.S. Open in 1969 and the Stardust World All-Around Championship in 1971.

Johnny Layton, born in Sedalia, Missouri, won the world's Three-Cushion championship 12 times, defeating such champions as Willie Hoppe, Welker Cochran, Jake Schaefer, Jr., and Augie Kieckhefer in the 1920s and '30s. Layton recorded the high Three-Cushion game mark of 50 points in 23 innings, a record which still stands today. He was credited with originating the method of using the diamond system, using table markers to indicate direction of ball rebounds, a style that he perfected through the application of his highly developed mathematical mind.

Ray Martin's world titles in straight pool in 1971, 1974 and 1978 make him one of only seven players in this century to win three or more world 14.1 titles. He has many nine-ball tournament wins to his credit as well, including the 1980 Caesars Tahoe Invitational, the 1981 ESPN King of the Hill, and the 1983 Music City Open. While concentrating today more on teaching than playing, Martin (born in 1936) is still a threat in straight pool tournaments, finishing fourth and fifth in the 1992 and 1993 BCA U.S. Opens. In collaboration with Rosser Reeves, Martin wrote *The 99 Critical Shots in Pool* (1977).

Ruth Mcginnis, who was born in 1910, began playing pool at age 7. At 14, she had defeated both Flower Sisters, then world champions at straight pool. She was acclaimed the world women's champion for the years 1932–40, and during that time she lost only 29 out of 1,532 exhibition matches. She entered the New York State pocket championship (until then restricted to men only) in 1942 and was invited to compete for the world title in 1948. Her high runs were 85 on a 10-foot table and 128 on a 9-foot table. She had a tournament high run of 125 and was inducted into the WPBA Hall of Fame in 1976. She promoted billiards by touring extensively with Willie Mosconi and appearing in several short films about pocket billiards. Her career outside of pool was as a teacher of special children. The best female player in the country from 1924 through 1960, Ruth died in 1974 in Honesdale, Pennsylvania.

Steve Mizerak, born in Perth Amboy, New Jersey, was the youngest inductee to the BCA Hall of Fame. In the brief span of his career, he has been champion four times of the U.S. Open, winning the title in 1970, 1971, 1972, and 1973. Mizerak also captured the PPPA World Open title in 1982 and 1983. Mizerak continues to finish near the top in several national tournaments each year.

Although **Jimmy Moore** never won a world title, he claimed the National Pocket Billiards Championship in a 3,000-point match win over Luther Lassiter in 1958. At the National Invitational Pocket Billiards Championship in New York City in 1965, he easily outdistanced a straight-pool field which included the strongest players of the period, such as Joe Balsis, Ed Kelly, Lou Butera, Luther Lassiter, and Eddie Taylor. He is a five-time runner-up in world 14.1 championship play. He posted high finishes in many other major events in the 1950s and '60s.

For most people, the name **Willie Mosconi** and the sport of Pocket Billiards are synonymous. And rightly so, since from 1940 to 1957 Mosconi had a near-stranglehold on the World Title, winning it 15 times in that period. Born in Philadelphia in 1913, Willie was a prodigy with the cue by the age of 7. At 20, he embarked on a hectic cross-country exhibition tour with his idol, Ralph Greenleaf, then World Champ and at the height of his game. The result, 57 wins for Greenleaf and an amazing

50 wins for the young Mosconi. One of the most astounding of Mosconi's many records is his yet-unbroken exhibition high run of 526 balls.

James Cisero Murphy was the first and only African-American ever to win a world or U.S. national billiard title. He started by taking the New York City championship at age 16. While in his 20s, he won the Eastern States 14.1 Championship six straight times against top competition but, because of his race, was not invited to compete in world title events until 1965, when he won the Burbank World Invitational 14.1 tournament, beating Joe Balsis, Jimmy Moore, and Luther Lassiter. Murphy remains the only player in the history of pocket billiard competition to win a world title on his first attempt. He continued to place near the top in straight pool events during the 1960s and, two decades later, had a winning record in the 1983 BCA U.S. Open 14.1 Championship. He posted several competitive high runs of over 250 balls.

Ben Nartzik will always be remembered for his tireless crusade to revive billiards from its severe doldrums in the 1950s. Nartzik deserves a lion's share of the credit for ridding the game of its "pool hall" image and reestablishing its status as a "gentleman's sport." Under his leadership, the BCA was able to help both the Boys Club of America and the Association of College Unions organize billiard programs and run successful annual tournaments. Nartzik recognized the potential of the industry and bought the National Billiard Chalk Co. of Chicago.

Charlie Peterson earned the title "Missionary of Billiards" for his untiring efforts to promote the game throughout the United States. In addition to being the world's fancy-shot champion and, for years, holder of the Red Ball title, Peterson made scores of personal appearances at colleges and universities across the country and was the guiding spirit of the Intercollegiate and Boys' Clubs of America tournaments. Peterson died at the age of 83, after a life devoted to winning friends for the sport of billiards.

Michael Phelan is considered by many to be the Father of American Billiards. Player, inventor, manufacturer, and tireless popularizer of billiards, Phelan played in and won the first billiard stakes match in 1859. He holds many patents for table designs and cushions and is credited as being the first to put diamonds on tables. Phelan also is the author of *Billiards Without A Master* (1850), the first American book on billiards. He set the trend for lavish billiard rooms through his New York room on Broadway.

Andrew Ponzi was born Andrew D'Allesandro in Philadelphia, Pennsylvania. He acquired the name Ponzi after a witness to his cue prowess compared the likelihood of beating D'Allesandro with beating the infamous "Ponzi Scheme," an early version of the pyramid game. A dazzling offensive player, Ponzi competed in the game's Golden Era, the 1930s and '40s, against the likes of Mosconi, Crane, Caras, Rudolph, and Greenleaf. Despite that stiff competition, Ponzi captured World 14.1 titles in 1934, 1940, and 1943.

Called the Stradivari of his trade by those who know, **Herman Rambow** crafted custom cues for the greatest players in billiards over the course of a 65-year career. Captains of industry and celebrities of the entertainment world also beat a path to his door to have the privilege of paying from $50 to $300 for one of his perfectly-balanced "Rambow Specials." It was Herman who perfected the jointed cue by inserting a countersunk screw in the recessed butt end, making an extra-sturdy connection. Only death at age 86 stopped the craftsman from his labor of love. To billiard cognoscenti the world over, there will never be another Rambow.

Erwin Rudolph was born in Cleveland. Rudolph did not participate in his first world 14.1 championship until he was 24 years old. Five years later, in 1926, Rudolph gained national acclaim by ending Ralph Greenleaf's six-year reign as world champion. Rudolph's win over Greenleaf came in a challenge match. After losing his world title to Thomas Hueston, Rudolph regained the Crown by winning the 1933 World Championship. He won his third World Title in 1933 and, at age 47, captured his fourth and final world crown by defeating a young Irving Crane in the finals of the 1941 World Championship in Philadelphia. At the time of his death in 1957, he held the record for fastest game in a world tournament, scoring 125 points in just 32 minutes. (The record has since been eclipsed.)

A player whose super-brilliance with a billiard cue won for him the sobriquet of "Wizard," so runs the lead of a 1909 newspaper article singing the praises of **Jake Schaefer, Sr.** From the last quarter of the 19th century through the first decade of the 20th, Schaefer, Sr. was one of the most feared names in Balkline Billiards. Derivations of the game were invented just to stymie his genius—all unsuccessfully. He traveled throughout the world winning matches and gathering fans. On March 11, 1908, though desperately ill, he successfully defended his title in his final match for the 18.1 championship against Willie Hoppe by a score of 500 to 423.

Billiard historians generally rank **Jake Schaefer, Jr.**, as the greatest of the American Balkline players. He was the world champion at 18.2 in 1921, 1925, 1926, 1927, and 1929–33. He held the 18.1 honors in 1926–27 and the 28.2 title in 1937–38. At the 18.2 game, he holds four records which have never been equaled in the United States: best game average, 400 (from the break); grand average, tournament, 57.14; grand average, match, 93.25; high run, match, 432.

Mike Sigel, at 35, became the youngest male elected to the BCA Hall of Fame. Born in Rochester, New York. Sigel began playing pool at 13 and turned professional when he was 20. A natural right-hander who shoots left-handed, Sigel won his first major tournament, the U.S. Open 9-Ball Championship, in 1975. His career blossomed quickly, and Sigel was perhaps the game's dominant player in the 1980s. He

amassed 38 major 14.1 and 9-Ball championships in that decade. Sigel has won three World 14.1 Crowns (1979, 1981, and 1985) and one World 9-Ball title (1985), as well as numerous national titles.

Frank Taberski grew up in Schenectady, New York. At the age of 26, he attended a pocket billiard championship in New York City, and came home convinced he played as well as the champions. The next year, he entered and placed third behind Johnny Layton. From then on, he was almost invincible. In those days, 450-point challenge matches were the means of competition; the prize was a ruby-and-diamond-studded gold medal with the proviso that any one who won 10 consecutive challenge matches could keep it. Alfredo DeOro had come closest with five straight defenses. By 1918, Taberski had accomplished the impossible, and the medal was his.

Eddie Taylor is a two-time world all-around tournament champion. Although he lost to Hall-of-Famer Luther Lassiter in 1963 in the Johnston City, Illinois, all-around finals, Taylor defeated Lassiter in the all-around finals in Johnston City in 1964. He defeated Danny Jones and Mike Eufemia at the 1967 Stardust Open finals in Las Vegas and finished 7th in 196767 World 14.1 championship in New York. A Tennessee native, the "Knoxville Bear" was inducted into the Knoxville Sports Hall of Fame in 1987. Taylor was an active promoter of billiards in Boys Clubs of America and is regarded as one of the greatest one-pocket and bank pool players of all time.

Walter Tevis is best remembered as the author of two popular novels about pool, *The Hustler* and *The Color of Money*. Both books were made into enormously successful movies starring Paul Newman. *The Hustler* documented pool culture in the United States in the late 1950s and *The Color of Money* followed up on the same theme 25 years later. Both movies were directly responsible for igniting strong uptrends in pocket billiards during the years immediately following their releases. Tevis wrote numerous short stories and several other novels including *The Man Who Fell To Earth* (a science fiction thriller) and *The Queen's Gambit* (a portrait of a female chess master). He was a Milton scholar and held two master's degrees (from the University of Kentucky and the Writers' Workshop at the University of Iowa). He taught creative writing at Ohio University from 1965 to 1978. His works have been translated into many languages and are popular all over the world.

Learning the basics of pool at an early age from his father in his hometown of Owensboro, Kentucky, **Nick Varner** displayed his great overall talents in 14.1, 9-Ball, One Pocket, and Bank Pool by claiming the 1969 and 1970 national ACU-I collegiate titles, the World 14.1 Championship in 1980 and 1986, and the BCA National 8-Ball Championship in 1980. Accumulating over 20 major titles in his career, he became only the second man to earn over $100,000 in prize winnings in the memorable 1989 season in which he won 8 of the 16 major 9-Ball events. Winner of the Player of the Year in 1980 and 1989, and the first honoree of the MPBA Sportsperson of the Year in 1991, Nick has always been an exemplary role model and has enriched the sport of pocket billiards through his many years of dedication to excellence and sportsmanship.

Perhaps the most recognizable figure in the history of pool, **Rudolph "Minnesota Fats" Wanderone** was elected to the Hall of Fame for Meritorious Service. Although he never actually won a designated "world championship," Wanderone, the game's leading comic, orator, and publicity generator, has probably done more for the game in terms of sheer exposure than any other player. Initially nicknamed "Brooklyn Fats," and "New York Fats," Wanderone dubbed himself "Minnesota Fats" after the film version of *The Hustler* hit movie screens around the country in the early 1960s. Since that time, he became known around the world as pool's foremost side show. Fats, whose exact age was a mystery, hosted a national television show, *Celebrity Billiards*, during the 1960s. He stopped playing in tournaments around that time.

Dallas West, the only player to appear in every BCA U.S. Open straight pool championship, was born in 1941 in Rockford, Illinois. By age 13, he had run 97 balls at straight pool. The holder of several state pool titles, West was the U.S. Open champion in 1975 and 1983. An expert 9-ball player, he earned second place in the 1995 WPA World Championship. He also plays top-level three cushions. West has shared his extensive knowledge of straight pool on video-tapes, explaining in detail how long runs are made. He has been winning tournaments for over 20 years and has earned the respect of the best players in the game for his positive attitude, gentlemanly behavior, and competitive spirit.

Dorothy Wise was born in Spokane, Washington. In her early years, there were very few national tournaments for women. Since she was in many local and state tournaments, she became the self-proclaimed world champion. When the BCA staged the first national tournament for women in 1967, she immediately entered. For the next five years, she proved herself most worthy as she won five consecutive U.S. Open titles.

Harold Worst of Grand Rapids, Michigan, was only 19 years old when he played the great Willie Hoppe, winner of 51 major billiard champion-ships, in a demonstration game in Detroit in 1949. Hoppe soon took an interest in Worst's playing potential, and under his guidance, Worst won the world title for Three-Cushion billiards in Argentina in 1954, the youngest player to compete in world competition. He successfully defended this title for many years. Equally skilled at pocket billiards, Worst dominated play to win the All-Around titles in both the 1965 Johnston City, Illinois, and 1965 Stardust Open championships.

Pool & Billiard Magazine's **Player of the Year Awards**

This section presents one hundred and twenty years of the cream of the crop. Each year, the top billiard player receives the *Pool & Billiard Magazine* Player of the Year Award. In the old days, this award was strictly a male preserve, but since the late 1960s, women have come into their own.

1878	Cyrille Dion	1903	Grant Eby
1879	Samuel F. Knight	1904	Alfredo de Oro
1880	Alonzo Morris	1905	Jerome Keough
1881	Gottlieb Wahlstrom	1906	John Horgan
1882	Albert Frey	1907	Thomas Hueston
1883	Albert Frey	1908	Frank Sherman
1884	J. L. Malone	1909	John Kling
1885	J. L. Malone	1910	Jerome Keough
1886	Albert Frey	1911	Alfredo de Oro
1887	Alfredo de Oro	1912	Edward Ralph
1888	Frank Powers	1913	Benjamin Allen
1889	Alfredo de Oro	1914	Benjamin Allen
1890	H. Manning	1915	Emmet Blankenship
1891	Frank Powers	1916	John Layton
1892	Alfredo de Oro	1917	Frank Taberski
1893	Alfredo de Oro	1918	Frank Taberski
1894	Alfredo de Oro	1919	Ralph Greenleaf
1895	William Clearwater	1920	Ralph Greenleaf
1896	Frank Stewart	1921	Ralph Greenleaf
1897	Grant Eby	1922	Ralph Greenleaf
1898	Jerome Keough	1923	Ralph Greenleaf
1899	Alfredo de Oro	1924	Ralph Greenleaf
1900	Alfredo de Oro	1925	Frank Taberski
1901	Frank Sherman	1926	Ralph Greenleaf
1902	William Clearwater	1927	Erwin Rudolph

1928	Ralph Greenleaf	1958	Art Cranfield
1929	Ralph Greenleaf	1959	Luther Lassiter
1930	Erwin Rudolph	1960	Irving Crane
1931	Ralph Greenleaf	1961	Luther Lassiter
1932	Ralph Greenleaf	1962	Jack Briet
1933	Erwin Rudolph	1963	Luther Lassiter
1934	Andrew Ponzi	1964	Luther Lassiter
1935	James Caras	1965	Joe Balsis
1936	James Caras	1966	Cicero Murphy
1937	Ralph Greenleaf	1967	Dorothy Wise
1938	James Caras	1967	James Caras
1939	James Caras	1968	Dorothy Wise
1940	Andrew Ponzi	1968	Joe Balsis
1941	Willie Mosconi	1969	Dorothy Wise
1942	Irving Crane	1969	Ed Kelley
1943	Andrew Ponzi	1970	Dorothy Wise
1944	Willie Mosconi	1970	Steve Mizerak
1945	Willie Mosconi	1971	Dorothy Wise
1946	Irving Crane	1971	Steve Mizerak
1947	Willie Mosconi	1972	Jean Balukas
1948	Willie Mosconi	1972	Steve Mizerak
1949	James Caras	1973	Jean Balukas
1950	Willie Mosconi	1973	Lou Butera
1951	Willie Mosconi	1974	Jean Balukas
1952	Willie Mosconi	1974	Ray Martin
1953	Willie Mosconi	1975	Jean Balukas
1954	Willie Mosconi	1975	Dallas West
1955	Irving Crane	1976	Jean Balukas
1956	Willie Mosconi	1976	Tom Jennings
1957	Willie Mosconi	1977	Jean Balukas

1977	Tom Jennings	1988	Earl Strickland
1978	Jean Balukas	1989	Loree Jon Jones
1978	Ray Martin	1989	Nick Varner
1979	Jean Balukas	1990	Ewa Mataya*
1979	Steve Mizerak	1990	Earl Strickland (tie)
1980	Jean Balukas	1990	Kim Davenport (tie)
1980	Nick Varner	1991	Robin Bell
1981	Loree Jon Jones	1991	Buddy Hall
1981	Mike Sigel	1992	Vivian Villarreal
1982	Vicki Paski	1992	Johnny Archer
1982	Nick Varner	1993	Loree Jon Jones
1983	Jean Balukas	1993	Johnny Archer
1983	Mike Sigel	1994	Jeanette Lee
1984	Jean Balukas	1994	Nick Varner
1984	Earl Strickland	1995	Loree Jon Jones
1985	Jean Balukas	1995	Efren Reyes
1985	Wade Crane	1996	Allison Fisher
1986	Jean Balukas	1996	Johnny Archer (Pro Billiards Tour)
1986	Mike Sigel	1996	C. J. Wiley (Professional Cuesports Association)
1987	Jean Balukas	1997	Allison Fisher
1987	Earl Strickland	1997	Jose Parica
1988	Loree Jon Jones		

* Ewa has also won the Billiards Digest Player of the Year Award in 1990 and 1992.

Ewa's Tournament Titles

Swedish National Champion (1980 and 1981)

European Champion (1981)

World Open 9-Ball Champion (1983 and 1984)

ESPN Team Challenge Champion (1987)

World 8-Ball Champion (1988)

International 9-Ball Champion (1988)

U.S. Open Champion (1988 and 1991)

Cleveland Open Champion (1990)

Sands Regent Classic Champion (1990)

Rocket City Invitational Champion (1990)

East Coast Classic Champion (1990)

National 10-Ball Champion (1990)

WPBA National Champion (1991)

WPA World 9-Ball Champion (1994)

Houston Classic Champion (1995)

Nordic Masters Champion (1997)

Brunswick Boston Classic Champion (1998)

The BCA General Rules of Pocket Billiards

These rules cover the basics. Each game has its own additional rules, but what you'll find in this appendix are the overall rules used in every game. I should stress that these are not always the rules used by professionals, by leagues, or in games among friends or strangers. Some variations of particular rules are more commonly accepted than those listed in this appendix. Still, these rules are, in the main, very common ones. When specific other rules are not being used, or when the players haven't decided on a particular rule before the violation comes up, the BCA rules are usually the default set.

Thanks to Jason Akst, public relations director, and the Billiard Congress of America for permission to reprint the rules here. (Sections 1 and 2, in case you wonder, deal with rules for tournaments and instructions for referees. The general rules begin with Section 3.)

General Rules of Pocket Billiards

3.1. TABLES, BALLS, EQUIPMENT. All games described in these rules are designed for tables, balls and equipment meeting the standards prescribed in the BCA EQUIPMENT SPECIFICATIONS.

3.2. RACKING THE BALLS. When racking the balls a triangle must be used, and the apex ball is to be spotted on the foot spot. All the balls must be lined up behind the apex ball and pressed together so that they all have contact with each other.

3.3. STRIKING THE CUE BALL. Legal shots require that the cue ball be struck only with the cue tip. Failure to meet this requirement is a foul.

3.4. FAILURE TO POCKET A BALL. If a player fails to pocket a ball on a legal shot, then the player's inning is over, and it is the opponent's turn at the table.

3.5. LAG FOR BREAK. The following procedure is used for the lag for the opening break. Each player should use balls of equal size and weight (preferably cue balls but, when not available, nonstriped object balls). With the balls in hand behind the head string, one player to the left and one player to the right of the head spot, the balls are shot simultaneously to the foot cushion and back to the head end of the table. The player whose ball is the closest to the innermost edge of the head cushion wins the lag. The lagged ball must contact the foot cushion at least once. Other cushion contacts are immaterial, except as prohibited below.

It is an automatic loss of the lag if: (a) the ball crosses into the opponent's half of the table, (b) the ball fails to contact the foot cushion, (c) the ball drops into a pocket, (d) the ball jumps the table, (e) the ball touches the long cushion, (f) the ball rests within the corner pocket and past the nose of the head cushion, or (g) the ball contacts the foot rail more than once. If both players violate automatic-loss lag rules, of if the referee is unable to determine which ball is closer, the lag is a tie and is replayed.

3.6. OPENING BREAK SHOT. The opening break shot is determined by either lag or lot. The player winning the lag or lot has the choice of performing the opening break shot or assigning it to the opponent.

3.7. CUE BALL ON OPENING BREAK. The opening break shot is taken with cue ball in hand behind the head string. The object balls are positioned according to specific game rules. On the opening break, the game is considered to have commenced once the cue ball has been struck by the cue tip and crosses the head string.

3.8. DEFLECTING THE CUE BALL ON THE GAME'S OPENING BREAK. On the break shot, stopping or deflecting the cue ball after it has crossed the head string and prior to hitting the racked balls is considered a foul and loss of turn. The opponent has the option of receiving cue ball in hand behind the head string or passing the cue ball in hand behind the head string back to the offending player. (Exception: 9-Ball, see rule 5.3: "cue ball in hand anywhere on the table.") A warning must be given that second violation during the match will result in the loss of the match by forfeiture. (See Rule 3.28.)

3.9. CUE BALL IN HAND BEHIND THE HEAD STRING. This situation applies in specific games whereby the opening break is administered or a player's scratching is penalized by the incoming player having cue ball in hand behind the head string. The incoming player may place the cue ball anywhere behind the head string.

The shooting player may shoot at any object ball as long as the base of the object ball is on or below the head string. He may not shoot at any ball, the base of which is above the head string, unless he first shoots the cue ball below the head string and then by hitting a rail causes the cue ball to come back above the head string and hit the object ball. The base of the ball (the point of the ball touching the table) determines whether it is above or below the head string.

If the incoming player inadvertently places the cue ball on or below the head string, the referee of the opposing player must inform the shooting player of improper positioning of the cue ball before the shot is made. If the opposing player does not so inform the shooting player before the shot is made, the shot is considered legal. If the shooting player is informed of improper positioning, he must then reposition the cue ball. If the player positions the cue ball completely and obviously outside the kitchen and shoots the cue ball, it is a foul.

When the cue ball is in hand behind the head string, it remains in hand *(not in play)* until the player drives the cue ball past the head string by striking it with his cue tip.

The cue ball may be *adjusted* by the player's hand, cue, etc. so long as it remains in hand. Once the cue ball is in play per the above, it may not be impeded in any way by the player; to do so is to commit a foul.

3.10. POCKETED BALLS. A ball is considered pocketed if as a result of an otherwise legal shot, it drops off the bed of the table into the pocket and remains there. (A ball that drops out of a ball return system onto the floor is not to be considered as a ball that has not remained pocketed.) A ball that rebounds from a pocket back onto the table bed is not a pocketed ball.

3.11. POSITION OF BALLS. The position of a ball is judged by where its base (or center) rests.

3.12. FOOT ON FLOOR. Player must have at least one foot in contact with the floor at the moment the cue tip contacts the cue ball, or the shot is a foul. Foot attire must be normal in regard to size, shape and manner in which it is worn.

3.13. SHOOTING WITH BALLS IN MOTION. It is a foul if a player shoots while the cue ball or any object ball is in motion (a spinning ball is in motion).

3.14. COMPLETION OF STROKE. A stroke is not complete (and therefore is not counted) until all balls on the table have become motionless after the stroke (a spinning ball is in motion).

3.15. HEAD STRING DEFINED. The area behind the head string does not include the head string. Thus an object ball that is dead center on the head string is playable when specific game rules require that a player must shoot at a ball past the head string. Likewise, the cue ball when being put in play behind the head string (cue ball in hand behind the head string), may not be placed directly on the head string; it must be behind it.

3.16. GENERAL RULE, ALL FOULS. Though the penalties for fouls differ from game to game, the following apply to all fouls: (a) player's inning ends; (b) if on a stroke, the stroke is invalid and any pocketed balls are not counted to the shooter's credit; and (c) any ball(s) is respotted only if the rules of the specific game require it.

3.17. FAILURE TO CONTACT OBJECT BALL. It is a foul if on a stroke the cue ball fails to make contact with any legal object ball first. Playing away from a touching ball does not constitute having hit that ball.

3.18. LEGAL SHOT. Unless otherwise stated in a specific game rule, a player must cause the cue ball to contact a legal object ball and then (a) pocket a numbered ball; or (b) cause the cue ball or any numbered ball to contact a cushion. Failure to meet these requirements is a foul.

3.19. CUE BALL SCRATCH. It is a foul (scratch) if on a stroke, the cue ball is pocketed. If the cue ball touches an object ball that was already pocketed (for example, in a pocket full of object balls), the shot is a foul.

3.20. FOULS BY TOUCHING BALLS. It is a foul to strike, touch, or in any way make contact with the cue ball in play or any object balls in play with anything (the body, clothing, chalk, mechanical bridge, cue shaft, etc.) *except* the cue tip (while attached to the cue shaft), which may contact the cue ball in the execution of a legal shot. Whenever a referee is presiding over a match, any object ball moved during a standard foul must be returned as closely as possible to its original position as judged by the referee, and the incoming player does not have the option of restoration. (Also see Rule 1.16.)

3.21. FOUL BY PLACEMENT. Touching any object ball with the cue ball while it is in hand is a foul.

3.22. FOULS BY DOUBLE HITS. If the cue ball is touching the required object ball prior to the shot, the player may shoot toward it, providing that any normal stroke is employed. If the cue stick strikes the cue ball more than once on a shot, or if the cue stick in is contact with the cue ball when or after the cue ball contacts an object ball, the shot is foul. (See Rule 2.20. For judging this kind of shot.) If a third ball is close by, care should be taken not to foul that ball under the first part of this rule.

3.23. PUSH SHOT FOULS. It is a foul if the cue ball is pushed by the cue tip, with contact being maintained for more than the momentary time commensurate with a stroked shot. (Such shots are usually referred to as push shots.)

3.24. PLAYER RESPONSIBILITY FOULS. The player is responsible for chalk, bridges, files and any other items or equipment he brings to, uses at, or causes to approximate the table. If he drops a piece of chalk, or knocks off a mechanical bridge head, as examples, he is guilty of a foul should such an object make contact with any ball in play (or the cue ball only if no referee is presiding over the match).

3.25. ILLEGAL JUMPING OF BALL. It is a foul if a player strikes the cue ball below center ("digs under" it) and intentionally causes it to rise off the bed of the table in an effort to clear an obstructing ball. Such jumping action may occasionally occur accidentally, and such "jumps" are not to be considered fouls on their face; they may still be ruled foul strokes, if for example, the ferrule or cue shaft makes contact with the cue ball in the course of the shot.

3.26. JUMP SHOTS. Unless otherwise stated n rules for a specific game it is legal to cause the cue ball to rise off the bed of the table by elevating the cue stick on the shot, and forcing the cue ball to rebound from the bed of the table. Any miscue when executing a jump shot is a foul.

3.27. BALLS JUMPED OFF TABLE. Balls coming to rest other than on the bed of the table after a stroke (on the cushion top, rail surface, floor, etc.) are considered jumped balls. Balls may bounce on the cushion tops and rails of the table in play without being jumped balls if they return to the bed of the table under their own power and without touching anything not a part of the table. The table shall consist of the permanent part of the table proper. (Balls that strike or touch anything not a part of the table, such as the light fixture, chalk on the rails and cushion tops, etc., shall be considered jumped balls even though they might return to the bed of the table after contacting items which are not parts of the table proper.)

In all pocket billiard games, when a stroke results in the cue ball or any object ball being a jumped ball off the table, the stroke is a foul. All jumped object balls are spotted (except in Nine-Ball) when all balls have stopped moving. See specific game rules for putting the cue ball in play after a jumped cue ball foul.

3.28. SPECIAL INTENTIONAL FOUL PENALTY. The cue ball in play shall not be intentionally struck with anything other than a cue's attached cue tip (such as the ferrule, shaft, etc.). While such contact is automatically a foul under the provisions of Rule 3.19., if the referee deems the contact to be intentional, he shall warn the player once during a match that a second violation during that match will result in the loss of the match by forfeiture. If a second violation does occur, the match must be forfeited.

3.29. ONE FOUL LIMIT. Unless specific game rules dictate otherwise, only one foul is assessed on a player in each inning; if different penalties can apply, the most severe penalty is the factor determining which foul is assessed.

3.30. BALLS MOVING SPONTANEOUSLY. If a ball shifts, settles, turns or otherwise moves "by itself", the ball shall remain in the position it assumed and play continues. A hanging ball that falls into a pocket "by itself" after being motionless for 5 seconds or longer shall be replaced as closely as possible to its position prior to falling, and play shall continue.

If an object ball drops into a pocket "by itself" as a player shoots at it, so that the cue ball passes over the spot the ball had been on, unable to hit it, the cue ball and object ball are to be replaced to their positions prior to the stroke, and the player may shoot again. Any other object balls disturbed on the stroke are also to be replaced to their original positions before the shooter replays.

3.31. When specific game rules call for spotting balls, they shall be replaced on the table on the long string after the stroke is complete. A single ball is placed on the foot spot; if more than one ball is to be spotted, they are placed on the long string in ascending numerical order, beginning on the foot spot and advancing toward the foot rail.

When balls on or near the foot spot or long string interfere with the spotting of balls, the balls to be spotted are placed on the long string as close as possible to the foot spot without moving the interfering balls. Spotted balls are to be placed as close as possible or frozen (at the referee's discretion) to such interfering balls, except when the cue ball is interfering; balls to be spotted against the cue ball are placed as close as possible without being frozen.

If there is insufficient room on the long string between the foot spot and the foot rail cushion for balls that must be spotted, such balls are then placed on the extension of the long string "in front" of the foot spot (between the foot spot and the center spot), as near as possible to the foot spot and in the same numerical order as they were spotted "behind" the foot spot (lowest numbered ball closest to the foot spot).

3.32. JAWED BALLS. If two or more balls are locked between the jaws or sides of the pocket, with one or more suspended in air, the referee shall inspect the balls in position and follow this procedure: he shall visually (or physically if he desires) project each ball directly downward from its locked position; any ball that in his judgement would fall in the pocket if so moved directly downward is a pocketed ball, while any ball that would come to rest on the bed of the table is not pocketed. The balls are then placed according to the referee's assessment, and play continues according to specific game rules as if no locking or jawing of balls had occurred.

3.33. ADDITIONAL POCKETED BALLS. If extra balls are pocketed on a legal scoring stroke, they are counted in accord with the scoring rules for the particular game.

3.34. NON-PLAYER INTERFERENCE. If the balls are moved (or a player bumped such that play is directly affected) by a non-player during the match, the balls shall be replaced as near as possible to their original positions immediately prior to the incident, and play shall resume with no penalty on the player affected. If the match is officiated, the referee shall replace the balls. This rule shall also apply to "act of God" interference, such as earthquake, hurricane, light fixture falling, power failure, etc. If the balls cannot be restored to their original positions, replay the game with the original player breaking. This rule is not applicable to 14.1 Continuous where the game consists of successive racks: the rack in progress will be discontinued and a completely new rack will be started with the requirements of the normal opening break (players lag for break). Scoring of points is to be resumed at the score as it stood at the moment of game disruption.

3.35. BREAKING SUBSEQUENT RACKS. In a match that consists of short rack games, the winner of each game breaks in the next. The following are common options that may be designated by tournament officials in advance: (a) Players alternate break. (b) Loser breaks. (c) Player trailing in games score breaks the next game.

3.36. PLAY BY INNINGS. During the course of play, players alternate turns (innings) at the table, with a player's inning ending when he either fails to legally pocket a ball, or fouls.

When an inning ends free of a foul, the incoming player accepts the table in position.

3.37. OBJECT BALL FROZEN TO CUSHION OR CUE BALL. This rule applies to any shot where the cue ball's first contact with a ball is with one that is frozen to a cushion or to the cue ball itself. After the cue ball makes contact with the frozen object ball, the shot must result in either (a) a ball being pocketed, or (b) the cue ball contacting a cushion, or (c) the frozen ball being caused to contact a cushion attached to a separate rail, or (d) another object ball being caused to contact a cushion with which it was not already in contact. Failure to satisfy one of those four requirements is a foul. (Note: 14.1 and other games specify additional requirements and applications of this rule; see specific game rules.)

A ball which is touching a cushion at the start of a shot and then is forced into a cushion attached to the same rail is not considered to have been driven to that cushion unless it leaves the cushion, contacts another ball, and then contacts the cushion again.

An object ball is not considered frozen to a cushion unless it is examined and announced as such by either the referee or one of the players prior to that object ball being involved in a shot.

3.38. PLAYING FROM BEHIND THE STRING. When a player has the cue ball in hand behind the string (in the kitchen), he must drive the cue ball to a point outside the kitchen before it contacts either a cushion or an object ball. Failure to do so is a foul if a referee is presiding over a match. If no referee, the opponent has the option to call it either a foul or to require the offending player to replay the shot again with the balls restored to their positions prior to the shot (and with no foul penalty imposed).

Exception: if an object ball lies on or outside the head string (and is thus playable) but so close that the cue ball contacts it before the cue ball is out of the kitchen, the ball can be legally played.

If, with cue ball in hand behind the headstring and while the shooter is attempting a legitimate shot, the cue ball accidentally hits a ball behind the head string, and the cue ball crosses the line, it is a foul. If with cue ball in hand behind the head string, the shooter causes the cue ball to accidentally hit an object ball, the cue ball does not cross the headstring, the following applies: the incoming player has the option of calling a foul and having cue ball in hand, having the balls returned to their original position, and having the offending player replay the shot.

If a player under the same conditions intentionally causes the cue ball to contact an object ball behind the headstring, it is unsportsmanlike conduct.

3.39. CUE BALL IN HAND FOUL. During cue ball in hand placement, the player may use his hand or any part of his cue (including the tip) to position the cue ball. When placing the cue ball in position, any forward stroke motion contacting the cue ball will be a foul, if not a legal shot.

3.40. INTERFERENCE. If the nonshooting player distracts his opponent or interferes with his play, he has fouled. If a player shoots out of turn, or moves any ball except during his inning, it is considered to be interference.

3.41. DEVICES. Players are not allowed to use a ball, the triangle or any other width-measuring device to see if the cue ball or an object ball would travel through a gap, etc. Only the cue stick may be used as an aid to judge gaps, etc., so long as the cue is held by the hand. To do so otherwise is a foul and unsportsmanlike conduct.

3.42. ILLEGAL MARKING. If a player intentionally marks the table in any way to assist in executing the shot, whether by wetting the cloth, by placing a cube of chalk on the rail, or by any other means, he has fouled. If the player removes the mark prior to the shot, no penalty is imposed.

Index

C

Unique Pool Tables Web site, 406
United States Confederation of Billiard Sports (USCBS), 26
United States Snooker Association Web site, 388
Upscale One Pocket Web site, 396
upscale rooms, 32-34
USCBS (United States Confederation of Billiard Sports), 26

V

V bridges, *see* open bridges
V-Que Billiard's Supply Company Web site, 398
vacuuming tables (chalk dust), 180
Varner, Nick, 416-417
Veritscapes Web site, 406
vertical axis, 184
video games, 102
videos (information resources), 385-386, 407
Viking Cue Manufacturing Web site, 393
Virtual Billiards Web site, 398
Virtual International Pool Ladder Web site, 404
Virtual Pool from Macplay Web site, 404
visualizing the shot, 174
Vitalie Manufacturing Web site, 406
Vogel Titanium Cues Web site, 393

W-Z

wall decorations, 105
wall racks (cues), costs, 95
Wanderone, Rudolph "Minnesota Fats", 20, 417

warmup strokes, *see* feathering
warped racks, 229
Watertown Billiards Web site, 398
WCBS (World Confederation of Billiard Sports), 24
Web sites (information resources)
  accessories, 386
  associations/leagues, 386-388
  billiard supply stores, 388-391
  clubs, 399-403
  cue cases, 393
  cue gloves, 394
  cue stands, 394
  cue tips, 394
  cues, 392-393
  device aids, 394
  distributors, 394-395
  furniture, 395
  instructional materials, 395-396
  magazines/publications, 396-397
  mail order, 397-398
  maintenance, 398
  players, 398-399
  pockets, 399
  pro shops, 399-403
  schools, 403
  scuffers, 403
  software, 403-404
  tables, 404-406
  videos, 407
weight (cues), 77
West, Dallas, 417
white ball (Carom), 367
Willie Holt Ireland, Ltd. Web site, 406
wing balls, 345
winner breaks, 350
winning 8-Ball, 336-338
Winning Garb Web site, 386
winning gracefully, 48

Wise, Dorothy, 417
Women & Billiards Online Magazine Web site, 397
Women's Professional Billiard Association (WPBA), 11, 26, 36, 112
  Web site, 388
women's tour, 10-11
wooden racks, 229
wool (table cloth), 66
World All-Around Pool Championship, The, 20
world championship, 17
World Confederation of Billiard Sports (WCBS), 24
  Web site, 387
World Pool-Billiard Association Web site, 387
World Registry (rankings) Web site, 399
Worldwide Billiards, Inc. Web site, 395
Worst, Harold, 37, 417
WPBA (Women's Professional Billiard Association), 11, 26, 36, 112
  Player Profiles Web site, 399
wrap (cue butt), 74-75

X system (bank shots), 247-248